Constitutional
Law
and
Criminal
Justice

Constitutional Law
and
Criminal
Justice

Cliff Roberson

CRC Press
Taylor & Francis Group
Boca Raton   London   New York

CRC Press is an imprint of the
Taylor & Francis Group, an **informa** business

AN AUERBACH BOOK

Auerbach Publications
Taylor & Francis Group
6000 Broken Sound Parkway NW, Suite 300
Boca Raton, FL 33487-2742

© 2009 by Taylor & Francis Group, LLC
Auerbach is an imprint of Taylor & Francis Group, an Informa business

International Standard Book Number-13: 978-1-4200-8610-2 (Hardcover)

Library of Congress Cataloging-in-Publication Data

Roberson, Cliff, 1937-
    Constitutional law and criminal justice / Cliff Roberson.
        p. cm.
    Includes bibliographical references and index.
    ISBN 978-1-4200-8610-2 (hardcover : acid-free paper)
        1. Constitutional law--United States. 2. Constitutional law—United States--Cases. 3. Civil rights--United States. 4. Criminal justice, Administration of--United States. 5. Criminal procedure--United States. I. Title.

KF4550.R57 2009
342.73--dc22   2008051530

Visit the Taylor & Francis Web site at
http://www.taylorandfrancis.com

and the Auerbach Web site at
http://www.auerbach-publications.com

This book is dedicated to the men and women serving and those who have served in our criminal justice system. We, as Americans, are truly fortunate to have had fine devoted professionals ever tending that fine blue line. For your anonymous help in our times of need, and to perhaps make up some for the thanks that we have failed to express, thank you.

Table of Contents

6 Fifth Amendment Issues   141

List of Illustrations

Preface

Constitutional Law and Criminal Justice is designed to provide students and persons interested in both our Constitution and criminal justice with an easy-to-read work on the relationship between the two. While I have attempted to remove any indication of my political viewpoints or opinions of the court decisions from the discussion, some may have crept in, for which I apologize in advance. The Constitution is not a perfect document, but it far exceeds anything else available today to ensure basic human rights to the people it serves. A complete copy of the U.S. Constitution is contained in Appendix A.

Often, I see or hear the statement: "The judge threw out the evidence based on technicalities." When I see this statement in newspapers or hear it from individuals, I consider it a statement from someone who is uneducated as to the importance of our Constitution. Judges do not exclude evidence for technical reasons; judges exclude evidence based on violations of constitutional rights. The violation of a constitutional right is never a mere technical violation.

Many cases and excerpts of cases are included in the text. In many instances, the cases or excerpts were edited to enhance the understanding of the material. I have taken great effort not to change the meanings of the material so edited. Lawyers, including myself, tend to put in too many citations and extraneous matters. Judges are no exception. The average U.S. Supreme Court decision is approximately 50 pages. Accordingly, editing is necessary.

Even though I am listed as the sole author of the text, numerous persons assisted in the preparation of the manuscript, including the editor at Taylor & Francis, Carolyn Spence, and the person who corrected my grammar and most of my errors, Judith Simon. Thanks to both of you for your assistance and encouragement. Comments and suggestions for improvement regarding the contents of the material may be forwarded to me by e-mail at croberson@kaplan.edu.

The Author

Cliff Roberson, LLM, PhD, is editor-in-chief of the *Professional Issues in Criminal Justice Journal* and is an emeritus professor of criminal justice at Washburn University. His previous academic experiences include associate vice president for academic affairs, Arkansas Tech University; dean of arts and sciences, University of Houston, Victoria; director of programs, National College of District Attorneys; professor of criminology and director of Justice Center, California State University, Fresno; and assistant professor of criminal justice, St. Edwards University, Austin, Texas. He has authored or coauthored 52 books and texts, including, with Dilip Das, *An Introduction to Comparative Legal Models of Criminal Justice* (CRC Press, 2009).

Dr. Roberson's nonacademic experience includes U.S. Marine Corps service as an infantry officer, trial and defense counsel, military judge as a marine judge advocate, and director of the Military Law Branch, U.S. Marine Corps. Other legal employment experiences include trial supervisor, Office of State Counsel for Offenders, Texas Board of Criminal Justice, and judge *pro tem* in the California courts. Dr. Roberson is admitted to practice before the U.S. Supreme Court, U.S. Court of Military Appeals, U.S. Tax Court, state and federal courts in California and Texas, Supreme Court of Texas, and Supreme Court of California.

His educational background includes a PhD in human behavior, U.S. International University; LLM in criminal law, criminology, and psychiatry, George Washington University; JD, American University; BA in political science, University of Missouri; and one year of postgraduate study at the University of Virginia School of Law.

Introduction to the U.S. Constitution

1

Introduction

Any study on the impact of the U.S. Constitution on the criminal justice system will consist mostly of a study of the first ten amendments to the Constitution, the Bill of Rights. Generally, the Bill of Rights is studied in separate segments. As noted by Amar (1998), students study the First, Ninth, and Tenth Amendments in an introductory course in constitutional law. The Fourth, Fifth, Sixth, and Eighth Amendments are studied in a course on criminal procedure, and the Fourth is also studied in courses on evidence. The due process clause of the Fifth Amendment is also studied in courses on property law. The Seventh Amendment is normally studied in a course in civil procedure. Amar notes that the Second and Third Amendments are generally ignored. In this chapter, we will briefly examine all the amendments to introduce the Bill of Rights as a whole document rather than separate amendments. In later chapters we will examine in more detail those amendments that significantly impact the criminal justice system.

The U.S. Supreme Court traditionally decides more business- and corporate-related cases than those involving criminal justice. Each year, the Court receives about 10,000 petitions for review. The Court accepts less than 2 percent of the petitions, and most of those will be in areas other than criminal justice. A review of the Court's last 20 years indicates that the Court will decide fewer than 20 cases involving criminal justice issues each year.

Original Constitution

By "original constitution" I am referring to the constitution as first proposed by the Philadelphia convention. This constitution focused primarily on the organizational structure of the new government and the self-governance issues of federalism, separation of powers, bicameralism, and how the constitution could be amended. The general consensus is that the Bill of Rights that was drafted by the first Congress had little to say on those issues and instead focused on the rights of individuals and minority groups. Amar (1998) disagrees with this consensus and contends that the Bill of Rights includes structural ideas that are interconnected with the language of the

Photo 1.1 Courtroom where the U.S. Supreme Court has sat since 1935. (Photo by Cliff Roberson.)

amendments. His ideas will be discussed later in the text when the individual amendments are explored.

The original constitution contained no bill of rights. Because the records of the Philadelphia convention are fragmentary, it can only be speculated as to why they were left out of the constitution (Cohen and Danelski, 2002). Shortly before the convention closed, a motion was raised to appoint a committee to prepare a Bill of Rights to attach to the constitution. This motion did not receive a favorable vote from any of the states. During the ratification process, promises were made to include a bill of rights to protect individual liberties.

Bill of Rights

The original bill of rights proposed by the first Congress included 12 amendments. The first proposed amendment attempted to control the size of Congress, and it failed by one state to be ratified. The second proposed amendment provided that if the compensation of members of Congress was raised, that the raise would not be effective until after an election of representatives was held. This proposed amendment was designed to limit the right of Congress and the Senate to grant themselves unjustified pay raises at public expense. The proposed amendment was not ratified until 1992 and is the present Twenty-seventh Amendment. The other ten amendments were ratified, renumbered, and became known as the Bill of Rights.

First Amendment

What is now considered the First Amendment was the original third proposed amendment. The present First Amendment states:

> Congress shall make no law respecting an establishment of religion, or prohibiting the free exercise thereof; or abridging the freedom of speech, or of the press; or the right of the people peaceably to assemble, and to petition the Government for a redress of grievances.

While the First Amendment is broad enough to protect the rights of unpopular minorities, according to Amar (1998), it was designed to protect the rights of the majority against Congress. He notes that words are designed to restrain Congress, not the people. There is an argument by many that the words "the right of the people" refer to the majority of people and not just to individuals. In 1980, the Supreme Court in the case of *Richmond Newspapers v. Virginia* held that the First Amendment also protected the right of the press to attend criminal trials.

Second Amendment

The present Second and Third Amendments are often referred to as the military amendments. The Second Amendment reads as follows:

> A well regulated Militia, being necessary to the security of a free State, the right of the people to keep and bear Arms, shall not be infringed.

The Supreme Court held in *United States v. Cruikshank* (1876) that the right to bear arms for lawful purposes under the Second Amendment is not a right granted by the Constitution, and the Second Amendment only means that such right shall not be infringed by Congress. Other cases have held that the Second Amendment does not apply to states and does not confer absolute individual right to bear any type of firearm; rather, the Second Amendment only confers the collective right of keeping and bearing arms, which must bear reasonable relationship to preservation or efficiency or well-regulated militia (see *Love v. Pepersack*, 1995).

The Iowa Supreme Court noted that the right to bear arms under the Second Amendment is not an absolute right, because constitutional protection extends only to situations bearing some "reasonable relationship" to preservation or efficiency of a well-regulated militia; a statute prohibiting possession or transportation of firearms by convicted felons is not overbroad because it brings within its protection those convicted of nonviolent as well as violent crimes (*State v. Rupp*, 1979).

In 1995, a convicted felon applied to a federal court to have his right to own and possess firearms restored pursuant to 18 USCS § 925(c). A U.S. Court of Appeals held that he did not suffer violation of his Second Amendment rights when the Bureau of Alcohol, Tobacco, and Firearms refused to process his application for relief from firearm disability because Congress had eliminated appropriations for investigating and acting on such applications (*Rice v. Department of Alcohol, Tobacco and Firearms*, 1995).

Gun control is a controversial subject. Often politicians will state that they are either in favor of gun control or against it. The National Rifle Association (NRA) spends large amounts of money each year to protect the right of people to own weapons, and other public interest groups spend large sums to support the reduction in the number of firearms available. The authority of states to regulate gun control appears to be clear. It appears that under the Constitution, this should be a state, not federal, issue. Regardless of your beliefs on gun control, few people, if any, would advocate no restrictions on gun control. For example, even the NRA would support keeping guns out of the hands of eight-year-olds or seriously deranged individuals. So when the issue of gun control is discussed, the real question presented is not whether there should be gun control, but the permissible limits of the control.

In June 2008, for the first time in Supreme Court history, the Court addressed the substantive rights of citizens to possess a firearm unconnected with service in a militia, and to use that arm for traditionally lawful purposes, such as self-defense within the home.

District of Columbia v. Heller, 2008 U.S. LEXIS 5268 (2008)
Justice Scalia delivered the opinion of the Court:

> We consider whether a District of Columbia prohibition on the possession of usable handguns in the home violates the Second Amendment to the Constitution.
>
> The District of Columbia generally prohibits the possession of handguns. It is a crime to carry an unregistered firearm, and the registration of handguns is prohibited. Wholly apart from that prohibition, no person may carry a handgun without a license, but the chief of police may issue licenses for 1-year periods. District of Columbia law also requires residents to keep their lawfully owned firearms, such as registered long guns, unloaded and dissembled or bound by a trigger lock or similar device unless they are located in a place of business or are being used for lawful recreational activities. There are minor exceptions to all of these prohibitions, none of which is relevant here.
>
> Respondent Dick Heller is a D.C. special police officer authorized to carry a handgun while on duty at the Federal Judicial Center. He applied for a registration certificate for a handgun that he wished to keep at home, but the District refused. He thereafter filed a lawsuit in the Federal District Court for

the District of Columbia seeking, on Second Amendment grounds, to enjoin the city from enforcing the bar on the registration of handguns, the licensing requirement insofar as it prohibits the carrying of a firearm in the home without a license, and the trigger-lock requirement insofar as it prohibits the use of functional firearms within the home.

We turn first to the meaning of the Second Amendment.

The Second Amendment provides: "A well regulated Militia, being necessary to the security of a free State, the right of the people to keep and bear Arms, shall not be infringed." In interpreting this text, we are guided by the principle that the Constitution was written to be understood by the voters; its words and phrases were used in their normal and ordinary as distinguished from technical meaning. Normal meaning may of course include an idiomatic meaning, but it excludes secret or technical meanings that would not have been known to ordinary citizens in the founding generation.

The two sides in this case have set out very different interpretations of the Amendment. Petitioners and today's dissenting Justices believe that it protects only the right to possess and carry a firearm in connection with militia service. Respondent argues that it protects an individual right to possess a firearm unconnected with service in a militia, and to use that arm for traditionally lawful purposes, such as self-defense within the home.

The Second Amendment is naturally divided into two parts: its prefatory clause and its operative clause. The former does not limit the latter grammatically, but rather announces a purpose. The Amendment could be rephrased, "Because a well regulated Militia is necessary to the security of a free State, the right of the people to keep and bear Arms shall not be infringed." Although this structure of the Second Amendment is unique in our Constitution, other legal documents of the founding era, particularly individual-rights provisions of state constitutions, commonly included a prefatory statement of purpose.

Logic demands that there be a link between the stated purpose and the command. The Second Amendment would be nonsensical if it read, "A well regulated Militia, being necessary to the security of a free State, the right of the people to petition for redress of grievances shall not be infringed." That requirement of logical connection may cause a prefatory clause to resolve an ambiguity in the operative clause.

"Right of the People." The first salient feature of the operative clause is that it codifies a "right of the people." The unamended Constitution and the Bill of Rights use the phrase "right of the people" two other times, in the First Amendment's Assembly-and-Petition Clause and in the Fourth Amendment's Search-and-Seizure Clause. The Ninth Amendment uses very similar terminology ("The enumeration in the Constitution, of certain rights, shall not be construed to deny or disparage others retained by the people"). All three of these instances unambiguously refer to individual rights, not "collective" rights, or rights that may be exercised only through participation in some corporate body.

Three provisions of the Constitution refer to "the people" in a context other than "rights"—the famous preamble ("We the people"), § 2 of Article I (providing that "the people" will choose members of the House), and the Tenth Amendment (providing that those powers not given the Federal Government remain with "the States" or "the people"). Those provisions arguably refer to "the people" acting collectively—but they deal with the exercise or reservation of powers, not rights. Nowhere else in the Constitution does a "right" attributed to "the people" refer to anything other than an individual right.

What is more, in all six other provisions of the Constitution that mention "the people," the term unambiguously refers to all members of the political community, not an unspecified subset. Second Amendments, and to whom rights and powers are reserved in the Ninth and Tenth Amendments, refers to a class of persons who are part of a national community or who have otherwise developed sufficient connection with this country to be considered part of that community.

This contrasts markedly with the phrase "the militia" in the prefatory clause. As we will describe below, the "militia" in colonial America consisted of a subset of "the people"—those who were male, able bodied, and within a certain age range. Reading the Second Amendment as protecting only the right to "keep and bear Arms" in an organized militia therefore fits poorly with the operative clause's description of the holder of that right as "the people."

We start therefore with a strong presumption that the Second Amendment right is exercised individually and belongs to all Americans.

"Keep and bear Arms." We move now from the holder of the right—"the people"—to the substance of the right: "to keep and bear Arms." The term was applied, then as now, to weapons that were not specifically designed for military use and were not employed in a military capacity.

Some have made the argument, bordering on the frivolous, that only those arms in existence in the 18th century are protected by the Second Amendment. We do not interpret constitutional rights that way. Just as the First Amendment protects modern forms of communications, the Second Amendment extends, prima facie, to all instruments that constitute bearable arms, even those that were not in existence at the time of the founding.

The phrase "keep arms" was not prevalent in the written documents of the founding period that we have found, but there are a few examples, all of which favor viewing the right to "keep Arms" as an individual right unconnected with militia service. William Blackstone (Amar, 1998), for example, wrote that Catholics convicted of not attending service in the Church of England suffered certain penalties, one of which was that they were not permitted to "keep arms in their houses." "Keep arms" was simply a common way of referring to possessing arms, for militiamen and everyone else.

At the time of the founding, as now, to "bear" meant to "carry." When used with "arms," however, the term has a meaning that refers to carrying for a particular purpose—confrontation. Although the phrase implies that the carrying of the weapon is for the purpose of "offensive or defensive action," it in no way connotes participation in a structured military organization.

From our review of founding-era sources, we conclude that this natural meaning was also the meaning that "bear arms" had in the 18th century. In numerous instances, "bear arms" was unambiguously used to refer to the carrying of weapons outside of an organized militia. The most prominent examples are those most relevant to the Second Amendment: nine state constitutional provisions written in the 18th century or the first two decades of the 19th, which enshrined a right of citizens to "bear arms in defense of themselves and the state" or "bear arms in defense of himself and the state." It is clear from those formulations that "bear arms" did not refer only to carrying a weapon in an organized military unit.

By the time of the founding, the right to have arms had become fundamental for English subjects. Blackstone, whose works, we have said, "constituted the preeminent authority on English law for the founding generation," cited the arms provision of the Bill of Rights as one of the fundamental rights of Englishmen. Thus, the right secured in 1689 as a result of the Stuarts' abuses was by the time of the founding understood to be an individual right protecting against both public and private violence.

The prefatory clause reads: "A well regulated Militia, being necessary to the security of a free State...."

"Well-regulated Militia." In *United States v. Miller*, we explained that "the Militia comprised all males physically capable of acting in concert for the common defense." That definition comports with founding-era sources. Finally, the adjective "well-regulated" implies nothing more than the imposition of proper discipline and training.

"Security of a free State." The phrase "security of a free state" meant "security of a free polity," not security of each of the several States. Joseph Story wrote in his treatise on the Constitution (Levy, 1998) that "the word 'state' is used in various senses and in its most enlarged sense, it means the people composing a particular nation or community. The militia is the natural defence of a free country." It is true that the term "State" elsewhere in the Constitution refers to individual States, but the phrase "security of a free state" and close variations seem to have been terms of art in 18th-century political discourse, meaning a "free country" or free polity. Moreover, the other instances of "state" in the Constitution are typically accompanied by modifiers making clear that the reference is to the several States—"each state," "several states," "any state," "that state," "particular states," "one state," "no state." And the presence of the term "foreign state" in Article I and Article III shows that the word "state" did not have a single meaning in the Constitution.

Relationship between Prefatory Clause and Operative Clause. We reach the question, then: Does the preface fit with an operative clause that creates an individual right to keep and bear arms? It fits perfectly, once one knows the history that the founding generation knew and that we have described above. That history showed that the way tyrants had eliminated a militia consisting of all the able-bodied men was not by banning the militia but simply by taking away the people's arms, enabling a select militia or standing army to suppress political opponents. This is what had occurred in England that prompted codification of the right to have arms in the English Bill of Rights.

We turn finally to the law at issue here. As we have said, the law totally bans handgun possession in the home. It also requires that any lawful firearm in the home be disassembled or bound by a trigger lock at all times, rendering it inoperable.

As the quotations earlier in this opinion demonstrate, the inherent right of self-defense has been central to the Second Amendment right. The handgun ban amounts to a prohibition of an entire class of "arms" that is overwhelmingly chosen by American society for that lawful purpose. The prohibition extends, moreover, to the home, where the need for defense of self, family, and property is most acute. Under any of the standards of scrutiny that we have applied to enumerated constitutional rights, banning from the home the most preferred firearm in the nation to keep and use for protection of one's home and family would fail constitutional muster.

Few laws in the history of our Nation have come close to the severe restriction of the District's handgun ban. And some of those few have been struck down.

We must also address the District's requirement (as applied to respondent's handgun) that firearms in the home be rendered and kept inoperable at all times. This makes it impossible for citizens to use them for the core lawful purpose of self-defense and is hence unconstitutional. The District argues that we should interpret this element of the statute to contain an exception for self-defense. But we think that is precluded by the unequivocal text, and by the presence of certain other enumerated exceptions: "Except for law enforcement personnel..., each registrant shall keep any firearm in his possession unloaded and disassembled or bound by a trigger lock or similar device unless such firearm is kept at his place of business, or while being used for lawful recreational purposes within the District of Columbia." The nonexistence of a self-defense exception is also suggested by the D.C. Court of Appeals' statement that the statute forbids residents to use firearms to stop intruders.

In sum, we hold that the District's ban on handgun possession in the home violates the Second Amendment, as does its prohibition against rendering any lawful firearm in the home operable for the purpose of immediate self-defense. Assuming that Heller is not disqualified from the exercise of Second Amendment rights, the District must permit him to register his handgun and must issue him a license to carry it in the home.

We are aware of the problem of handgun violence in this country, and we take seriously the concerns raised by the many who believe that prohibition of handgun ownership is a solution. The Constitution leaves the District of Columbia a variety of tools for combating that problem, including some measures regulating handguns. But the enshrinement of constitutional rights necessarily takes certain policy choices off the table. These include the absolute prohibition of handguns held and used for self-defense in the home. Undoubtedly some think that the Second Amendment is outmoded in a society where our standing army is the pride of our Nation, where well-trained police forces provide personal security, and where gun violence is a serious problem. That is perhaps debatable, but what is not debatable is that it is not the role of this Court to pronounce the Second Amendment extinct.

It is so ordered.

Justice Stevens, with whom Justice Souter, Justice Ginsburg, and Justice Breyer join, dissenting:

> The question presented by this case is not whether the Second Amendment protects a "collective right" or an "individual right." Surely it protects a right that can be enforced by individuals. But a conclusion that the Second Amendment protects an individual right does not tell us anything about the scope of that right.
>
> Guns are used to hunt, for self-defense, to commit crimes, for sporting activities, and to perform military duties. The Second Amendment plainly does not protect the right to use a gun to rob a bank; it is equally clear that it does encompass the right to use weapons for certain military purposes. Whether it also protects the right to possess and use guns for nonmilitary purposes like hunting and personal self-defense is the question presented by this case. The text of the Amendment, its history, and our decision in *United States v. Miller*, 307 U.S. 174 (1939), provide a clear answer to that question.
>
> The Second Amendment was adopted to protect the right of the people of each of the several States to maintain a well-regulated militia. It was a response to concerns raised during the ratification of the Constitution that the power of Congress to disarm the state militias and create a national standing army posed an intolerable threat to the sovereignty of the several States. Neither the text of the Amendment nor the arguments advanced by its proponents evidenced the slightest interest in limiting any legislature's authority to regulate private civilian uses of firearms. Specifically, there is no indication that the Framers of the Amendment intended to enshrine the common-law right of self-defense in the Constitution.
>
> In 1934, Congress enacted the National Firearms Act, the first major federal firearms law. Upholding a conviction under that Act, this Court held that, "in the absence of any evidence tending to show that possession or use of a 'shotgun having a barrel of less than eighteen inches in length' at this time has some reasonable relationship to the preservation or efficiency of a well regulated militia, we cannot say that the Second Amendment guarantees the right to keep and bear such an instrument." *Miller*, 307 U.S., at 178. The view of the Amendment we took in *Miller*—that it protects the right to keep and bear arms for certain military purposes, but that it does not curtail the Legislature's power to regulate the nonmilitary use and ownership of weapons—is both the most natural reading of the Amendment's text and the interpretation most faithful to the history of its adoption.

Third Amendment

The Third Amendment is the second of the military amendments. That amendment reads as follows:

> No Soldier shall, in time of peace be quartered in any house, without the consent of the Owner, nor in time of war, but in a manner to be prescribed by law.

This amendment is probably the most overlooked amendment, and it is rarely discussed in criminal justice classes. The Supreme Court has, however, used the Third Amendment to bolster its decisions that there is a right of privacy implied in the Constitution.

One interesting case involving the amendment and criminal justice was *Engblom v. Carey* (1982). In that case, the State of New York evicted striking correctional officers from their prison-owned residences, at the Mid-Orange Correctional Facility in Warwick, New York, where (1) monthly rent was charged for furnished rooms, (2) officers did not maintain separate residences or have alternative housing available, and (3) prison department's regulations repeatedly refer to occupants as tenants. The State then quartered National Guard personnel, who were working in place of the striking workers, in the residences. The U.S. Court of Appeals held that the correctional workers had established a reasonable expectation of privacy protected by the Third Amendment in their rented residences. The court, in holding that the actions of the state constituted a violation of the Third Amendment, stated that the amendment's reference to the word *house* was a term that encompasses the various modern forms of dwelling. The court also held that National Guardsmen are "soldiers" within meaning of the Third Amendment. The court noted that aside from the lower court's opinion in this case, there were no reported opinions involving the literal application of the Third Amendment.

In *Griswold v. Connecticut* (1965), the Supreme Court noted that a zone of privacy was created by the Third Amendment's prohibition against quartering of soldiers in any house in time of peace without the owner's consent. It was in the *Griswold* decision that the Court held that there was an implied right of privacy in the federal Constitution.

Fourth Amendment

The Fourth Amendment is one of those key amendments that have significant impact on criminal justice. This amendment is discussed extensively in other chapters. The amendment reads as follows:

> The right of the people to be secure in their persons, houses, papers, and effects, against unreasonable searches and seizures, shall not be violated, and no Warrants shall issue, but upon probable cause, supported by Oath or affirmation, and particularly describing the place to be searched, and the persons or things to be seized.

Fifth Amendment

The Fifth Amendment is another of the key amendments involved in criminal justice. The rights protected under the amendment include the right against self-incrimination, requirement for a grand jury indictment, and protection against double jeopardy. Each of these rights will be discussed extensively in other chapters. Also included in the amendment is the first due process clause. This due process clause is normally referred to as the federal due process clause. For reasons that will be discussed later, this due process clause is a protection against the actions of the federal government and not state governments. The due process protection against state and local governments is contained in the Fourteenth Amendment. The restriction against the taking of privately owned property is an important protection and is explored in classes on property law. The Fifth Amendment reads as follows:

> No person shall be held to answer for a capital, or otherwise infamous crime, unless on a presentment or indictment of a Grand Jury, except in cases arising in the land or naval forces, or in the Militia, when in actual service in time of War or public danger; nor shall any person be subject for the same offense to be twice put in jeopardy of life or limb; nor shall be compelled in any criminal case to be a witness against himself, nor be deprived of life, liberty, or property, without due process of law; nor shall private property be taken for public use, without just compensation.

Sixth Amendment

The Sixth Amendment is primarily known as the "right to counsel" amendment. Other criminal justice protections included in the amendment are the right to a speedy and public trial, by an impartial jury, and the right to be tried in the judicial district in which the crime occurred. This amendment will also be discussed in detail later in the book. The Sixth Amendment reads as follows:

> In all criminal prosecutions, the accused shall enjoy the right to a speedy and public trial, by an impartial jury of the State and district wherein the crime shall have been committed, which district shall have been previously ascertained by law, and to be informed of the nature and cause of the accusation; to be confronted with the witnesses against him; to have compulsory process for obtaining witnesses in his favor, and to have the Assistance of Counsel for his defense.

Seventh Amendment

As noted by the Supreme Court, the thrust of the Seventh Amendment is to preserve the right to a civil jury trial as it existed in 1791 (*Parklane Hosiery Co. v. Shore*, 1979). The Seventh Amendment provides for rights in civil cases and, therefore, will not be discussed again in the text. The amendment reads as follows:

In Suits at common law, where the value in controversy shall exceed twenty dollars, the right of trial by jury shall be preserved, and no fact tried by a jury, shall be otherwise re-examined in any Court of the United States, than according to the rules of the common law.

Eighth Amendment

The Eighth Amendment contains the protection against "cruel and unusual" punishment and will be discussed in detail in a later chapter. The amendment reads as follows:

Excessive bail shall not be required, nor excessive fines imposed, nor cruel and unusual punishments inflicted.

To allege a violation of the amendment, a plaintiff must allege that an agent of the state committed an act as punishment that was shocking to the conscience (*Barrett v. City of Allentown*, 1993). As one appellate court noted, the simple misuse of a state's prosecutorial machinery does not constitute the type of cruel and unusual punishment that the Eighth Amendment was meant to prohibit (*Bacon v. Patera*, 1985).

The amendment also protects a pretrial detainee's right not to be punished, and that right is as expansive as a convicted prisoner's Eighth Amendment rights (*Swofford v. Mandrell*, 1992).

The amendment does not apply to disciplinary action in a school setting (*Ramon by Ramon v. Soto*, 1989). In addition, the amendment applies only to punitive sanctions, not to remedial sanctions imposed by a union on its members (*United States v. International Brotherhood of Teamsters*, 1991). The cruel and unusual punishment clause protects only people who have been convicted of crime and does not protect homeless people whom county sheriffs remove from their campsite on private land (*D'Aguanno v. Gallagher*, 1995). Later, when this issue is revisited, the constitutionality of the death penalty will also be explored.

Ninth Amendment

The purpose of the Ninth Amendment is to guarantee to individuals those rights inherent to citizenship in democracy that is not specifically enumerated in the Bill of Rights (*United States v. Cook*, 1970). The Ninth Amendment is another amendment that has only limited involvement with the criminal justice system. That amendment reads as follows:

The enumeration in the Constitution, of certain rights, shall not be construed to deny or disparage others retained by the people.

The Ninth Amendment does not confer substantive rights in addition to those conferred by other portions of our governing law (*Gibson v. Matthews*, 1991). Also, the amendment does not withdraw rights expressly granted to federal government (*Ashwander v. Tennessee Valley Authority*, 1936). One appellate court noted that no constitutional right exists under the Ninth Amendment, or any other provision of the Constitution of the United States, "to trust the Federal Government and to rely on the integrity of its pronouncements" (*MAPCO, Inc. v. Carter*, 1978).

Do we need a Supreme Court case to inform us that there is no constitutional right to trust the federal government or rely on its integrity?

Tenth Amendment

The Supreme Court has stated that the Tenth Amendment is the essence of the federal system, and the states must be equally free to engage in any activity that their citizens choose for common weal, no matter how unorthodox or unnecessary anyone else, including judiciary, deems state involvement to be (*Garcia v. San Antonio Metropolitan Transit Authority*, 1985). The purpose of the Tenth Amendment was to allay fears that national government might seek to exercise powers not granted, and that states might not be able to exercise fully their reserved rights (*United States v. Darby*, 1941). The amendment reads as follows:

> The powers not delegated to the United States by the Constitution, nor prohibited by it to the States, are reserved to the States respectively, or to the people.

Under this amendment, the federal government can claim no powers that are not granted to it by U.S. Constitution, and powers actually granted must be such as are expressly given, or given by necessary implication (*Martin v. Hunter's Lessee*, 1816). As noted later in this chapter, the Tenth Amendment restricts the ability of Congress to take the gun control issue from the states.

The Supreme Court has stated that the Tenth Amendment is to be considered fairly and liberally so as to give effect to its scope and meaning; the Tenth Amendment discloses widespread fear that national government might, under pressure of supposed general welfare, attempt to exercise powers that had not been granted, and framers intended that no such assumption should ever find justification in organic act, and that if, in the future, further powers seemed necessary, they should be granted by people in a manner provided for amending that act (*Kansas v. Colorado*, 1907).

Application of the Bill of Rights to State and Local Prosecutions

The Supreme Court held in *Barron v. Baltimore* (1833) that the first ten amendments to the federal Constitution were limitations solely on the

Photo 1.2 U.S. Supreme Court building. (Photo by Cliff Roberson.)

federal government. When the Fourteenth Amendment was ratified in 1868, the courts began to use the due process clause of that amendment to apply most of the limitations contained in the Bill of Rights against the states and local governments. This issue is explored in detail in Chapter 2.

Supreme Law of the Land

In 1918, Congress passed a statute, the Migratory Bird Treaty Act, which implemented a treaty with Great Britain. The treaty and act were designed to protected migratory birds and provided restrictions on the killing of ducks as they migrated to and from Canada. At the time, the State of Missouri had a state law that regulated duck hunting within the state, and the state statute conflicted with the act. The State of Missouri filed a court action in an attempt to have the act declared unconstitutional as a violation of the Tenth Amendment (*Missouri v. Holland*, 1920).

Holland was a U.S. game warden. The Supreme Court upheld the Migratory Bird Treaty Act and stated that the power to make the treaty had been expressly delegated to the United States under U.S. Constitution Article II, § 2 and Article VI. The Court noted that the treaty did not contravene any prohibitory words found in the federal Constitution, nor was the subject matter, the regulation of migratory birds, forbidden by some invisible radiation from the general terms of the Tenth Amendment.

The Supreme Court also noted in the case that the Constitution made the "supreme law of the land" to consist of three things: (1) the Constitution, (2) the laws of the United States that are made in accordance with the Constitution, and (3) all treaties made or which shall be made under the authority of the United States. Accordingly, if any state law or local ordinance conflicts with U.S. Constitution validly enacted federal laws, or valid treaties, the state law or local ordinance is unconstitutional.

Overview of the Judiciary

The United States has a dual court system: the federal and the state. Basically, the federal system handles matters concerning federal issues, and the state systems handle issues concerning state and local issues. This is a general rule and there are some exceptions that will be discussed later. For a court to have authority to take any action in a case or dispute, the court must have jurisdiction. There are two types of jurisdiction: jurisdiction over the person and jurisdiction over the subject matter. The court must have both types to take any legal action in the case or dispute.

Jurisdiction over the person is usually obtained by having the individual in court or by service of process on the individual. Generally, determining personal jurisdiction is not as complicated as determining whether a court has jurisdiction over the subject matter. A general statement is that state courts have subject matter jurisdiction over state matters and federal courts

Photo 1.3 Bryon White Federal Court building in Denver, Colorado. (Photo by Cliff Roberson.)

have subject matter jurisdiction over federal matters. There are other restrictions on subject matter jurisdiction. For example, a state court in Texas has no jurisdiction to decide a divorce case in Nevada, nor does a probate court in California have jurisdiction to try a murder case in California.

State or Federal Issue

In examining jurisdiction in criminal cases, the below general rules apply:

- If the act is a violation of a federal law, the case will be tried in a federal court.
- If the act is a violation of a state law, the case will be tried in a state court.

If an act violates both state and federal law, a case may be tried in both courts. For example, if a police officer unlawfully beats a suspect, the officer's conduct is a violation of a state criminal statute on battery, and the officer may be tried in state court. The same conduct may involve a violation of the suspect's federal civil rights, and the officer may also be tried in federal criminal court. It would not be a violation of the officer's protection against double jeopardy because in state court the officer was tried for violation of a state offense, battery, and in federal court the officer was tried for a violation of the federal civil rights legislation. For example, in 2007, a professional football player was tried in federal court for being involved in dog fighting. After the player pleaded guilty to that offense, the state then indicted him for violating state statutes by financing a dog-fighting enterprise.

Most criminal cases are tried in state courts. The state criminal courts in the cities of New York, Chicago, Houston, and Los Angeles each adjudicate more criminal cases each year than are tried in all the federal courts combined.

Frequently, a state criminal case may involve a federal issue. In the famous case of *Miranda v. Arizona* (1966), Ernesto Miranda was tried in an Arizona state criminal court for rape. After he was convicted in state court, he appealed to federal court and claimed that his rights under the U.S. Constitution were violated by his in-custody interrogation. By alleging a federal issue, he was allowed to collaterally appeal to a federal court.* Had he claimed only that his rights under the Arizona state constitution had been violated, this would have been a state issue and the Arizona Supreme Court decision would have been final.

In *Doe v. Norris* (1988), the Tennessee Supreme Court reviewed the constitutionality of a practice by its Department of Corrections, Division of

---

* An appeal of a state criminal trial issue into federal court is considered a collateral appeal because direct appeals of state convictions are available only in the state system.

Youth Services, of commingling juvenile "status offenders" with delinquent offenders in secure correctional facilities. The state court in condemning the practice held that federal courts' interpretations of the due process clauses of the U.S. Constitution established only a minimum level of protection, and the Tennessee Supreme Court, as the final arbiter of the Tennessee Constitution, is always free to expand the minimum level of protection mandated by the federal Constitution. The court found the defendants' practice to be unconstitutional under the Tennessee Constitution, even though at the time the practice was considered constitutional under the federal Constitution.

Appellate Courts

Appellate courts are divided into two basic categories:

- Courts of last resort: These courts are established in the state's constitution and have final jurisdiction over appeals. Except in the states of New York, Oklahoma, and Texas, the court of last resort is the State Supreme Court. In New York it is the Court of Appeals, and in Oklahoma and Texas it is the Court of Criminal Appeals. In Texas and Oklahoma there are state supreme courts, but they handle only civil issues.
- Intermediate appellate courts: These courts hear initial appeals from trial courts, the outcome of which can be subject to further review by the state's courts of last resort.

In 2008, there were 1,335 state appellate judges or justices in the state courts. Most term lengths vary among states from four to sixteen years; only Rhode Island selects judges to serve for life, while Massachusetts and Puerto Rico mandate terms that last until retirement at age 70. Federal judges for courts established pursuant to Article III of the Constitution are appointed for life (http://www.ojp.usdoj.gov/bjs/courts.htm#judges, accessed January 30, 2008).

New York State Court of Appeals

Rather than examine all state appellate court systems, the New York system was selected to provide the reader with an overview of the state appellate systems. The Court of Appeals, New York State's highest court, is composed of a chief judge and six associate judges, each appointed to a 14-year term. New York's highest appellate court was established to articulate statewide principles of law in the context of deciding particular lawsuits. The court thus generally focuses on broad issues of law as distinguished from individual factual disputes.

There is one term of the Court of Appeals each year, commencing in January and continuing throughout the year in monthly sessions, usually excluding July. Oral arguments at the Court of Appeals are held during nine calendar months, and the court usually sits in late August to hear and decide cases related to primary elections.

Necessity for Criminal Leave Application

There is no appeal of right except in cases involving the death penalty. A death penalty case shall be appealed directly from the trial court. Appeals in all other cases must be from order of intermediate appellate court and may be taken only if a certificate is issued pursuant to statutes.

Article III Federal Courts

Article III courts are those that were established by Section 1, Article III of the U.S. Constitution. That section provides, in part, that the judicial power of the federal government shall be vested in one Supreme Court and in such inferior courts as the Congress may from time to time establish. The justices and judges appointed pursuant to Article III hold their offices, subject to good behavior, for life. Congress has also created courts under the authority of Article I of the U.S. Constitution. The Article I or legislative courts do not have full judicial power, and the judges generally serve for a period of years rather than for life. Article I courts include the U.S. Court of Military Appeals, U.S. Tax Court, and U.S. Court of Veterans' Appeals. The Article III federal courts are the U.S. Supreme Court, U.S. Courts of Appeals, U.S. District Courts, and bankruptcy courts.

Under the U.S. Constitution, the president appoints federal judges with the "advice and consent" of the Senate. The president usually consults senators or other elected officials concerning candidates for vacancies on the federal courts.

The Department of Justice is responsible for prosecuting federal crimes and for representing the government in civil cases. Each federal district court has a U.S. attorney who is appointed by the president with the advice and consent of Congress. The U.S. attorney acts as the prosecutor for federal cases in the district court. The United States Marshals Service provides security for federal courthouses and judges.

Organization of Federal Courts

Article III, Section 1, U.S. Constitution

The judicial Power of the United States, shall be vested in one supreme Court, and in such inferior Courts as the Congress may from time to time ordain and establish. The Judges, both of the supreme and inferior Courts, shall hold their Offices during good Behavior, and shall, at stated Times, receive for their Services a Compensation which shall not be diminished during their Continuance in Office.

Article III, Section 2, U.S. Constitution

The judicial Power shall extend to all Cases, in Law and Equity, arising under this Constitution, the Laws of the United States, and Treaties made, or which shall be made, under their Authority; to all Cases affecting Ambassadors, other public Ministers and Consuls; to all Cases of admiralty and maritime Jurisdiction; to Controversies to which the United States shall be a Party; to Controversies between two or more States; between a State and Citizens of another State; between Citizens of different States; between Citizens of the same State claiming Lands under Grants of different States, and between a State, or the Citizens thereof, and foreign States, Citizens or Subjects.

Congress has established two levels of federal courts under the Supreme Court: the trial courts and the appellate courts. The United States District Courts are the trial courts of the federal court system. Within limits set by Congress and the Constitution, the district courts have jurisdiction to hear nearly all categories of federal cases, including both civil and criminal matters. There are 94 federal judicial districts, including at least one district in each state, the District of Columbia, and Puerto Rico. Each district includes a United States bankruptcy court as a unit of the district court. Three territories of the United States—the Virgin Islands, Guam, and the Northern Mariana Islands—have district courts that hear federal cases, including bankruptcy cases.

There are two special trial courts that have nationwide jurisdiction over certain types of cases. The Court of International Trade addresses cases involving international trade and customs issues. The United States Court of Federal Claims has jurisdiction over most claims for money damages against the United States, disputes over federal contracts, and unlawful "takings" of private property.

The 94 judicial districts are organized into 12 regional circuits, each of which has a United States Court of Appeals. A court of appeals hears appeals from the district courts located within its circuit, as well as appeals from decisions of federal administrative agencies. In addition, the Court of Appeals for the Federal Circuit has nationwide jurisdiction to hear appeals in specialized cases, such as those involving patent laws and cases decided by the Court of International Trade or the Court of Federal Claims (see Figure 1.1).

Court of appeals, district court, and Court of International Trade judges have life tenure, and they may retire if they are at least 65 years old and meet certain years of service requirements. Most Article III judges who are eligible

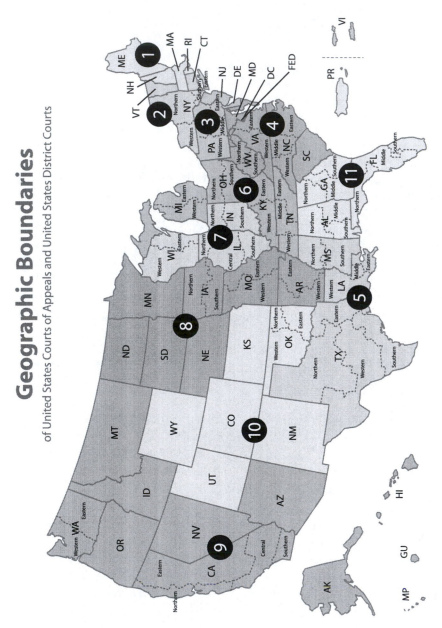

Figure 1.1 U.S. Circuit Court map provided by the U.S. Supreme Court.

to retire decide to continue to hear cases on a full- or "senior judges."

Supreme Court Procedures

A term of the Supreme Court begins, by statute, on the first M..

Usually Court sessions continue until late June or early July. The term is divided between "sittings," when the justices hear cases and deliver opinions, and intervening "recesses," when they consider the business before the Court and write opinions. Sittings and recesses alternate at approximately two-week intervals.

With rare exceptions, each side is allowed 30 minutes of argument, and up to 24 cases may be argued at one sitting. Because the majority of cases involve the review of a decision of some other court, there is no jury and no witnesses are heard. For each case, the Court has before it a record of prior proceedings and printed briefs containing the arguments of each side.

During the intervening recess period, the justices study the argued and forthcoming cases and work on their opinions. Each week the justices must also evaluate more than 130 petitions seeking review of judgments of state and federal courts to determine which cases are to be granted full review with oral arguments by attorneys.

When the Court is sitting, public sessions begin promptly at 10 a.m. and continue until 3 p.m., with a one-hour lunch recess starting at noon. No public sessions are held on Thursdays or Fridays. On Fridays during and preceding argument weeks, the justices meet to discuss the argued cases and to discuss and vote on petitions for review.

When the Court is in session, the 10 a.m. entrance of the justices into the courtroom is announced by the marshal. Those present, at the sound of the gavel, arise and remain standing until the robed justices are seated following the traditional chant:

> The Honorable, the Chief Justice and the Associate Justices of the Supreme Court of the United States. Oyez! Oyez! Oyez! All persons having business before the Honorable, the Supreme Court of the United States, are admonished to draw near and give their attention, for the Court is now sitting. God save the United States and this Honorable Court!

Prior to hearing oral argument, other business of the Court is transacted. On Monday mornings this includes the release of an order list, a public report of Court actions, including the acceptance and rejection of cases, and the admission of new members to the Court bar. Opinions are typically released on Tuesday and Wednesday mornings and on the third Monday of each sitting, when the Court takes the bench but no arguments are heard.

he Court maintains this schedule each term until all cases ready for omission have been heard and decided. In May and June the Court sits only to announce orders and opinions. The Court recesses at the end of June, but the work of the justices is unceasing.

During the summer they continue to analyze new petitions for review, consider motions and applications, and make preparations for cases scheduled for fall argument.

The Court's caseload has increased steadily to a current total of more than 7,000 cases on the docket per term. The increase has been rapid in recent years. In 1960, only 2,313 cases were on the docket, and in 1945, only 1,460. Plenary review, with oral arguments by attorneys, is granted in about 100 cases per term. Formal written opinions are delivered in 80 to 90 cases. Approximately 50 to 60 additional cases are disposed of without granting plenary review. The publication of a term's written opinions, including concurring opinions, dissenting opinions, and orders, approaches 5,000 pages. Some opinions are revised a dozen or more times before they are announced.

The information for this section was taken from a booklet prepared by the Supreme Court of the United States.

Judicial Authority and Power

Before a court can hear a case, or "exercise its jurisdiction," certain conditions must be met:

- Federal courts and the majority of state courts exercise only judicial powers. This means that the judges may interpret the law only through the resolution of actual legal disputes, referred to as cases or controversies. Generally, a court cannot attempt to correct a problem on its own initiative, or to answer a hypothetical legal question.
- When there is an actual case or controversy, the plaintiff in a federal lawsuit also must have legal standing to ask the court for a decision. That means the plaintiff must have been aggrieved, or legally harmed in some way, by the defendant. In a criminal case, the plaintiff in a federal case is the United States, and in state cases, the state. This is based on the concept that the United States or the state was harmed by a criminal act.
- The case must present a category of dispute that the law in question was designed to address, and it must be a complaint that the court has the power to remedy. In other words, in federal cases the court must be authorized, under the Constitution or a federal law, to hear the case and grant appropriate relief to the plaintiff.
- The case cannot be moot; that is, it must present an ongoing problem for the court to resolve.

- The federal courts have limited jurisdiction because they may only decide certain types of cases as provided by Congress or as identified in the Constitution. Generally, state major trial courts are considered the courts of general jurisdiction, and therefore it is assumed that they have jurisdiction.

In general, federal courts may decide cases that involve the United States government, the United States Constitution or federal laws, or controversies between states or between the United States and foreign governments. A case that raises a federal issue may be filed in federal court. In criminal cases, this might include a claim by the government that someone has violated federal laws, or a challenge to actions taken by a federal agency.

The litigation process in federal and state courts is referred to as an adversarial system because it relies on the litigants to present their dispute before a neutral fact finder. In criminal cases, it is the United States, State of _____, or Commonwealth of _____ v. the defendant.

Supreme Court Justices (2008–2009 Term)

Chief Justice

John G. Roberts, Jr., chief justice of the United States, was born in Buffalo, New York, January 27, 1955. He received an AB from Harvard College in 1976 and a JD from Harvard Law School in 1979. He served as a law clerk for Judge Henry J. Friendly of the United States Court of Appeals for the Second Circuit from 1979 to 1980, and as a law clerk for Associate Justice William H. Rehnquist of the Supreme Court of the United States during the 1980 term. He was special assistant to the attorney general, U.S. Department of Justice, from 1981 to 1982; associate counsel to President Ronald Reagan, White House Counsel's Office, from 1982 to 1986; and principal deputy solicitor general, U.S. Department of Justice, from 1989 to 1993. From 1986 to 1989 and 1993 to 2003, he practiced law in Washington, D.C. He was appointed to the United States Court of Appeals for the District of Columbia Circuit in 2003. President George W. Bush nominated him as chief justice of the United States, and he took his seat on September 29, 2005.

Associate Justices

John Paul Stevens, associate justice, was born in Chicago, Illinois, April 20, 1920. He received an AB from the University of Chicago, and a JD from Northwestern University School of Law. He served in the United States Navy from 1942 to 1945, and was a law clerk to Associate Justice Wiley Rutledge

Photo 1.4 Picture of Supreme Court justices (2008–2009 term).

of the Supreme Court of the United States during the 1947 term. He was admitted to law practice in Illinois in 1949. He was associate counsel to the Subcommittee on the Study of Monopoly Power of the Judiciary Committee of the U.S. House of Representatives, 1951–1952, and a member of the Attorney General's National Committee to Study Antitrust Law, 1953–1955. He was second vice president of the Chicago Bar Association in 1970. From 1970 to 1975, he served as a judge of the United States Court of Appeals for the Seventh Circuit. President Ford nominated him as an associate justice of the Supreme Court, and he took his seat on December 19, 1975.

Antonin G. Scalia, associate justice, was born in Trenton, New Jersey, March 11, 1936. He received his AB from Georgetown University and the University of Fribourg, Switzerland, and his LLB from Harvard Law School, and was a Sheldon Fellow of Harvard University from 1960 to 1961. He was in private practice in Cleveland, Ohio, from 1961 to 1967; a professor of law at the University of Virginia from 1967 to 1971; a professor of law at the University of Chicago from 1977 to 1982; and a visiting professor of law at Georgetown University and Stanford University. He was chairman of the American Bar Association's Section of Administrative Law, 1981–1982, and its Conference of Section Chairmen, 1982–1983. He served the federal government as general counsel of the Office of Telecommunications Policy from 1971 to 1972, chairman of the Administrative Conference of the United States from 1972 to 1974, and assistant attorney general for the Office of Legal Counsel from 1974 to 1977. He was appointed judge of the United States Court of Appeals for the District of Columbia Circuit in 1982. President Reagan nominated him as an associate justice of the Supreme Court, and he took his seat on September 26, 1986.

Anthony M. Kennedy, associate justice, was born in Sacramento, California, July 23, 1936. He received his BA from Stanford University and the London School of Economics, and his LLB from Harvard Law School. He was in private practice in San Francisco, California, from 1961 to 1963, as well as in Sacramento, California, from 1963 to 1975. From 1965 to 1988, he was a professor of constitutional law at the McGeorge School of Law, University of the Pacific. He has served in numerous positions during his career, including a member of the California Army National Guard in 1961, the board of the Federal Judicial Center from 1987 to 1988, and two committees of the Judicial Conference of the United States: the Advisory Panel on Financial Disclosure Reports and Judicial Activities, subsequently renamed the Advisory Committee on Codes of Conduct, from 1979 to 1987, and the Committee on Pacific Territories from 1979 to 1990, which he chaired from 1982 to 1990. He was appointed to the United States Court of Appeals for the Ninth Circuit in 1975. President Reagan nominated him as an associate justice of the Supreme Court, and he took his seat on February 18, 1988.

David Hackett Souter, associate justice, was born in Melrose, Massachusetts, September 17, 1939. He graduated from Harvard College, from which he received his AB. After two years as a Rhodes Scholar at Magdalen College, Oxford, he received an AB in jurisprudence from Oxford University and an MA in 1989. After receiving an LLB from Harvard Law School, he was an associate at Orr and Reno in Concord, New Hampshire, from 1966 to 1968, when he became an assistant attorney general of New Hampshire. In 1971, he became deputy attorney general, and in 1976, attorney general of New Hampshire. In 1978, he was named an associate justice of the Superior Court of New Hampshire and was appointed to the Supreme Court of New Hampshire as an associate justice in 1983. He became a judge of the United States Court of Appeals for the First Circuit on May 25, 1990. President George H.W. Bush nominated him as an associate justice of the Supreme Court, and he took his seat on October 9, 1990.

Clarence Thomas, associate justice, was born in the Pin Point community of Georgia near Savannah, June 23, 1948. He attended Conception Seminary and received an AB, cum laude, from Holy Cross College, and a JD from Yale Law School in 1974. He was admitted to law practice in Missouri in 1974, and served as an assistant attorney general of Missouri from 1974 to 1977, as an attorney with the Monsanto Company from 1977 to 1979, and as legislative assistant to Senator John Danforth from 1979 to 1981. From 1981 to 1982, he served as assistant secretary for civil rights, U.S. Department of Education, and as chairman of the U.S. Equal Employment Opportunity Commission from 1982 to 1990. He became a judge of the United States Court of Appeals for the District of Columbia Circuit in 1990. President George H.W. Bush nominated him as an associate justice of the Supreme Court, and he took his seat on October 23, 1991.

Ruth Bader Ginsburg, associate justice, was born in Brooklyn, New York, March 15, 1933. She received her BA from Cornell University, attended Harvard Law School, and received her LLB from Columbia Law School. She served as a law clerk to the Honorable Edmund L. Palmieri, judge of the United States District Court for the Southern District of New York, from 1959 to 1961. From 1961 to 1963, she was a research associate and then associate director of the Columbia Law School Project on International Procedure. She was a professor of law at Rutgers University School of Law from 1963 to 1972 and Columbia Law School from 1972 to 1980, and a fellow at the Center for Advanced Study in the Behavioral Sciences in Stanford, California, from 1977 to 1978. In 1971, she was instrumental in launching the Women's Rights Project of the American Civil Liberties Union, and served as the ACLU's General Counsel from 1973 to 1980 and on the National Board of Directors from 1974 to 1980. She was appointed a judge of the United States Court of Appeals for the District of Columbia Circuit in 1980. President Clinton nominated her as an associate justice of the Supreme Court, and she took her seat on August 10, 1993.

Stephen G. Breyer, associate justice, was born in San Francisco, California, August 15, 1938. He received an AB from Stanford University, a BA from Magdalen College, Oxford, and an LLB from Harvard Law School. He served as a law clerk to Associate Justice Arthur Goldberg of the Supreme Court of the United States during the 1964 term; as a special assistant to the assistant U.S. attorney general for antitrust, 1965–1967; as an assistant special prosecutor of the Watergate Special Prosecution Force, 1973; as special counsel of the U.S. Senate Judiciary Committee, 1974–1975; and as chief counsel of the committee, 1979–1980. He was an assistant professor, professor of law, and lecturer at Harvard Law School, 1967–1994; a professor at the Harvard University Kennedy School of Government, 1977–1980; and a visiting professor at the College of Law, Sydney, Australia, and at the University of Rome. From 1980 to 1990, he served as a judge of the United States Court of Appeals for the First Circuit, and as its chief judge, 1990–1994. He also served as a member of the Judicial Conference of the United States, 1990–1994, and of the United States Sentencing Commission, 1985–1989. President Clinton nominated him as an associate justice of the Supreme Court, and he took his seat on August 3, 1994.

Samuel Anthony Alito, Jr., associate justice, was born in Trenton, New Jersey, April 1, 1950. He received his BA from Princeton University and a JD from Yale University. He served as a law clerk for Leonard I. Garth of the

United States Court of Appeals for the Third Circuit from 1976 to 1977. He was assistant U.S. attorney, District of New Jersey, 1977–1981; assistant to the solicitor general, U.S. Department of Justice, 1981–1985; deputy assistant attorney general, U.S. Department of Justice, 1985–1987; and U.S. attorney, District of New Jersey, 1987–1990. He was appointed to the United States Court of Appeals for the Third Circuit in 1990. President George W. Bush nominated him as an associate justice of the Supreme Court, and he took his seat on January 31, 2006.

Sandra Day O'Connor (retired), associate justice, was born in El Paso, Texas, March 26, 1930. She received her BA and LLB from Stanford University. She served as deputy county attorney of San Mateo County, California, from 1952 to 1953, and as a civilian attorney for Quartermaster Market Center, Frankfurt, Germany, from 1954 to 1957. From 1958 to 1960, she practiced law in Maryvale, Arizona, and served as assistant attorney general of Arizona from 1965 to 1969. She was appointed to the Arizona State Senate in 1969, and was subsequently reelected to two 2-year terms. In 1975 she was elected Judge of the Maricopa County Superior Court and served until 1979, when she was appointed to the Arizona Court of Appeals. President Reagan nominated her as an associate justice of the Supreme Court, and she took her seat on September 25, 1981. Justice O'Connor retired from the Supreme Court on January 31, 2006.

The information on the justices was taken from a booklet prepared by the Supreme Court of the United States and published with funding from the Supreme Court Historical Society (www.supremecourt.gov/about/bio-graphiescurrent.pdf).

Capstone Case: *United States v. Lopez,* 514 U.S. 549 (1995)

Does the federal government have the authority to pass a statute that prohibits the possession of a firearm in or near school property? (The factual material in this section was obtained from the U.S. Courts website at http://www.uscourts.gov/outreach/topics/lopez/index.html, accessed on August 1, 2008.)

Note that the cases in the text have been edited and the internal citations have been removed.

Background

The dispute in *United States v. Lopez* illustrates the different interpretations of the commerce clause of the U.S. Constitution. In *Lopez*, the Supreme Court addressed the issue of whether the commerce clause provides Congress with the authority to pass the Gun Free School Zones Act of 1990. The act prohibited the possession of firearms in areas on or near school property. Congress had used the commerce clause of the Constitution as its authority for enacting the legislation. The Court was asked to determine whether the possession of firearms on or near school grounds has an impact on interstate commerce.

The federal government is considered a limited government of enumerated powers. Its powers are restricted to those explicitly (directly) granted in the Constitution. Article I, Section 8 of the Constitution is the main source of the federal government's congressional/legislative powers. In addition to providing Congress with certain powers, these enumerated powers serve as a limitation on the powers of state governments. Some examples include the power to regulate interstate commerce, establish an army and navy, and print and coin money.

The Tenth Amendment states that any powers that the Constitution does not give to the federal government or explicitly prohibit the states from exercising belong to the state governments. This amendment preserves federalism by ensuring that power is shared between the federal government and the state governments.

The interstate commerce clause (commerce clause) of Article I, Section 8 gives Congress the explicit power to regulate commerce among the states. Before the Constitution was written in 1787, each state had almost complete control of its economic policy. As a result, states often taxed goods from out of state, prevented certain goods from being shipped across their territories, and engaged in other such activities that generally had an adverse impact on the economy of the young United States. To alleviate some of these problems, the framers wrote a Constitution permitting Congress to regulate interstate commerce (which includes commerce between two or more states). The hope was that with a uniform regulation, as opposed to 13 different commercial regulations, the American economy would grow stronger. Intrastate commerce (commerce solely within a state) was left to state regulation. Due to the fact that there is not an accepted definition of what constitutes interstate commerce, the commerce clause is an occasional source of controversy between the federal and state governments.

Many individuals consider that this clause permits Congress to regulate anything that even remotely touches upon interstate commerce. They argue that American society, especially its economy, has become so interconnected since the days when the Constitution was written that everything now has an impact on interstate commerce. Therefore, Congress can regulate almost any type of activity, including passing criminal laws preventing certain activities. In essence, they argue that the evolution of the economy has given Congress the *de facto* power to legislate on any subject. This ability, known as police power, has traditionally been reserved to the states.

Others contend that Congress has no such power. They point out that the Constitution created a limited government specifically for the purposes of preventing the federal government from assuming such broad police powers.

Moreover, they question at what point an activity sufficiently touches upon interstate commerce to permit it to be regulated under the commerce clause. Although such people agree that, technically, almost anything in modern society has some connection to interstate commerce, they claim that if the connection is too remote, this could allow Congress to exercise a general police power that violates the principles of federalism. Some even take issue with the definition of commerce itself, arguing that it does not affect all economic activity, i.e., manufacturing, but only the physical transfer of goods across state lines.

In his dissent in the case of *New State Ice Co. v. Liebmann* (1932), Justice Louis Brandeis made perhaps the best argument for federalism. He stated: "It is one of the happy incidents of the federal system that a single courageous State may, if its citizens choose, serve as a laboratory; and try novel social and economic experiments without risk to the rest of the country."

It was Brandeis's view that federalism recognizes that not all laws are in the best interests of every citizen nationwide. While the principles of federalism delegate to the federal government the power to make laws that require national uniformity, e.g., citizenship laws, they give states the latitude to be responsive to local needs, interests, and values.

By allowing citizens of each state to live under a government that they believe best represents them, federalism helps to ensure the freedoms of all Americans. For these reasons, it is worthwhile for Americans to familiarize themselves with the boundaries that federalism sets between national and state power.

Facts of the Case

The Gun Free School Zones Act of 1990 was enacted to prevent the possession of firearms near a school. The act forbade any individual to "knowingly ... possess a firearm at a place that the individual knows, or has a reasonable cause to believe, is a school zone" (18 USC 922(q)(1)(A)). Any individual found in violation of this act would be guilty of committing a federal crime and could face imprisonment.

An anonymous tipster informed school officials at Edison High School (located in San Antonio, Texas) that one of its students, twelfth-grader Alfonso Lopez, brought a gun to school. Lopez was placed under arrest after a search by school officials found a .38-caliber handgun and five bullets in his possession. Although Lopez was originally charged with violating a Texas law prohibiting firearms on school property, his case was removed to federal court, where a grand jury indicted him of violating the Gun Free School Zones Act of 1990.

Lopez's counsel sought to quash the indictment on constitutional grounds. He argued that although Congress looked to its authority to regulate interstate commerce to justify this act, the act had nothing to do with interstate commerce. In essence, the counsel argued that Congress had usurped the power of the states by passing an ordinary criminal act under the guise of its authority to regulate commerce.

Majority Opinion

The decision was 5–4, meaning that five justices voted for the majority decision, which held that Congress did not have the authority to enact the legislation, and four justices voted against the decision, which declared the act unconstitutional. Chief Justice William Rehnquist, writing for the majority of the Court, which included Justices Sandra Day O'Connor, Antonin Scalia, Anthony Kennedy, and Clarence Thomas, held that the act was not supported by the commerce clause of Article I, Section 8. After reviewing the history of the Court's commerce clause jurisprudence, the Court stated that Congress does not have the authority to regulate everything that remotely touches upon interstate commerce. The Court held that the constitutional test for whether Congress can regulate an economic activity under the commerce clause is determined by whether the action has a "substantial effect" upon interstate commerce. Although the Court recognized that great deference should be given to Congress in determining what affects interstate commerce, it could not ignore the fact that the connection between guns in school and interstate commerce was so remote that its effect was nowhere near substantial. For these reasons, the Court exercised an independent review of Congress's findings and held that the act was unconstitutional because the act exceeded the authority of Congress under the commerce clause.

Concurring Opinions

Concurring opinions support the conclusion of the majority's decision but offer different reasoning for that conclusion.

In a concurring opinion, joined by Justice Sandra Day O'Connor, Justice Anthony Kennedy reiterated the importance of deferring to Congress's findings regarding what activities have an impact on interstate commerce. Yet, Justice Kennedy held that independent judicial review is sometimes appropriate. When, as in this case, there appears to be no reasonable connection between a regulation and interstate commerce, the Court must strike down the law.

In a separate concurrence, Justice Clarence Thomas argued that the Court should reexamine its commerce clause jurisprudence. In particular, he argued that interstate commerce has a very specific definition. According to Justice Thomas, this definition does not necessarily permit Congress to regulate activities, such as manufacturing, that, although substantially affecting interstate commerce, occur completely intrastate.

Dissents

Justice John Paul Stevens dissented, arguing that the majority's holding in Lopez was a retreat from recent commerce clause jurisprudence. Moreover, he argued that the Court should not substitute its personal feelings about what affects interstate commerce for the findings of the people's elected representatives.

Justice David Souter dissented, arguing that as long as Congress made a rational argument, even if it was not the best one, that gun violence in schools could affect interstate commerce, the Court should defer to its findings. Justice Souter found Congress's justifications rational, and so argued for deference to them.

Justice Stephen Breyer, joined by Justices David Souter, Ruth Bader Ginsburg, and John Paul Stevens, dissented, arguing that gun violence in schools has a demonstrable impact on interstate commerce. For example, Justice Breyer argued that gun violence increases insurance premiums and affects where people want to live. Moreover, he argued that such violence in schools impairs the education process. Because an educated populace is necessary for the U.S. economy to function, he stated that Congress could rationally conclude that gun violence has an adverse impact on interstate commerce. Congress chose to address this issue with the Gun Free School Zones Act of 1990, and the Court should defer to its judgment.

Subsequent Congressional Action

After the decision in *Lopez*, Congress amended the Gun Free School Zones Act of 1990 to permit prosecutions of individuals who possess a firearm on or near school property if the firearm was involved in interstate commerce. Although the Supreme Court has not yet ruled on this matter, the amended statute was held to be constitutional by the Eighth and Ninth Circuits. See *United States v. Dorsey*, 418 F.3d 1038 (2005, 9th Cir.); *United States v. Danks*, 221 F.3d 1037 (1999, 8th Cir.).

Questions in Review

1. Why is there a dual court system in the United States?
2. How does a state criminal case get into federal court?
3. If a criminal case is tried in the Southern District Court for the State of Florida, which U.S. Court of Appeals, if any, will decide the appeal?

4. Could Congress enact legislation requiring states to provide free textbooks to high school students? Justify your opinion.
5. Federal District Court Judge Brown is convicted of failure to pay state income tax. How could she be removed from office?

The Concept of Due Process

2

Nor be deprived of life, liberty, or property, without due process of law.

—Excerpt from the Fifth Amendment, U.S. Constitution

Nor shall any State deprive any person of life, liberty, or property, without due process of law.

—Excerpt from the Fourteenth Amendment, U.S. Constitution

Introduction

The concept of due process is difficult to understand, but its understanding is essential to understanding constitutional law's impact on criminal justice. There are two due process clauses in the U.S. Constitution. Generally, the due process clause in the Fifth Amendment is considered as a restraint on the federal government, and the due process clause in the Fourteenth Amendment applies to states and local governments. In the criminal justice area, due process is classified as either procedural due process or substantive due process. Procedural due process refers to the means or methods by which an individual exercises his or her due process rights. Substantive due process refers to the actual rights themselves, such as the right to a fair hearing or right to notice.

As noted in Chapter 1, the Supreme Court has held that the protections contained in the U.S. Constitution's Bill of Rights were restraints on the federal government and not on the states. The due process clause of the Fourteenth Amendment has, however, been construed to provide most of those Bill of Rights' protections to individuals involved in a state justice system.

Defining Due Process

What constitutes due process is not an easy question to answer. Probably the easy explanation of what constitutes due process is the statement by Justice Felix Frankfurter in his concurring opinion in the Supreme Court case *Joint Anti-Fascist Refugee Committee v. McGrath* (1951, pp. 162–63):

> The requirement of "due process" is not a fair-weather or timid assurance. It must be respected in periods of calm and in times of trouble; it protects aliens

33

Photo 2.1 Justice Frankfurter (November 15, 1882–February 22, 1965) was born to a Jewish family in Vienna, Austria. He immigrated with his family to the United States in 1894, and grew up on New York City's Lower East Side. He attended New York Law School, but in 1902 transferred to Harvard Law School, where he became an editor of the *Harvard Law Review*. He was appointed an associate justice by President Franklin Roosevelt in 1939 and served until 1962. (Photograph by Harris and Ewing, Collection of the Supreme Court of the United States.)

as well as citizens. But "due process," unlike some legal rules, is not a technical conception with a fixed content unrelated to time, place and circumstances. Expressing as it does in its ultimate analysis respect enforced by law for that feeling of just treatment which has been evolved through centuries of Anglo-American constitutional history and civilization, "due process" cannot be imprisoned within the treacherous limits of any formula. Representing a profound attitude of fairness between man and man, and more particularly between the individual and government, "due process" is compounded of history, reason, the past course of decisions, and stout confidence in the strength of the democratic faith which we profess. Due process is not a mechanical instrument. It is not a yardstick. It is a process. It is a delicate process of adjustment inescapably involving the exercise of judgment by those whom the Constitution entrusted with the unfolding of the process.

Other notable explanations of the due process concept are listed below:

- "The essential elements of due process of law are notice, an opportunity to be heard, and the right to defend in an orderly proceeding" (*Fiehe v. R. E. Householder Co.*, 1929, p. 7).
- "Due process of law implies and comprehends the administration of laws equally applicable to all under established rules which do not violate fundamental principles of private rights, and in a competent tribunal possessing jurisdiction of the cause and proceeding upon justice. It is founded upon the basic principle that every man shall have his day in court, and the benefit of the general law which proceeds only upon notice and which hears and considers before judgment is rendered" (*State v. Green*, 1950, p. 903).
- "Aside from all else, 'due process' means fundamental fairness and substantial justice" (*Black's Law Dictionary*, 1961, p. 500).

Early History of Due Process Clause

The concept of due process can be traced back to English common law (Orth, 2003). The Magna Carta was signed in 1215 at Runnymede by King John. The Magna Carta's Article 32 provided, in part, that "no freeman shall be taken, or imprisoned, or disseised, or outlawed, or exiled, or any wise destroyed; nor shall we go upon him, nor send upon him, but by the lawful judgment of his peers or by the law of the land." According to Lord Coke (pronounced Cook), the words "due process of law" are equivalent in meaning to the words "law of the land," contained in Article 32 (Levy, 1988, pp. 304–5).

In 1246, the church in England introduced its inquisitional oath procedure, whereby members of the church were required to state under oath as to whether or not they had committed certain acts of treason against the king or the church. When Henry II became king, he condemned the procedure as repugnant to the ancient customs and in violation of the law of the land. In 1354, the English Parliament reenacted and revised Article 32 of the Magna Carta. The revised article for the first time used the phrase "by due process of law" (Levy, 1988, pp. 303–4).

One of the first American cases involving the concept of due process was the 1693 case of Sir Thomas Lawrence. Sir Lawrence was the secretary of the Maryland colony, a judge, and a member of the governor's council. After he denounced the Maryland colonial government, he was accused of having in his possession a treasonable letter. The council summoned him for an examination and demanded that he produce the letter. When he refused to produce it, the council had him searched and found the letter. He was convicted of unspecified crimes, deprived of his office, and jailed for treason without a trial. Lawrence appealed his conviction to the state assembly. The assembly freed him and restored him to his office holding that his treatment violated the "law of the land" (Levy, 1988).

States and the Fourteenth Amendment

As noted in Chapter 1, the Supreme Court held in *Barron v. Baltimore* (1833) that the first ten amendments to the federal constitution were limitations solely on the federal government and were not limitations on the power of a state. When the Fourteenth Amendment was ratified in 1868, the courts begin to use the due process clause of that amendment to apply most of the limitations and individual protections contained in the Bill of Rights against the states and local governments. The Fourteenth Amendment was designed as an antislavery amendment. It is the first section of the amendment that contains the due process clause. Section 1 of the amendment reads as follows:

> All persons born or naturalized in the United States, and subject to the jurisdiction thereof, are citizens of the United States and of the State wherein they reside. No State shall make or enforce any law which shall abridge the privileges or immunities of citizens of the United States; nor shall any State deprive any person of life, liberty, or property, without due process of law; nor deny to any person within its jurisdiction the equal protection of the laws.

The first case in which the Supreme Court considered the relationship between the Fourteenth Amendment and the Bill of Rights was *Hurtado v. California* (1884). An "information" was filed by the State of California against defendant Hurtado, charging him with murder. In California, an accused may be charged by an information, which is a sworn statement charging the defendant with a violation of a specified crime or crimes. Without any investigation by a grand jury, the defendant was arraigned and pleaded not guilty. He was found guilty by a verdict of murder in the first degree and was then

Photo 2.2 Each Monday when the U.S. Supreme Court is in session, its opinions are announced at its public session on "decision day." Individuals may obtain copies of a decision on decision day from a special office in the Supreme Court building. Two attorneys are currently receiving one of the recent opinions from the office. (Photograph by Cliff Roberson.)

sentenced to death. The defendant appealed the judgment on the ground that he was not legally indicted by or presented to a grand jury in violation of the Fifth Amendment, and that the proceedings violated due process of law, as they were in conflict with the Fourteenth Amendment of the Constitution. In *Hurtado*, the Supreme Court stated that the words "due process of law" in the Fourteenth Amendment do not necessarily require an indictment by a grand jury in a prosecution by a state for murder. The *Hurtado* case pointed out that the Court was not going to accept all the individual protections in the Bill of Rights as necessary requirements to constitute due process.

The first case to apply one of the guarantees of the Bill of Rights to the states was *Chicago, Burlington, and Quincy R.R. v. Chicago* (1897). The Supreme Court held in the case that the "due process of law" required the state to pay compensation to the owner of private property taken for public use. In the case, the city had taken land from the railroad company for the purpose of building a public street.

The guarantees of freedom of speech and press were applied against a state in *Gitlow v. New York* (1925). The Supreme Court stated in Gitlow (at p. 666):

> For present purposes we may and do assume that freedom of speech and of the press—which are protected by the First Amendment from abridgment by

Congress—are among the fundamental personal rights and "liberties" protected by the due process clause of the Fourteenth Amendment from impairment by the States.

Application of the Bill of Rights to the States

From the date of the *Hurtado* case, the Supreme Court has struggled with the concept of due process and determining which Bill of Rights protections are necessary to constitute due process in state criminal courts. The approaches to this issue include the following:

- The fundamental rights
- Justice Hugo Black's total incorporation
- Selective incorporation

In the *Hurtado* case, the Court adopted the "fundamental rights interpretation" of the Fourteenth Amendment's due process clause. Under the fundamental rights concept, the Fourteenth Amendment is viewed as incorporating those rights included in the Bill of Rights that are so rooted in the traditions and conscience of the people to be considered as fundamental rights. The right to a grand jury indictment was not included in those rights, even though that was one of the fundamental rights set forth in the Magna Carta.

The fundamental rights interpretation was used by Justice Benjamin Cardozo in *Snyder v. Massachusetts* (1934). Snyder was charged with murder and attempted robbery of a gas station in Somerville, Massachusetts. His counsel argued on appeal that the denial of his request to be present when the jury viewed the crime scene was a denial of due process under the Fourteenth Amendment. The counsel contended that Snyder had a right to be present, and the failure of the trial court to allow his presence put him at a disadvantage despite the fact that Snyder's defense counsel was present. The Supreme Court denied the appeal. Justice Cardozo stated, in part:

> A state may regulate the procedure of its courts in accordance with its own conception of policy and fairness unless it offends some principle of justice ranked as fundamental.
>
> ... Due process of law requires that the proceedings shall be fair, but fairness is a relative, not an absolute concept. It is fairness with reference to particular conditions or particular results. The due process clause does not impose upon the states a duty to establish ideal systems for the administration of justice, with every modern improvement and with provision against every possible hardship that may befall. (pp. 103–4).

The fundamental rights interpretation prevailed until the 1960s; there was a notable shift from what constitutes a fundamental right from 1930 to

Photo 2.3 Associate Justice Benjamin N. Cardozo (May 24, 1870–July 9, 1938) was a well-known American lawyer and jurist, remembered for his significant influence on the development of American common law in the 20th century. Although Cardozo served on the Supreme Court of the United States from 1932 until his death in 1938, the majority of his landmark decisions were delivered during his 18-year tenure on the New York Court of Appeals. (Photograph by Harris and Ewing, Collection of the Supreme Court of the United States.)

1960. As the Supreme Court became more involved in state criminal trials, the Court determined that more of the rights contained in the Bill of Rights were fundamental. In 1932 in *Powell v. Alabama*, the Court held that the right to counsel was a fundament right for indigents who did not understand the process.

In 1937, the Court backtracked and held in *Palko v. Connecticut* that the due process clause did not include the protection against double jeopardy.

The *Palko* decision was, however, overruled in *Benton v. Maryland* (1969). In *Benton*, a Maryland state court tried the accused on charges of burglary and larceny. He was found not guilty of larceny, but was convicted of the burglary and was sentenced to ten years in prison. Because both the grand and trial juries in the case had been unconstitutionally selected, the Maryland Court of Appeals returned the case to the trial court for a new trial. Benton was reindicted and retried on both charges. At the second trial, Benton contended that it was a violation of his protection against double jeopardy to be tried again on the larceny charge because he was found not guilty of it at the first trial. He was found guilty of both offenses and given concurrent sentences of 15 years on the burglary count and 5 years for larceny.

The Supreme Court reversed Benton's conviction in an opinion written by Justice Marshall. The Court stated that the double jeopardy prohibition of the Fifth Amendment represents a fundamental ideal in our constitutional heritage, and it applies to the states through the Fourteenth Amendment.

The total incorporation approach was championed by Justice Hugo Black. He contended that the due process clause of the Fourteenth Amendment should be read to include all the protections contained in the Bill of Rights. In his dissenting opinion in *Adamson v. California* (1947, pp. 71–72), Black stated:

> In my study of the historical events that culminated in the Fourteenth Amendment, and the expressions of those who sponsored and favored, as well as those who opposed its submission and passage, it persuades me that one of the chief objects that the provisions of the Amendment's first section, separately, and as a whole, were intended to accomplish was to make the Bill of Rights applicable to the states. With full knowledge of the import of the *Barron* decision, the framers and backers of the Fourteenth Amendment proclaimed its purpose to be to overturn the constitutional rule that case had announced. This historical purpose has never received full consideration or exposition in any opinion of this Court interpreting the Amendment.

The total incorporation approach never received the support of a majority of the Court. But between the years 1947 and 1969, the Supreme Court by the process of selective incorporation incorporated almost all of the important guarantees of the Bill of Rights. The total incorporation approach's criticism of the fundamental rights approach, however, probably led to the demise of the fundamental rights approach.

Even though the *Palko* case was later overruled, it is considered as the case that introduced the selective incorporation approach. The selected incorporation approach, which is used today, is a compromise between the total incorporation and the fundamental rights approaches. The selective approach accepts the premise from the fundamental rights approach that not all rights contained in the Bill of Rights are fundamental to due process.

Photo 2.4 Associate Justice Hugo LaFayette Black (February 27, 1886–September 25, 1971) was a politician and jurist. Justice Black represented the state of Alabama in the United States Senate from 1926 to 1937, and served as an associate justice of the Supreme Court of the United States from 1937 to 1971. He was regarded as one of the most influential Supreme Court justices in the 20th century. Black was appointed by President Franklin D. Roosevelt. He was the first of nine Roosevelt nominees to the Court, and with the exception of William O. Douglas, he outlasted them all. Justice Black is noted for his advocacy of a literalist reading of the United States Constitution and of the position that the liberties guaranteed in the Bill of Rights were imposed on the states ("incorporated") by the Fourteenth Amendment. (Photograph by Harris and Ewing, Collection of the Supreme Court of the United States.)

Whereas the fundamental approach looked only to the character of the specific right in a particular case, the selective incorporation approach requires that the Court examine the total right guaranteed by a particular Bill of Rights provision to determine if that provision is fundamental to due process. For example, under the fundamental rights approach, if there was a claim that a certain action by the police violated the defendant's rights again self-incrimination, the Court would examine whether that particular aspect of the right was a fundamental right of the defendant. Under the selective incorporation approach, the Court would look at the entire clause against self-incrimination to determine if self-incrimination in general was a due process right.

The following Bill of Rights protections have been selectively incorporated by the Fourteenth Amendment and are held enforceable against the states to the same standards that the rights protect the individual from federal encroachment:

First Amendment:
  Free speech (*Gitlow v. New York*, 1925)
  Freedom of press (*Near v. Minnesota*, 1931)
  Freedom to assembly (*Dejonge v. Oregon*, 1937)
Fourth Amendment:
  General right to privacy (*Griswold v. Connecticut*, 1965)
  Protection against unreasonable searches and seizures (*Wolf v. Colorado*, 1949).
  Exclusionary rule (*Mapp v. Ohio*, 1961)
  Requirement of probable cause to arrest (*Terry v. Ohio*, 1961)
Fifth Amendment:
  Protection against self-incrimination (*Malloy v. Hogan*, 1968)
  Protection against double jeopardy (*Benton v. Maryland*, 1969)
Sixth Amendment:
  Right to trial by jury in serious cases (*Duncan v. Louisiana*, 1968)
  Right to speedy trial (*Klopfer v. North Carolina*, 1967)
  Right to be informed of nature of charges (*Connally v. General Construction Co.*, 1926)
  Right to confront and cross-examine adverse witnesses (*Pointer v. Texas*, 1965)
  Right to subpoena witnesses in a criminal case (*Washington v. Texas*, 1967)
Eighth Amendment:
  Protection against "cruel and unusual" punishment (*Robinson v. California*, 1962)

The following rights, although required in federal criminal proceedings, have not been imposed on the states:

Fifth Amendment:
   Right to grand jury indictment (*Hurtado v. California*, 1884)
Sixth Amendment:
   Right to jury trial in minor criminal cases (*Duncan v. Louisiana*, 1968)
Eighth Amendment:
   Prohibition against excessive bail (The Court has never decided this issue, but indicated in *Schilb v. Kuebel* (1971) that it would apply to the states.)

Regarding the prohibition against excessive bail, Justice Harry Blackmun in *Schilb v. Kuebel* (p. 485) stated:

> Bail, of course, is basic to our system of law, and the Eighth Amendment's proscription of excessive bail has been assumed to have application to the States through the Fourteenth Amendment. But we are not at all concerned here with any fundamental right to bail or with any Eighth Amendment–Fourteenth Amendment question of bail excessiveness.

Due Process beyond the Bill of Rights

Does the due process clause of the Fourteenth Amendment provide additional protections other than those rights set forth in the Bill of Rights? Stated in a different manner, can police conduct violate the due process requirements of the Fourteenth Amendment without violating one of the specific protections listed in the Bill of Rights? This issue was addressed by the Supreme Court in the case of *Rochin v. California* (1952). Defendant Rochin was convicted of possession of morphine. Rochin, on appeal, claimed that the evidence against him was obtained in violation of the due process clause of the Fourteenth Amendment.

Facts

Having "some information that Rochin was selling narcotics," three deputy sheriffs of the County of Los Angeles, on the morning of July 1, 1949, entered the two-story dwelling house in which Rochin lived with his mother, common-law wife, brothers, and sisters. Finding the outside door open, they entered and then forced open the door to Rochin's room on the second floor. Inside they found the petitioner sitting partly dressed on the side of the bed, upon which his wife was lying. On a "night stand" beside the bed the deputies spied two capsules. When asked "Whose stuff is this?" Rochin seized the capsules and put them in his mouth. A struggle ensued, in the course of which the three officers "jumped upon him" and attempted to extract the capsules. The force they applied proved unavailing against Rochin's resistance. He was handcuffed and taken to a hospital. At the direction of one of the officers, a doctor forced an emetic solution through a tube into Rochin's stomach against his will. This "stomach pumping" produced vomiting. In the vomited matter were found two capsules that proved to contain morphine (p. 187). (This case was decided by the Court before the exclusionary rule was imposed upon the states by the *Mapp v. Ohio* (1961) decision.)

Court's Opinion

Justice Flex Frankfurter delivered the opinion of the Court. He stated that "even though the concept of due process of law is not final and fixed, these limits are derived from considerations that are fused in the whole nature of our judicial process" (p. 171). According to the justice, the considerations are deeply rooted in reason and in the compelling traditions of the legal profession. The due process clause places upon the Supreme Court the duty of exercising a judgment, within the narrow confines of judicial power in reviewing State convictions, upon interests of society pushing in opposite directions. Justice Frank Frankfurter stated in his opinion:

> Due process of law, according to the justice, thus conceived is not to be derided as resort to a revival of "natural law." To believe that this judicial exercise of judgment could be avoided by freezing "due process of law" at some fixed stage of time or thought is to suggest that the most important aspect of constitutional adjudication is a function for inanimate machines and not for judges, for whom the independence safeguarded by Article III of the Constitution was designed and who are presumably guided by established standards of judicial behavior. Even cybernetics has not yet made that haughty claim. To practice the requisite detachment and to achieve sufficient objectivity no doubt demands of judges the habit of self-discipline and self-criticism, incertitude that one's own views are incontestable and alert tolerance toward views not shared. But these are precisely the presuppositions of our judicial process. They are precisely the qualities society has a right to expect from those entrusted with ultimate judicial power.
>
> Applying these general considerations to the circumstances of the present case, we are compelled to conclude that the proceedings by which this conviction was obtained do more than offend some fastidious squeamishness or private sentimentalism about combating crime too energetically. This is conduct that shocks the conscience. Illegally breaking into the privacy of the petitioner, the struggle to open his mouth and remove what was there, the forcible extraction of his stomach's contents—this course of proceeding by agents of government to obtain evidence is bound to offend even hardened sensibilities. They are methods too close to the rack and the screw to permit of constitutional differentiation (pp. 171–72).

The Supreme Court found no distinction between a verbal confession extracted by physical abuse and a confession wrested from a defendant's body by physical abuse. Moreover, the Court found that the police officers' conduct, by illegally violating the defendant's privacy, struggling to open his mouth, and forcibly extracting his stomach's contents, shocked the conscience. The Court ruled that the coerced evidence was inadmissible under the due process clause of the Fourteenth Amendment—and that the due process clause included more protections than those specifically listed in the Bill of Rights.

The test formulated by Justice Frankfurter in *Rochin* provides that it is a violation of due process when the police conduct departs from the fundamental standards of decency and fairness of the English-speaking peoples and shocks the judicial conscience (Dunne, 1977, p. 288). The abortion case, *Roe v. Wade* (1973), which held that women have certain abortion rights, discusses the right of privacy and includes that the right of privacy was incorporated into the due process clause of the Fourteenth Amendment.

Procedural Due Process

Procedural due process refers to the means or methods by which an individual exercises his or her due process rights. As the Supreme Court noted in *Fuentes v. Shevin* (1972), the central meaning of procedural due process is clear: "Parties whose rights are to be affected are entitled to be heard; and in order that they may enjoy that right they must first be notified." The Court also stated that it was equally fundamental that the right to notice and an opportunity to be heard "must be granted at a meaningful time and in a meaningful manner" (p. 570). Procedural due process rights include the right to a fair hearing, the right to be heard, and the right to notice.

Substantive Due Process

Substantive due process refers to the actual rights themselves, such as the right to a fair hearing or right to notice. A U.S. District Court defined substantive due process: "The right not to be subject to arbitrary or capricious action by a state either by legislative or administrative action is commonly referred to as substantive due process" (*Vandergriff v. City of Chattanooga*, 1998, p. 929). The U.S. Court of Appeals, Seventh Circuit, stated: "Only laws that affect fundamental rights come within the purview of the substantive due process doctrine" (*National Paint and Coatings Association v. City of Chicago*, 1995).

Some of the more basic substantive due process rights of a defendant include the right to a speedy trial, freedom from illegal searches, the right to confrontation of witnesses, the right to be tried in the judicial district in which the crime occurred, protection against self-incrimination, the right to a fair and impartial jury, and the right to counsel.

Police Power

The police power of a state or a political subdivision of a state refers to the power of the state or subdivision to place restraints on the personal freedom and property rights of persons for the protection of the public safety, health, and morals. Another definition of police power was explained by a state court in *Marshall v. Kansas City* (1962, p. 884):

> Police power is the exercise of the sovereign right of a government to promote order, safety, health, morals, and the general welfare of society, within constitutional limits. The police power is an essential attribute of government without which constitutional guaranties of personal and property rights would be ineffective and meaningless. In their very nature, neither the police power nor constitutional limitations can be absolute; they are necessarily relative and dependent in the complexities of modern life.

When a state prohibits certain conduct such as speeding in a school zone, protesting in a school building, or selling obscene materials, the state is exercising its police power. A similar process occurs when a city or county regulates the sale of fireworks within city limits. Any exercise of the sovereign right of a state or political subdivision must not unconstitutionally abridge any substantive due process rights. For example, a city ordinance that prohibited people of certain nationality or religion from living in one sector of the city violates the substantive due process rights of the restricted individuals.

Vagueness

> The root of the vagueness doctrine is a rough idea of fairness. It is not a principle designed to convert into a constitutional dilemma the practical difficulties in drawing criminal statutes both general enough to take into account a variety of human conduct and sufficiently specific to provide fair warning that certain kinds of conduct are prohibited.
>
> —Justice Byron White in *Colten v. Kentucky*, 1972

It is a basic principle of constitutional due process that a law is void for vagueness if its prohibitions are not clearly defined. Vague laws offend several important values. First, if we assume that a person is free to decide between lawful and unlawful conduct, then we should insist that laws give the person of ordinary intelligence a reasonable opportunity to know what is prohibited, so that he or she may act accordingly. Vague laws may trap the innocent by not providing fair warning. Second, if arbitrary and discriminatory enforcement is to be prevented, laws must provide explicit standards for those who apply them. "A vague law impermissibly delegates basic policy matters to policemen, judges, and juries for resolution on an ad hoc and subjective basis, with the attendant dangers of arbitrary and discriminatory application" (*Papachristou v. City of Jacksonville*, 1972).

In *Grayned v. City of Rockford* (1972), Defendant Grayned, a demonstrator, was convicted of violating an antipicketing and an antinoise ordinance while demonstrating in front of a school. Grayned challenged the constitutionality of the two ordinances in the state supreme court, which held that both ordinances were constitutional on their face. On appeal, the U.S. Supreme Court reversed his conviction to the antipicketing ordinance, holding that it was unconstitutional. The antinoise ordinance stated:

> No person, while on public or private grounds adjacent to any building in which a school or any class thereof is in session, shall willfully make or assist in the making of any noise or diversion which disturbs or tends to disturb the peace or good order of such school session or class thereof. (Rockford, Illinois, Code of Ordinances, ch. 28, § 19.2(a))

The antipicketing ordinance provided, in part:

A person commits disorderly conduct when he knowingly:

> ...
> (i) Pickets or demonstrates on a public way within 150 feet of any primary or secondary school building while the school is in session and one-half hour before the school is in session and one-half hour after the school session has been concluded, provided that this subsection does not prohibit the peaceful picketing of any school involved in a labor dispute.... (Rockford, Illinois, Code of Ordinances, ch. 28, § 18.1(i))

The Supreme Court held that the antinoise ordinance was not impermissibly vague because it was written specifically for the school context, where the prohibited disturbances were easily measured by their impact on the school. The antinoise ordinance was narrowly tailored to further the city's compelling interest in having an undisrupted school session and did not unnecessarily interfere with First Amendment rights. The antinoise ordinance did not punish the defendant because of what he was saying, but represented a considered legislative judgment that demonstrating should be restricted at a particular time and place, to protect the schools.

In *Winters v. New York* (1948), the defendant was convicted under New York Penal Law § 1141(2), "for the distribution of magazines principally made up of criminal news or stories of deeds of bloodshed or lust, so massed as to become vehicles for inciting violence and depraved crimes against the person." The Court reversed the defendant's conviction, holding that the statute was too vague and indefinite. The Court ruled that the statute failed to give fair notice of what acts would be punished and was unconstitutional. The Court opined that the statute was so vague that an honest distributor of publications could not know whether he was violating the statute.

The Court stated that when a statute uses words of "no determinative meaning," or the language is so general and indefinite as to embrace not only acts commonly recognized as reprehensible, but also others that it is unreasonable to presume were intended to be made criminal, it will be declared void for uncertainty. Justice Frankfurter in dissent stated: "What makes an indefinite law constitutionally vague is hard to define" (p. 521).

Equal Protection of the Law

Even before the adoption of the Fourteenth Amendment, equal protection was an established principle in the United States. In his first inaugural address, President Thomas Jefferson advised the listeners to keep in mind the "sacred principle ... that though the will of the majority is in all cases to prevail, that will to be rightful, must be reasonable; that the minority possess their equal rights, which equal laws must protect, and to violate [those equal rights] would be oppression" (Padover, 1943, p. 384).

The Fourteenth Amendment prohibits the states from denying persons equal protection of the law. As a general rule, the equal protection clause permits states to treat people differently if there is a valid reason for the classification. For example, the City of San Francisco could not prohibit the operation of laundries in the city based on the owner's racial background.

In *Lindsley v. Natural Carbonic Gas Co.* (1911), the Supreme Court discussed the equal protection clause. The Court's decision is summarized in the following paragraphs. The equal protection clause of the Fourteenth Amendment admits of a wide exercise of discretion, and only avoids a classification that is purely arbitrary or does not have a reasonable basis. A classification having a reasonable basis will not violate the amendment just because it was not made with mathematical nicety or it results in some inequality.

The Court will assume the existence at the time the statute was enacted of any state of facts that can reasonably be conceived and which will support a classification in a state statute attacked as denying equal protection of the law. The burden of showing that a classification in a state statute denies equal protection of the law and does not rest on a reasonable basis is on the party claiming that the statute is unconstitutional.

If two teenagers have consensual sex, is it constitutionally permissible for the state to prosecute the male for statutory rape and not the female? Consider the case of *Michael M. v. Superior Court of Sonoma County* (1981).

When the defendant was just over 17 years old, he was charged in a criminal complaint in state court for violating California Penal Code § 261.5 by having unlawful sexual intercourse with a female under the age of 18. Section 261.5 made men alone criminally liable for the act of sexual intercourse.

Defendant Michael appealed his conviction, contending that the statute unlawfully discriminated against men. The U.S. Supreme Court rejected his contention that the penal code section violated the equal protection clause of the Fourteenth Amendment. The Court noted that California had a strong, legitimate interest in preventing illegitimate pregnancies because of the social and economic problems such pregnancies caused it and the woman to suffer. The Court further held that the statute was sufficiently related to that state interest. The Court stated that the statute did not impermissibly discriminate between the genders by punishing only the male when both parties were under the age of 18.

In *Craig v. Boren* (1976), the Supreme Court held that an Oklahoma state statute that permitted females over 18 years of age to purchase 3.2 percent beer, but required that males could not purchase the beer until they were over 21 years of age, was unconstitutional. In *Loving v. Virginia* (1967) the Court held that a Virginia statute that prohibited interracial marriages was a violation of the due process clause.

Capstone Case: *Medina v. California,* 505 U.S. 437 (1992)

Can a state place the burden of establishing that a defendant is incompetent to be tried on the state?

Justice Anthony Kennedy delivered the opinion of the U.S. Supreme Court. (Note that the cases in the text have been edited and the internal citations have been removed.)

In 1984, petitioner Teofilo Medina, Jr., stole a gun from a pawnshop in Santa Ana, California. In the weeks that followed, he held up two gas stations, a drive-in dairy, and a market, murdered three employees of those establishments, attempted to rob a fourth employee, and shot at two passers-by who attempted to follow his getaway car. Petitioner was apprehended less than one month after his crime spree began and was charged with a number of criminal offenses, including three counts of first-degree murder. Before trial, petitioner's counsel moved for a competency hearing, on the ground that he was unsure whether petitioner had the ability to participate in the criminal proceedings against him.

Under California law, a person cannot be tried or adjudged to punishment while such person is mentally incompetent. A defendant is mentally incompetent if, as a result of mental disorder or developmental disability, the defendant is unable to understand the nature of the criminal proceedings or to assist counsel in the conduct of a defense in a rational manner. The statute establishes a presumption that the defendant is competent, and the party claiming incompetence bears the burden of proving that the defendant is incompetent by a preponderance of the evidence.

Based on our review of the historical treatment of the burden of proof in competency proceedings, the operation of the challenged rule, and our precedents, we cannot say that the allocation of the burden of proof to a criminal defendant to prove incompetence offends some principle of justice so rooted in the traditions and conscience of our people as to be ranked as fundamental. Historical practice is probative of whether a procedural rule can be characterized as fundamental. The rule that a criminal defendant who is incompetent should not be required to stand trial has deep roots in our common-law heritage. Blackstone acknowledged that a defendant who became mad after the commission of an offense should not be arraigned for it because he is not able to plead to it with that advice and caution that he ought, and if he became mad after pleading, he should not be tried, for how can he make his defense?

By contrast, there is no settled tradition on the proper allocation of the burden of proof in a proceeding to determine competence. Petitioner concedes that the common-law rule on this issue at the time the Constitution was adopted is not entirely clear.

Petitioner further contends that the burden of proof should be placed on the State because we have allocated the burden to the State on a variety of other issues that implicate a criminal defendant's constitutional rights. The decisions upon which petitioner relies, however, do not control the result here, because they involved situations where the government sought to introduce inculpatory evidence obtained by virtue of a waiver of, or in violation of, a defendant's constitutional rights. In such circumstances, allocating the burden of proof to the government furthers the objective of deterring lawless conduct by police and prosecution. No such purpose is served by allocating the burden of proof to the government in a competency hearing.

In light of our determination that the allocation of the burden of proof to the defendant does not offend due process, it is not difficult to dispose of petitioner's challenge to the presumption of competence. Under California law, a defendant is required to make a threshold showing of incompetence before a hearing is required and, at the hearing, the defendant may be prevented from making decisions that are normally left to the discretion of a competent defendant. Petitioner argues that, once the trial court has expressed a doubt as to the defendant's competence, a hearing is held, and the defendant is deprived of his right to make determinations reserved to competent persons, it is irrational to retain the presumption that the defendant is competent.

In rejecting this contention below, the California Supreme Court observed that the primary significance of the presumption of competence is to place on defendant (or the People, if they contest his competence) the burden of rebutting it and that, by its terms, the presumption of competence is one which affects the burden of proof. We see no reason to disturb the California Supreme Court's conclusion that, in essence, the challenged presumption is a restatement of the burden of proof, and it follows from what we have said that the presumption does not violate the Due Process Clause.

Nothing in today's decision is inconsistent with our long-standing recognition that the criminal trial of an incompetent defendant violates due process. Rather, our rejection of petitioner's challenge is based on a determination that the California procedure is constitutionally adequate to guard against such results, and reflects our considered view that traditionally, due process has required that only the most basic procedural safeguards be observed; more subtle balancing of society's interests against those of the accused has been left to the legislative branch.

The judgment of the Supreme Court of California is affirmed.

Questions in Review

1. Explain the difference between substantive due process and procedural due process.
2. What are the most common substantive due process rights? Procedural due process rights?
3. Explain the present test the Supreme Court uses to determine if a protection in the Bill of Rights applies to a state criminal proceeding.
4. Explain why it is important that a criminal law specifically define what conduct it prohibits.
5. May a state require male teenage drivers to attend traffic school and not place a similar requirement on female teenage drivers? Why?
6. Why does the U.S. Constitution have two due process clauses?

Fourth Amendment

3

History

> The right of the people to be secure in their persons, houses, papers, and effects, against unreasonable searches and seizures, shall not be violated, and no Warrants shall issue, but upon probable cause, supported by Oath or affirmation, and particularly describing the place to be searched, and the persons or things to be seized.

> **—U.S. Constitution, Amendment IV**

The use of the phrase "of the people" in the amendment is interesting because when the same phrase is used in the First, Second, Ninth, and Tenth Amendments it refers to the collective people, same as in the Preamble's phrase "We the people of the United States ...." At the time the amendment was drafted, the Virginia prototype of the protection against unreasonable searches and seizures provided that "every freeman has a right to be secure from all unreasonable searches and seizures of his person...." New Hampshire had a similar provision in its state constitution. Only the Pennsylvania Constitution of 1776 used the phrase "of the people."

There is a conflict among scholars as to whether James Madison's use of the phrase was simply sloppy wording or a way of reminding us that we must be especially watchful of government efforts to use its search and seizure powers to interfere with the people's political activities (Amar, 1998, p. 65). Because the phrase "of the people" is immediately qualified by the use of the more individualistic language of "persons" twice in the amendment and nowhere else in the Constitution, the courts have accepted the phrase to protect the individual private rights of persons and have not considered the phrase to refer to the people solely in the collective sense.

Overview of the Amendment

The Fourth Amendment contains two different commands. The first clause protects us against unreasonable searches and seizures by the government. The second clause, often referred to as the warrant clause, sets forth the requirement to obtain a warrant. To better understand the parameters of the amendment, it is diagrammed below:

1. The right of the people to be secure in their:
   a. persons
   b. houses
   c. papers
   d. effects
   against unreasonable searches and seizures, shall not be violated, and
2. no warrants shall issue, but
   a. upon probable cause
   b. supported by oath or affirmation,
   and
   c. particularly describing the
      (1) place to be searched
      (2) and the persons or things to be seized.

Justice Charles E. Moylan, Jr., of the Maryland Court of Special Appeals, a former mentor of the author, has developed a unique approach to studying Fourth Amendment issues. Judge Moylan's approach is to ask the following three questions:

- Is the Fourth Amendment applicable? (If the amendment is not applicable, then there is no Fourth Amendment issue. Instances of inapplicability include open fields, consent, and plain view.)
- If the Fourth Amendment is applicable, has it been complied with? (If so, evidence will not be excluded. If not, go to question 3.)
- If the Fourth Amendment is applicable and it has not been complied with, what sanctions will the court impose? (See discussion on the exclusionary rule and its exceptions.)

What Constitutes a Search?

Determining if specific government conduct constitutes a search is part of Judge Moylan's first question of whether the amendment is applicable to the situation. If the conduct does not amount to a search, then the Fourth Amendment's restrictions on searches do not apply. Also, if the conduct is not that of government agents or individuals acting on behalf of the government, then the search restrictions of the amendment do not apply.

In *Katz v. United States* (1967), defendant Katz was convicted of transmitting wagering information by telephone in violation of a federal statute. At the trial, the government introduced evidence of Katz's end of telephone conversations, which were overheard by FBI agents who had attached an

Photo 3.1 The great hall of the U.S. Supreme Court building. The Court personnel are preparing for the annual reception of the Supreme Court Historical Society, held each June in the Supreme Court building. (Photograph by Cliff Roberson.)

electronic listening and recording device to the outside of the public telephone booth where he had placed his calls. The Supreme Court reversed his conviction, finding that a person in a telephone booth could rely upon the protection of Amendment IV. The Court stated that a person who occupied a telephone booth, shut the door behind him, and paid the toll that permitted him to place a call was entitled to assume that the words he uttered into the mouthpiece would not be broadcast to the world. The Court held that the actions of the government constituted a search.

The Court stated that the Fourth Amendment protects people, not places. And what a person knowingly exposes to the public, even in his own home or office, is not a subject of Fourth Amendment protection. But what he seeks to preserve as private, even in an area accessible to the public, may be constitutionally protected. The government's activities in attaching an electronic listening and recording device to the outside of a public telephone booth from which Katz placed his calls constituted a "search and seizure" within the meaning of the Fourth Amendment; the fact that the electronic device employed did not penetrate the wall of the booth had no constitutional significance. According to the Court, the Fourth Amendment governs not only the seizure of tangible items, but extends as well to the recording of oral statements, overheard without any technical trespass under local property law.

The Court noted that searches without a warrant are assumed to be unreasonable under the Fourth Amendment, subject only to a few specifically established and well-delineated exceptions, such as searches incident to a lawful arrest or searches with the suspect's consent.

As the result of the *Katz* case, a generally accepted definition of what constitutes a search is as follows:

> A search is a government intrusion into an area where a person has a reasonable expectation of privacy.

Under this definition, there must be:

- a government intrusion
- into an area
- where a person has a reasonable expectation of privacy.

Reasonable Expectation of Privacy

What constitutes a reasonable expectation of privacy is an area that has been subject to many court decisions. By "reasonable" the courts have determined that this must be an expectation that the public accepts. This is an objective, not subjective, test. Some of the cases that have examined this issue include the following:

Samson v. California (2006): A parolee who accepted a clear and unambiguous search condition of parole had a significantly diminished expectation of privacy.

United States v. Banks (2008a): A hotel occupant, who had been evicted from his room in the hotel, had no reasonable expectation of privacy involving his personal possessions that were left in the hotel room.

Garcia v. Dykstra (2008): Defendant had a reasonable expectation of privacy that the contents of a closed, locked storage unit within a gated storage complex would remain free from public inspection. The opening and visual examination of the contents of the storage unit was a search. In this case, a key to the lock was found in front of the storage unit, and the key was given to the police, who used it to open the unit and look in.

Sherbrooke v. City of Pelican Rapids (2008): The recording of the defendant's conversation with his attorney was not an unconstitutional search because the driver had no reasonable expectation of privacy during the call, which he placed in the presence of police officers.

Warner v. McCunney (2008): After a couple was found murdered in their home, and a daughter later found some bullets in a hallway closet, the state trooper who headed the murder investigation was contacted by the daughter and given permission to search the house.

While searching a store room, the members of a forensic team found a plastic container with bullets similar in caliber to those used to kill the couple. Defendant Warner, the son, was charged with murder. He had resided at his deceased father's residence occasionally during the two decades that preceded his father's death; he had not slept overnight at the residence since 1993 or 1994. About one month before his father's murder, Warner had placed some of his personal belongings in a small, second-floor storage room in the residence. The door to the room was unlocked, and the room was accessible to anyone in the house. Some of Warner's belongings were in open boxes; some were in a small, plastic container with drawers. Although the top and sides of the container were opaque, the front of the container was clear. Nothing in the record indicates that the plastic container was locked. At the time of the search, the property was under the control of the executors of the father's estate, one of whom was Warner's sister. The court concluded that the defendant did not have a reasonable expectation of privacy in his late father's house, where the defendant did not lawfully reside in the house, and the house was under the control of a personal representative of the estate.

Plain View

Items in plain view are not considered as a search because there is no reasonable expectation of privacy in such items.

United States v. Banks (2008b): Defendant was found guilty in the U.S. District Court for the Southern District of Iowa under 18 USCS § 922(g) of being a felon in possession of a firearm. He was sentenced to 100 months' imprisonment. On appeal, the U.S. Court of Appeals held that there was no illegal search. The court stated that observing objects in plain view violates no reasonable expectation of privacy, which obviates the need for a search warrant. Ordinarily, a warrant is necessary before police may open a closed container because by concealing the contents from plain view, the possessor creates a reasonable expectation of privacy. However, the contents of some containers are treated similarly to objects in plain view. No warrant is required to open a gun case or similar containers that by their very nature cannot support a reasonable expectation of privacy because their contents can be inferred from their outward appearance. No warrant is necessary to search a bag whose size and shape suggests it contains a gun. This exception is limited to those rare containers that are designed for a single purpose because the distinctive configuration of such containers proclaims their contents; consequently, the contents cannot fairly be said to have been removed from a searching officer's view. Individuals, therefore, possess a lesser expectation of privacy in the contents of such containers when the container is observed from a lawful vantage point.

United States v. Susini (2008): Two officers knocked on the defendant's door and informed the defendant that police had received an anonymous tip that he was conducting a marijuana-growing operation. The defendant and his wife verbally consented to a search, and the wife signed the consent form. In the bedroom, police found blank credit cards on the floor, and in the closet, a machine for embossing names on the cards. The sole issue on appeal was whether the district court erred in holding the search and seizures legal.

Court decision:

The Fourth Amendment of the United States Constitution protects an individual's right to be free from unreasonable searches and seizures. At the forefront of this Fourth Amendment protection is reasonableness. Consensual searches have consistently been held to be reasonable. The only restraint on a validly authorized search conducted pursuant to consent is that the scope of the search be limited to the terms of its authorization. Permission to conduct a general search includes permission to search any compartment or container therein that might reasonably contain the objects of the search.

Generally speaking, there is no reasonable expectation of privacy in objects that are exposed to the public. Thus, it is well-settled that objects falling in the plain view of an officer who has a right to be in the position to have that view are subject to seizure and may be introduced into evidence. The "plain view" doctrine allows a warrantless seizure where (1) an officer was lawfully located in the place from which the seized object could be plainly viewed and had a lawful right of access to the object itself; and (2) the incriminating character of the item is immediately apparent. For an item's incriminating character to be "immediately apparent," the police merely need probable cause to believe that the item is contraband. Probable cause merely requires that the facts available to the officer would warrant a man of reasonable caution in the belief ... that certain items may be contraband ...; it does not demand any showing that such a belief be correct or more likely true than false. A practical, nontechnical probability that incriminating evidence is involved is all that is required.

Construing the facts in the light most favorable to the government, as the prevailing party below, the evidence shows that the officers went to Susini's residence based on a tip that there was a marijuana growing operation taking place. Since they did not have a warrant to search the residence, they knocked and asked for permission. Both Susini and his wife gave verbal consent to search the residence and Susini's wife signed a consent to search form. There was testimony that, as part of a grow operation, there are pots, plants, lights, and tampering with electricity. While the officers were in the bedroom, one of them observed gray electrical lines leading into the closet. On this record, since the officers had a general consent to search the residence, and pots, plants, and other evidence of a dismantled grow operation could have been in the closet, the officers were not acting outside the scope of the consent to search when they looked in the closet.

As for suppression of the credit cards, the evidence shows that, while in the process of performing a consensual search, one of the officers heard a loud noise coming from the rear of the residence. Taking the facts in the light most favorable to the government, when the officers responded to that area of the home, the officers found Susini standing in the bedroom with a large amount of embossed, but not imprinted, credit cards at his feet. Officer Rodriguez testified that he immediately recognized the credit cards to be contraband. The officers had permission to be in the residence; therefore, even though they had initially entered to look for evidence of a marijuana growth operation, it was lawful for them to seize the credit cards on the floor because they were in plain view.

We likewise discern no error in the decision to deny suppression of the machine. In light of the fact that the officers had already found hundreds of embossed, but not imprinted, credit cards in plain view in the home, it was reasonable for the officers to believe that the machine they found in the closet was incriminating evidence. Therefore, the officers had probable cause to believe that the machine was contraband and to seize it. The fact that they did not immediately recognize what it was, or that it was contraband, is not dispositive, given the existence of this probable cause.

Government Intrusion

In addition to the reasonableness requirement, to constitute a search there must be a government intrusion. As will be discussed later, the courts have construed the government intrusion element to mean an intrusion by a law enforcement officer or an agent of a law enforcement officer. For example, a teacher's intrusion is generally not considered a government intrusion.

The Supreme Court discussed government intrusion in the case of *Skinner v. Railway Labor Executives' Association* (1989). The question was whether regulations requiring drug testing on train engineers was legal.

Justice Anthony Kennedy delivered the opinion of the Court:

The Federal Railroad Safety Act of 1970 authorizes the Secretary of Transportation to "prescribe, as necessary, appropriate rules, regulations, orders, and standards for all areas of railroad safety." 84 Stat. 971, 45 U.S.C. 431(a). Finding that alcohol and drug abuse by railroad employees poses a serious threat to safety, the Federal Railroad Administration (FRA) has promulgated regulations that mandate blood and urine tests of employees who are involved in certain train accidents. The FRA also has adopted regulations that do not require, but do authorize, railroads to administer breath and urine tests to employees who violate certain safety rules. The question presented by this case is whether these regulations violate the Fourth Amendment.

The problem of alcohol use on American railroads is as old as the industry itself, and efforts to deter it by carrier rules began at least a century ago. For many years, railroads have prohibited operating employees from possessing alcohol or being intoxicated while on duty and from consuming alcoholic beverages while subject to being called for duty. More recently, these proscriptions have been expanded to forbid possession or use of certain drugs. These restrictions are embodied in "Rule G," an industry-wide operating rule promulgated by the Association of American Railroads, and are enforced, in various formulations, by virtually every railroad in the country. The customary sanction for Rule G violations is dismissal.

... After occurrence of an event which activates its duty to test, the railroad must transport all crew members and other covered employees directly involved in the accident or incident to an independent medical facility, where both blood and urine samples must be obtained from each employee. After the samples have been collected, the railroad is required to ship them by prepaid air freight to the FRA laboratory for analysis. 219.205(d). There, the samples are analyzed using "state-of-the-art equipment and techniques" to detect and measure alcohol and drugs. The FRA proposes to place primary reliance on analysis of blood samples, as blood is "the only available body fluid ... that can provide a clear indication not only of the presence of alcohol and drugs but also their current impairment effects." 49 Fed. Reg. 24291 (1984). Urine samples are also necessary, however, because drug traces remain in the urine longer than in blood, and in some cases it will not be possible to transport employees to a medical facility before the time it takes for certain drugs to be eliminated from the bloodstream. In those instances, a "positive urine test, taken with specific information on the pattern of elimination for the particular drug and other information on the behavior of the employee and the circumstances of the accident, may be crucial to the determination of" the cause of an accident.

The regulations require that the FRA notify employees of the results of the tests and afford them an opportunity to respond in writing before preparation of any final investigative report. See 219.211(a)(2). Employees who refuse to provide required blood or urine samples may not perform covered service for nine months, but they are entitled to a hearing concerning their refusal to take the test. 219.213.

Subpart D of the regulations, which is entitled "Authorization to Test for Cause," is permissive. It authorizes railroads to require covered employees to submit to breath or urine tests in certain circumstances not addressed by Subpart C. Breath or urine tests, or both, may be ordered (1) after a reportable accident or incident, where a supervisor has a "reasonable suspicion" that an employee's acts or omissions contributed to the occurrence or severity of the accident or incident, 219.301(b)(2); or (2) in the event of certain specific rule violations, including noncompliance with a signal and excessive speeding, 219.301(b)(3). A railroad also may require breath tests where a supervisor has a "reasonable suspicion" that an employee is under the influence of alcohol, based upon specific, personal observations concerning the appearance, behavior, speech, or body odors of the employee. 219.301(b)(1). Where impairment is suspected, a railroad, in addition, may require urine tests, but only if two supervisors make the appropriate determination, 219.301(c)(2)(i), and, where the supervisors suspect impairment due to a substance other than alcohol, at least one of those supervisors must have received specialized training in detecting the signs of drug intoxication, 219.301(c)(2)(ii).

Subpart D further provides that whenever the results of either breath or urine tests are intended for use in a disciplinary proceeding, the employee must be given the opportunity to provide a blood sample for analysis at an independent medical facility. 219.303(c). If an employee declines to give a blood sample, the railroad may presume impairment, absent persuasive evidence to the contrary, from a positive showing of controlled substance residues in the urine. The railroad must, however, provide detailed notice of this presumption to its employees, and advise them of their right to provide a contemporaneous blood sample....

Although the Fourth Amendment does not apply to a search or seizure, even an arbitrary one, effected by a private party on his or her own initiative, the Amendment protects against such intrusions if the private party acted as an instrument or agent of the Government. A railroad that complies with the provisions of Subpart C of the regulations does so by compulsion of sovereign authority, and the lawfulness of its acts is controlled by the Fourth Amendment. Petitioners contend, however, that the Fourth Amendment is not implicated by Subpart D of the regulations, as nothing in Subpart D compels any testing by private railroads.

We are unwilling to conclude, in the context of this facial challenge, that breath and urine tests required by private railroads in reliance on Subpart D will not implicate the Fourth Amendment. Whether a private party should be deemed an agent or instrument of the Government for Fourth Amendment purposes necessarily turns on the degree of the Government's participation in the private party's activities, a question that can only be resolved in light of all the circumstances. The fact that the Government has not compelled a private party to perform a search does not, by itself, establish that the search is a private one. Here, specific features of the regulations combine to convince us that the Government did more than adopt a passive position toward the underlying private conduct.

... We are unwilling to accept petitioners' submission that tests conducted by private railroads in reliance on Subpart D will be primarily the result of private initiative. The Government has removed all legal barriers to the testing authorized by Subpart D, and indeed has made plain not only its strong preference for testing, but also its desire to share the fruits of such intrusions. In addition, it has mandated that the railroads not bargain away the authority to perform tests granted by Subpart D. These are clear indices of the Government's encouragement, endorsement, and participation, and suffice to implicate the Fourth Amendment.

Our precedents teach that where, as here, the Government seeks to obtain physical evidence from a person, the Fourth Amendment may be relevant at several levels. The initial detention necessary to procure the evidence may be a seizure of the person, if the detention amounts to a meaningful interference with his freedom of movement.

Obtaining and examining the evidence may also be a search, if doing so infringes an expectation of privacy that society is prepared to recognize as reasonable.

We have long recognized that a compelled intrusion into the body for blood to be analyzed for alcohol content must be deemed a Fourth Amendment search. In light of our society's concern for the security of one's person, it is obvious that this physical intrusion, penetrating beneath the skin, infringes an expectation of privacy that society is prepared to recognize as reasonable. The ensuing chemical analysis of the sample to obtain physiological data is a further invasion of the tested employee's privacy interests. Much the same is true of the breath-testing procedures required under Subpart D of the regulations. Subjecting a person to a breathalyzer test, which generally requires the production of alveolar or "deep lung" breath for chemical analysis implicates similar concerns about bodily integrity and, like the blood-alcohol test we considered in *Schmerber*, should also be deemed a search.

Unlike the blood-testing procedure at issue in *Schmerber*, the procedures prescribed by the FRA regulations for collecting and testing urine samples do not entail a surgical intrusion into the body. It is not disputed, however, that chemical analysis of urine, like that of blood, can reveal a host of private medical facts about an employee, including whether he or she is epileptic, pregnant, or diabetic. Nor can it be disputed that the process of collecting the sample to be tested, which may in some cases involve visual or aural monitoring of the act of urination, itself implicates privacy interests. As the Court of Appeals for the Fifth Circuit has stated:

> There are few activities in our society more personal or private than the passing of urine. Most people describe it by euphemisms if they talk about it at all. It is a function traditionally performed without public observation; indeed, its performance in public is generally prohibited by law as well as social custom.

Because it is clear that the collection and testing of urine intrudes upon expectations of privacy that society has long recognized as reasonable, the Federal Courts of Appeals have concluded unanimously, and we agree, that these intrusions must be deemed searches under the Fourth Amendment.

In view of our conclusion that the collection and subsequent analysis of the requisite biological samples must be deemed Fourth Amendment searches, we need not characterize the employer's antecedent interference with the employee's freedom of movement as an independent Fourth Amendment seizure. As our precedents indicate, not every governmental interference with an individual's freedom of movement raises such constitutional concerns that there is a seizure of the person. For present purposes, it suffices to note that any limitation on an employee's freedom of movement that is necessary to obtain the blood, urine, or breath samples contemplated by the regulations must be considered in assessing the intrusiveness of the searches effected by the Government's testing program.

To hold that the Fourth Amendment is applicable to the drug and alcohol testing prescribed by the FRA regulations is only to begin the inquiry into the standards governing such intrusions. For the Fourth Amendment does not proscribe all searches and seizures, but only those that are unreasonable. What is reasonable, of course, depends on all of the circumstances surrounding the search or seizure and the nature of the search or seizure itself. Thus, the permissibility of a particular practice is judged by balancing its intrusion on the individual's Fourth Amendment interests against its promotion of legitimate governmental interests.

In most criminal cases, we strike this balance in favor of the procedures described by the Warrant Clause of the Fourth Amendment. Except in certain well-defined circumstances, a search or seizure in such a case is not reasonable unless it is accomplished pursuant to a judicial warrant issued upon probable cause. We have recognized exceptions to this rule, however, when special needs, beyond the normal need for law enforcement, make the warrant and probable-cause requirement impracticable. When faced with such special needs, we have not hesitated to balance the governmental and privacy interests to assess the practicality of the warrant and probable-cause requirements in the particular context.

The Government's interest in regulating the conduct of railroad employees to ensure safety, like its supervision of probationers or regulated industries, or its operation of a government office, school, or prison, likewise presents "special needs" beyond normal law enforcement that may justify departures from the usual warrant and probable-cause requirements. The hours of service employees covered by the FRA regulations include persons engaged in handling orders concerning train movements, operating crews, and those engaged in the maintenance and repair of signal systems. It is undisputed that these and other covered employees are engaged in safety-sensitive tasks. The FRA so found, and respondents conceded the point at oral argument. As we have recognized, the whole premise of the Hours of Service Act is that the length of hours of service has direct relation to the efficiency of the human agencies upon which protection of life and property necessarily depends. It must be remembered that the purpose of the act was to prevent the dangers which must necessarily arise to the employee and to the public from continuing men in a dangerous and hazardous business for periods so long as to render them unfit to give that service which is essential to the protection of themselves and those entrusted to their care.

The FRA has prescribed toxicological tests, not to assist in the prosecution of employees, but rather to prevent accidents and casualties in railroad operations that result from impairment of employees by alcohol or drugs. This governmental interest in ensuring the safety of the traveling public and of the employees themselves plainly justifies prohibiting covered employees from using alcohol or drugs on duty, or while subject to being called for duty. This interest also requires and justifies the exercise of supervision to assure that the restrictions are in fact observed. The question that remains, then, is whether the Government's need to monitor compliance with these restrictions justifies the privacy intrusions at issue absent a warrant or individualized suspicion.

An essential purpose of a warrant requirement is to protect privacy interests by assuring citizens subject to a search or seizure that such intrusions are not the random or arbitrary acts of government agents. A warrant assures the citizen that the intrusion is authorized by law, and that it is narrowly limited in its objectives and scope. A warrant also provides the detached scrutiny of a neutral magistrate, and thus ensures an objective determination whether an intrusion is justified in any given case. In the present context, however, a warrant would do little to further these aims. Both the circumstances justifying toxicological testing and the permissible limits of such intrusions are defined narrowly and specifically in the regulations that authorize them, and doubtless are well known to covered employees. Indeed, in light of the standardized nature of the tests and the minimal discretion vested in those charged with administering the program, there are virtually no facts for a neutral magistrate to evaluate.

We have recognized, moreover, that the government's interest in dispensing with the warrant requirement is at its strongest when, as here, the burden of obtaining a warrant is likely to frustrate the governmental purpose behind the search. As the FRA recognized, alcohol and other drugs are eliminated from the bloodstream at a constant rate and blood and breath samples taken to measure whether these substances were in the bloodstream when a triggering event occurred must be obtained as soon as possible. Although the metabolites of some drugs remain in the urine for longer periods of time and may enable the FRA to estimate whether the employee was impaired by those drugs at the time of a covered accident, incident, or rule violation, the delay necessary to procure a warrant nevertheless may result in the destruction of valuable evidence.

The Government's need to rely on private railroads to set the testing process in motion also indicates that insistence on a warrant requirement would impede the achievement of the Government's objective. Railroad supervisors, like school officials and hospital administrators are not in the business of investigating violations of the criminal laws or enforcing administrative codes, and otherwise have little occasion to become familiar with the intricacies of this Court's Fourth Amendment jurisprudence. "Imposing unwieldy warrant procedures ... upon supervisors, who would otherwise have no reason to be familiar with such procedures, is simply unreasonable."

In sum, imposing a warrant requirement in the present context would add little to the assurances of certainty and regularity already afforded by the regulations, while significantly hindering, and in many cases frustrating, the objectives of the Government's testing program. We do not believe that a warrant is essential to render the intrusions here at issue reasonable under the Fourth Amendment.

Our cases indicate that even a search that may be performed without a warrant must be based, as a general matter, on probable cause to believe that the person to be searched has violated the law. When the balance of interests precludes insistence on a showing of probable cause, we have usually required some quantum of individualized suspicion before concluding that a search is reasonable. We made it clear, however, that a showing of individualized suspicion is not a constitutional floor, below which a search must be presumed unreasonable. In limited circumstances, where the privacy interests implicated by the search are minimal, and where an important governmental interest furthered by the intrusion would be placed in jeopardy by a requirement of individualized suspicion, a search may be reasonable despite the absence of such suspicion. We believe this is true of the intrusions in question here.

By and large, intrusions on privacy under the FRA regulations are limited. To the extent transportation and like restrictions are necessary to procure the requisite blood, breath, and urine samples for testing, this interference alone is minimal given the employment context in which it takes place. Ordinarily, an employee consents to significant restrictions in his freedom of movement where necessary for his employment, and few are free to come and go as they please during working hours. Any additional interference with a railroad employee's freedom of movement that occurs in the time it takes to procure a blood, breath, or urine sample for testing cannot, by itself, be said to infringe significant privacy interests....

In *New Jersey v. T. L. O.* (1985) a New Jersey high school teacher discovered a 14-year-old freshman smoking in a lavatory in violation of a school rule and brought her to the principal's office. When questioned by an assistant vice principal, the student denied that she had been smoking and claimed that she did not smoke at all, and the assistant vice principal then demanded to see her purse, opened the purse, found a pack of cigarettes, and upon removing the cigarettes, noticed a pack of cigarette rolling papers, which is closely associated with the use of marijuana. The assistant vice principal proceeded to search the purse thoroughly and found a small amount of marijuana, a pipe, a number of empty plastic bags, a substantial quantity of money in $1 bills, an index card containing a list of those students who owed the student money, and two letters that implicated the student in marijuana dealing. A New Jersey juvenile court admitted the evidence in delinquency proceedings against the student, holding that a school official may properly conduct a search of a student's person if the official has a reasonable suspicion that a crime has been or is in the process of being committed, or reasonable cause to believe that the search is necessary to maintain school discipline or enforce school policy, and that the search in this case was a reasonable one under this standard. The court found the student to be a delinquent and sentenced her to a year's probation.

The Supreme Court held that:

1. The Fourth Amendment's prohibition on unreasonable searches and seizures applies to searches conducted by public school officials.
2. School officials need not obtain a warrant before searching a student who is under their authority.

3. School officials need not strictly adhere to the requirement that searches be based on probable cause to believe that the subject of the search has violated or is violating the law, and that the legality of their search of a student should depend simply on the reasonableness, under all the circumstances, of the search.
4. The search in this case was not unreasonable under the Fourth Amendment.

Protected Areas

The traditional approach to the question of what is protected by the Fourth Amendment was to examine whether the intrusion was into a "constitutionally protected area." This approach was known as the property approach and was based on the following phrase in the amendment: "the right of the people to be secure in their persons, houses, papers, and effects." The property approach was rejected in *Katz v. United States* (1967). As noted in the *Katz* case, the Court adopted the privacy approach. That approach examines whether the individual had a reasonable expectation of privacy.

Generally, a person has a right of expectation in his or her residence and the surrounding living space (cartilage). This right was recognized prior to the adoption of the U.S Constitution. In 1763, William Pitt in his address before the English House of Commons stated:

> The poorest man may in his cottage bid defiance to all the forces of the Crown. It may be frail; its roof may shake; the wind may blow through it; the storm may enter; but the King of England cannot enter—all his force dares not cross the threshold of the ruined tenement. (As quoted in Hendrie, 1998, p. 26)

The Court has used a very broad definition of what constitutes a residence under the privacy approach. One of the leading cases on this issue is *Stoner v. California* (1964).

Justice Potter Stewart delivered the opinion of the Court:

> The defendant was convicted of armed robbery after a jury trial in the Superior Court of Los Angeles County, California. At the trial several articles which had been found by police officers in a search of the defendant's hotel room during his absence were admitted into evidence over his objection. We granted certiorari, limiting review "to the question of whether evidence was admitted which had been obtained by an unlawful search and seizure. For the reasons which follow, we conclude that the defendant's conviction must be set aside.
>
> The essential facts are not in dispute. On the night of October 25, 1960, the Budget Town Food Market in Monrovia, California, was robbed by two men, one of whom was described by eyewitnesses as carrying a gun and wearing horn-rimmed glasses and a grey jacket. Soon after the robbery a checkbook belonging to the defendant was found in an adjacent parking lot and turned

over to the police. Two of the stubs in the checkbook indicated that checks had been drawn to the order of the Mayfair Hotel in Pomona, California. Pursuing this lead, the officers learned from the Police Department of Pomona that the defendant had a previous criminal record, and they obtained from the Pomona police a photograph of the defendant. They showed the photograph to the two eyewitnesses to the robbery, who both stated that the picture looked like the man who had carried the gun. On the basis of this information the officers went to the Mayfair Hotel in Pomona at about 10 o'clock on the night of October 27. They had neither search nor arrest warrants. There then transpired the following events, as later recounted by one of the officers:

"We approached the desk, the night clerk, and asked him if there was a party by the name of Joey L. Stoner living at the hotel. He checked his records and stated 'Yes, there is.' And we asked him what room he was in. He stated he was in Room 404 but he was out at this time.

"We asked him how he knew that he was out. He stated that the hotel regulations required that the key to the room would be placed in the mail box each time they left the hotel. The key was in the mail box, that he therefore knew he was out of the room.

"We asked him if he would give us permission to enter the room, explaining our reasons for this.

Q. What reasons did you explain to the clerk?

A. We explained that we were there to make an arrest of a man who had possibly committed a robbery in the City of Monrovia, and that we were concerned about the fact that he had a weapon. He stated 'In this case, I will be more than happy to give you permission and I will take you directly to the room.'

Q. Is that what the clerk told you?

A. Yes, sir.

Q. What else happened?

A. We left one detective in the lobby, and Detective Oliver, Officer Collins, and myself, along with the night clerk, got on the elevator and proceeded to the fourth floor, and went to Room 404. The night clerk placed a key in the lock, unlocked the door, and says, 'Be my guest.'"

The officers entered and made a thorough search of the room and its contents. They found a pair of horn-rimmed glasses and a grey jacket in the room, and a .45-caliber automatic pistol with a clip and several cartridges in the bottom of a bureau drawer. The defendant was arrested two days later in Las Vegas, Nevada. He waived extradition and was returned to California for trial on the charge of armed robbery. The gun, the cartridges and clip, the horn-rimmed glasses, and the grey jacket were all used as evidence against him at his trial.

The search of the defendant's room by the police officers was conducted without a warrant of any kind, and it therefore "can survive constitutional inhibition only upon a showing that the surrounding facts brought it within one of the exceptions to the rule that a search must rest upon a search warrant...." The District Court of Appeal thought the search was justified as an incident to a lawful arrest. But a search can be incident to an arrest only if it is substantially contemporaneous with the arrest and is confined to the immediate vicinity of the arrest.... Whatever room for leeway there may be in these concepts, it is clear that the search of the defendant's hotel room in Pomona, California, on October 27 was not incident to his arrest in Las Vegas, Nevada, on October 29. The search was completely unrelated to the arrest, both as to time and as to place....

Even if it be assumed that a state law which gave a hotel proprietor blanket authority to authorize the police to search the rooms of the hotel's guests could survive constitutional challenge, there is no intimation in the California cases cited by the respondent that California has any such law. Nor is there any substance to the claim that the search was reasonable because the police, relying upon the night clerk's expressions of consent, had a reasonable basis for the belief that the clerk had authority to consent to the search. Our decisions make clear that the rights protected by the Fourth Amendment are not to be eroded by strained applications of the law of agency or by unrealistic doctrines of "apparent authority." ...

It is important to bear in mind that it was the defendant's constitutional right which was at stake here, and not the night clerk's nor the hotel's. It was a right, therefore, which only the defendant could waive by word or deed, either directly or through an agent. It is true that the night clerk clearly and unambiguously consented to the search. But there is nothing in the record to indicate that the police had any basis whatsoever to believe that the night clerk had been authorized by the defendant to permit the police to search the defendant's room.

It is true, that when a person engages a hotel room he undoubtedly gives "implied or express permission" to "such persons as maids, janitors or repairmen" to enter his room "in the performance of their duties." But the conduct of the night clerk and the police in the present case was of an entirely different order. In a closely analogous situation the Court has held that a search by police officers of a house occupied by a tenant invaded the tenant's constitutional right, even though the search was authorized by the owner of the house, who presumably had not only apparent but actual authority to enter the house for some purposes, such as to "view waste." *Chapman v. United States*, 365 U.S. 610. The Court pointed out that the officers' purpose in entering was not to view waste but to search for distilling equipment, and concluded that to uphold such a search without a warrant would leave tenants' homes secure only in the discretion of their landlords.

No less than a tenant of a house, or the occupant of a room in a boarding house, *McDonald v. United States*, 335 U.S. 451, a guest in a hotel room is entitled to constitutional protection against unreasonable searches and

Photo 3.2 Inside courtyard of the Supreme Court building. (Photo by Cliff Roberson.)

seizures. That protection would disappear if it were left to depend upon the unfettered discretion of an employee of the hotel. It follows that this search without a warrant was unlawful. Since evidence obtained through the search was admitted at the trial, the judgment must be reversed....

Probable Cause

What constitutes probable cause was discussed by the Supreme Court in *Draper v. United States* (1959). Draper was convicted of knowingly concealing and transporting narcotic drugs in Denver, Colorado, in violation of 21 USC 174. His conviction was based in part on the use in evidence of two envelopes containing 865 grains of heroin and a hypodermic syringe that had been taken from his person, following his arrest, by the arresting officer. He appealed his conviction claiming that the seizure of the drugs violated the Fourth Amendment. Justice Charles Whittaker delivered the Court's opinion:

> The evidence offered at the hearing on the motion to suppress was not substantially disputed. It established that one Marsh, a federal narcotic agent with 29 years' experience, was stationed at Denver; that one Hereford had been engaged as a "special employee" of the Bureau of Narcotics at Denver for about six months, and from time to time gave information to Marsh regarding

violations of the narcotic laws, for which Hereford was paid small sums of money, and that Marsh had always found the information given by Hereford to be accurate and reliable. On September 3, 1956, Hereford told Marsh that James Draper recently had taken up abode at a stated address in Denver and "was peddling narcotics to several addicts" in that city. Four days later, on September 7, Hereford told Marsh "that Draper had gone to Chicago the day before [September 6] by train and that he was going to bring back three ounces of heroin and that he would return to Denver either on the morning of the 8th of September or the morning of the 9th of September also by train." Hereford also gave Marsh a detailed physical description of Draper and of the clothing he was wearing, and said that he would be carrying "a tan zipper bag," and that he habitually "walked real fast."

On the morning of September 8, Marsh and a Denver police officer went to the Denver Union Station and kept watch over all incoming trains from Chicago, but they did not see anyone fitting the description that Hereford had given. Repeating the process on the morning of September 9, they saw a person, having the exact physical attributes and wearing the precise clothing described by Hereford, alight from an incoming Chicago train and start walking "fast" toward the exit. He was carrying a tan zipper bag in his right hand and the left was thrust in his raincoat pocket. Marsh, accompanied by the police officer, overtook, stopped and arrested him. They then searched him and found the two "envelopes containing heroin" clutched in his left hand in his raincoat pocket, and found the syringe in the tan zipper bag. Marsh then took Draper into custody.

The crucial question for us then is whether knowledge of the related facts and circumstances gave Marsh "probable cause" within the meaning of the Fourth Amendment, and "reasonable grounds" to believe that Draper had committed or was committing a violation of the narcotic laws. If it did, the arrest, though without a warrant, was lawful and the subsequent search of petitioner's person and the seizure of the found heroin were validly made incident to a lawful arrest, and therefore the motion to suppress was properly overruled and the heroin was competently received in evidence at the trial....

Petitioner does not dispute this analysis of the question for decision. Rather, he contends (1) that the information given by Hereford to Marsh was "hearsay" and, because hearsay is not legally competent evidence in a criminal trial, could not legally have been considered, but should have been put out of mind by Marsh in assessing whether he had "probable cause" and "reasonable grounds" to arrest petitioner without a warrant, and (2) that, even if hearsay could lawfully have been considered, Marsh's information should be held insufficient to show "probable cause" and "reasonable grounds" to believe that Draper had violated or was violating the narcotic laws and to justify his arrest without a warrant.

Considering the first contention, we find Draper entirely in error. There is a large difference between the two things to be proved; guilt and probable cause....

Nor can we agree with petitioner's second contention that Marsh's information was insufficient to show probable cause and reasonable grounds to believe that petitioner had violated or was violating the narcotic laws and to justify his arrest without a warrant. The information given to narcotic agent Marsh by "special employee" Hereford may have been hearsay to Marsh, but coming from one employed for that purpose and whose information had always been found accurate and reliable, it is clear that Marsh would have been derelict in his duties had he not pursued it. And when, in pursuing that information, he saw a man, having the exact physical attributes and wearing the precise clothing and carrying the tan zipper bag that Hereford had described, alight from one of the very trains from the very place stated by Hereford and start to walk at a "fast" pace toward the station exit, Marsh had personally verified every facet of the information given him by Hereford except whether petitioner had accomplished his mission and had the three ounces of heroin on his person or in his bag. And surely, with every other bit of Hereford's information being thus personally verified, Marsh had "reasonable grounds" to believe that the remaining unverified bit of Hereford's information—that Draper would have the heroin with him—was likewise true.

In dealing with probable cause, ... as the very name implies, we deal with probabilities. These are not technical; they are the factual and practical considerations of everyday life on which reasonable and prudent men, not legal technicians, act. Probable cause exists where the facts and circumstances within the arresting officers' knowledge and of which they had reasonably trustworthy information are sufficient in themselves to warrant a man of reasonable caution in the belief that an offense has been or is being committed.

We believe that, under the facts and circumstances here, Marsh had probable cause and reasonable grounds to believe that petitioner was committing a violation of the laws of the United States relating to narcotic drugs at the time he arrested him. The arrest was therefore lawful, and the subsequent search and seizure, having been made incident to that lawful arrest, were likewise valid. It follows that petitioner's motion to suppress was properly denied and that the seized heroin was competent evidence lawfully received at the trial.

Affirmed.

Where the facts are not in conflict, the issue of probable cause is a question of law. Probable cause for an arrest warrant is shown if a person of ordinary caution or prudence would be led to believe and conscientiously entertain a strong suspicion of the guilt of the accused. Probable cause may exist even though there may be some room for doubt. The test in such a case is not whether the evidence upon which the officer made the arrest or a search warrant is requested is sufficient to convict, but only whether the prisoner should stand trial. Moreover, information from a citizen who purports to be the victim of a robbery or an assault has been held sufficient even though his reliability has not been previously tested. A victim is more than a mere informer who gives a tip to law enforcement officers that a person is engaged in a course of criminal conduct.

The following general rules regarding probable cause apply to both searches and arrests:

- Probable cause may be based on hearsay information.
- The phrase "person of reasonable caution" or "ordinary prudent and cautious person" does not refer to a person with special legal training. It refers to the average person "on the street" who, under the circumstances, would believe that the individual being arrested had committed the offense or that items to be seized would be found in a particular place.
- The experience of the police officer may be considered in determining whether the officer had probable cause. Accordingly, what may be insufficient to establish probable cause to an untrained person may be sufficient to establish for a specially trained officer.
- "Reasonable ground" and "probable cause" are used interchangeably in many courts.
- Probable cause requires an "honest and reasonable" belief.
- Proof beyond a reasonable doubt is not required—only that it is more probable than not, i.e., more than 50 percent certainty that the person has committed a crime or that the items to be seized will be found in a certain place.
- Probable cause must exist before the search or the arrest. A search or arrest cannot be justified by the facts that are discovered during the search or arrest. For example, you cannot justify a search of a person by the fact that during the search drugs were discovered on the person.
- Probable cause may be established by (1) the officer's own knowledge of certain facts and circumstances, (2) information given by informants, or (3) information plus corroboration.
- If the information on which probable cause is based is provided by an informant, additional corroboration is normally required. This is based on the questionable status of informants. The informant's information may be corroborated by a showing that the informant has been reliable in the past or gives a precise description of the alleged wrongdoing. The Supreme Court applies the "totality of the circumstances analysis" in informant cases to determine if there is sufficient corroboration to constitute probable cause (*Illinois v. Gates*, 1983). Under this analysis, the Court looks at all the facts to determine if sufficient corroboration is present to establish probable cause.
- Probable cause may be required in the following four basic situations: arrests with warrant, arrests without warrant, searches and seizures with warrant, and searches and seizures without warrant.

Warrants

A warrant is defined as an official judicial document issued by a judicial officer authorizing a government official to conduct a search or to seize a person or item of property. For a copy of a search warrant and the documents accompanying it, see Appendix B.

The warrant clause of the Fourth Amendment requires that no warrant shall issue but upon probable cause supported by oath or affirmation, and particularly describing the place to be searched or the persons or things to be seized. The general rules regarding warrants include the following:

- The warrant must be issued by a neutral and detached magistrate. A magistrate is a judicial officer, usually a judge, who has authority to issue warrants.
- A judge who receives compensation based on the number of warrants he issues is not a neutral and detached magistrate because he has a financial interest in issuing warrants.
- An attorney general for a state may not issue a warrant because he or she is the chief criminal justice officer for the state and, therefore, is not neutral.
- The magistrate, not the police officer, is the individual who makes the decision as to whether there is sufficient probable cause to justify a warrant.
- The magistrate makes the decision regarding the existence of probable cause based on sworn statement or statements furnished by the police.
- The existence of probable cause must be determined based on facts, not opinions, included in the warrant.
- A search warrant is valid for only a limited time, whereas an arrest warrant is valid until the warrant is recalled.
- If the facts in the affidavit are based on information from an informer, there must be other facts to substantiate the information, or other facts that establish the trustworthiness of the informer.
- A search warrant must describe in detail the place to be searched and the items to be seized.
- Erroneous facts in the affidavit will not affect the validly of the warrant, if the police or person submitting the warrant had an honest and reasonable belief in the truth of the facts.

Sufficiency of the Affidavit

In *Franks v. Delaware* (1978), the defendant alleged that the police had made false statements in the affidavit that was used to establish probable cause. The

Supreme Court held that where a defendant makes a substantial preliminary showing that a false statement knowingly and intentionally, or with reckless disregard for the truth, was included by an affiant in a search warrant affidavit, and if the allegedly false statement is necessary to the finding of probable cause, that a hearing be held at the defendant's request. In the event that at the hearing the allegation of perjury or reckless disregard is established by the defendant by a preponderance of the evidence, and, with the affidavit's false material set to one side, the affidavit's remaining content is insufficient to establish probable cause, the search warrant must be voided and the fruits of the search excluded to the same extent as if probable cause were lacking on the face of the affidavit.

A hearing to determine if the police used false information is called a *Franks* hearing based on the *Franks v. Delaware* case. To apply the *Franks* rule, a defendant must establish that the police knowingly and intentionally, or with reckless disregard for the truth, used the statement in the affidavit. An honest and reasonable mistake is not grounds for invoking the *Franks* rule.

Mistakes in the Place to Be Searched

Mistakes in issuing or executing a warrant can affect its validity. Often the courts will overlook mistakes if it appears that the mistake does not make the warrant too general or give too much discretion to the searching officers. One of the leading cases on this issue is *Maryland v. Garrison* (1987).

Justice John Paul Stevens delivered the opinion of the Court:

Baltimore police officers obtained and executed a warrant to search the person of Lawrence McWebb and "the premises known as 2036 Park Avenue third floor apartment." When the police applied for the warrant and when they conducted the search pursuant to the warrant, they reasonably believed that there was only one apartment on the premises described in the warrant. In fact, the third floor was divided into two apartments, one occupied by McWebb and one by respondent Garrison. Before the officers executing the warrant became aware that they were in a separate apartment occupied by respondent, they had discovered the contraband that provided the basis for respondent's conviction for violating Maryland's Controlled Substances Act. The question presented is whether the seizure of that contraband was prohibited by the Fourth Amendment....

There is no question that the warrant was valid and was supported by probable cause.... The trial court found, and the two appellate courts did not dispute, that after making a reasonable investigation, including a verification of information obtained from a reliable informant, an exterior examination of the three-story building at 2036 Park Avenue, and an inquiry of the utility company, the officer who obtained the warrant reasonably concluded that there was only one apartment on the third floor and that it was occupied by McWebb.... When six Baltimore police officers executed the warrant, they fortuitously encountered McWebb in front of the building and used his key to gain admittance to the first-floor hallway and to the locked door at the top of the stairs to the third floor. As they entered the vestibule on the third floor, they encountered respondent, who was standing in the hallway area. The police could see into the interior of both McWebb's apartment to the left and respondent's to the right, for the doors to both were open. Only after respondent's apartment had been entered and heroin, cash, and drug paraphernalia had been found did any of the officers realize that the third floor contained two apartments. As soon as they became aware of that fact, the search was discontinued. All of the officers reasonably believed that they were searching McWebb's apartment. No further search of respondent's apartment was made.

The matter on which there is a difference of opinion concerns the proper interpretation of the warrant. A literal reading of its plain language, as well as the language used in the application for the warrant, indicates that it was intended to authorize a search of the entire third floor. This is the construction adopted by the intermediate appellate court and it also appears to be the construction adopted by the trial judge. One sentence in the trial judge's oral opinion, however, lends support to the construction adopted by the Court of Appeals, namely, that the warrant authorized a search of McWebb's apartment only. Under that interpretation, the Court of Appeals concluded that the warrant did not authorize the search of respondent's apartment and the police had no justification for making a warrantless entry into his premises.

In our view, the case presents two separate constitutional issues, one concerning the validity of the warrant and the other concerning the reasonableness of the manner in which it was executed. We shall discuss the questions separately.

I

The Warrant Clause of the Fourth Amendment categorically prohibits the issuance of any warrant except one "particularly describing the place to be searched and the persons or things to be seized." The manifest purpose of this particularity requirement was to prevent general searches. By limiting the authorization to search to the specific areas and things for which there is probable cause to search, the requirement ensures that the search will be carefully tailored to its justifications, and will not take on the character of the wide-ranging exploratory searches the Framers intended to prohibit. Thus, the scope of a lawful search is "defined by the object of the search and the places in which there is probable cause to believe that it may be found. Just as probable cause to believe that a stolen lawnmower may be found in a garage will not support a warrant to search an upstairs bedroom, probable cause to believe that undocumented aliens are being transported in a van will not justify a warrantless search of a suitcase."

In this case there is no claim that the "persons or things to be seized" were inadequately described or that there was no probable cause to believe that those things might be found in "the place to be searched" as it was described in the warrant. With the benefit of hindsight, however, we now know that the description of that place was broader than appropriate because it was based on the mistaken belief that there was only one apartment on the third floor of the building at 2036 Park Avenue. The question is whether that factual mistake invalidated a warrant that undoubtedly would have been valid if it had reflected a completely accurate understanding of the building's floor plan.

Plainly, if the officers had known, or even if they should have known, that there were two separate dwelling units on the third floor of 2036 Park Avenue, they would have been obligated to exclude respondent's apartment from the scope of the requested warrant. But we must judge the constitutionality of their conduct in light of the information available to them at the time they acted. Those items of evidence that emerge after the warrant is issued have no bearing on whether or not a warrant was validly issued. Just as the discovery of contraband cannot validate a warrant invalid when issued, so is it equally clear that the discovery of facts demonstrating that a valid warrant was unnecessarily broad does not retroactively invalidate the warrant. The validity of the warrant must be assessed on the basis of the information that the officers disclosed, or had a duty to discover and to disclose, to the issuing Magistrate. On the basis of that information, we agree with the conclusion of all three Maryland courts that the warrant, insofar as it authorized a search that turned out to be ambiguous in scope, was valid when it was issued.

II

The question whether the execution of the warrant violated respondent's constitutional right to be secure in his home is somewhat less clear. We have no difficulty concluding that the officers' entry into the third-floor common area was legal; they carried a warrant for those premises, and they were accompanied by McWebb, who provided the key that they used to open the door giving access to the third-floor common area. If the officers had known, or should have known, that the third floor contained two apartments before they entered the living quarters on the third floor, and thus had been aware of the error in the warrant, they would have been obligated to limit their search to McWebb's apartment. Moreover, as the officers recognized, they were required to discontinue the search of respondent's apartment as soon as they discovered that there were two separate units on the third floor and therefore were put on notice of the risk that they might be in a unit erroneously included within the terms of the warrant. The officers' conduct and the limits of the search were based on the information available as the search proceeded. While the purposes justifying a police search strictly limit the permissible extent of the search, the Court has also recognized the need to allow some latitude for honest mistakes that are made by officers in the dangerous and difficult process of making arrests and executing search warrants. In *Hill v. California*, 401 U.S. 797 (1971), we considered the validity of the arrest of a man named Miller based on the mistaken belief that he was Hill. The police had probable cause to arrest Hill and they in good faith believed that Miller was Hill when they found him in Hill's apartment.

The upshot was that the officers in good faith believed Miller was Hill and arrested him. They were quite wrong as it turned out, and subjective good-faith belief would not in itself justify either the arrest or the subsequent search. But sufficient probability, not certainty, is the touchstone of reasonableness under the Fourth Amendment and on the record before us the officers' mistake was understandable and the arrest a reasonable response to the situation facing them at the time. Id., at 803–804.

While Hill involved an arrest without a warrant, its underlying rationale that an officer's reasonable misidentification of a person does not invalidate a valid arrest is equally applicable to an officer's reasonable failure to appreciate that a valid warrant describes too broadly the premises to be searched. Under the reasoning in Hill, the validity of the search of respondent's apartment pursuant to a warrant authorizing the search of the entire third floor depends on whether the officers' failure to realize the overbreadth of the warrant was objectively understandable and reasonable. Here it unquestionably was. The objective facts available to the officers at the time suggested no distinction between McWebb's apartment and the third-floor premises.

For that reason, the officers properly responded to the command contained in a valid warrant even if the warrant is interpreted as authorizing a search limited to McWebb's apartment rather than the entire third floor. Prior to the officers' discovery of the factual mistake, they perceived McWebb's apartment and the third-floor premises as one and the same; therefore their execution of the warrant reasonably included the entire third floor. Under either interpretation of the warrant, the officers' conduct was consistent with a reasonable effort to ascertain and identify the place intended to be searched within the meaning of the Fourth Amendment.

Using Informants to Establish Probable Cause

In numerous cases, the Supreme Court has held that informants are generally unreliable, and that if the facts in the affidavit are based solely on information obtained by an informant, there must be additional facts that establish the informant as reliable, or that tend to prove the accuracy of the information. For example, an affidavit that contains the statement that the police officer "believes that the informant is telling the truth" is only an opinion and is not a fact that the magistrate may use to determine the reliability of the informant. Compare that with the statement "The informant has provided information on four different occasions, and on each occasion her information was found to be correct." The latter statement contains facts, not opinions, and can be used by the magistrate to determine the reliability of the informant. The leading case involving the use of informants to establish probable cause is *Illinois v. Gates* (1983).

Justice William Rehnquist delivered the opinion of the Court:

Respondents Lance and Susan Gates were indicted for violation of state drug laws after police officers, executing a search warrant, discovered marijuana and other contraband in their automobile and home. Prior to trial the Gates

Photo 3.3 Chief Justice William Rehnquist (October 1, 1924–September 3, 2005) served as an associate justice on the Supreme Court of the United States and later as the chief justice of the United States. Considered a conservative and strict constructionist, Rehnquist favored a federalism under which the states meaningfully exercised governmental power. (Photograph by Dane Penland, Smithsonian Institution, courtesy of the Supreme Court of the United States.)

moved to suppress evidence seized during this search. The Illinois Supreme Court affirmed the decisions of lower state courts granting the motion.... It held that the affidavit submitted in support of the State's application for a warrant to search the Gates' property was inadequate under this Court's decisions in *Aguilar v. Texas*, 378 U.S. 108 (1964), and *Spinelli v. United States*, 393 U.S. 410 (1969)....

We now turn to the question presented in the State's original petition for certiorari, which requires us to decide whether respondents' rights under the

Fourth and Fourteenth Amendments were violated by the search of their car and house. A chronological statement of events usefully introduces the issues at stake. Bloomingdale, Ill., is a suburb of Chicago located in Du Page County. On May 3, 1978, the Bloomingdale Police Department received by mail an anonymous handwritten letter which read as follows:

> This letter is to inform you that you have a couple in your town who strictly make their living on selling drugs. They are Sue and Lance Gates, they live on Greenway, off Bloomingdale Rd. in the condominiums. Most of their buys are done in Florida. Sue his wife drives their car to Florida, where she leaves it to be loaded up with drugs, then Lance flies down and drives it back. Sue flies back after she drops the car off in Florida. May 3 she is driving down there again and Lance will be flying down in a few days to drive it back. At the time Lance drives the car back he has the trunk loaded with over $100,000.00 in drugs. Presently they have over $100,000.00 worth of drugs in their basement.
>
> They brag about the fact they never have to work, and make their entire living on pushers.
>
> I guarantee if you watch them carefully you will make a big catch. They are friends with some big drug dealers, who visit their house often.

The letter was referred by the Chief of Police of the Bloomingdale Police Department to Detective Mader, who decided to pursue the tip. Mader learned, from the office of the Illinois Secretary of State, that an Illinois driver's license had been issued to one Lance Gates, residing at a stated address in Bloomingdale. He contacted a confidential informant, whose examination of certain financial records revealed a more recent address for the Gates, and he also learned from a police officer assigned to O'Hare Airport that "L. Gates" had made a reservation on Eastern Airlines Flight 245 to West Palm Beach, Fla., scheduled to depart from Chicago on May 5 at 4:15 p.m.

Mader then made arrangements with an agent of the Drug Enforcement Administration for surveillance of the May 5 Eastern Airlines flight. The agent later reported to Mader that Gates had boarded the flight, and that federal agents in Florida had observed him arrive in West Palm Beach and take a taxi to the nearby Holiday Inn. They also reported that Gates went to a room registered to one Susan Gates and that, at 7 o'clock the next morning, Gates and an unidentified woman left the motel in a Mercury bearing Illinois license plates and drove northbound on an interstate highway frequently used by travelers to the Chicago area. In addition, the DEA agent informed Mader that the license plate number on the Mercury was registered to a Hornet station wagon owned by Gates. The agent also advised Mader that the driving time between West Palm Beach and Bloomingdale was approximately 22 to 24 hours.

Mader signed an affidavit setting forth the foregoing facts, and submitted it to a judge of the Circuit Court of Du Page County, together with a copy of the anonymous letter. The judge of that court thereupon issued a search warrant for the Gates' residence and for their automobile. The judge, in deciding to issue the warrant, could have determined that the modus operandi of the

Gates had been substantially corroborated. As the anonymous letter predicted, Lance Gates had flown from Chicago to West Palm Beach late in the afternoon of May 5th, had checked into a hotel room registered in the name of his wife, and, at 7 o'clock the following morning, had headed north, accompanied by an unidentified woman, out of West Palm Beach on an interstate highway used by travelers from South Florida to Chicago in an automobile bearing a license plate issued to him.

At 5:15 a.m. on March 7, only 36 hours after he had flown out of Chicago, Lance Gates, and his wife, returned to their home in Bloomingdale, driving the car in which they had left West Palm Beach some 22 hours earlier. The Bloomingdale police were awaiting them, searched the trunk of the Mercury, and uncovered approximately 350 pounds of marijuana. A search of the Gates' home revealed marijuana, weapons, and other contraband. The Illinois Circuit court ordered suppression of all these items, on the ground that the affidavit submitted to the Circuit Judge failed to support the necessary determination of probable cause to believe that the Gates' automobile and home contained the contraband in question. This decision was affirmed in turn by the Illinois Appellate Court ... and by a divided vote of the Supreme Court of Illinois....

The Illinois Supreme Court concluded—and we are inclined to agree—that, standing alone, the anonymous letter sent to the Bloomingdale Police Department would not provide the basis for a magistrate's determination that there was probable cause to believe contraband would be found in the Gates' car and home. The letter provides virtually nothing from which one might conclude that its author is either honest or his information reliable; likewise, the letter gives absolutely no indication of the basis for the writer's predictions regarding the Gates' criminal activities. Something more was required, then, before a magistrate could conclude that there was probable cause to believe that contraband would be found in the Gates' home and car....

The Illinois Supreme Court also properly recognized that Detective Mader's affidavit might be capable of supplementing the anonymous letter with information sufficient to permit a determination of probable cause.... In holding that the affidavit in fact did not contain sufficient additional information to sustain a determination of probable cause, the Illinois court applied a "two-pronged test," derived from our decision in *Spinelli v. United States*, 393 U.S. 410 (1969). The Illinois Supreme Court, like some others, apparently understood *Spinelli* as requiring that the anonymous letter satisfy each of two independent requirements before it could be relied on. 85 Ill. 2d, at 383, 423 N. E. 2d, at 890. According to this view, the letter, as supplemented by Mader's affidavit, first had to adequately reveal the "basis of knowledge" of the letter writer—the particular means by which he came by the information given in his report. Second, it had to provide facts sufficiently establishing either the "veracity" of the affiant's informant, or, alternatively, the "reliability" of the informant's report in this particular case.

The Illinois court, alluding to an elaborate set of legal rules that have developed among various lower courts to enforce the "two-pronged test," found that the test had not been satisfied. First, the "veracity" prong was not satisfied because, "[t]here was simply no basis for concluding that the anonymous person who wrote the letter to the Bloomingdale Police Department was credible." The court indicated that corroboration by police of details contained in the letter might never satisfy the "veracity" prong, and in any event, could not do so if, as in the present case, only "innocent" details are corroborated. In addition, the letter gave no indication of the basis of its writer's knowledge of the Gates' activities. The Illinois court understood *Spinelli* as permitting the detail contained in a tip to be used to infer that the informant had a reliable basis for his statements, but it thought that the anonymous letter failed to provide sufficient detail to permit such an inference. Thus, it concluded that no showing of probable cause had been made.

We agree with the Illinois Supreme Court that an informant's "veracity," "reliability," and "basis of knowledge" are all highly relevant in determining the value of his report. We do not agree, however, that these elements should be understood as entirely separate and independent requirements to be rigidly exacted in every case, which the opinion of the Supreme Court of Illinois would imply. Rather, as detailed below, they should be understood simply as closely intertwined issues that may usefully illuminate the common-sense, practical question whether there is "probable cause" to believe that contraband or evidence is located in a particular place.

This totality-of-the-circumstances approach is far more consistent with our prior treatment of probable cause than is any rigid demand that specific "tests" be satisfied by every informant's tip. Perhaps the central teaching of our decisions bearing on the probable-cause standard is that it is a "practical, nontechnical conception." ... "In dealing with probable cause, ... as the very name implies, we deal with probabilities. These are not technical; they are the factual and practical considerations of everyday life on which reasonable and prudent men, not legal technicians, act." Our observation in *United States v. Cortez*, 449 U.S. 411, 418 (1981), regarding "particularized suspicion," is also applicable to the probable-cause standard:

> As these comments illustrate, probable cause is a fluid concept—turning on the assessment of probabilities in particular factual contexts—not readily, or even usefully, reduced to a neat set of legal rules. Informants' tips doubtless come in many shapes and sizes from many different types of persons. As we said in *Adams v. Williams*, 407 U.S. 143, 147 (1972): "Informants' tips, like all other clues and evidence coming to a policeman on the scene, may vary greatly in their value and reliability." Rigid legal rules are ill-suited to an area of such diversity. One simple rule will not cover every situation.

Moreover, the "two-pronged test" directs analysis into two largely independent channels—the informant's "veracity" or "reliability" and his "basis of knowledge." ... There are persuasive arguments against according these two elements such independent status. Instead, they are better understood as relevant considerations in the totality-of-the-circumstances analysis that traditionally has guided probable-cause determinations: a deficiency in one may be compensated for, in determining the overall reliability of a tip, by a strong showing as to the other, or by some other indicia of reliability....

For all these reasons, we conclude that it is wiser to abandon the "two-pronged test" established by our decisions in *Aguilar* and *Spinelli*. In its place we reaffirm the totality-of-the-circumstances analysis that traditionally has informed probable-cause determinations…. The task of the issuing magistrate is simply to make a practical, common-sense decision whether, given all the circumstances set forth in the affidavit before him, including the "veracity" and "basis of knowledge" of persons supplying hearsay information, there is a fair probability that contraband or evidence of a crime will be found in a particular place. And the duty of a reviewing court is simply to ensure that the magistrate had a "substantial basis for … concluding" that probable cause existed…. We are convinced that this flexible, easily applied standard will better achieve the accommodation of public and private interests that the Fourth Amendment requires than does the approach that has developed from *Aguilar* and *Spinelli*….

… The judgment of the Supreme Court of Illinois therefore must be Reversed.

Arrests

An arrest (seizure of a person) is the taking of a person into custody so that the person may be held to answer for the commission of a crime. The four essential elements required for an arrest are as follows:

1. Intention to arrest
2. Authority to arrest
3. Seizure and detention
4. An understanding by the arrestee that he or she is being arrested

General rules regarding an arrest warrant are as follows:

- A warrant must describe the offense charged and contain the name of the accused, or if the name is unknown, a description of the accused.
- The warrant also must indicate the time of issuance, the city or county and state where it is issued, and the duty of the arresting officer to bring the defendant before the magistrate.
- It is directed to, and thus may be acted on by, any peace officer in the jurisdiction. (Note: A warrant issued by a state court is directed to any peace officer in the state.)
- Arrest warrants, unlike search warrants, are valid until they are recalled by the court.
- The arrest warrant can specify the amount of bail needed by the accused to be released.
- The officer making the arrest pursuant to a warrant need not have the warrant in his or her presence, as long as the officer is aware of its contents.

- If the officer has the warrant, he or she must display it if requested. If the officer does not have the warrant in his or her presence, the officer must explain to the defendant the reason for the arrest.
- The officer must have an intention to arrest a person. There can be no accidental arrests. This is a subjective requirement.
- The person arrested may only be subjected to such restraint as is reasonable for his arrest and detention.
- Booking, being merely a ministerial function, is not part of the arrest process, and delay in or an absence of booking will not affect an otherwise legal arrest.
- Where the arrest is lawful, subsequent unreasonable delay in taking the person before a magistrate will not affect the legality of the arrest.
- The officer making the arrest must have the authority to make the arrest.
- There must be a seizure and detention of the person to constitute an arrest.
- Merely telling a person that he or she is under arrest is not an arrest unless it is accompanied by an actual seizure of the person or by the person's submission to the officer's will and control.
- A police officer's uniform is sufficient indicia of authority to make the arrest (*People v. Superior Court of San Mateo County*, 1973).
- Miranda warnings are not required for questions asked during the booking process. The preliminary questions asked an accused with respect to his name and address, which are part of the booking proceedings, do not amount to an interrogation to elicit incriminating testimony or admissions from the defendant (*People v. Weathington*, 1979).

In *People v. Superior Court of San Mateo County* (1973), the defendant drove a motor vehicle off the shoulder of a road. A police officer observed that the defendant smelled of alcohol and had red, glassy eyes and slurred speech. The defendant was arrested for driving while under the influence. At the hospital a blood test was administered while the defendant was unconscious. The respondent superior court granted the defendant's motion to suppress the blood test as evidence, holding that the defendant was not placed under lawful arrest by the officer. On appeal, the appellate court held that the defendant was lawfully arrested at the scene of the accident. Where an officer informed the person to be arrested of the intention and authority to arrest him, to require that the officer closely attend to that person to the exclusion of the officer's duty to obtain aid for accident victims and to prevent further injuries would be wrong. The court concluded that failure to maintain close police custody over the hospitalized suspect, or to place a police hold on him, did not reasonably or retroactively affect the validity of an otherwise lawful arrest at the accident scene.

A police officer may make a seizure by a show of authority and without the use of physical force, but there is no seizure without actual submission; otherwise, there is at most an attempted seizure, so far as the Fourth Amendment is concerned (*California v. Hodari D.*, 1991).

Capstone Case: *Atwater v. City of Lago Vista,* 149 L. Ed. 2d 549 (2001)

Should the police be allowed to arrest a person who has committed an offense for which the punishment includes only a fine?

One of the most controversial cases decided by the U.S. Supreme Court in recent years was the *Atwater* case, decided in 2001.

Gail Atwater was driving her pickup in Lago Vista, Texas, with her three-year-old son and five-year-old daugther, when she was stopped by the police. None of them were wearing seatbelts. Police officer Turek observed the violations and pulled Atwater over. According to Atwater's civil rights complaint, Turek approached the truck and yelled something to the effect of "We have met before" and "You are going to jail." Turek called for backup and asked Atwater for her driver's license and insurance papers. Atwater stated that her purse had been stolen the day before and she did not have the papers. Turek said that he had heard that story two hundred times. Atwater claimed that she asked if she could take her crying and frightened children to a nearby friend's house. Atwater claimed that Turek stated that she was not going anywhere. Atwater's friend arrived and took the children. Atwater was then arrested and released on $310 bond. Atwater later pleaded guilty to a misdemeanor seatbelt violation and paid a $50 fine.

Atwater filed suit against Turek and the city under 42 USCS 1983, alleging civil rights violation.

The U.S. Supreme Court, in a 5–4 decision, held that a police officer could arrest under the Fourth Amendment without a warrant for a misdemeanor not amounting to or involving a breach of peace. The majority opinion stated that there was no dispute that Atwater had committed a crime in the presence of a police officer, and Turek was authorized to make a custodial arrest without balancing the costs and benefits or determining whether Atwater's arrest was in some sense necessary. The court stated that the standard of probable cause applies to all arrests, without the need to balance the interests and circumstances involved in particular situations. (Note: Failure to wear a seatbelt was punishable only by a fine.)

Justice Souter wrote the Court's majority opinion. He stated:

A responsible Fourth Amendment balance is not well served by standards requiring sensitive, case-by-case determinations of government need, lest every discretionary judgment in the field be converted into an occasion for constitutional review. Often enough, the Fourth Amendment has to be applied on the spur (and in the heat) of the moment, and the object in implementing its command of reasonableness is to draw standards sufficiently clear and simple to be applied with a fair prospect of surviving judicial second-guessing months and years after an arrest or search is made. Courts attempting to strike a reasonable Fourth Amendment balance thus credit the Government's side with an essential interest in readily administrable rules. Fourth Amendment rules ought to be expressed in terms that are readily applicable by the police in the context of the law enforcement activities in which they are necessarily engaged and not qualified by all sorts of ifs, ands, and buts.

Questions in Review

1. What is required before a search warrant may be issued by a magistrate?
2. What constitutes a search?
3. What constitutes an arrest?
4. Why do the courts require corroboration of an informant's statement to constitute probable cause?
5. Define probable cause.

Fourth Amendment Issues

4

Introduction

Chapter 3 explored the wording of the Fourth Amendment, what constitutes a search or an arrest, and the warrant requirements. The discussion of the Fourth Amendment will continue in this chapter as we examine other Fourth Amendment issues.

Most arrests are accomplished without a warrant; however, in the area of searches, the general rule is that you must get a warrant unless you cannot. When a search is conducted under a warrant, the trial court will presume that the search was authorized and legal. And the burden of establishing that the search was not valid is upon the person attacking the search, which in most cases will be the defendant. If, however, the search is without a warrant, then the trial court will presume that the search is not valid and the prosecution has the burden to establish its legality.

Searches without Warrants

There are several recognized exceptions to the warrant requirement for searches. Those exceptions will be explored in this section. It is important to ascertain whether probable cause is needed prior to the warrantless search.

With Probable Cause

The two common situations where the police are allowed to search without a warrant, but are required to have probable cause, are searches based on exigent circumstances and vehicle searches. The basis for an approval of a search under exigent circumstances is that it is impractical or impossible to get a warrant. The basis for a warrantless search of a vehicle is that there is a lesser expectation of privacy in a vehicle on a public road, and that to hold the vehicle while waiting for a warrant would cause an inconvenience to both the police and the driver.

Exigent circumstances include the following:

- Where it would be impractical for the police to obtain a search warrant. For example, if the police want to take a blood sample from an apparent intoxicated driver, if they wait for a warrant, the alcohol in the blood may dissipate before the warrant is issued.
- Where an emergency situation justifies the warrantless search.

In both of the two described exigent circumstances situations, probable cause is required, and only the necessity to obtain a warrant is excused.

An unconsented intrusion into a person's body by a person at the direction of law enforcement is a search. The courts have also held that because the intrusions into a human body involve an area where a person has significantly heightened privacy, the police must be justified in believing that the intrusion will result in the discovery of evidence (*People v. Burgner*, 1986). However, if a medical person orders a blood sample for medical purposes, generally the sample will be admissible in evidence because it was not a "search" within the Fourth Amendment, but a medical diagnosis. Any intrusions into a person's body must be under acceptable medical standards.

As a general rule, the only time the police may go into a private residence to arrest a felon without a warrant is under the hot pursuit exception or exigent circumstances, and the action is considered necessary to prevent harm to people or the immediate destruction of evidence. If an armed individual is being chased by the police after an armed robbery and the individual enters a private residence, the police would be justified in entering the residence to apprehend the individual. If, however, the individual was not chased into the private residence, but the police are aware of his or her location within the residence, generally the police will be required to obtain a warrant before searching the private residence. In the latter situation, because there is no hot pursuit, the police could surround the home and wait for a warrant. The courts have shown a general reluctance to approve warrantless searches of private residences.

In *United States v. Ponder* (2007), a caller told the police that shots had been fired. When police officers arrived on the scene, the officers observed a bloodied, vandalized vehicle with smashed windows. The car owner informed the officers that two brothers had vandalized his vehicle and threatened him with a gun. The owner then took police to where he believed they would be. The police arrived at the defendant's brother's house and saw two males sitting on the porch. As the officers approached, the brother went inside and the defendant remained on the porch. The officers noticed that the defendant's hand was bloody and arrested him. The police entered the home to search for the brother and discovered two guns. The appellate court found that exigent circumstances supported the warrantless entry because it was reasonable for the officers to fear that the brother had both a weapon and a willingness to use it because the victim had indicated that the defendant and the brother were the individuals who had illegally fired shots near his home less than an hour earlier. The officers did not intentionally create an exigent situation, but rather, the exigent situation naturally arose when they observed the brother flee into the house.

The warrantless search, but with probable cause, of a vehicle on public roads is based on the premise that there is a lesser expectation of privacy in the vehicle than there would be in a home or similar place. The warrantless search of the vehicle is applicable only when the vehicle is on a public road or other public place, such as the parking lot of a mall. The police generally need a warrant or exigent circumstances to search a vehicle parked on private property. In most states, if the officer has probable cause to search a vehicle, then the officer may open any container in the vehicle. For example, if the officer is searching for drugs, he or she may look, with probable cause, into a briefcase in the vehicle trunk. If, however, the officer has probable cause to search for illegal immigrants in the vehicle; the officer may look in the trunk, but not in a briefcase in the trunk, because of the old adage that "you cannot find an elephant in a matchbox."

For purposes of a search warrant requirement, what about motor homes? Is it a vehicle or a home? Generally, if the motor home is on a public road or parked in a grocery store parking lot, it is subject to being searched without a warrant if probable cause exists. If, however, the motor home is on blocks on private land, it is considered as a home (*California v. Carney*, 1985).

Probable Cause Not Needed

Searches Incident to Arrest

When a person is legally arrested, the individual may be searched. As long as the arrest is legal, no probable cause is needed to search him or her. In *State v. Oyenusi* (2006), a New Jersey appellate court discussed the right to search pursuant to an arrest. The court stated:

> The issue presented by this appeal is whether law enforcement officers may conduct a warrantless search of the contents of a container in the possession of an arrestee even if the arrestee no longer has access to the container when the search is conducted. We conclude that such a search, if conducted contemporaneously with the arrest, is a valid search incident to an arrest under both the Fourth Amendment to the United States Constitution and Article I, paragraph 7 of the New Jersey Constitution.
>
> Defendant and his brother Babatunde Oyenusi were indicted on two counts of Medicaid fraud, in violation of N.J.S.A. 30:4D-17, N.J.S.A. 2C:2-6 and N.J.S.A. 2C:2-7; second-degree theft by deception, in violation of N.J.S.A. 2C:20-4, N.J.S.A. 2C:2-6 and N.J.S.A. 2C:2-7; second-degree misconduct by a corporate official, in violation of N.J.S.A. 2C:21-9c; and conspiracy to commit the foregoing offenses, in violation of N.J.S.A. 2C:5-2.

Codefendants moved to suppress evidence obtained in a search incident to Babatunde's arrest. After an evidentiary hearing, the trial court denied the motion. Codefendants were subsequently tried jointly, which resulted in a guilty verdict against defendant on all charges.

The trial court sentenced the defendants to concurrent five-year terms of imprisonment for theft by deception and misconduct by a corporate official, and a three-year concurrent term for one count of Medicaid fraud. The court also imposed a $75,000 fine and required the defendants to pay the state $152,215 in restitution.

The leading case dealing with the permissible scope of a search incident to an arrest under the Fourth Amendment is *Chimel v. California*, [citations omitted]. The Court in *Chimel* held that when the police arrest a suspect, they may conduct a search of his "person and the area 'within his immediate control'— construing that phrase to mean the area from within which he might gain possession of a weapon or destructible evidence." The Supreme Court of the United States has repeatedly reaffirmed the *Chimel* test for determining the validity of a search incident to an arrest.

The authorization to search incident to an arrest is based on the need to disarm the arrestee and preserve evidence for later use at trial. However, the validity of such a search does not depend on what a court may later decide was the probability in a particular arrest situation that weapons or evidence would in fact be found upon the person of the suspect. A custodial arrest of a suspect based on probable cause is a reasonable intrusion under the Fourth Amendment; that intrusion being lawful, a search incident to the arrest requires no additional justification.

The authority to search an arrestee and the area within his immediate control includes the authority to search a container found in the arrestee's possession.

The search that is the subject of this appeal was conducted on February 10, 1996, pursuant to a warrant for Babatunde's arrest. This warrant was not based on evidence of the Medicaid fraud scheme for which the defendant was convicted, but instead on evidence of Babatunde's participation in the sale of stolen prescription drugs through pharmacies.

The arrest was made outside of Babatunde's Newark residence by Division of Criminal Justice investigators. At the time of Babatunde's arrest, he was carrying two white plastic bags. The arresting officers took the bags from Babatunde, placed handcuffs on him, and then looked inside the bags, which were not sealed or otherwise secured. One of the bags contained a typewriter, and the other a notebook, blank prescription pads, Medicaid eligibility cards under various names, and some prescriptions ostensibly written by doctors. The items found in the second bag were subsequently used by the state to prove the defendant's involvement in the Medicaid fraud scheme.

At the suppression hearing, one of the arresting officers was asked how much time elapsed between Babatunde's arrest and the examination of the contents of the bags, in response to which he said: "Not much. I mean, we arrested him out on the street, looked in the bags on the street. We did it all right there."

A search incident to an arrest may be valid under some circumstances even though it is not conducted contemporaneously with the arrest. In *United States v. Edwards*, the Court upheld the validity of the seizure and subsequent search of clothing taken from an arrestee in jail approximately ten hours after his arrest.

Once the accused is lawfully arrested and is in custody, the effects in his possession at the place of detention that were subject to search at the time and place of his arrest may lawfully be searched and seized without a warrant even though a substantial period of time has elapsed between the arrest and subsequent administrative processing, on the one hand, and the taking of the property for use as evidence, on the other. The court upheld the conviction and the legality of the search.

If the individual is arrested in a car, generally the police may search the entire passenger compartment of the automobile. In most states, the police may also search the trunk of the vehicle and any containers in the car. Several states have placed restrictions on searching packages within the automobile.

If the individual is arrested in a home, the police may not search the entire house, but may search the area within the immediate control of the accused at the time of the arrest. The rationale for this rule in the search of the immediate area is to keep the accused from obtaining a weapon or destroying the evidence (lunge distance). Apparently, it does not matter that the search is conducted after the accused is under control and cannot reach those areas.

Actual case: Consider the fact situation in *Chimel v. California* (1969) where the police went to the defendant's home with an arrest warrant to arrest him for an alleged burglary. When the defendant returned from work, the police arrested him. Police then asked for permission to "look around." Even though the defendant objected, the officers conducted a search. They looked through the entire house and had the defendant's wife open drawers and physically remove contents of the drawers so they could view items. Police seized a number of coins and medals, among other things, that the state later used to convict the defendant of burglary.
Question: Was this search a valid search incident to an arrest?
Court decision: There was no justification for searching any room other than that in which the arrest occurred. Even searching through desk drawers or other closed or concealed areas of the room where the arrest occurred was not appropriate. Extending the search to the entire house was not proper, and the conviction was reversed.

If, however, under the *Chimel* fact situation, during the search the police hear a noise in another room of the home, may the police search other parts of the home? The courts will allow the police to search other parts of the home, if there is a valid question regarding the safety of the officers.

Searches of Probationers and Parolees

As the court noted in *United States v. Godsey* (2007, p. 876), probationers do not enjoy the absolute liberty to which every citizen is entitled, but only conditional liberty dependent on observance of special (probation) restrictions. The Supreme Court has upheld the search of probationers without a warrant and without probable cause, concluding that the state regulation under which the search was conducted was justified by the "special needs" of a state's probation system.

As the Supreme Court noted in *Morrissey v. Brewer* (1972, p. 484), parolees, who are on the "continuum" of state-imposed punishments, have fewer expectations of privacy than probationers, because parole is more akin to imprisonment than probation is. "The essence of parole is release from prison, before the completion of sentence, on the condition that the prisoner abides by certain rules during the balance of the sentence."

Samson v. California (2006) centered around a California law that required all parolees to agree in writing to submit to searches and seizures by parole officers or police officers at any time of day or night, with or without a search warrant and with or without cause. Samson was a parolee who had signed such a waiver. A police officer approached Samson while he was walking down the street, and after the officer learned that Samson had no outstanding warrants, he decided to search Samson based solely on his status as a parolee. During the search, the officer recovered methamphetamine. At trial, Samson moved to suppress this evidence on the grounds that the search was arbitrary and capricious. The trial court admitted the evidence and Samson was convicted.

The United States Supreme Court upheld the conviction finding the state's interest to be substantial and Samson's interest to be diminished based on his status as a parolee; the Court ruled the search was reasonable. The court concluded that a parolee search supported by neither individualized suspicion nor special needs could nonetheless be reasonable.

In *United States v. Knights* (2001), the California court's order sentencing respondent Knights to probation for a drug offense included the condition that Knights submit to search at anytime, with or without a search or arrest warrant or reasonable cause, by any probation or law enforcement officer. Subsequently, a sheriff's detective, with reasonable suspicion, searched Knights's apartment. Based in part on items recovered, a federal grand jury indicted Knights for conspiracy to commit arson, for possession of an unregistered destructive device, and for being a felon in possession of ammunition.

The U.S. Supreme Court held that the warrantless search of Knights, supported by reasonable suspicion and authorized by a probation condition, satisfied the Fourth Amendment. Because nothing in Knights's probation condition limited searches to those with a "probationary" purpose,

Photo 4.1 One of two circular staircases in the U.S. Supreme Court building. The staircase is five stories high and is supported only by overlapping steps and their extensions into the wall. (Photograph by Cliff Roberson.)

the question before the Court was whether the Fourth Amendment imposed such a limitation. The Court stated that the Fourth Amendment's touchstone is reasonableness, and a search's reasonableness is determined by assessing, on the one hand, the degree to which it intrudes upon an individual's privacy and, on the other, the degree to which it is needed to promote legitimate governmental interests. Knights' status as a probationer subject to a search condition informed both sides of that balance. The sentencing judge reasonably concluded that the search condition would further the two primary goals of probation—rehabilitation and protecting society from future criminal violations. Knights was unambiguously informed of the search condition. Thus, Knights' reasonable expectation of privacy was significantly diminished. In assessing the governmental interest, it must be remembered that the very assumption of probation is that the probationer is more likely than others to violate the law. The state's interest in apprehending criminal law violators, thereby protecting potential victims, may justifiably focus on probationers in a way that it does not on the ordinary citizen. On balance, no more than reasonable suspicion was required to search this probationer's house. The degree of individualized suspicion required is a determination that a sufficiently high probability of criminal conduct makes the intrusion on the individual's privacy interest reasonable. Although the Fourth Amendment ordinarily requires probable cause, a lesser degree satisfies the Constitution when the balance of governmental and private interests makes such a standard reasonable. The same circumstances that lead to the conclusion that reasonable suspicion is constitutionally sufficient also render a warrant requirement unnecessary.

No Reasonable Expection of Privacy Situations

Often the courts will state that consent searches and the open fields exception are searches that do not require warrants or probable cause. But if you examine the Supreme Court's definition of what constitutes a search, they do not qualify as searches because there is no reasonable expectation of privacy. The most common situations in this area are discussed in this section.

Consent Searches

When an individual consents to a search, he or she waives search protections under the Fourth Amendment. In *United States v. Ziegler* (2007), the defendant claimed that a police officer, lacking a warrant, violated the Fourth Amendment by directing his employer's employees to enter the defendant's private office and search his computer. The appellate court found that the use of a password on the computer and the lock on his private office door were sufficient evidence of a subjective expectation of privacy in his office and the computer, and that his expectation of privacy in his office was reasonable given that he did not share his office with coworkers and kept it locked. The court held, however, that the employer could give valid consent to a search of the contents of the hard drive of the defendant's workplace computer because the computer was the type of workplace property that remained within the control of the employer even if the defendant had placed personal items in it, and that the employees who copied the hard drive received consent to search the office and the keys to the office from the employer.

Rules pertaining to consent searches include the following:

- Searches conducted by means of consent are valid so long as the consent is voluntary (*United States v. Kapperman*, 1985, p. 783).
- Whether an individual's consent to a warrantless search was given voluntarily is a question of fact that must be decided in light of the totality of the circumstances (*United States v. Gonzalez*, 1996, p. 828).
- An individual who does not understand English did not give effective consent when he was asked in English for permission to search (*United States v. Gonzalez*, 1996, p. 828).
- Relevant factors in determining voluntariness, none of which is dispositive, include (1) the voluntariness of the defendant's custodial

status, (2) the presence of coercive police procedure, (3) the extent
and level of the defendant's cooperation with police, (4) the defendant's awareness of his right to refuse to consent to the search, (5)
the defendant's education and intelligence, and (6) the defendant's
belief that no incriminating evidence will be found (*United States v.
Chemaly*, 1984, p. 1352).

- While knowledge of the right to refuse consent is one factor to be
  taken into account, the government need not establish such knowledge as the sine qua non of an effective consent (*Schneckloth v.
  Bustamonte*, 1973, p. 227).
- The government bears the burden of establishing that the consent
  to search was not a function of acquiescence to a claim of lawful
  authority but rather was given freely and voluntarily (*United States v.
  Hidalgo*, 1993, p. 1571).
- The government may satisfy its burden of establishing consent to a
  warrantless search by showing permission to search was obtained
  from a third party who possessed common authority over the premises searched. Proof of voluntary consent to justify a warrantless
  search is not limited to proof that consent was given by the defendant, but may show that permission to search was obtained from
  a third party who possessed common authority over or other sufficient relationship to the premises or effects sought to be inspected
  (*Schneckloth v. Bustamonte*, 1973, pp. 245–46).
- "The Fourth Amendment does not assure a defendant that no government search of his house will occur unless he consents, rather the
  Fourth Amendment guarantees only no such search will occur that
  is unreasonable. The fundamental objective that alone validates all
  unconsented government searches is the seizure of persons who have
  committed or are about to commit crimes, or of evidence related to
  crimes and of the many factual determinations that must regularly
  be made by agents of the government, the Fourth Amendment does
  not require the agents always be correct, but that they always be reasonable" (*Brinegar v. United States*, 1949, p. 173).

Open Fields

Traditionally "open fields" were not considered as protected from searches by
the Fourth Amendment. In *Oliver v. United States* (1984), the Supreme Court
discussed whether the open fields doctrine was still viable. In that case, acting
on reports that marijuana was being raised on the petitioner's farm, narcotics
agents of the Kentucky State Police went to the farm to investigate. Arriving
at the farm, they drove past the petitioner's house to a locked gate with a
"No Trespassing" sign, but with a footpath around one side. The agents then

walked around the gate and along the road and found a field of marijuana over a mile from the petitioner's house. Oliver was arrested and indicted for manufacturing a controlled substance in violation of a federal statute. After a pretrial hearing, the district court suppressed evidence of the discovery of the marijuana field, holding that Oliver had a reasonable expectation that the field would remain private and that it was not an open field that invited casual intrusion. The court of appeals reversed, holding that the open fields doctrine of *Hester v. United States* (1924) permits police officers to enter and search a field without a warrant.

The open fields doctrine was founded upon the explicit language of the Fourth Amendment, whose special protection accorded to "persons, houses, papers, and effects" does "not extend to the open fields" (*Hester v. United States*, 1924, p. 59). The court stated that open fields are not "effects" within the meaning of the Fourth Amendment, the term *effects* being less inclusive than "property" and not encompassing open fields. The court then concluded that the government's intrusion upon open fields is not one of those "unreasonable searches" proscribed by the amendment.

The Court reasoned that since *Katz v. United States* (1967), the touchstone of Fourth Amendment analysis has been whether a person has a "constitutionally protected reasonable expectation of privacy" (p. 360). The amendment does not protect the merely subjective expectation of privacy, but only those expectations that society is prepared to recognize as reasonable. Because open fields are accessible to the public and the police in ways that a home, office, or commercial structure would not be, and because fences or "No Trespassing" signs do not effectively bar the public from viewing open fields, the asserted expectation of privacy in open fields is not one that society recognizes as reasonable. Moreover, the common law, by implying that only the land immediately surrounding and associated with the home warrants the Fourth Amendment protections that attach to the home, conversely implies that no expectation of privacy legitimately attaches to open fields.

Plain View

If the property can be viewed without intruding upon a person's privacy rights, then there is no reasonable expectation of privacy. In *Commonwealth v. Johnson* (2007), on September 11, 2004, there was a shooting at 53rd and Market Streets in West Philadelphia. Johnson was arrested in connection with the shooting several days later. While in custody Johnson admitted to detectives that he had a gun at his apartment. On the morning of September 15, 2004, appellee signed a consent to search form permitting police officers to search his apartment for a "9 millimeter handgun." That same morning, when the police went and searched that location they did not find a handgun. It was agreed that the officers had authority to search for only the handgun.

While searching the back bedroom of the apartment, Detective Thomas Augustine discovered an open spiral bound notebook on the dresser, on top of which lay the first page of a handwritten letter. Upon reading the letter, Detective Augustine realized it pertained to the underlying matter and seized the letter as evidence. The narrow issue that is presented by this case entails simply whether a police officer, pursuant to the plain view doctrine, may properly read the exposed pages of a letter, and then make a warrantless seizure of that letter should its contents prove incriminating.

The appellate court noted that the plain view doctrine permits the warrantless seizure of evidence in plain view when (1) an officer views the object from a lawful vantage point, and (2) it is immediately apparent to him that the object is incriminating. In determining whether the incriminating nature of an object is immediately apparent to the police officer, the court stated that it would look to the totality of the circumstances. An officer can never be 100 percent certain that a substance in plain view is incriminating, but his belief must be supported by probable cause.

The court noted that the plain view doctrine functions differently depending upon the thing that is perceived. The court stated:

> If a police officer spies a pistol on a table, its potentially incriminating nature is not only "immediately apparent," it is very likely instantaneous. In contrast, if it is a sheet of paper on the table, there is nothing inherently incriminating in paper alone and nothing may be "immediately apparent." On the other hand, if the paper contains writing, the writing itself may be incriminating. However, the incriminating nature of writing is not perceived until it is read. Only then does its incriminating nature become "immediately apparent." We see no sense in imposing some artificial limit on the number of words that may be read before the incriminating nature of a document is no longer "immediately apparent."
>
> The incriminating nature of a letter cannot be known until the key words are read and it should not matter whether they occur in the first sentence of the letter or the last. We will not restrict a police officer either to the first few words of a letter, where the eyes are naturally drawn, or to those that "jump off the page." Simply stated, it seems foolish to tell our police officers that they may observe items in plain view, but that they must not look too closely. If a letter is left lying open on a table, we find that its entire contents are exposed to plain view and the letter is subject to seizure under that doctrine. (pp. 1225–26)

In *Gibson v. Commonwealth* (2007), the defendant contended that the police violated his constitutional rights by using a flashlight to illuminate contraband in his pocket during night hours. The officer testified that when he encountered the defendant it was dark and that he scanned the defendant with a flashlight. The scan revealed a pocket bulge in the right side of the defendant's pants. The bulge was significant enough so the pocket remained exposed to public view even though the officer had not touched the defendant. The officer stated he was able to shine the light right into the pocket while the defendant turned his back to the officer. It was at that point that the officer spotted a green leafy substance that the officer suspected was marijuana. In using a flashlight to view the defendant's pocket, the officer did no more than illuminate what the defendant had exposed to plain view. The officer's use of a flashlight to illuminate the interior of the defendant's pants did not change the plain view nature of the discovery. The court upheld the defendant's conviction.

Consider the fact situation in *Szlemko v. State* (2007). In the early morning hours of January 21, 2005, Officer Whisenant of the Harrison Police Department was on patrol when he noticed a pickup truck parked in the drive-thru lane behind the closed Baskin Robbins. Officer Whisenant testified that, because there had been a series of break-ins in the past several months, he went to investigate. He saw no exterior lights and only a minimal light inside the drive-thru window. As he pulled up to the window, he noticed that the light emitted from a computer screen. Officer Whisenant saw several pictures of young girls flashing across the screen in a slide-show manner. He testified that, in one of the pictures, he saw two topless girls who appeared to be eight years old or younger in a bathtub.

As judge in the case, would you hold that it was a search or that the material on the computer was in plain view?

The appellate court held that the plain view doctrine may be used to uphold a warrantless seizure of items where, first, the officers were lawfully located in a place to plainly view the object and, second, the object was in plain view and its incriminating nature was immediately apparent. The court upheld the validity of the search.

Abandoned of Property

Property that has been voluntarily abandoned raises two interesting issues:

1. **Does an individual still have a property interest in abandoned property?**
2. **Do you have a reasonable expectation of privacy of the contents of your trashcan that is on the curb to be picked by the trash collector?**

In *California v. Greenwood* (1988), acting on information indicating that respondent Greenwood might be engaged in narcotics trafficking, police twice obtained from his regular trash collector garbage bags left on the curb in front of his house. On the basis of items in the bags that were indicative of narcotics use, the police obtained warrants to search the house, discovered controlled substances during the searches, and arrested respondents on felony narcotics

Photo 4.2 Associate Justice Byron "Whizzer" White (June 8, 1917–April 15, 2002) authored the Court's opinion in the *California v. Greenwood* case. Justice White won fame both as a football running back and as an associate justice of the Supreme Court of the United States. He was a college classmate and later a member of the campaign staff of President John F. Kennedy. He was appointed as associate justice by Kennedy in 1962, and he served until his retirement in 1993. (Photograph by Harris and Ewing, Collection of the Supreme Court of the United States.)

charges. Finding that probable cause to search the house would not have existed without the evidence obtained from the trash searches, the state superior court dismissed the charges and concluded that the warrantless trash search violated the Fourth Amendment and the California constitution.

The arrestees claimed that they had an expectation of privacy in the trash that was searched by the police because it was in opaque bags on the street for collection at a fixed time, and there was little likelihood that it would be inspected by anyone. The Court held that the Fourth Amendment does not prohibit the warrantless search and seizure of garbage left for collection outside the curtilage of a home (living area surrounding the home). Because respondents voluntarily left their trash for collection in an area particularly suited for public inspection, their claimed expectation of privacy in the inculpatory items they discarded was not objectively reasonable. The Court noted that it was common knowledge that plastic garbage bags left along a public street are readily accessible to animals, children, scavengers, snoops, and other members of the public. Moreover, respondents placed their refuse at the curb for the express purpose of conveying it to a third party, the trash collector, who might himself have sorted through it or permitted others, such as the police, to do so. The police cannot reasonably be expected to avert their eyes from evidence of criminal activity that could have been observed by any member of the public.

The Supreme Court did not address the issue of a reasonable expectation of privacy in the trash before it is placed on the curb for collection. *State v. Ronngren* (1985) involved the search of a garbage bag that a dog, acting "at the behest of no one" (p. 228), had dragged from the defendants' yard into the yard of a neighbor. The neighbor then deposited the bag in his own trashcan, which he later permitted the police to search. The North Dakota Supreme Court held that the search of the garbage bag did not violate the defendants' Fourth Amendment rights.

Even the refuse of prominent Americans has not been invulnerable. In 1975, for example, a reporter for a weekly tabloid seized five bags of garbage from the sidewalk outside the home of Secretary of State Henry Kissinger (*Washington Post*, July 9, 1975, p. A1, col. 8). A newspaper editorial criticizing this journalistic "trash-picking" observed that evidently everybody does it (*Washington Post*, July 10, 1975, p. A18, col. 1).

Aerial Observations

In *California v. Ciraolo* (1986), the Santa Clara, California, police received an anonymous telephone tip that marijuana was growing in the defendant's backyard, which was enclosed by two fences and shielded from view at ground level. Officers who were trained in marijuana identification secured a private airplane, flew over the defendant's house at an altitude of 1,000 feet, and readily identified marijuana plants growing in the yard. A search warrant was later obtained on the basis of one of the officer's naked-eye observations; a photograph of the surrounding area taken from the airplane was attached as an exhibit. The warrant was executed, and marijuana plants were seized. After the California trial court denied the defendant's motion to suppress the evidence of the search, he pleaded guilty to a charge of cultivation of marijuana.

The U.S Supreme Court, in an opinion by Chief Justice Warren Burger, held that the Fourth Amendment was not violated by the naked-eye aerial observation of the respondent's backyard. The Court noted that the touchstone of Fourth Amendment analysis is whether a person has a constitutionally protected reasonable expectation of privacy, which involves the two inquiries of whether the individual manifested a subjective expectation of privacy in the object of the challenged search, and whether society is willing to recognize that expectation as reasonable. In pursuing the second inquiry, the Court stated that the test of legitimacy was not whether the individual chooses to conceal assertedly "private activity," but whether the government's intrusion infringes upon the personal and societal values protected by the Fourth Amendment.

The Court held that the defendant's expectation of privacy from all observations of his backyard was unreasonable, that the backyard and its crop were within the "curtilage" of the respondent's home did not itself bar all police observation. The mere fact that an individual has taken measures to restrict some views of his activities does not preclude an officer's observation from a public vantage point where he has a right to be and which renders the activities clearly visible. The police observations here took place within public navigable airspace, in a physically nonintrusive manner. The police were able to observe the plants readily discernible to the naked eye as marijuana, and it was irrelevant that the observation from the airplane was directed at identifying the plants and that the officers were trained to recognize marijuana. Any member of the public flying in this airspace who cared to glance down could have seen everything that the officers observed. The Fourth Amendment simply does not require police traveling in the public airways at 1,000 feet to obtain a warrant to observe what is visible to the naked eye.

Student Searches

Any discussion of student searches should begin with a discussion of the U.S. Supreme Court case *New Jersey v. T. L. O.* (1985). A teacher at a New Jersey high school, upon discovering that a 14-year-old freshman and her companion were smoking cigarettes in a school lavatory in violation of a school rule, took them to the principal's office, where they met with the assistant vice principal. In response to the assistant vice principal's questioning, T.L.O. denied

Photo 4.3 Chief Justice Warren Burger (September 17, 1907–June 25, 1995) was the author of the Court's opinion in *California v. Ciraolo*. He was chief justice of the United States from 1969 to 1986. Although Burger was a conservative and considered a strict constructionist, under his leadership, the United States Supreme Court delivered a variety of transformative decisions on abortion, capital punishment, religious establishment, and school desegregation. (Photograph by Robert Oakes, National Geographical Society, courtesy of the Supreme Court of the United States.)

that she had been smoking and claimed that she did not smoke. The assistant vice principal demanded to see her purse. In her purse, he found a pack of cigarettes and a package of cigarette rolling papers commonly associated with the use of marijuana. He then proceeded to search the purse thoroughly and found some marijuana, a pipe, plastic bags, a fairly substantial amount of money, an index card containing a list of students who owed her money, and two letters that implicated her in marijuana dealing. The state brought delinquency charges against T.L.O. in juvenile court, which held that the Fourth Amendment applied to searches by school officials, but that the search in question was a reasonable one, and adjudged her to be a delinquent. The New Jersey Supreme Court reversed and ordered the suppression of the evidence found in her purse, holding that the search of the purse was unreasonable.

The U.S. Supreme Court held that the Fourth Amendment's prohibition on unreasonable searches and seizures applies to searches conducted by public school officials and was not limited to searches carried out by law enforcement officers. Nor were school officials exempt from the amendment's limitations by virtue of their authority over schoolchildren.

The Supreme Court also held that schoolchildren have legitimate expectations of privacy. They may find it necessary to carry with them a variety of legitimate, noncontraband items, and there was no reason to conclude that they have necessarily waived all rights to privacy in such items by bringing them onto school grounds. But the Court held that in determining if a search was legal, the courts must strike a balance between schoolchildren's legitimate expectations of privacy and the school's equally legitimate need to maintain an environment in which learning can take place, requiring some easing of the restrictions to which searches by public authorities are ordinarily subject. The Court held that school officials need not obtain a warrant before searching a student who is under their authority. And school officials need not be held subject to the requirement that searches be based on probable cause to believe that the subject of the search has violated or is violating the law. Rather, the legality of a search of a student should depend simply on the reasonableness, under all the circumstances, of the search. Determining the reasonableness of any search involves a determination of whether the search was justified at its inception and whether, as conducted, it was reasonably related in scope to the circumstances that justified the interference in the first place. Under ordinary circumstances the search of a student by a school official will be justified at its inception where there are reasonable grounds for suspecting that the search will turn up evidence that the student has violated or is violating either the law or the rules of the school. And such a search will be permissible in its scope when the measures adopted are reasonably related to the objectives of the search and not excessively intrusive in light of the student's age and sex and the nature of the infraction.

The Supreme Court held that under these standards, the search in the case was not unreasonable for Fourth Amendment purposes. First, the initial search for cigarettes was reasonable. The report to the assistant vice principal that T.L.O. had been smoking warranted a reasonable suspicion that she had cigarettes in her purse, and thus the search was justified despite the fact that the cigarettes, if found, would constitute mere evidence of a violation of the no-smoking rule. Second, the discovery of the rolling papers then gave rise to a reasonable suspicion that the respondent was carrying marijuana as well as cigarettes in her purse, and this suspicion justified the further exploration that turned up more evidence of drug-related activities.

Arrests without Warrants

The U.S. Supreme Court requires, except for recognized exceptions, that officers obtain warrants before conducting a search. Most arrests are, however, without warrants. For example, the below federal law allows an FBI Agent to arrest certain individuals without warrants.

18 USCS § 3052: Powers of Federal Bureau of Investigation

The Director, Associate Director, Assistant to the Director, Assistant Directors, inspectors, and agents of the Federal Bureau of Investigation of the Department of Justice may carry firearms, serve warrants and subpoenas issued under the authority of the United States and make arrests without warrant for any offense against the United States committed in their presence, or for any felony cognizable under the laws of the United States if they have reasonable grounds to believe that the person to be arrested has committed or is committing such felony.

The statutory authority of FBI officers and agents to make felony arrests without a warrant is restricted to offenses committed "in their presence" or to instances where they have "reasonable grounds to believe that the person to be arrested has committed or is committing" a felony (18 USC § 3052).

Evidence sufficient to establish guilt is not required. However, there must be more than good faith on the part of the arresting officers. Probable cause exists if the facts and circumstances known to the officer warrant a prudent person in believing that the offense has been committed. If the officer acts with probable cause, he or she is protected even though it turns out that the citizen is innocent. And while a search without a warrant is, within limits, permissible if incident to a lawful arrest, if an arrest without a warrant is to support an incidental search, it must be made with probable cause.

Selected Court Cases on Arrests

A person is seized by the police and thus entitled to challenge the government's action under the Fourth Amendment when the officer, "by means of physical force or show of authority," terminates or restrains the person's freedom of movement (*Florida v. Bostick*, 1991, p. 434).

The law is settled that in Fourth Amendment terms a traffic stop entails a seizure of the driver "even though the purpose of the stop is limited and the resulting detention quite brief" (*Delaware v. Prouse*, 1979, p. 653).

Stopping an automobile and detaining its occupants constitutes a seizure within the meaning of the Fourth and Fourteenth Amendments (*Colorado v. Bannister*, 1980, p. 4).

One officer testified that he stopped a defendant two days prior to his arrest, obtained his name and information regarding a pending case, and learned that the defendant had previously been in jail. Another officer conducted a criminal history check of a defendant, and that officer learned that the defendant had several violent arrests and a conviction. The officer further testified that under New Jersey law, a person with a criminal record could not obtain a permit to carry a handgun. Taken together, these facts demonstrated that the officers had enough information at the time of arrest indicating that the defendant did not possess permits for the firearms in his possession and that his possession of the firearms was not legal (*United States v. Booker*, 2008, p. 19).

Terry Stops

The 1968 case of *Terry v. Ohio* developed the concept of "stop and frisk." In the *Terry* case, a Cleveland, Ohio, detective (McFadden), on a downtown beat that he had been patrolling for many years, observed two strangers (Terry and another man, Chilton) on a street corner. He saw them proceed alternately back and forth along an identical route, pausing to stare in the same store window, which they did for a total of about 24 times. Each completion of the route was followed by a conference between the two on a corner, at one of which they were joined by a third man (Katz), who left swiftly. Suspecting the two men of "casing a job, a stick-up," the officer followed them and saw them rejoin the third man a couple of blocks away in front of a store. The officer approached the three, identified himself as a policeman, and asked their names. The men "mumbled something," whereupon McFadden spun Terry around, patted down his outside clothing, and found in his overcoat pocket, but was unable to remove, a pistol. The officer ordered the three into the store. He removed Terry's overcoat, took out a revolver, and ordered the three to face the wall with their hands raised. He patted down the outer clothing

Photo 4.4 Chief Justice Earl Warren (March 19, 1891–July 9, 1974), who wrote the Court's opinion in *Terry v. Ohio*, was a district attorney, attorney general of California, governor of California, and chief justice of the United States (1953–1969). Chief Justice Warren is regarded as one of the most influential Supreme Court justices in the history of the United States, and perhaps the most controversial. (Photograph by Abdon Daoud Ackad, Collection of the Supreme Court of the United States.)

of Chilton and Katz and seized a revolver from Chilton's outside overcoat pocket. He did not put his hands under the outer garments of Katz (because he discovered nothing in his pat-down that might have been a weapon), or under Terry's or Chilton's outer garments until he felt the guns. The three were taken to the police station. Terry and Chilton were charged with carrying concealed weapons. The defense moved to suppress the weapons. Though the trial court rejected the prosecution theory that the guns had been seized during a search incident to a lawful arrest, the court denied the motion to

suppress and admitted the weapons into evidence on the ground that the officer had cause to believe that Terry and Chilton were acting suspiciously, that
their interrogation was warranted, and that the officer for his own protection
had the right to pat down their outer clothing, having reasonable cause to
believe that they might be armed. The court distinguished between an investigatory "stop" and an arrest, and between a "frisk" of the outer clothing for
weapons and a full-blown search for evidence of crime. Terry and Chilton
were found guilty, an intermediate appellate court affirmed, and the state
supreme court dismissed the appeal on the ground that "no substantial constitutional question" was involved.

The Supreme Court upheld the conviction and stated that the search was
not unreasonable under the Fourth Amendment. Chief Justice Earl Warren
wrote the majority opinion for the Supreme Court. The key points in his
opinion include the following:

- The Fourth Amendment right against unreasonable searches and seizures, made applicable to the states by the Fourteenth Amendment,
  protects people, not places, and therefore applies as much to the citizen on the streets as well as at home or elsewhere.
- The issue in this case is not the abstract propriety of the police conduct, but the admissibility against Terry of the evidence uncovered
  by the search and seizure.
- The exclusionary rule cannot properly be invoked to exclude the
  products of legitimate and restrained police investigative techniques,
  and the Court's approval of such techniques should not discourage
  remedies other than the exclusionary rule to curtail police abuses for
  which that is not an effective sanction.
- The Fourth Amendment applies to stop-and-frisk procedures such
  as those followed here.
- Whenever a police officer accosts an individual and restrains his
  freedom to walk away, he has "seized" that person within the meaning of the Fourth Amendment.
- A careful exploration of the outer surfaces of a person's clothing in
  an attempt to find weapons is a "search" under that amendment.
- Where a reasonably prudent officer is warranted in the circumstances
  of a given case in believing that his safety or that of others is endangered, he may make a reasonable search for weapons of the person
  believed by him to be armed and dangerous regardless of whether he
  has probable cause to arrest that individual for crime or the absolute
  certainty that the individual is armed.
- Though the police must whenever practicable secure a warrant to
  make a search and seizure, that procedure cannot be followed where

swift action based upon on-the-spot observations of the officer on the beat is required.

- The reasonableness of any particular search and seizure must be assessed in light of the particular circumstances against the standard of whether a man of reasonable caution is warranted in believing that the action taken was appropriate.
- The officer here was performing a legitimate function of investigating suspicious conduct when he decided to approach Terry and his companions.
- An officer justified in believing that an individual whose suspicious behavior he is investigating at close range is armed may, to neutralize the threat of physical harm, take necessary measures to determine whether that person is carrying a weapon.
- A search for weapons in the absence of probable cause to arrest must be strictly circumscribed by the exigencies of the situation.
- An officer may make an intrusion short of arrest where he has reasonable apprehension of danger before being possessed of information justifying arrest.
- The officer's protective seizure of Terry and his companions and the limited search that he made were reasonable, both at their inception and as conducted.
- The actions of Terry and his companions were consistent with the officer's hypothesis that they were contemplating a daylight robbery and were armed.
- The officer's search was confined to what was minimally necessary to determine whether the men were armed, and the intrusion, which was made for the sole purpose of protecting himself and others nearby, was confined to ascertaining the presence of weapons.
- The revolver seized from Terry was properly admitted into evidence against him because the search that led to its seizure was reasonable under the Fourth Amendment.

Selected Court Cases on *Terry* Stops

A traffic stop is an investigatory detention that we analyze according to the principles set forth in *Terry v. Ohio*. *Terry* sets up a two-prong test of the reasonableness of investigatory detentions and weapons searches. First, we must decide whether the detention was justified at its inception. Second, the officer's actions must be reasonably related in scope to the circumstances that justified the interference in the first place. At both stages, the reasonableness of the officer's suspicions is judged by an objective standard taking the totality of the circumstances and information available to the officers into account. (*United States v. Johnson*, 2004, p. 1189)

A radio broadcast instructed police officers to look out for two armed robbery suspects in a Crown Victoria car that was tan on one side and black on top with smoked-out windows. Forty minutes later, within two blocks of the robbery, police saw the defendant's car, a Crown Victoria with dark-tinted windows and dark blue in color, with a white driver's side door. Police stopped the car. The appearance of a defendant, one of two occupants, closely matched the description of one of the suspects. When the defendant, who was told to exit the car, learned he would be patted down for officer safety, he tried to run. In restraining the defendant, police felt a gun in his pocket and retrieved it. On appeal, the court held that the minor differences between the lookout description of the car and the defendant's car did not dispel the reasonable suspicion that the officers had to justify the *Terry* stop of the defendant (*United States v. Abdus-Price*, 2008).

A defendant argued that a police officer lacked reasonable suspicion to stop and attempt to frisk him. He claimed that it was only as a result of the illegal stop that his gun was ultimately discovered and that his confession was extracted. The court ruled that the seizure itself constituted a *Terry* stop. A defendant was in a car bearing Massachusetts plates, oddly parked near an alleged crime scene associated with a Massachusetts suspect; two individuals were in the back seat at a very early hour of the morning. The defendant left the car as the officer approached, walking in the opposite direction and ignoring directions to stop. Further, the defendant was wearing a leather coat in July, a fact that the officer reasonably considered curious and perhaps suggestive of hidden weapons (*United States v. Stroman*, 2007).

Traffic Stops

The legality of a traffic stop is to be examined under the two-prong test announced in *Terry v. Ohio* (1968). First, the stop must be justified at its inception. Second, the officer's conduct during detention must be reasonably related in scope to the circumstances that justified the initial stop. The touchstone of the Fourth Amendment is reasonableness (*Florida v. Jimeno*, 1991).

An officer may detain the driver and vehicle if the officer develops reasonable suspicion that the driver is engaged in criminal activity. An investigative detention may be expanded beyond its original purpose if during the initial stop the detaining officer acquires reasonable suspicion of criminal activity (*United States v. Villa-Chaparro*, 1997). Reasonable suspicion is based on the totality of circumstances. "The reasonable suspicion calculus turns on whether the specific articulable facts, when viewed together through the lens of a reasonable law enforcement officer, justified a brief roadside detention" (*United States v. Doyle*, 1997, p. 1376).

In *United States v. Hall* (2008), the court found that the police officers did not violate a defendant's Fourth Amendment rights by stopping his vehicle because the officers had a reasonable suspicion that the defendant had committed a traffic violation with the heavy window tinting on his vehicle. The defendant's tinted windows prevented anyone from viewing the interior of the vehicle, and such tinting was, with limited exception, a violation of Pennsylvania law. The Court noted that viewing these facts from the perspective of a reasonable law enforcement officer on the scene, the window tint on the defendant's vehicle was sufficient to establish reasonable suspicion that the defendant had violated a traffic ordinance.

In *State v. Bomboy* (2007), two officers lawfully stopped a defendant's vehicle for a license plate illumination violation and on reasonable suspicion that he was driving on a suspended license. One officer saw a substance in the vehicle that he recognized as methamphetamine, and after the defendant was removed from the vehicle and arrested, the officer took the methamphetamine. The trial court granted the defendant's motion to suppress on the ground that there were no exigent circumstances justifying the seizure. On appeal, the court affirmed. Under the *Garcia, Gomez,* and *Jones* cases, New Mexico Constitution Article II, § 10 required a warrant or a recognized exception to the warrant requirement to justify the officer's seizure of the methamphetamine from the defendant's vehicle following the defendant's arrest outside the vehicle. Because there was no warrant and no exception to the warrant requirement shown, the seizure was unlawful. The fact that the officer saw the methamphetamine in plain view did not justify the warrantless seizure.

The *Bomboy* case was not followed by the Pennsylvania Supreme Court in *Commonwealth v. McCree* (2007). In that case, an undercover officer asked a man who had just sold her prescription drugs if he could get her more pills. He said he could, entered a car, and spoke to defendant, who was in the driver's seat. Officers approached the car; one of them saw the defendant shove an amber container under a seat cushion on top of the driver's seat. The officer asked the defendant to exit the car, and then reached under the cushion and recovered a pill bottle containing prescription drugs. The officer saw and retrieved two more pill bottles from a door pocket; they also contained prescription drugs. The high court noted that the notion of privacy in Pennsylvania Constitution Article I, § 8 was greater than that of the Fourth Amendment. However, police access to the vehicle was authorized by Pennsylvania's limited automobile exception, as police did not know in advance the car would be there, and seizure of the pill bottles was authorized by the plain view exception, as the officer was lawfully present when he saw the defendant place the pill container—which was immediately incriminating in nature, due to the undercover officer's prior drug buy—under his seat cushion and when he saw the pill bottles in the door pocket.

Scope of the Search

Search of a Residence

As a general rule, during a search pursuant to a warrant, executing officers are permitted to open any containers in which objects named by the warrant "may reasonably be found" (*United States v. Newman*, 1982, p. 92). As the Supreme Court reasoned, when officers are executing a warrant, distinctions among closets, drawers, and containers must give way to the interest in the prompt and efficient completion of the task at hand (*United States v. Ross*, 1982, p. 821). When determining whether a locked space may reasonably be opened during the course of a search pursuant to a warrant, the court's inquiry is normally guided by a comparison of the dimensions of the locked space to the dimensions of the items sought in the search warrant. For example, if the warrant authorized the officers to search an entire residence for evidence including documents, keys, drugs, and drug paraphernalia, the officers would probably be authorized to search the entire contents of the house.

If the officers know or should know that there are separate dwellings contained in the property to be searched, they are obligated to either limit the search to those areas clearly covered by the warrant or to discontinue entirely their search (*United States v. Ritter*, 2005). The purpose of the multiunit dwelling rule is to prevent executing officers from searching separate units of a multiunit dwelling upon a mere showing that one of the units, not specifically identified, contained the contraband sought. To hold otherwise would contravene the Fourth Amendment's particularity requirement by expanding the area to be searched beyond that for which probable cause exists.

Search of Students

Under the T.L.O. framework, the search of a student by a public school official must also be permissible in its scope. A search is permissible in its scope if the measures adopted are reasonably related to the objectives of the search and not excessively intrusive in light of the age and sex of the student and the nature of the infraction.

As to scope of search, courts have looked to a number of factors. Many have considered, for example, the importance of the governmental interest at stake. For example, a search to find drugs may be more extensive than a strip search aimed at finding stolen money. In *Beard v. Whitmore Lake School District* (2005), the appellate court noted that a search undertaken to find money serves a less weighty governmental interest than a search undertaken for items that pose a threat to the health or safety of students, such as drugs or weapons. Other courts have considered the size of the contraband to be found. In *Williams v. Ellington* (1991), the appellate court held that a personally intrusive search was legal in light of the item sought—a small vial containing suspected narcotics. Some courts have also considered the physical setting and circumstances surrounding a search in determining the search's overall reasonableness (*Singleton v. Board of Education*, 1995).

Vehicle Searches

In *United States v. Gonzalez* (2008), Gonzalez consented to a search of his van. The officer removed a piece of plastic molding and found drugs beneath it. Gonzalez contended that his consent did not include the right to damage his van and that the search went beyond the scope of the consent. The appellate court stated that it would apply an objective reasonableness standard to determine if the scope of the search extended beyond that consented to and was thus an unauthorized search. The court agreed that Gonzalez's consent to search could not be reasonably understood as authorizing the officer to damage the van. Yet, the record did not support a finding that there was any damage to the van during the consensual search. The court noted that it appeared that the subject piece of plastic molding became dislodged in response to a slight exploratory touch or manipulation by the officer, and that its falling off created an opening through which suspicious-looking packages were readily visible. To the extent that screws and other parts ultimately needed to be removed to gain access to the packages, these steps were taken only later, after the officer had obtained a search warrant. In other words, the court stated that any actions that might be construed as resulting in damage to the van were not taken pursuant to Gonzalez's consent, but were authorized by the warrant-issuing magistrate. The appellate court affirmed the district court's denial of the motion to suppress the evidence.

Wiretaps

The interception of conversations by use of electronic devices is a "search" within the meaning of the Fourth Amendment. Title III of the Omnibus Crime Control and Safe Streets Act of 1968 (Title III) applies where the evidentiary use of wiretap evidence is in issue. "Title III incorporates the Fourth Amendment's protections by placing probable cause and particularity conditions on the issuance of a wiretap." Accordingly, surveillance that is properly authorized and carried out under Title III complies with the Fourth Amendment. The federal procedures for electronic surveillance are governed by 18 USC § 2518.

A wiretap warrant can only be issued upon a showing of probable cause, "the probable cause required for an electronic surveillance search is no different from that which is necessary to obtain a warrant for a physical search"

(*Commonwealth v. Wallace*, 1986). The facts as set forth within the four corners of the affidavit and the reasonable inferences therefrom must be sufficient to establish probable cause, and the affidavits accompanying warrant applications must be considered as a whole.

Drafting an affidavit for a wiretap is very difficult. Courts have recognized that the nature of electronic surveillance makes precise descriptions of anticipated conversations impracticable (*United States v. Gambale*, 1985). In *Gambale*, the court rejected the defendants' argument that conversations to be intercepted had to be described with the same degree of particularity as would be required to justify more traditional searches of places for physical evidence. Recognizing that "conversations are not like physical evidence" because "they cannot be described with as much precision, nor can an applicant for a surveillance order know of their actual content in advance, because it is virtually impossible for an applicant to predict exactly what will be said concerning a specific crime," the courts instead have adopted a flexible, pragmatic approach to the particularity requirement in the context of electronic surveillance. Thus, where a continuing course of criminal conduct is involved, a surveillance order must necessarily be framed flexibly enough to permit interception of any statements concerning a specified pattern of crime. Although the nature and type of the anticipated conversations must be described, the actual content need not and cannot be stated because the conversations have not yet taken place at the time the application is made, and it is virtually impossible for an applicant to predict exactly what will be said concerning a specific crime. The order must be broad enough to allow interception of any statements concerning a specified pattern of crime.

The key question is whether a magistrate, reading the warrant, would understand what limits were placed on the authority to intercept—that is, whether the warrant's description of the communications authorized to be intercepted is sufficiently particular to give clear direction as to which communications could be lawfully intercepted and recorded and which could not. As *Gambale* and other cases have recognized, the same kind of language that can be used to describe particular existing places or things is not suited to describing conversations or other communications that do not yet exist. Even descriptions of physical objects that may or will exist in the future must necessarily be more general and, therefore, less particular than descriptions of already existing and observable objects. Similarly, descriptions of past recorded conversations can be more particular than descriptions of yet-to-occur conversations.

One limitation that is frequently contained in a wiretap warrant to provide direction to executing officers is to describe communications that may and may not be intercepted by reference to the participants. For example, the warrant could identify specific persons, notably co-conspirators, whose communications with the target can be expected, on the basis of reliable information, to be about criminal activity.

Another useful limitation is to describe, categorically by necessity, what content of communications can be the subject of interception. For instance, where there is probable cause to believe the target is a drug dealer, the warrant may authorize the interception of conversations about drug dealing. With regard to content, however, there are two difficulties. The first is generality. An obvious way to keep the topical description of the type of communication that may be intercepted from being too broad is to relate it to the probable cause showing that it supports the issuance of the warrant. Where the information developed in the preapplication investigation supports a conclusion that Smith and Jones are distributing cocaine, the targeted communications can be described as "conversations concerning the distribution of cocaine by Smith and Jones."

The other difficulty is ambiguity. For instance, conversations concerning the distribution of cocaine are not likely to involve the actual use of the word *cocaine*. It is unlikely in the extreme that sophisticated drug dealers will speak over the telephone in explicit terms about their criminal activity. The problem is not slang, but code. Common slang terms could be particularly enumerated, *blow, candy, snow*, etc., and interceptions could be limited to those in which either the word *cocaine* itself or an itemized slang substitute was used. But drug dealers are probably no more likely to use a well-known synonym for cocaine as they are to use the word itself.

Rather, what they are likely to do is to code their messages. "I need to get some flowers to send to my girlfriend" may be about roses, but it also may be a coded request between knowing confederates for replenishment of a drug supply. Where probable cause supports the issuance of a warrant to intercept telephone conversations about distributing cocaine, it is necessary and proper to intercept the statement "I need to get some flowers to send to my girlfriend" when it is in fact a statement about distributing cocaine. Whether it is or not can only be determined by inference from context interpreted in the light of experience. In other words, whether to understand the statement as one about cocaine and not roses is, in the end, a judgment call. The soundness of such judgment calls can be reviewed retrospectively. Prospectively, however, it is not practicable to insist that a warrant accurately predict what form of words will be used to convey the substance of a message that may be intercepted.

Thus, the substance of communications to be intercepted can be described in advance, but the words in which that substance will be expressed cannot be. The particularity requirement must be understood and applied harmoniously with this reality.

Cellular Telephones

Prior to 1986 the federal Wiretapping and Electronic Surveillance statute protected the "privacy of wire and oral communication" when obtained by electronic surveillance. The interception of such communication was illegal, with strict exceptions for police surveillance (18 USC § 2510). The federal statute was generally viewed as establishing the lowest level of protection, with states being able to provide greater protection if they so choose (*Commonwealth v. Vitello*, 1975). The federal statute did not cover, however, radio transmissions, only land-based wire communication. In 1981, the FCC authorized cellular communication. At that time, given that cellular calls traveled over radio waves and land-line calls over wires, the federal statute was interpreted not to apply to calls between two cellular phones. The statute was updated in 1986, and now clearly covers cellular telephones under the expanded definition of wire communication in 18 USC §2510(1).

Capstone Case: *Virginia v. Moore,* 128 S. Ct. 1598 (2008)

When a motorist is stopped for driving with a suspended license and the state statute provides that the individual is to be cited and released, is the search legal where the police arrest and then search the individual as an incident to the arrest?

On February 20, 2003, two City of Portsmouth, Virginia, police officers stopped a car driven by David Lee Moore. They had heard over the police radio that a person known as "Chubs" was driving with a suspended license, and one of the officers knew Moore by that nickname. The officers determined that Moore's license was in fact suspended and arrested him for the misdemeanor of driving on a suspended license, which is punishable under Virginia law by a year in jail and a $2,500 fine. The officers subsequently searched Moore and found that he was carrying 16 grams of crack cocaine and $516 in cash.

Under state law, the officers should have issued Moore a summons instead of arresting him. Driving on a suspended license, like some other misdemeanors, is not an arrestable offense except as to those who "fail or refuse to discontinue" the violation, and those whom the officer reasonably believes to be likely to disregard a summons, or likely to harm themselves or others.

Moore was charged with possessing cocaine with the intent to distribute it in violation of Virginia law. He filed a pretrial motion to suppress the evidence from the arrest search.

Virginia law does not, as a general matter, require suppression of evidence obtained in violation of state law. Moore argued, however, that suppression was required by the Fourth Amendment. The trial court denied the motion, and after a bench trial found Moore guilty of the drug charge and sentenced him to a five-year prison term. The conviction was reversed by the Virginia Appellate Court on Fourth Amendment grounds. The Virginia Supreme Court reasoned that because the arresting officers should have issued Moore a citation under state law, and the Fourth Amendment does

not permit search incident to citation, the arrest search violated the Fourth
Amendment. The U.S. Supreme Court granted certiorari to review the federal constitutional question regarding the admissibility of the search.

The U.S. Supreme Court, in holding the search constitutional, stated:

> Even if we thought that state law changed the nature of the Virginia
> Commonwealth's interests for purposes of the Fourth Amendment, we would
> adhere to the probable-cause standard. In determining what is reasonable
> under the Fourth Amendment, we have given great weight to the "essential
> interest in readily administrable rules." In *Atwater*, we acknowledged that
> nuanced judgments about the need for warrantless arrest were desirable, but
> we nonetheless declined to limit to felonies and disturbances of the peace the
> Fourth Amendment rule allowing arrest based on probable cause to believe a
> law has been broken in the presence of the arresting officer. The rule extends
> even to minor misdemeanors, we concluded, because of the need for a bright-
> line constitutional standard. If the constitutionality of arrest for minor offenses
> turned in part on inquiries as to risk of flight and danger of repetition, offi-
> cers might be deterred from making legitimate arrests. We found little to jus-
> tify this cost, because there was no "epidemic of unnecessary minor-offense
> arrests," and hence "a dearth of horribles demanding redress."
>
> Incorporating state-law arrest limitations into the Constitution would pro-
> duce a constitutional regime no less vague and unpredictable than the one
> we rejected in *Atwater*. The constitutional standard would be only as easy to
> apply as the underlying state law, and state law can be complicated indeed. The
> Virginia statute in this case, for example, calls on law enforcement officers to
> weigh just the sort of case-specific factors that *Atwater* said would deter legit-
> imate arrests if made part of the constitutional inquiry. It would authorize
> arrest if a misdemeanor suspect fails or refuses to discontinue the unlawful
> act, or if the officer believes the suspect to be likely to disregard a summons.
> *Atwater* specifically noted the "extremely poor judgment" displayed in arrest-
> ing a local resident who would "almost certainly" have discontinued the
> offense and who had "no place to hide and no incentive to flee." It nonethe-
> less declined to make those considerations part of the constitutional calculus.
> *Atwater* differs from this case in only one significant respect: It considered
> (and rejected) federal constitutional remedies for all minor-misdemeanor
> arrests; Moore seeks them in only that subset of minor-misdemeanor arrests
> in which there is the least to be gained—that is, where the State has already
> acted to constrain officers' discretion and prevent abuse. Here we confront
> fewer horrible than in *Atwater*, and less of a need for redress.
>
> Finally, linking Fourth Amendment protections to state law would cause
> them to vary from place to place and from time to time. Even at the same place
> and time, the Fourth Amendment's protections might vary if federal officers
> were not subject to the same statutory constraints as state officers. In *Elkins v.
> United States*, 364 U.S. 206 (1960), we noted the practical difficulties posed by
> the "silver-platter doctrine," which had imposed more stringent limitations on
> federal officers than on state police acting independent of them. It would be

strange to construe a constitutional provision that did not apply to the States at all when it was adopted to now restrict state officers more than federal officers, solely because the States have passed search-and-seizure laws that are the prerogative of independent sovereigns.

We reaffirm against a novel challenge what we have signaled for more than half a century. When officers have probable cause to believe that a person has committed a crime in their presence, the Fourth Amendment permits them to make an arrest, and to search the suspect in order to safeguard evidence and ensure their own safety. The judgment of the Supreme Court of Virginia is reversed, and the case is remanded for further proceedings not inconsistent with this opinion.

Questions in Review

1. What are the differences between a standard search warrant and a warrant to wiretap telephones?
2. Why are "open fields" not considered searches within the Fourth Amendment's restrictions?
3. What are the requirements before an individual may be stopped and patted down under the *Terry* case?
4. How does a *Terry* stop and frisk differ from a normal search of an individual?
5. Under what circumstances may a teacher search a student?

Exclusionary Rule 5

Suppression of evidence has always been our last resort, not our first impulse. The exclusionary rule generates "substantial social costs," which sometimes include setting the guilty free and the dangerous at large. We have therefore been cautious against expanding it, and have repeatedly emphasized that the rule's costly toll upon truth-seeking and law enforcement objectives presents a high obstacle for those urging its application. We have rejected indiscriminate application of the rule and have held it to be applicable only where its remedial objectives are thought most efficaciously served—that is, where its deterrence benefits outweigh its substantial social costs.

—Justice Scalia in *Hudson v. Michigan* (2006, p. 588)

Introduction

Traditionally the sanction by the courts for violation of a defendant's constitutional rights is by use of the exclusionary rule. The primary purpose of the exclusionary rule is to deter police misconduct. Although it may apply to certain situations involving violations of the Fifth and Sixth Amendments, primarily the exclusionary rule is used for violations of an individual's Fourth Amendment rights. For that reason, it is discussed in the text following our coverage of the Fourth Amendment. As will be noted later in this section, it is not a popular remedy with many criminal justice professionals.

Mapp v. Ohio

On May 23, 1957, three Cleveland police officers arrived at the appellant's residence in that city pursuant to information that a person, who was wanted for questioning in connection with a recent bombing, was hiding out in the home and that there was a large amount of police paraphernalia being hidden in the home. Miss Mapp and her daughter by a former marriage lived on the top floor of the two-family dwelling. Upon their arrival at that house, the officers knocked on the door and demanded entrance but the appellant, after telephoning her attorney, refused to admit them without a search warrant. The officers advised their headquarters of the situation and undertook a surveillance of the house.

The officers again sought entrance some three hours later when four or more additional officers arrived on the scene. When Miss Mapp did not come to the door immediately, at least one of the several doors to the house was forcibly opened and the policemen gained admittance. Meanwhile, Miss Mapp's attorney arrived, but the officers, having secured their own entry, and continuing in their defiance of the law, would permit him neither to see Miss Mapp nor to enter the house. It appeared that Miss Mapp was halfway down the stairs from the upper floor to the front door when the officers broke into the hall. She demanded to see the search warrant. A paper, claimed to be a warrant, was held up by one of the officers. She grabbed the "warrant" and placed it in her bosom. A struggle ensued in which the officers recovered the piece of paper, and as a result of which they handcuffed the appellant because she had been "belligerent" in resisting their official rescue of the "warrant" from her person. Running roughshod over the appellant, a policeman "grabbed" her, "twisted her hand," and she "yelled and pleaded with him" because "it was hurting." The appellant, in handcuffs, was then forcibly taken upstairs to her bedroom where the officers searched a dresser, a chest of drawers, a closet, and some suitcases. They also looked into a photo album and through personal papers belonging to the appellant. The search spread to the rest of the second floor, including the child's bedroom, the living room, the kitchen, and a dinette. The basement of the building and a trunk found therein were also searched. The obscene materials for possession of which she was ultimately convicted were discovered in the course of that widespread search. The materials were pictures of her daughter. The supposed search warrant was never entered into evidence and apparently did not exist.

The Supreme Court stated:

> If letters and private documents can thus be seized and held and used in evidence against a citizen accused of an offense, the protection of the Fourth Amendment declaring his right to be secure against such searches and seizures is of no value, and, so far as those thus placed are concerned, might as well be stricken from the Constitution. The efforts of the courts and their officials to bring the guilty to punishment, praiseworthy as they are, are not to be aided by the sacrifice of those great principles established by years of endeavor and suffering which have resulted in their embodiment in the fundamental law of the land. (*Mapp v. Ohio*, 1961, pp. 663–64)

Justice Tom Clark concluded the majority opinion of the court with the following statement:

> The ignoble shortcut to conviction left open to the State tends to destroy the entire system of constitutional restraints on which the liberties of the people rest. Having once recognized that the right to privacy embodied in the Fourth Amendment is enforceable against the States, and that the right to be secure

against rude invasions of privacy by state officers is, therefore, constitutional in origin, we can no longer permit that right to remain an empty promise. Because it is enforceable in the same manner and to like effect as other basic rights secured by the Due Process Clause, we can no longer permit it to be revocable at the whim of any police officer who, in the name of law enforcement itself, chooses to suspend its enjoyment. Our decision, founded on reason and truth, gives to the individual no more than that which the Constitution guarantees him, to the police officer no less than that to which honest law enforcement is entitled, and, to the courts, that judicial integrity so necessary in the true administration of justice. (p. 665)

Brief History of the Rule

In *Weeks v. United States* (1914), the U.S. Supreme Court adopted the federal exclusionary rule for evidence that was unlawfully seized from a home without a warrant in violation of the Fourth Amendment. The Court began applying the same rule to the states, through the Fourteenth Amendment in *Mapp v. Ohio* (1961). In *Mapp*, the Court suggested a broad application of the exclusionary rule with the statement: "All evidence obtained by searches and seizures in violation of the Constitution is, by that same authority, inadmissible in a state court" (p. 655).

In *Whiteley v. Warden, Wyoming State Penitentiary* (1971), the Court treated identification of a Fourth Amendment violation as synonymous with application of the exclusionary rule to evidence secured incident to that violation. But the Court rejected the broad application of the exclusionary rule in *Arizona v. Evans* (1995, p. 13). In *Evans*, the Court stated that "whether the exclusionary sanction is appropriately imposed in a particular case is an issue separate from the question whether the Fourth Amendment rights of the party seeking to invoke the rule were violated by police conduct. In other words, exclusion may not be premised on the mere fact that a constitutional violation was a 'but-for' cause of obtaining evidence." In *Evans*, the Court stated it would not mechanically apply the exclusionary rule to every item of evidence that has a causal connection with police misconduct, and the exclusionary rule has never been applied except where its deterrence benefits outweigh its substantial social costs.

Standing to Object

A defendant may not claim a violation of his Fourth Amendment rights based only on the introduction of evidence procured through an illegal search and seizure of a third person's property or premises (*United States v. DeLuca*, 2001). Before a defendant may object that the evidence was the result of an illegal search, the defendant's rights must have been violated. For example,

Photo 5.1 Justice Sandra Day O'Connor (March 26, 1930–) served as an associate justice of the Supreme Court of the United States from 1981 until her retirement from the bench in 2005. She was the first woman to serve on the Supreme Court and was a crucial swing vote on the Court for many years because of her case-by-case approach to jurisprudence and her relatively moderate political views. (Photograph by Eileen Colton, Collection of the Supreme Court of the United States.)

the police illegally search a house belonging to Brown and find material that is incriminating to Covington. If both Brown and Covington were tried in a criminal case, the results of the search would be inadmissible against Brown because his rights were violated. But as to Covington, the evidence would be admissible against him because his rights were not violated. Covington would not have a standing to object to the search of Brown's residence. Some recent cases involving the standing to object include the following:

When a police officer makes a traffic stop, the driver of the car is seized within the meaning of the Fourth Amendment. The same is true of a passenger. A passenger is seized as well and has standing to challenge the constitutionality of the stop (*Brendlin v. California*, 2007).

To suppress evidence as the fruit of an unlawful detention, a defendant must first establish that the detention violated his Fourth Amendment rights. A defendant must then demonstrate that a factual nexus exists between the Fourth Amendment violation and the challenged evidence. If a defendant adduces the requisite proof, the burden shifts to the government to show that the evidence is not fruit of the poisonous tree. To satisfy the nexus requirement, the defendant must show the evidence he seeks to suppress would never have been found but for his, and only his, unlawful detention. Absent a nexus between the defendant's allegedly illegal arrest and the discovered contraband, the defendant simply has no constitutional claim (*United States v. Nava-Ramirez*, 2000).

In *United States v. Olivares-Rangel* (2007), the government admitted that the defendant was unlawfully arrested. The issue was whether evidence of a defendant's identity could ever be suppressed as the "fruit" of an unlawful arrest. The appellate court found that the normal Fourth Amendment exclusionary rule applied to determine if challenged identity-related evidence was excludable. But as to his fingerprints, the appellate court stated that if they were obtained merely as part of routine booking, they were unrelated to the unlawful arrest, but if they were obtained to develop evidence of criminal conduct, they were suppressible.

The defendant's motion to suppress evidence that a highway patrol officer seized from him, the contents of a briefcase, was unsuccessful because he denied owning the briefcase when he was stopped. Accordingly, he lacked standing to object to the search of it (*United States v. Decoud*, 2006).

A known associate of the defendant had rented a car. When the rental car was stopped by the police, defendant was the only person in the vehicle. A search of the rental vehicle produced cocaine, heroin, and $1,200. The court found that the defendant, an unauthorized driver, only had standing to challenge the search of a rental automobile if he received permission to use the rental car from the authorized renter, his associate. Because the defendant failed to show that he received his associate's permission to use the car, the district court properly concluded that he lacked standing to challenge the search (*United States v. Thomas*, 2006).

The defendant was the owner of a residence that was the subject of a government's search warrant. As the owner of that real property and residence, he has standing to object to any unlawful search and seizure on his property (*Agnello v. United States*, 1925).

In *Jones v. United States* (1960) the Supreme Court found that the defendant had a standing to object where he was in the apartment with permission of the owner, slept there occasionally, possessed a key, and kept a change of clothes within. In *United States v. Pollard* (2000), an appellate court held that the defendant had standing where the defendant had been friends with the lessee for seven years, spent the night occasionally, left clothes there, ate meals therein, and could stay there when the lessee was away. However in *Minnesota v. Carter* (1998), a court found no standing where the defendants were not overnight guests, and merely visited the premises to conduct illegal business. Proof that a defendant could come and go from the premises at will is not enough to have standing without the additional proof of a preexisting relationship (*United States v. McRae*, 1998).

Fruit of the Poisonous Tree

The common phrase "fruit of the poisonous tree" is based on a rule of evidence announced by the U.S. Supreme Court. As the Court restated the rule in *Wong Sun v. United States* (1963, p. 487):

> In order to make effective the fundamental constitutional guarantees of sanctity of the home and inviolability of the person, … evidence seized during an unlawful search could not constitute proof against the victim of the search. The exclusionary prohibition extends as well to the indirect as the direct products of such invasions.

The fruit of the poisonous tree rule, like many other rules, has numerous exceptions. In *Hudson v. Michigan* (2006, pp. 588–89), the U.S. Supreme Court stated:

> We have never held that evidence is fruit of the poisonous tree simply because it would not have come to light but for the illegal actions of the police. We have not … mechanically applied the exclusionary rule to every item of evidence that has a causal connection with police misconduct. Rather, but-for cause, or causation in the logical sense alone can be too attenuated to justify exclusion. Even in the early days of the exclusionary rule, we declined to hold that all evidence is fruit of the poisonous tree simply because it would not have come to light but for the illegal actions of the police. Rather, the more apt question in such a case is whether, granting establishment of the primary illegality, the evidence to which instant objection is made has been come at by exploitation of that illegality or instead by means sufficiently distinguishable to be purged of the primary taint.

Exceptions to the Rule

The most popular exceptions to the exclusionary rule are the following:

- Good faith exception
- Purged taint exception
- Independent source exception
- Inevitable discovery
- Impeachment of defendant at trial

Good Faith Exception

The U.S. Supreme held in *United States v. Leon* (1984) that the Fourth Amendment exclusionary rule should not be applied to bar the use of evidence obtained by officers acting in reasonable reliance on a search warrant issued by a detached and neutral magistrate but ultimately found to be invalid, except where:

1. The magistrate issuing the warrant was deliberately misled by false information.
2. The magistrate wholly abandoned his or her detached or neutral role.
3. There was so little indicia of probable cause contained in the affidavit that it was entirely unreasonable for the officers to believe the warrant was valid.
4. The warrant so lacked specificity that officers could not determine the place to be searched or the items to be seized.

The *Leon* good faith exception applies when an affidavit does not supply a substantial basis for the determination of probable cause but does provide some indicia of probable cause sufficient to render official reliance reasonable. The Court has implied that the good faith exception in *Leon* is based on the concept that the marginal or nonexistent benefits produced by suppressing evidence obtained in objectively reasonable reliance on a subsequently invalidated search warrant cannot justify the substantial costs of exclusion.

In *United States v. Cos* (2006), the defendant attempted to suppress a gun police officers found when they searched his apartment, and the district court granted the motion based on its finding that the officers who searched the apartment did not reasonably believe that defendant was in the apartment, and a woman who gave the police permission to conduct the search did not have actual or apparent authority to give consent. The government asked the court to reconsider its ruling, arguing that police acted in good faith because they stopped the search and obtained a search warrant as soon as they found the gun, and because violation of the defendant's Fourth Amendment rights was made by the woman who gave police permission to search the defendant's apartment. The U.S. District Court for New Mexico held that the good faith exception to the exclusionary rule applied when police relied on a mistake made by a judge or magistrate who issued a search warrant, but because here the officers entered the defendant's apartment without a search warrant and did not act in an objectively reasonable manner when they entered the apartment based on permission granted by a woman about whom they knew virtually nothing, the good faith exception did not apply.

One U.S. District Court noted:

> Application of the good faith exception to a warrant search does not erase an underlying Fourth Amendment violation; it is simply a determination that there exists an exception to the exclusionary rule. Suppression of evidence obtained pursuant to a warrant is ordered on a case-by-case basis and only in those unusual cases in which exclusion will further the purposes of the exclusionary rule. Application of the good faith exception creates no new infringement on a defendant's constitutional rights because no new constitutional wrong is committed when evidence seized contrary to the Fourth Amendment is admitted into evidence. (*United States v. Mettetal*, 2000, p. 21605)

Purged Taint

The purged taint exception is based on the concept that the connection has been broken between the unlawful police conduct and the tainted evidence (Roberson, 2003). For example, in *Brown v. Illinois* (1975), following an illegal arrest, the defendant gave inculpatory statements after he was read his constitutional rights. The statements were admitted at trial on the basis that the Miranda warnings, by themselves, were sufficient to purge the taint of the illegal arrest, making admissible that which would normally be excluded. The Supreme Court held that the Miranda warnings could neither automatically nor by themselves protect an accused's Fourth Amendment rights. Whether a confession was freely given or improperly coerced, the Court held, had to be determined on a case-by-case basis. The Court directed the trial court to examine factors such as the temporal proximity of the arrest to the confession, the intervening circumstances, and particularly, the purpose and flagrancy of the official misconduct.

The exception was created by the Supreme Court in the case of *Wong Sun v. United States* (1963). In *Wong Sun*, two defendants were arrested after a suspect under surveillance was held with narcotics, and had led the federal agents to defendants. The challenged evidence included the heroin surrendered to the police and the statements made orally by the second defendant in his bedroom at the time of his arrest, and pretrial unsigned confessions of both defendants. The appeals court held that the arrests were illegal for lack of probable cause, but that the challenged evidence was not fruit of the illegal arrests and, therefore, was admissible. The Supreme Court stated:

> A court need not hold that all evidence is "fruit of the poisonous tree" simply because it would not have come to light but for the illegal actions of the police. Rather, the more apt question in such a case is whether, granting establishment of the primary illegality, the evidence to which an objection is made has been come at by exploitation of that illegality or instead by means sufficiently distinguishable to be purged of the primary taint. (p. 487)

Independent Source

The independent source exception is based on the concept that even if the police obtained the evidence by conduct that violated the defendant's constitutional rights, they could have obtained the evidence from a source that was not connected to the illegal actions. Justice Oliver Wendell Holmes discussed this exception in *Silverthorne Lumber Co. v. United States* (1920). In that case, the government agencies illegally entered the company offices and took the documents. Later, the government subpoenaed certain documents from the lumber company. The company refused to obey the subpoena and contempt proceedings were instituted against the company for failure to obey the court subpoenas. The district court concluded that originally the papers were seized in violation of the owners' constitutional rights; however, the district court ordered the owners to comply with the subpoenas. The Supreme Court stated that illegal action of subordinate public officials in their seizure of the papers cannot forever prevent the United States from later securing them by legal process. The Court noted:

> The lumber company, not being entitled to object under the Fifth Amendment to the use as evidence of the papers in question, could not object to lawful, sufficiently definite subpoenas to produce ... if knowledge of them is gained from an independent source they may be proved like any others, but the knowledge gained by the government's own wrong cannot be used by it to seek by subpoena evidence to be used in a criminal prosecution and to obtain an order commanding compliance with such subpoena. (p. 389)

Inevitable Discovery

The inevitable discovery exception rests upon the principle that the remedial purposes of the exclusionary rule are not served by suppressing evidence discovered through a later, lawful seizure that is genuinely independent of an earlier, tainted one (*Murray v. United States*, 1988).

The Supreme Court noted in *Murray* (p. 539) that the inevitable discovery doctrine, with its distinct requirements, was in reality an extrapolation from the independent source doctrine: "Since the tainted evidence would be admissible if in fact discovered through an independent source, it should be admissible if it inevitably would have been discovered."

In *Murray*, the federal agents obtained a warrant to search a warehouse. Prior to obtaining the warrant, however, the agents had entered the warehouse and observed covered bales of marijuana. The Court noted that if warrantless entry did not contribute to the issuance of the warrant, then the evidence was admissible. The Court noted that the agents had not revealed their warrantless entry to the magistrate from whom they sought the warrant and did not include in their application any recitations of their observations in the warehouse. The Court remanded the case to the district court for a determination as to whether the agents would have sought a warrant if they had not earlier entered the warehouse.

In *Nix v. Williams* (1984), Williams challenged his conviction for first-degree murder of a young girl. At his first trial, the conviction was reversed on the grounds that the evidence of his incriminating statements, which led the police to the victim's body, should have been excluded because the evidence was the product of unlawful questioning by the police. At his second trial, no such evidence was admitted, but the trial court admitted evidence of the body's location and condition on the theory that the body would have been discovered in any event, even had the incriminating statements not been elicited from him. The Supreme Court held that there was an inevitable discovery exception to the exclusionary rule. At the time that the illegal information was obtained from Williams, search parties were near the location where the body was found. The Court concluded that the record supported a finding that the victim's body would inevitably have been discovered and approved his conviction.

Impeachment of Defendant

In *Harris v. New York* (1971), the police took a statement from the accused (Harris) regarding his involvement in a drug deal. Later he was indicated by the State of New York for selling heroin. The prosecutor determined that Harris's statement was inadmissible to establish evidence of his guilt because he was not properly warned under the Miranda requirements. After the prosecution rested, Harris took the stand and testified that he was never involved with drugs. The prosecution then used his pretrial statement to impeach his testimony.

The U.S. Supreme Court held that statements made by an accused to police under circumstances rendering the statements inadmissible to establish the prosecution's case in chief under *Miranda v. Arizona* (1966) were admissible for purposes of impeaching the accused's credibility, where such statements were inconsistent with the accused's trial testimony bearing directly on the crimes charged, and although the police did not warn the

Photo 5.2 Main reading room of the Supreme Court Library. (Photograph by Cliff Roberson.)

accused of his right to appointed counsel before they questioned him when he was taken into custody, the accused made no claim that his statements to the police were coerced or involuntary. The Court noted that the exclusionary rule should not be used as a shield to protect lies by an accused when he is testifying in his defense.

The History of a Grand Old Building

The Supreme Court building, constructed between 1932 and 1935, was designed by noted architect Cass Gilbert, who is best known as the architect for the Woolworth building in New York. The first session of the Supreme Court was convened on February 1, 1790, but it took some 145 years for the Supreme Court to find a permanent residence. During those years the Supreme Court lived a nomadic existence. Initially meeting in the Royal Exchange building in New York, the Court established chambers in Independence Hall and later in City Hall when the national capitol moved to Philadelphia in 1790. The Court moved again when the federal government moved in 1800 to the permanent capital in Washington. Because no provision had been made for a Supreme Court building, Congress lent the Court space in the new Capitol building. The Court convened for a short period in a private home after the British had used Supreme Court documents to set fire to the Capitol during the War of 1812. Following this episode, the Court returned to the capitol and met from 1819 to 1860 in a chamber that has been restored as the Old Supreme Court Chamber. Then from 1860 to 1935, the Court sat in what is now known as the Old Senate Chamber. Finally in 1929, former President William Howard Taft, who was chief justice from 1921 to 1930, persuaded Congress to end this arrangement and authorize a permanent home for the Court.

At the laying of the cornerstone for the building on October 13, 1932, Chief Justice Charles Evans Hughes stated, "The Republic endures and this is the symbol of its faith." The building was designed on a scale in keeping with the importance and dignity of the Court and the judiciary as a coequal, independent branch of the federal government and as a symbol of "the national ideal of justice in the highest sphere of activity." Sixteen marble columns at the main west entrance support the portico, and on the architrave above is incised "Equal Justice Under Law." Capping the entrance is the pediment filled with a sculpture group by Robert Aitken, representing Liberty Enthroned guarded by Order and Authority. Cast in bronze, the west entrance doors, sculpted by John Donnelly, Jr., depict historic scenes in the development of the law. The east entrance's architrave bears the legend "Justice the Guardian of Liberty." A sculpture group by Herman A. McNeil is located above the east entrance that represents great lawgivers, Moses, Confucius, and Solon, flanked by symbolic groups representing means of enforcing the law, tempering justice with mercy, carrying on civilization, and settlement of disputes between states.

The Supreme Court building is located at 1st and East Capitol Streets, NE. Self-guided exhibits on the main level are available for touring Monday through Friday, 9:00 a.m. to 4:30 p.m. Lectures on the Supreme Court are presented on the main level every hour on the half-hour, Monday through Friday, 9:00 a.m. to 3:30 pm. For more information, call 202-479-3000.

Source: National Registry of Historical Places, http://www.nps.gov/nr/travel/wash/dc78.htm, accessed June 17, 2008.

Noncriminal Trial Proceedings

As a general rule, the exclusionary rule has not been applied to noncriminal trial proceedings. For example, it does not apply in civil trials.

Civil Tax Proceedings

In *United States v. Janis* (1976), Janis, a taxpayer, filed suit for refund of $4,940, which had been seized from him by the California State Police under a defective warrant directing a search for bookmaking paraphernalia. The money was then levied upon by the Internal Revenue Service (IRS) under an assessment for wagering taxes. The District Court rendered judgment for Janis on the ground that substantially all the evidence utilized by the IRS in making the assessment was illegally obtained.

The U.S. Supreme Court reversed and remanded the case. The Court held that the exclusionary rule should not be extended to forbid the use in the civil proceeding evidence seized by a criminal law enforcement agent of another sovereign. The Court's ruling was based on the ground that the exclusion of the evidence in the instant case had not been shown to have a sufficient likelihood of deterring the conduct of the state police so that it outweighed the societal costs imposed by the exclusion. This was a 5–4 decision by the U.S. Supreme Court, it involved police misconduct by state police, and the IRS proceedings were in federal court. The Court left open the question as to whether the rule would have applied had the misconduct been by a federal officer. The Supreme Court has never directly applied the exclusionary rule in a civil case except as noted in the next section.

Quasi-Criminal Proceedings

Quasi-criminal proceedings are civil in nature, but are founded on criminal misconduct. For example, a civil forfeiture action in a court designed to cause the forfeiture of property used in a criminal activity is considered a quasi-criminal proceeding. The Court has excluded illegally seized evidence in a quasi-criminal proceeding where the defendant was threatened with forfeiture of his car as a penalty for a criminal violation (*One 1958 Plymouth Sedan v. Pennsylvania*, 1965). It appears that in suits for penalties and forfeitures incurred by the commission of offenses against the law, quasi-criminal in nature, the courts will treat those as criminal proceedings for all the purposes of determining if the exclusionary rule applies.

Deportation Hearings

In *Immigration and Naturalization Service v. Lopez-Mendoza* (1984), respondent illegal aliens were arrested by the Immigration and Naturalization Service (INS). At their deportation hearings, they attempted to suppress evidence of their status under the exclusionary rule because their status was discovered during an illegal arrest. On appeal, the Supreme Court held that the exclusionary rule did not apply to civil proceedings such as the petitioner's deportation hearing, because the purpose of the exclusionary rule was to deter police misconduct, and that did not exist in this situation. The Supreme Court opined that application of the exclusionary rule to civil deportation proceedings could be justified only if the rule was likely to add significant protection to Fourth Amendment rights. The Court noted that if the evidence of their illegal status was excluded, the rule would have allowed them to continue breaking the law, something that the exclusionary rule was never designed to do.

Probation Revocation Hearings

In *Pennsylvania Board of Probation and Parole v. Scott* (1998), the Supreme Court ruled that the exclusionary rule did not bar the introduction at parole revocation hearings of evidence obtained in violation of such Fourth Amendment rights of parolees for the following reasons:

1. Application of the exclusionary rule would hinder the functioning of state parole systems, because the rule, which precludes consideration of reliable, probative evidence, imposes significant costs by detracting from the truth-finding process and allowing many who would otherwise be incarcerated to escape the consequences of their actions.
2. The rule is incompatible with the traditionally flexible, nonadversarial administrative process of parole revocation proceedings, because the rule frequently requires extensive litigation to determine whether particular evidence must be excluded.
3. The deterrence benefits of applying the rule to parole revocation hearings would not outweigh these costs because, in view of the significant deterrence already provided by the applicability of the rule in criminal trials, any additional deterrence resulting from applying the rule to parole revocation hearings would be minimal concerning a search by (a) a police officer, regardless of whether the officer is aware of the parolee's status, or (b) a parole officer.

Situations Where the Rule Has Not Been Applied

Violation of the Knock-and-Announce Requirement

The common-law principle that law enforcement officers must announce their presence and provide residents an opportunity to open the door is an ancient one. In *Hudson v. Michigan* (2006), the police obtained a warrant authorizing a search for drugs and firearms at the home of defendant Hudson. They discovered both. Large quantities of drugs were found, including cocaine rocks in Hudson's pocket. A loaded gun was lodged between the cushion and armrest of the chair in which he was sitting. Hudson was charged under Michigan law with unlawful drug and firearm possession.

When police arrived to execute a search warrant for drugs and firearms at defendant's home, they announced their presence but waited only a short time before turning the knob of the unlocked front door and entering the home. Police discovered large quantities of drugs and a loaded gun. The state conceded that the entry was a violation of the "knock and announce" rule. The Supreme Court determined that the exclusionary rule was inapplicable and suppression of the evidence was not warranted because, *inter alia*:

1. Violation of the knock-and-announce rule did not require the suppression of all evidence found in the search.
2. The constitutional violation of an illegal manner of entry was not a but-for cause of obtaining the evidence.
3. The interests that were violated, preventing the government from seeing or taking evidence described in a warrant, had nothing to do with the seizure of the evidence.
4. The social costs of applying the exclusionary rule to knock-and-announce violations were considerable, the incentive for such violations was minimal to begin with, and the extant deterrences against them were substantial.

Searches Based on Erroneous Information

Consider this fact situation: An accused was arrested when, during a routine traffic stop, a check on the police computer indicated an outstanding misdemeanor warrant for the accused's arrest. A subsequent search of the accused's vehicle revealed a bag of marijuana, and the accused was charged with possession of the drug. It was later discovered that the misdemeanor warrant had been quashed prior to the arrest. The accused sought suppression of the marijuana as the fruit of an unlawful arrest. Should the evidence be suppressed?

The Supreme Court in *Arizona v. Evans* (1995) stated that the exclusionary rule did not require the suppression of the evidence seized in violation of the federal Constitution's Fourth Amendment, where the erroneous information upon which the police based their actions resulted from clerical errors of court employees. The Court concluded that the exclusionary rule was historically designed as a means of deterring police misconduct, not mistakes by court employees. And there was no basis for believing that application of the exclusionary rule in such circumstances would have a significant effect on court employees responsible for informing the police that a warrant has been quashed (p. 15).

Exclusionary Rule and the Fifth Amendment

Testimony from a witness can at times constitute a tainted fruit of the poisonous tree. However, the attenuated taint exception is applied more generously when the challenged derivative evidence is live-witness testimony than when it is documentary evidence (*United States v. Ramirez-Sandoval*, 1989). A Court's decision regarding the possible attenuation of taint as to witness testimony should be based on (1) the witness's willingness to testify, (2) the role played by the illegality, (3) the proximity between the illegal behavior and the testimony, and (4) the police's motivation (*United States v. Reyes*, 1998, p. 954).

The U.S. Supreme Court indicated its reluctance to use the exclusionary rule in cases involving the Fifth Amendment in *United States v. Ceccolini* (1977). The Court noted that the greater the willingness of the witness to freely testify, the greater the likelihood that he or she will be discovered by legal means and, concomitantly, the smaller the incentive to conduct an illegal search to discover the witness. The Court also noted that witnesses are not like guns or documents that remain hidden from view until one turns over a sofa or opens a filing cabinet. Witnesses can, and often do, come forward and offer evidence entirely of their own volition. And evaluated properly, the degree of freedom necessary to dissipate the taint will very likely be found more often in the case of live-witness testimony than other kinds of evidence. The time, place, and manner of the initial questioning of the witness may be such that any statements are truly the product of detached reflection and a desire to be cooperative on the part of the witness. And the illegality that led to the discovery of the witness very often will not play any meaningful part in the witness's willingness to testify.

The Court noted that the fact that the name of a potential witness was disclosed to police is of no evidentiary significance, per se, because the living witness is an individual human personality whose attributes of will, perception, memory, and volition interact to determine what testimony he or she will give. The uniqueness of this human process distinguishes the evidentiary character of a witness from the relative immutability of inanimate evidence (p. 277).

Exclusionary Rule and the Sixth Amendment

The Supreme Court has held that the Sixth Amendment requires the suppression of any confession that federal agents deliberately elicit from a defendant after he has been indicted and in the absence of his counsel (*Massiah v. United States*, 1964). In relying on *Massiah*, the Supreme Court has held that "if police initiate interrogation after a defendant's assertion, at an arraignment or similar proceeding, of his right to counsel, any waiver of the defendant's right to counsel for that police-initiated interrogation is invalid" (*Michigan v. Jackson*, 1986, p. 636). From the *Massiah* and *Jackson* cases, it is clear that the Supreme Court will apply the exclusionary rule to the use in evidence of statements obtained by the police in violation of a defendant's Sixth Amendment right to counsel.

Capstone Case: *Groh v. Ramirez,* 540 U.S. 551 (2004)

The petitioner federal agent was sued in federal court in a civil action for violation of an individual's constitutional rights. The federal agent sought review of a U.S. Court of Appeals decision that held that the search of the respondent individuals' home was unconstitutional and that the federal agent was not entitled to qualified immunity.

Justice Stevens delivered the opinion of the Court:

Petitioner conducted a search of respondents' home pursuant to a warrant that failed to describe the "persons or things to be seized." The questions presented are (1) whether the search violated the Fourth Amendment, and (2) if so, whether petitioner nevertheless is entitled to qualified immunity, given that a Magistrate Judge (Magistrate), relying on an affidavit that particularly described the items in question, found probable cause to conduct the search.

Respondents, Joseph Ramirez and members of his family, live on a large ranch in Butte-Silver Bow County, Montana. Petitioner, Jeff Groh, has been a Special Agent for the Bureau of Alcohol, Tobacco and Firearms (ATF) since 1989. In February 1997, a concerned citizen informed petitioner that on a number of visits to respondents' ranch the visitor had seen a large stock of weaponry, including an automatic rifle, grenades, a grenade launcher, and a rocket launcher. Based on that information, petitioner prepared and signed an application for a warrant to search the ranch. The application stated that the search was for "any automatic firearms or parts to automatic weapons, destructive devices to include but not limited to grenades, grenade launchers, rocket launchers, and any and all receipts pertaining to the purchase or manufacture of automatic weapons or explosive devices or launchers." Petitioner supported the application with a detailed affidavit, which he also prepared and executed, that set forth the basis for his belief that the listed items were concealed on the ranch. Petitioner then presented these documents to a Magistrate, along with a warrant form that petitioner also had completed. The Magistrate signed the warrant form.

Although the application particularly described the place to be searched and the contraband petitioner expected to find, the warrant itself was less specific; it failed to identify any of the items that petitioner intended to seize. In the portion of the form that called for a description of the "person or property" to be seized, petitioner typed a description of respondents' two-story blue house rather than the alleged stockpile of firearms. The warrant did not incorporate by reference the itemized list contained in the application. It did, however, recite that the Magistrate was satisfied the affidavit established probable cause to believe that contraband was concealed on the premises, and that sufficient grounds existed for the warrant's issuance.

The day after the Magistrate issued the warrant, petitioner led a team of law enforcement officers, including both federal agents and members of the local sheriff's department, in the search of respondents' premises. Although respondent Joseph Ramirez was not home, his wife and children were. Petitioner states that he orally described the objects of the search to Mrs. Ramirez in person and to Mr. Ramirez by telephone. According to Mrs. Ramirez, however, petitioner explained only that he was searching for "an explosive device in a box." At any rate, the officers' search uncovered no illegal weapons or explosives. When the officers left, petitioner gave Mrs. Ramirez a copy of the search warrant, but not a copy of the application, which had been sealed. The following day, in response to a request from respondents' attorney, petitioner faxed the attorney a copy of the page of the application that listed the items to be seized. No charges were filed against the Ramirezes.

Respondents sued petitioner and the other officers under 42 USC § 1983, raising eight claims, including violation of the Fourth Amendment. The District Court found no Fourth Amendment violation, because it considered the case comparable to one in which the warrant contained an inaccurate address, and in such a case, the court reasoned, the warrant is sufficiently detailed if the executing officers can locate the correct house. The court added that even if a constitutional violation occurred, the defendants were entitled to qualified immunity because the failure of the warrant to describe the objects of the search amounted to a mere "typographical error."

The Court of Appeals affirmed the judgment with respect to all defendants and all claims, with the exception of respondents' Fourth Amendment claim against petitioner. On that claim, the court held that the warrant was invalid because it did not "describe with particularity the place to be searched and the items to be seized," and that oral statements by petitioner during or after the search could not cure the omission. The court observed that the warrant's facial defect "increased the likelihood and degree of confrontation between the Ramirezes and the police" and deprived respondents of the means "to challenge officers who might have exceeded the limits imposed by the magistrate." The court also expressed concern that "permitting officers to expand the scope of the warrant by oral statements would broaden the area of dispute between the parties in subsequent litigation." The court nevertheless concluded that all of the officers except petitioner were protected by qualified immunity. With respect to petitioner, the court read our opinion in *United States v. Leon* as precluding qualified immunity for the leader of a search who fails to "read the warrant and satisfy himself that he understands its scope and limitations, and that it is not defective in some obvious way." The court added that "the leaders of the search team must also make sure that a copy of the warrant is available to give to the person whose property is being searched at the commencement of the search, and that such copy has no missing pages or other obvious defects."

The warrant was plainly invalid. The Fourth Amendment states unambiguously that "no Warrants shall issue, but upon probable cause, supported by Oath or affirmation, and particularly describing the place to be searched, and the persons or things to be seized." The warrant in this case complied with the first three of these requirements: It was based on probable cause and supported by a sworn affidavit, and it described particularly the place of the search. On the fourth requirement, however, the warrant failed altogether. Indeed, petitioner concedes that "the warrant ... was deficient in particularity because it provided no description of the type of evidence sought."

The fact that the application adequately described the "things to be seized" does not save the warrant from its facial invalidity. The Fourth Amendment by its terms requires particularity in the warrant, not in the supporting documents. The Fourth Amendment requires that the warrant particularly describe the things to be seized, not the papers presented to the judicial officer ... asked to issue the warrant. And for good reason: "The presence of a search warrant serves a high function," and that high function is not necessarily vindicated when some other document, somewhere, says something about the objects of the search, but the contents of that document are neither known to the person whose home is being searched nor available for her inspection. We do not say that the Fourth Amendment prohibits a warrant from cross-referencing other documents. Indeed, most Courts of Appeals have held that a court may construe a warrant with reference to a supporting application or affidavit if the warrant uses appropriate words of incorporation, and if the supporting document accompanies the warrant. But in this case the warrant did not incorporate other documents by reference, nor did either the affidavit or the application (which had been placed under seal) accompany the warrant. Hence, we need not further explore the matter of incorporation.

Petitioner argues that even though the warrant was invalid, the search nevertheless was "reasonable" within the meaning of the Fourth Amendment. He notes that a Magistrate authorized the search on the basis of adequate evidence of probable cause, that petitioner orally described to respondents the items to be seized, and that the search did not exceed the limits intended by the Magistrate and described by petitioner. Thus, petitioner maintains, his search of respondents' ranch was functionally equivalent to a search authorized by a valid warrant.

We disagree. This warrant did not simply omit a few items from a list of many to be seized, or misdescribe a few of several items. Nor did it make what fairly could be characterized as a mere technical mistake or typographical error. Rather, in the space set aside for a description of the items to be seized, the warrant stated that the items consisted of a "single dwelling residence ... blue in color." In other words, the warrant did not describe the items to be seized at all. In this respect the warrant was so obviously deficient that we must regard the search as "warrantless" within the meaning of our case law. Because the right of a man to retreat into his own home and there be free from unreasonable governmental intrusion stands at the very core of the Fourth Amendment, our cases have firmly established the basic principle of Fourth Amendment law that searches and seizures inside a home without a warrant are presumptively unreasonable. Thus, absent exigent circumstances, a warrantless entry to search for weapons or contraband is unconstitutional even when a felony has been committed and there is probable cause to believe that incriminating evidence will be found within.

The uniformly applied rule is that a search conducted pursuant to a warrant that fails to conform to the particularity requirement of the Fourth Amendment is unconstitutional. That rule is in keeping with the well-established principle that except in certain carefully defined classes of cases, a search of private property without proper consent is "unreasonable" unless it has been authorized by a valid search warrant.

Petitioner asks us to hold that a search conducted pursuant to a warrant lacking particularity should be exempt from the presumption of unreasonableness if the goals served by the particularity requirement are otherwise satisfied. He maintains that the search in this case satisfied those goals—which he says are "to prevent general searches, to prevent the seizure of one thing under a warrant describing another, and to prevent warrants from being issued on vague or dubious information." But unless the particular items described in the affidavit are also set forth in the warrant itself (or at least incorporated by reference, and the affidavit present at the search), there can be no written assurance that the Magistrate actually found probable cause to search for, and to seize, every item mentioned in the affidavit.

For this reason petitioner's argument that any constitutional error was committed by the Magistrate, not petitioner, is misplaced. In *Massachusetts v. Sheppard*, we suggested that "the judge, not the police officers," may have committed "an error of constitutional dimension," because the judge had assured the officers requesting the warrant that he would take the steps necessary to conform the warrant to constitutional requirements. Thus, it was not unreasonable for the police in that case to rely on the judge's assurances that the warrant authorized the search they had requested. In this case, by contrast, petitioner did not alert the Magistrate to the defect in the warrant that petitioner had drafted, and we therefore cannot know whether the Magistrate was aware of the scope of the search he was authorizing. Nor would it have been reasonable for petitioner to rely on a warrant that was so patently defective, even if the Magistrate was aware of the deficiency.

We have long held, moreover, that the purpose of the particularity requirement is not limited to the prevention of general searches. A particular warrant also assures the individual whose property is searched or seized of the lawful authority of the executing officer, his need to search, and the limits of his power to search.

It is incumbent on the officer executing a search warrant to ensure the search is lawfully authorized and lawfully conducted. Because petitioner did not have in his possession a warrant particularly describing the things he intended to seize, proceeding with the search was clearly "unreasonable" under the Fourth Amendment. The Court of Appeals correctly held that the search was unconstitutional.

The Court of Appeals' decision is consistent with this principle. Petitioner mischaracterizes the court's decision when he contends that it imposed a novel proofreading requirement on officers executing warrants. The court held that officers leading a search team must "make sure that they have a proper warrant that in fact authorizes the search and seizure they are about to conduct." That is not a duty to proofread; it is, rather, a duty to ensure that the warrant conforms to constitutional requirements.

Having concluded that a constitutional violation occurred, we turn to the question whether petitioner is entitled to qualified immunity despite that violation. The answer depends on whether the right that was transgressed was "clearly established"—that is, "whether it would be clear to a reasonable officer that his conduct was unlawful in the situation he confronted."

Given that the particularity requirement is set forth in the text of the Constitution, no reasonable officer could believe that a warrant that plainly did not comply with that requirement was valid. Moreover, because petitioner himself prepared the invalid warrant, he may not argue that he reasonably relied on the Magistrate's assurance that the warrant contained an adequate description of the things to be seized and was therefore valid. In fact, the guidelines of petitioner's own department placed him on notice that he might be liable for executing a manifestly invalid warrant. An ATF directive in force at the time of this search warned: "Special agents are liable if they exceed their authority while executing a search warrant and must be sure that a search warrant is sufficient on its face even when issued by a magistrate." And even a cursory reading of the warrant in this case—perhaps just a simple glance— would have revealed a glaring deficiency that any reasonable police officer would have known was constitutionally fatal.

No reasonable officer could claim to be unaware of the basic rule, well established by our cases, that, absent consent or exigency, a warrantless search of the home is presumptively unconstitutional. Because not a word in any of our cases would suggest to a reasonable officer that this case fits within any exception to that fundamental tenet, petitioner is asking us, in effect, to craft a new exception. Absent any support for such an exception in our cases, he cannot reasonably have relied on an expectation that we would do so.

Accordingly, the judgment of the Court of Appeals is affirmed.

Questions in Review

1. What does the Supreme Court consider the primary purpose of the exclusionary rule?
2. Under what circumstances will the courts not apply the exclusionary rule?
3. Explain the "fruit of the poisonous tree" rule.
4. Under what circumstances may a prosecutor use a statement taken from a defendant in violation of her *Miranda* rights in a court case?
5. What is the Court's rationale for not using the exclusionary rule in deportation cases?

Fifth Amendment Issues

6

No person shall be held to answer for a capital, or otherwise infamous crime, unless on a presentment or indictment of a Grand Jury, except in cases arising in the land or naval forces, or in the Militia, when in actual service in time of War or public danger; nor shall any person be subject for the same offence to be twice put in jeopardy of life or limb; nor shall be compelled in any criminal case to be a witness against himself, nor be deprived of life, liberty, or property, without due process of law; nor shall private property be taken for public use, without just compensation.

—Fifth Amendment, U.S Constitution

Introduction

As noted in Chapter 2, the due process clause of the Fifth Amendment applies to the federal government and not to state criminal trials. For discussion on the due process clauses, review Chapter 2. The protections afforded an accused in criminal proceedings by the Fifth Amendment include the following rights, which are discussed in this chapter:

- The right to an indictment by a grand jury before being tried on a capital or otherwise infamous crime
- Double jeopardy
- Right against self-incrimination

Grand Jury

The right to a grand jury indictment prior to being tried on a capital or other infamous crime does not apply to the states. Criminal prosecutions by information rather than by grand jury indictment afford due process of law (*Eyman v. Alford*, 1969). As one court noted: "States are free to prosecute crimes on information, since the indictment clause of Constitution is not applicable to states" (*Buchannon v. Wainwright*, 1973, p. 1008). See Appendix C for a copy of an indictment that was issued by a federal grand jury in Virginia.

Grand juries are used in many states and in the federal system. In addition, some states use both the grand jury system and prosecutions by information, depending on either the type of crime or the decision of the prosecutor.

Infamous Crime

What constitutes an "infamous crime" to trigger the grand jury requirement in the federal system or in those states that use the infamous crime classification in their constitution? In *Ex parte Wilson* (1885), the Supreme Court stated that any crime punishable by imprisonment for term of years at hard labor is an infamous crime. In *Mackin v. United States* (1886), the Court stated that a crime in which the maximum punishment was imprisonment in state prison or penitentiary, with or without hard labor, is an infamous punishment. The Court noted that if penalty prescribed by statute does not include hard labor, offense does not become infamous just because a court may sentence a defendant to confinement in state jail or penitentiary, where employment of prisoners may be required as part of prison discipline (*Brede v. Powers*, 1923). The Court also held that any misdemeanor, regardless of character of particular offense so described, unless it is subject to punishment by imprisonment at hard labor or to some other punishment that, although not involving imprisonment in penitentiary, is deemed infamous, is not "infamous crime" within the meaning of the Fifth Amendment (*Duke v. United States*, 1937, p. 1243).

Discrimination in Selection of Grand Jury Members

Although states are not required to use the grand jury system, any racial discrimination in selection of a grand jury and its foreman violates the equal protection clause of the Fourteenth Amendment in state criminal cases. As one appellate court noted, a defendant has standing to challenge exclusion of cognizable groups from grand or petit juries under the Fifth and Fourteenth Amendments, even though the defendant is not a member of the excluded group (*United States v. Cabrera-Sarmiento*, 1982).

Evidence

The validity of a grand jury indictment is not affected by character of evidence considered by the grand jury. An indictment that is valid on its face is not subject to challenge on the ground that the grand jury acted on the basis of inadequate or incompetent evidence, or even on the basis of information obtained in violation of the defendant's Fifth Amendment privilege against self-incrimination (*United States v. Calandra*, 1974).

Absent evidence that suggests that a grand jury was misled into believing that a federal agent had firsthand knowledge of all that he related, indictment was not open to attack on the ground that the government presented only hearsay testimony of the federal agent to the grand jury when firsthand testimony was readily available (*United States v. Powers*, 1973).

Sufficiency of an Indictment

The two criteria by which sufficiency of indictment is tested are whether facts stated show essential elements of offense and whether facts alleged are sufficient to permit defendant to plead former jeopardy in subsequent prosecution (*Russell v. United States*, 1962). An indictment must inform the accused of the nature of the crime charged and its basis, so that he may prepare his defense, and an indictment must protect the accused against subsequent prosecution for the same offense (*United States v. Boston*, 1983). An indictment that enumerated each element of offense, notified the defendant of charges, and provided him with double jeopardy defense against future prosecution was constitutionally sufficient even if it contained technical errors (*United States v. Gonzales*, 1997).

When an indictment is filed with a trial court, no change can be made in the body of instrument, without resubmission of the case to the grand jury, unless the change is merely a matter of form (*Russell v. United States*, 1962). Dropping allegations from an indictment that are unnecessary to the offense that is clearly contained within the indictment does not constitute an unconstitutional amendment of the indictment (*United States v. Miller*, 1985). A conviction must be reversed when an essential element of felony indictment is amended other than by grand jury action (*United States v. Pandilidis*, 1975). Any amendment to indictment enabling prosecution to seek conviction on a charge not brought by the grand jury is prejudicial per se and violates the defendant's Fifth Amendment right not to be held to answer for infamous crime except by indictment of grand jury (*Watson v. Jago*, 1977).

Double Jeopardy

The concept that an individual should be protected from prosecution a second time for the same offense is derived from early English common law (*Ex parte Lange*, 1874). The prohibition is against being twice put in jeopardy. Common law not only prohibited a second punishment for the same offense, but it went further and forbid a second trial for the same offense, whether the accused had suffered punishment or not, and whether in the former trial he had been acquitted or convicted (*United States v. Ball*, 1896). The "twice put in jeopardy" language relates to potential risk that the accused for a second time will be convicted or punished of the "same offense" for which he or she was initially tried. Double jeopardy attaches in jury trial when the jury is impaneled and in bench trial when evidence is heard.

Application of Prohibition

The double jeopardy clause differs from procedural guarantees in that its practical result is to prevent a trial from taking place at all rather than to prescribe procedural rules that govern conduct of trial (*Blackledge v. Perry*, 1974). The double jeopardy clause protects against (1) second prosecution for the same offense after acquittal, (2) second prosecution for the same offense after conviction, and (3) multiple punishments for the same offense (*Ohio v. Johnson*, 1984).

The sweep of the double jeopardy clause of the Fifth Amendment, where it is applicable, is absolute, and there are no equities to be balanced in determining whether a second trial should be held. The clause has been declared constitutional policy, based on grounds that are not open to judicial examination (*Burks v. United States*, 1978). It applies to the states. As one court noted, a state may not put a defendant in jeopardy twice for the same offense; as a general rule under double jeopardy principles, the prosecutor is entitled to one, and only one, opportunity to require the accused to stand trial; the double jeopardy clause precludes prosecution from enhancing risk that an innocent defendant may be convicted by taking question of guilt to a series of persons empowered to make binding determinations (*Swisher v. Brady*, 1978).

What if the defendant fails to object to a second trial? Double jeopardy is a personal right that, if not affirmatively pleaded at the time of trial, will be regarded as waived (*United States v. Parker*, 2004). Jeopardy attaches when a jury is impaneled and sworn. An acquittal based on statute of limitations did not bear on the defendant's culpability, and as such did not trigger the protection of the double jeopardy clause (*Kruelski v. Conn. Superior Court*, 2003).

The double jeopardy clause does not bar the grand jury from returning an indictment when a prior grand jury has refused to do so (*United States v. Williams*, 1992). The Tennessee Sex Offender Registration and Monitoring Act, requiring sex offenders to register with law enforcement agencies and allowing officials to release such information for protection of the public, did not violate the double jeopardy clause because the act's purpose is not punitive and no affirmative restraint is imposed by it (*Cutshall v. Sundquist*, 1999).

The Fifth Amendment's protection against double jeopardy is fully applicable to juvenile court proceedings to the extent that jeopardy attaches during delinquency hearings if juvenile court, on the basis of the delinquency hearing, can impose severe restrictions upon the juvenile's liberty; once a minor has been placed under such risk of conviction, he cannot be retried for the same offense (*Jones v. Breed*, 1974).

Collateral Estoppel

The principle of collateral estoppel prevents introduction of evidence concerning prior similar acts, even those for which the defendant has been acquitted, as evidence of identity or motive, for any purpose (*Albert v. Montgomery*, 1984). The doctrine of collateral estoppel has the purpose of protecting litigants from the burden of relitigating an identical issue with the same party or his privy and of promoting judicial economy by preventing needless litigation. The need for the application of collateral estoppel in criminal cases arises primarily because of proliferation of overlapping and related statutory offenses from a single alleged criminal transaction (*Ashe v. Swenson*, 1970).

Hoag v. New Jersery (1958) involved the issue of collateral estoppel. In *Hoag*, a grand jury returned three indictments against the defendant, charging him with robbing three victims at a tavern. Although two witnesses had identified the petitioner from a police photograph, only one witness, a fourth victim of the robbery, identified him at trial. The jury acquitted the defendant. A later grand jury returned another indictment against him naming the fourth victim as the victim of the robbery. At trial, the state called only the fourth victim as a witness and the jury returned a verdict of guilty. The conviction was sustained on appeal. The appellate court held that his later prosecution and conviction did not violate due process, and he was not twice put in jeopardy for the same crime. Each of the four robberies, though taking place on the same occasion, was a separate offense. Double jeopardy did not apply. The Fourteenth Amendment did not prevent the state from allowing different offenses arising out of the same act or transaction to be prosecuted separately. Collateral estoppel was inapplicable because the first trial involved questions other than the petitioner's identity. There was no way of knowing upon which question the jury's verdict turned.

Collateral estoppel does not preclude a trial court from allowing introduction, during the second trial, of evidence admitted during the first trial (*Flittie v. Solem*, 1985). A defendant who was acquitted on two counts of a three-count indictment was not successful in invoking the collateral estoppel doctrine to preclude retrial on the third count after a jury was unable to reach a verdict on the third count and the judge declared a mistrial, because the jury in acquitting the defendant did not have to resolve any of the essential elements of the third count (*United States v. Medina*, 1983).

Self-Incrimination

The constitutional privilege against self-incrimination is designed to prevent use of the legal process to force from the lips of an accused individual the evidence necessary to convict him or to force him to produce and authenticate any personal documents or effects that might incriminate him, and thereby to avoid reprehensible methods of compelling production of incriminating evidence, by forcing prosecutors to search for independent evidence (*United States v. White*, 1944, p. 696).

The Fifth Amendment's privilege against self-incrimination was aimed at recurrence of the Inquisition and Star Chamber; prevention of that greater evil was deemed of more importance than occurrence of the lesser evil that privilege may, on occasion, save the guilty man from his just desserts (*Ullmann v. United States*, 1956, p. 423).

The Fifth Amendment's privilege against self-incrimination is liberally construed in favor of the right it was intended to protect, and the liberal construction is particularly warranted in prosecution of a witness for refusal to answer, because the respect normally accorded privilege is then buttressed by presumption of the defendant's innocence (*Quinn v. United States*, 1955).

The Fifth Amendment's strictures against self-incrimination, unlike the Fourth Amendment's strictures against unreasonable searches and seizures, are not removed by showing reasonableness. The Fifth Amendment privilege against self-incrimination protects compelled testimony, not disclosure of private information. The Fifth Amendment privilege against self-incrimination does not independently proscribe compelled production of every sort of incriminating evidence, but applies only when an accused is compelled to make testimonial communication that is incriminating (*Fisher v. United States*, 1976). The standards for admitting illegally obtained statements should be stricter than standards for admitting illegally obtained physical evidence because of trustworthiness implications of the Fifth Amendment, as distinguished from security implications of the Fourth Amendment (*United States v. Whitson*, 1978).

The U.S. Supreme Court noted in *United States v. Patane* (2004) that there was no reason to apply the "fruit of poisonous tree" doctrine when a police officer fails to give an arrestee his Miranda warnings and the arrestee's subsequent statement leads to seizure of physical evidence because, unlike unreasonable searches under the Fourth Amendment or actual violations of the due process clause or self-incrimination clause, there was nothing to deter because police do not violate an arrestee's constitutional rights or Miranda rule by failure to provide him his Miranda warnings.

Coverage of the Privilege

The Fifth Amendment privilege against self-incrimination does not automatically preclude self-incrimination, whether spontaneous or in response to questions put by government officials. It does not preclude a witness from testifying voluntarily in matters that may incriminate him, for those competent and free willed to do so may give evidence against the whole world, themselves included. It does not prohibit admissions of guilt by wrongdo-ers. It does guarantee the right to remain silent unless immunity is granted, proscribes only self-incrimination obtained by genuine compulsion of testi-mony, and absent some officially coerced self-accusation, is not violated by even the most damning admissions (*United States v. Washington*, 1977). The Fifth Amendment provision as to self-incrimination applies only to testimo-nial self-incrimination and not to production of incriminating physical evi-dence (*United States v. Thompson*, 1973).

A statement made during a 911 call identifying the defendant was not "testimonial," as it described a current emergency (*Davis v. Washington*, 2006). The Court in *Davis* noted that as for Fifth Amendment purposes, police officers can and will distinguish almost instinctively between ques-tions necessary to secure their own safety or the safety of the public and questions designed solely to elicit testimonial evidence from a suspect.

The Fifth Amendment right against self-incrimination did not apply where a prisoner was interviewed by a prison psychologist for purposes of evaluation for rehabilitation and training; the prisoner's right to assert the Fifth Amendment would be triggered, however, if the state attempted to use the evaluation in a subsequent criminal proceeding (*Briley v. Booker*, 1984). The privilege against self-incrimination does not apply to a resident alien during his investigation into whether he was subject to expulsion from the United States as a war criminal because of the real and substantial likelihood of his prosecution and conviction in several foreign countries for his par-ticipation in Nazi concentration camp executions in Lithuania during World War II (*United States v. Gecas*, 1997).

The privilege against self-incrimination does not extend to the right to refuse to file any tax return at all, and a blanket refusal to disclose any finan-cial information on the basis of the Fifth Amendment is equivalent to filing no return. A person is not prohibited from claiming Fifth Amendment privi-lege concerning a specific answer to selected individual questions, but he has the burden of asserting facts establishing that answer may incriminate, or at least it must be apparent from the context that such is the case. A claim of privilege is not allowed to avoid disclosure of information as to tax liability; claiming the right to refuse to disclose income information on grounds that it will establish tax liability, and thus potential for criminal prosecution for disobedience to tax laws, is a bootstrapping argument that could defeat the legitimate power of government to tax income (*State Department of Revenue v. Oliver*, 1981).

The Fifth Amendment privilege against self-incrimination relates only to testimonial or communicative acts on the part of person to whom privilege applies and does not apply to acts noncommunicative in nature as to the person asserting privilege, even though such acts are compelled to obtain the testimony of others (*Schmerber v. California*, 1966). A criminal suspect may properly be compelled to put on a shirt, provide a blood sample or hand-writing exemplar, or make a recording of his voice—even though such acts may provide incriminating evidence—for the act of exhibiting such physical characteristics is not the same as sworn communication by a witness that relates either expressed or implied assertions of fact or belief (*United States v. Hubbell*, 2000).

A chemical test that consisted of swabbing the defendant's hands, after his arrest and his refusal to answer questions concerning his handling of explosives, did not violate the defendant's privilege against self-incrimination, as swabbing did not provide testimonial or communicative evidence, and exigent circumstances existed, in that if the defendant had washed his hands before the test, any traces of explosive on them would have disappeared (*United States v. Bridges*, 1974). The privilege against self-incrimination was not violated by a trial judge's asking the accused to stand up after he was described and identified by a government witness, who did not know his name, at which point the judge asked the accused if he was the named defendant, to which the accused responded yes, because the accused's answer was nontestimonial, having been used exclusively for purposes of identification (*United States v. Silvestri*, 1986).

A state's "hit and run" statute, which required the driver of a motor vehicle involved in an accident resulting in damage to any property to stop at the scene and give his or her name and address, did not violate constitutional privilege against compulsory self-incrimination (*California v. Byers*, 1971).

Establishing Voluntariness of Statement

The burden is on the government to prove by a preponderance of evidence that a defendant's statements were voluntary (*United States v. Haswood*, 2003). There is a presumption that a custodial confession is involuntary and the prosecutor bears a heavy burden to show that such a statement was voluntarily, freely, and understandably given; the court must make independent determination based upon the totality of circumstances, resolving all doubts in favor of individual rights and constitutional safeguards (*Thomerson v. State*, 1981). The defendant may interrupt any interrogation and request counsel or voluntarily raise his rights; however, representation by an attorney does not mean that law enforcement officials cannot procure a statement from a defendant without notice to the attorney; notice or lack thereof to the attorney that interrogation is to commence and that the statement might be procured is but one important factor that should be considered by the trial court when examining the totality of circumstances to determine whether the state has met its burden of proof (*Kern v. State*, 1981).

A criminal defendant's rights under the Fifth and Fourteenth Amendments were violated by use of his confession obtained by police-instigated interrogation—without counsel present—after he requested an attorney (*Edwards v. Arizona*, 1981).

Miranda Warning

As the Supreme Court explained in *Johnson v. New Jersey* (1966), the prime purpose of rulings in *Escobedo v. Illinois* (1964) and *Miranda v. Arizona* (1966), both involving interrogation of suspects by police, is to guarantee full effectuation of privilege against self-incrimination, the mainstay of our adversary system of criminal justice; these rulings are designed in part to ensure that a person who responds to interrogation while in custody does so with intelligent understanding of his right to remain silent and of consequences that may flow from relinquishing it, and in this respect rulings secure the scrupulous observance of the principle that law will not suffer a prisoner to be made a deluded instrument of his own conviction.

In *Miranda v. Arizona* (1966), Ernesto Miranda was taken into custody on suspicion of kidnapping and rape. The Phoenix police placed him in a lineup, where the victim identified him. He was then interrogated by the police for about two hours. During the interrogation, he confessed to the rape. The Supreme Court agreed to hear the case, along with three other cases with similar issues. After the Supreme Court reversed the case, Miranda was retried without the use of his confession and was found guilty of the rape. He served seven years in prison. After release, he was killed in a bar fight. On his body, the police found autographed Miranda warning cards that he was trading for drinks.

Excepts from the Supreme Court's opinion are as follows:

> An understanding of the nature and setting of this in-custody interrogation is essential to our decisions today. The difficulty in depicting what transpires at such interrogations stems from the fact that in this country they have largely taken place incommunicado. From extensive factual studies undertaken in the early 1930's, including the famous Wickersham Report to Congress by a Presidential Commission, it is clear that police violence and the "third degree" flourished at that time. In a series of cases decided by this Court long after these studies, the police resorted to physical brutality—beating, hanging, whipping—and to sustained and protracted questioning incommunicado in order to extort confessions. The Commission on Civil Rights in 1961 found much evidence to indicate that some policemen still resort to physical force to obtain confessions. The use of physical brutality and violence is not, unfortunately, relegated to the past or to any part of the country. Only recently in Kings County, New York, the police brutally beat, kicked and placed lighted cigarette butts on the back of a potential witness under interrogation for the purpose of securing a statement incriminating a third party. (pp. 446–47)

To the contention that the third degree is necessary to get the facts, the reporters aptly reply in the language of the present Lord Chancellor of England (Lord Sankey): "It is not admissible to do a great right by doing a little wrong.... It is not sufficient to do justice by obtaining a proper result by irregular or improper means." Not only does the use of the third degree involve a flagrant violation of law by the officers of the law, but it involves also the dangers of false confessions, and it tends to make police and prosecutors less zealous in the search for objective evidence. As the New York prosecutor quoted in the report said, "It is a short cut and makes the police lazy and unenterprising." Or, as another official quoted remarked: "If you use your fists, you are not so likely to use your wits." We agree with the conclusion expressed in the report, that "The third degree brutalizes the police, hardens the prisoner against society, and lowers the esteem in which the administration of justice is held by the public." (p. 448)

Again we stress that the modern practice of in-custody interrogation is psychologically rather than physically oriented. As we have stated before, this Court has recognized that coercion can be mental as well as physical, and that the blood of the accused is not the only hallmark of an unconstitutional inquisition. Interrogation still takes place in privacy. Privacy results in secrecy and this in turn results in a gap in our knowledge as to what in fact goes on in the interrogation rooms. A valuable source of information about present police practices, however, may be found in various police manuals and texts which document procedures employed with success in the past, and which recommend various other effective tactics. These texts are used by law enforcement agencies themselves as guides. It should be noted that these texts professedly present the most enlightened and effective means presently used to obtain statements through custodial interrogation. By considering these texts and other data, it is possible to describe procedures observed and noted around the country. (p. 449)

To highlight the isolation and unfamiliar surroundings, the manuals instruct the police to display an air of confidence in the suspect's guilt and from outward appearance to maintain only an interest in confirming certain details. The guilt of the subject is to be posited as a fact. The interrogator should direct his comments toward the reasons why the subject committed the act, rather than court failure by asking the subject whether he did it. Like other men, perhaps the subject has had a bad family life, had an unhappy childhood, had too much to drink, had an unrequited desire for women. The officers are instructed to minimize the moral seriousness of the offense, to cast blame on the victim or on society. These tactics are designed to put the subject in a psychological state where his story is but an elaboration of what the police purport to know already—that he is guilty. Explanations to the contrary are dismissed and discouraged. The manuals suggest that the suspect be offered legal excuses for his actions in order to obtain an initial admission of guilt. Where there is a suspected revenge-killing, for example, the interrogator may say:

"Joe, you probably didn't go out looking for this fellow with the purpose of shooting him. My guess is, however, that you expected something from him and that's why you carried a gun—for your own protection. You knew him for what he was, no good. Then when you met him he probably started using foul, abusive language and he gave some indication that he was about to pull a gun on you, and that's when you had to act to save your own life. That's about it, isn't it, Joe?" (pp. 451–52)

Having then obtained the admission of shooting, the interrogator is advised to refer to circumstantial evidence which negates the self-defense explanation. This should enable him to secure the entire story. One text notes that "Even if he fails to do so, the inconsistency between the subject's original denial of the shooting and his present admission of at least doing the shooting will serve to deprive him of a self-defense 'out' at the time of trial." ...

The Fifth Amendment privilege is so fundamental to our system of constitutional rule and the expedience of giving an adequate warning as to the availability of the privilege so simple, we will not pause to inquire in individual cases whether the defendant was aware of his rights without a warning being given. Assessments of the knowledge the defendant possessed, based on information as to his age, education, intelligence, or prior contact with authorities, can never be more than speculation; a warning is a clearcut fact. More important, whatever the background of the person interrogated, a warning at the time of the interrogation is indispensable to overcome its pressures and to insure that the individual knows he is free to exercise the privilege at that point in time....

The warning of the right to remain silent must be accompanied by the explanation that anything said can and will be used against the individual in court. This warning is needed in order to make him aware not only of the privilege, but also of the consequences of forgoing it. It is only through an awareness of these consequences that there can be any assurance of real understanding and intelligent exercise of the privilege. Moreover, this warning may serve to make the individual more acutely aware that he is faced with a phase of the adversary system—that he is not in the presence of persons acting solely in his interest .... (pp. 454–55)

The circumstances surrounding in-custody interrogation can operate very quickly to overbear the will of one merely made aware of his privilege by his interrogators. Therefore, the right to have counsel present at the interrogation is indispensable to the protection of the Fifth Amendment privilege under the system we delineate today. Our aim is to assure that the individual's right to choose between silence and speech remains unfettered throughout the interrogation process. A once-stated warning, delivered by those who will conduct the interrogation, cannot itself suffice to that end among those who most require knowledge of their rights. A mere warning given by the interrogators is not alone sufficient to accomplish that end. Prosecutors themselves claim that the admonishment of the right to remain silent without more will benefit only the recidivist and the professional. Even preliminary advice given to the accused by his own attorney can be swiftly overcome by the secret interrogation process. Thus, the need for counsel to protect the Fifth Amendment privilege comprehends not merely a right to consult with counsel prior to questioning, but also to have counsel present during any questioning if the defendant so desires .... (pp. 478–58)

Accordingly we hold that an individual held for interrogation must be clearly informed that he has the right to consult with a lawyer and to have the lawyer with him during interrogation under the system for protecting the privilege we delineate today. As with the warnings of the right to remain silent and that anything stated can be used in evidence against him, this warning is an absolute prerequisite to interrogation. No amount of circumstantial evidence that the person may have been aware of this right will suffice to stand in its stead. Only through such a warning is there ascertainable assurance that the accused was aware of this right. (p. 471)

If an individual indicates that he wishes the assistance of counsel before any interrogation occurs, the authorities cannot rationally ignore or deny his request on the basis that the individual does not have or cannot afford a retained attorney. The financial ability of the individual has no relationship to the scope of the rights involved here. The privilege against self-incrimination secured by the Constitution applies to all individuals. The need for counsel in order to protect the privilege exists for the indigent as well as the affluent. In fact, were we to limit these constitutional rights to those who can retain an attorney, our decisions today would be of little significance. The cases before us as well as the vast majority of confession cases with which we have dealt in the past involve those unable to retain counsel. While authorities are not required to relieve the accused of his poverty, they have the obligation not to take advantage of indigence in the administration of justice. Denial of counsel to the indigent at the time of interrogation while allowing an attorney to those who can afford one would be no more supportable by reason or logic than the similar situation at trial .... (pp. 472–73)

The Supreme Court ruled that prior to any in-custody interrogation, an individual must be advised of his or her Miranda rights. To trigger the required warning, there must be interrogation and it must be in-custody. The Supreme Court noted in *Oregon v. Elstad* (1985) that the Miranda exclusionary rule may be triggered even in absence of violation of the Fifth Amendment; failure to administer Miranda warnings creates presumption of compulsion, and consequently unwarned statements that are otherwise voluntary within meaning of the Fifth Amendment must nevertheless be excluded from evidence under Miranda, even as to the defendant who has suffered no identifiable constitutional harm.

If errors are, however, made by law enforcement officers in administering the Miranda warnings, the Court stated that they should not be considered as the irremediable consequences of police infringement of the Fifth Amendment itself; though Miranda requires suppression of unwarned admission, admissibility of any subsequent statements should turn solely on whether they are knowingly and voluntarily made (*Oregon v. Elstad*, 1985).

Because of the unpopularity of the Miranda decision, the U.S. Congress has considered legislation that would have modified the Miranda requirement. The Supreme Court stated, however, that the admissibility in evidence of any statement given during custodial interrogation of a suspect depends on whether the police provided the suspect with four specific warnings— is a constitutional decision that may not be in effect overruled by an act of Congress, notwithstanding language in some of the Supreme Court's subsequent opinions that supports the view that Miranda protections are not constitutionally required (*Dickerson v. United States*, 2000).

The Warning

As a constitutional prerequisite to any questioning, an individual held for interrogation by a law enforcement officer must be warned, in clear and unequivocal terms, that:

1. He has right to remain silent,
2. Any statement he does make may be used as evidence against him, and
3. He has the right to the presence of an attorney, either retained or appointed.

The requirements of warnings to be given by police before in-custody interrogation of suspect and rules as to waiver of his rights are fundamental with respect to the Fifth Amendment privilege against self-incrimination, and not simply a preliminary ritual to existing methods of interrogation (*Miranda v. Arizona*, 1966).

The Miranda warnings need not be virtual incantation of precise language contained in *Miranda* opinion, if the police have fully conveyed to the defendant his or her rights as required by *Miranda* (*California v. Prysock*, 1981). In one case, a defendant signed an in-custody statement that did not contain all of the proper warnings against self-incrimination, and the government agent was allowed to testify to additional oral warnings that were given to show that the defendant had the benefit of all proper warnings before he made any statement (*Sanders v. United States*, 1968). Police interrogators are not obliged to administer new Miranda warnings every time a suspect is questioned with regard to crimes other than that for which he was arrested (*United States ex rel. Henne v. Fike*, 1977).

In-Custody Requirement

Being in-custody is a prerequisite of the Miranda requirement; a formal arrest is not necessary because custody occurs any time a person is physically deprived of his or her freedom of action in any significant way, or is led to believe, as a reasonable person, that he or she is so deprived (*State v. Philbrick*, 1981). "Custodial interrogation" means questions initiated by law enforcement officers after a person has been taken into custody or otherwise deprived of his freedom of action in any significant way (*United States v. Ali*, 1995). In determining whether a defendant was subject to custodial interrogation, the court looks to whether, under totality of circumstances, a reasonable person in the defendant's position would feel restraint on his freedom of movement to such an extent that he would not feel free to leave (*United States v. Oddo*, 2005).

As a general rule, for the court to conclude that the suspect was in custody, for purposes of applying the Miranda rule, it must be evident that, under the totality of circumstances, a reasonable person in the suspect's position would feel restraint on freedom of movement fairly characterized as that degree associated with formal arrest to such extent that he or she would not feel free to leave the place where interrogation is conducted (*California v. Beheler*, 1983). Whether the person is in custody is a question of law to be determined by the court before deciding whether to admit testimony obtained before the defendant was given the Miranda warning, and warnings are not required simply because questioning takes place in a station house or because a questioned person is one whom police suspect.

Miranda warnings must be given prior to any custodial interrogation regardless of whether an individual is suspected of committing a felony or misdemeanor (*State v. Buchholz*, 1984). The Miranda notice requirements are not dependent upon whether the suspect is the focus of investigation, but whether the suspect is in custody or has otherwise been deprived of his liberty in any significant way; police may not forcibly bring the suspect to the police station and submit him to interrogation for a lengthy period of time for the purpose of inducing an incriminating statement without according him his Miranda rights (*Moore v. Ballone*, 1981).

Miranda warnings are not required for statements made to police over the telephone; an individual is not in custody even though a complaint and arrest warrant have been issued (*Pasdon v. City of Peabody*, 2005). Tape-recorded conversations between a defendant and police officers during the time that a defendant had barricaded himself in a house did not violate constitutional rights because of lack of Miranda warnings before such conversations; the defendant had complete freedom to move about within the house, and although officers initiated phone calls, the defendant had control of such conversations during that time and was not in custody (*State v. Halvorson*, 1984).

Miranda warnings need not be given to a person detained pursuant to a valid investigatory stop until the stop matures into custodial interrogation (*United States v. Streifel*, 1986).

A plain-clothes agent of the Immigration and Naturalization Service was not required to give a defendant Miranda warnings when, after approaching him outdoors in a public place in front of the housing authority, the agent asked him his name and immigration status, because the defendant, who had no reason to believe that he could not leave or refuse to answer questions, was not in custody (*United States v. Guerrero-Hernandez*, 1996).

Where a police officer initially stopped a defendant's automobile because he knew the defendant's driver's license had been suspended, but then told the defendant that he had received reliable information that the defendant sometimes carried an illegal sawed-off shotgun, from the moment the shotgun was mentioned, the defendant was being interrogated by the officer and it was the officer's obligation to give the defendant the Miranda warning (*United States v. Jordan*, 1977).

Statements made by a motorist who was stopped by a police officer who then asked the motorist to recite the alphabet, inquired about alcohol consumption, and requested him to perform a simple balancing test were admissible, despite the absence of the Miranda warning, because ordinary traffic stops do not involve custody for purposes of Miranda requirement (*Pennsylvania v. Bruder*, 1988).

An appellate court held that a defendant was in custody while in his home and should have been advised of his Miranda rights when he was interrogated in a small room in his home by officers who did not inform him that he could leave or could refuse to answer questions. A defendant was an immigrant who had difficulty communicating in English (*United States v. Mahmood*, 2006). However, conversation between the defendant and police officers who had surrounded the defendant's home in an effort to arrest the defendant, where conversation was initiated by the defendant and resulted in the defendant providing police with keys to an automobile in which evidence was found, did not constitute custodial interrogation (*Berna v. State*, 1984).

An arrest of a defendant is not a condition precedent to custodial interrogation, and questioning in a setting as familiar to the defendant as his residence may still be custodial in character; questioning of a suspect in his own home during the middle of the night in the presence of four police officers investigating murder was custodial (*State v. Russo*, 1984).

A 5- to 10-minute police conversation with an 18-year-old defendant in a murder case that was conducted in the defendant's own home with both parents present was not considered a custodial interrogation; however, the subsequent hour-and-a-half questioning of him in a police cruiser was custodial interrogation, where the defendant was never asked if he wished to take a break or be returned home (*State v. Thibodeau*, 1985).

Miranda warnings to a prisoner were not required when conversation with the prisoner was nothing more than an on-the-scene inquiry to ascertain what happened, to determine who had been injured, and to find the weapons used in connection with a physical attack on a fellow prisoner; Miranda warnings are not required before a prisoner's conversation with a corrections officer where the prisoner is not questioned in a coercive environment (*United States v. Scalf*, 1984).

A high school student's rights were not violated by failure to give the Miranda warning when questioned by a school official and police liaison officer in a locked school restroom and in the school office because questioning on school grounds is not custodial interrogation, and because it was a school official and not the police officer who initiated questioning (*Cason v. Cook*, 1987).

What Constitutes Interrogation?

A defendant was not subjected to custodial interrogation or its functional equivalent when his mother asked to speak with him, thereby prompting the waiving of his Miranda rights and giving an incriminating statement, because officers testified that they gave her no promises and told her that she could not be asked to speak with the defendant on behalf of the state. The defendant voluntarily, knowingly, and intelligently waived his right to have counsel present at his interrogation and his right to remain silent when he reinitiated communication with police (*Roberson v. Commonwealth*, 2006).

A defendant's rights against self-incrimination were not violated where he stated to a friend visiting him in jail that he had committed murder and gave directions as to the location of the body, although he had not been given Miranda warnings, and the acquaintance was secretly acting as a police agent to gather information, because the questioning was not custodial in nature (*Alexander v. Connecticut*, 1990).

A police officer's statement to an arrestee prior to Miranda rights— "You're a liar"—did not constitute express questioning or interrogation but was declarative in nature; the question and the defendant's response—"You're right. I did it"—were properly admissible (*People v. Huffman*, 1984). However, a detective's initial question—"Do you know why you are here?"—to a defendant constituted custodial interrogation, and the detective's failure to advise the defendant of his rights until the defendant made the statement to him violated the defendant's Fifth Amendment privilege against self-incrimination (*People v. Lowe*, 1980).

Questioning conducted by medical professionals solely for the purpose of providing treatment, even where the medical professional is a public employee, and the fact that a law enforcement official eavesdropped without the medical professional's knowledge, does not transform the conversation into interrogation for law enforcement purposes, nor does it require suppression of statements made during the conversation (*United States v. Borchardt*, 1987).

When Interrogation Must Stop

If an individual undergoing custodial interrogation indicates in any manner, at any time prior to or during questioning, that he or she wishes to remain silent, interrogation must cease, because, at this point, the individual has shown that he or she intends to exercise his or her Fifth Amendment privilege. If the individual states that he or she wants an attorney, the interrogation must also cease until the attorney is present, and at that time the individual must have an opportunity to confer with the attorney and to have him present during any subsequent questioning. Furthermore, if the individual cannot obtain an attorney and he indicates that he wants one before speaking to the police, they must respect his decision to remain silent (*Fare v. Michael C.*, 1979).

Naval Investigative Service agents were not required, with respect to the Miranda right to counsel, to stop questioning a United States Navy member after he made the ambiguous remark "Maybe I should talk to a lawyer" (*Davis v. United States*, 1994).

An inmate's statement "I think I would like to talk to a lawyer" did not constitute unambiguous and unequivocal request for counsel within meaning of the U.S. Supreme Court precedent, and thus, there was no Miranda violation when police continued to question the inmate after the inmate made that statement (*Clark v. Murphy*, 2003).

A defendant's request for counsel when he was arraigned for a traffic offense did not constitute invocation of his Fifth Amendment right to counsel that prohibited police interrogation on unrelated and uncharged drugstore robberies (*Williamson v. Parke*, 1992).

The failure of a suspect who had consented to answer some or even the majority of questions put to him is not enough, standing alone, to indicate that the suspect desires to exercise his right to silence (*State v. Westmoreland*, 1985). The defendant's right to cut off questioning by police officers was not invoked, and the officers were justified in continuing interrogation when he responded to an officer's question by saying, "Why should I tell you about it when I can tell a jury about it" (*People v. Roark*, 1982). Silence by a defendant was not considered to have constituted exercise by him of his right to remain silent and to terminate questioning (*McClinnahan v. United States*, 1982).

Once a defendant has invoked his rights to counsel or to remain silent, the police may not restart the questioning until the defendant initiates the subsequent communication and demonstrates a desire to discuss the criminal investigation, and that as a separate matter and under particular facts and circumstances surrounding the case, the defendant's latest waiver is knowing and intelligent (*Oregon v. Bradshaw*, 1983).

Exceptions to the Rule

Public Safety Exception

A public safety exception to the Miranda warning requirement is applicable, regardless of motivation of the individual officer involved, where the accused is captured by an officer after chase through a supermarket, and where in frisking the accused the officer discovers an empty shoulder holster and asks where the gun is, the accused nods toward some empty cartons and answers, "The gun is over there," and officer retrieves it. The gun and the defendant's statement are admissible under exception (*New York v. Quarles*, 1984).

The response of a defendant who was arrested on suspicion of narcotics activity to the question before Miranda warnings were given as to whether he had a gun did not violate the defendant's privilege against self-incrimination as falling under the public safety exception to Miranda because it was appropriate for the arresting officer to determine whether the defendant carried a weapon that might pose a threat to the officer or innocent persons in the area (*United States v. Edwards*, 1989).

Where Vienna Convention Was Violated

In *Sanchez-Llamas v. Oregon* (2006), the defendant, a Mexican national, argued that his incriminating statements to police in an attempted murder case should have been suppressed, as he was not informed of his right under Vienna Convention Article 36 to have the Mexican consulate notified of his detention. The Supreme Court held that, even assuming that Vienna Convention Article 36 created judicially enforceable rights, suppression of evidence was not an appropriate remedy; the remedial objectives served by the exclusionary rule did not arise in the consular notification context.

Statements Made during Medical Treatment

A defendant's postarrest statements recounting events leading to his arrest made to a nurse while in the hospital emergency room for treatment of bullet wounds received during a narcotics raid were not subject to suppression either because he had not been given Miranda warnings or because statements were not voluntary (*United States v. Romero*, 1990). Miranda rules did not apply when questioning of a suspect who was in hospital under police guard was initiated and conducted by a nurse in the presence of a police officer who took note of the conversation, where neither the nurse's questions nor the suspect's responses were prompted or suggested by law enforcement officials, and the nurse was not acting as an agent or proxy for the police. The police officer had no obligation to warn the suspect of the officer's presence or to stop the suspect from speaking (*Commonwealth v. Allen*, 1985).

A defendant's statements as to his income tax evasion and money laundering schemes made to Internal Revenue Service agents during noncustodial interview without prior Miranda warnings were admissible, even though failure to give such warnings violated IRS procedure (*United States v. Bencs*, 1994).

The giving of Miranda warnings prior to the request to submit to chemical analysis of blood, breath, or urine under a state implied consent law is not required because evidence obtained in the implied consent context is not testimonial or communicative in nature and does not fall within privilege against self-incrimination (*Fulmer v. Jensen*, 1986). Police officers are also not required

to give Miranda warnings to a stopped driver before administering field dex-
terity tests because such tests do not constitute communicative or testimonial
acts implicating a driver's Fifth Amendment rights (*State v. Lombard*, 1985).
However, when defendants charged with driving while intoxicated are put in
custody, police officers must give Miranda warnings, including the right to
counsel, prior to administering a breathalyzer chemical test. If Miranda rights
have already been given, it is not necessary to again tell the defendant that he or
she has a right to counsel to advise the defendant whether or not he should take
the breathalyzer test (*State ex rel. Juckett v. Evergreen District Court*, 1984).

Undercover Agents

An undercover law enforcement officer posing as a fellow jail inmate was
not required, under Fifth Amendment privilege against self-incrimination,
to give Miranda warnings to an incarcerated suspect before the officer asked
questions that elicited an incriminating response, making incriminating
statements made by the suspect in such circumstances therefore not inadmissible at trial, because interests protected by Miranda are not implicated
in such circumstances (*Illinois v. Perkins*, 1990).

Deportation Proceedings

Failure to give Miranda warnings does not render a statement made pursuant
to custodial questioning inadmissible in deportation proceedings (*Chavez-
Raya v. Immigration and Naturalization Service*, 1975).

Initial Inquiry and Booking

An inquiry by police officers as to a defendant's name during the defendant's
arrest was not a breach of the defendant's Miranda rights because the question was not aimed at eliciting a criminal response but merely at corroborat-
ing information made available to police by the rental agency concerning a
suspected auto theft (*United States v. Feldman*, 1986).

A defendant's Miranda rights were not violated by an arresting police
officer's routine questions during booking to elicit the personal history of a
narcotics defendant, such as his name and what he was doing in the United
States, although the officer knew the defendant's identity and name, and the
defendant's use of an alias in response to the question was admissible (*United
States v. Carmona*, 1989).

A defendant's Miranda rights were not violated when the arresting officer asked the defendant about his limp during a booking procedure because
the question was designed to fulfill the government's obligation to provide
medical attention if necessary and fell under "routine booking" exception to
Miranda requirements (*United States v. Bishop*, 1995).

A defendant's responses to booking questions as to his employment status fell within an exception to the Miranda rule for questioning designed to

obtain only routine booking information (*United States v. Duarte*, 1998). The booking agent's questions to the defendant, who was charged with participating in a criminal drug conspiracy, requesting the defendant's name, date of birth, and Social Security number, fell within the booking exception to the Miranda warning requirement (*United States v. Reyes*, 2000).

Mere investigatory focus does not require the giving of Miranda warnings; thus, warnings were not prerequisite to inquiry as to whether a defendant was the driver of a car at the time of accident, which took place upon locating the defendant at the hospital, because the defendant was not in custody when he was asked the initial identifying question. However, although the initial question was not a result of custodial interrogation in a police-dominated atmosphere, because the defendant's detention at the hospital resulted from medical advice and not from any action by authorities, other evidence must be suppressed because the defendant had been placed under arrest (*State v. Fields*, 1980).

An officer may respond to a radio-dispatched description of a suspect by stopping a person fitting that description and may ask routine questions for the purpose of obtaining basic identifying information without giving Miranda warnings (*Hatcher v. State*, 1980). A convicted defendant need not be advised of his right to counsel and his right to remain silent prior to submitting to a routine, authorized presentence interview, even if the defendant is in custody at the time of the interview (*Baumann v. United States*, 1982).

In *Hiibel v. Sixth Judicial District Court* (2004), a police officer responded to a call reporting that a man assaulted a woman. The officer found Hiibel standing outside a parked truck with a woman inside the truck. The officer asked for his identification, and Hiibel refused to give him any. Hiibel was arrested and was convicted for obstructing the officer in carrying out his duties under Nevada Revised Statute § 171.123, a "stop and identify" statute that required the defendant to disclose his name. The Supreme Court held that the *Terry* stop, the request for identification, and the state's requirement of a response did not violate the Fourth Amendment or the Miranda requirements, because the request for identity had an immediate relation to the purpose, rationale, and practical demands of the *Terry* stop. Also, the request for identification was reasonably related in scope to the circumstances that justified the *Terry* stop. The Court also determined that the defendant's conviction did not violate the Fifth Amendment's prohibition on compelled self-incrimination because disclosure of his name presented no reasonable danger of incrimination.

Failure to Advise Defendant of Other Suspected Crimes

If the defendant is arrested and advised that he or she is suspected of a crime, is there a requirement that the defendant also be advised as to other

crimes that he or she may have committed? The Supreme Court looked at this issue in *Colorado v. Spring* (1987). Defendant Spring was arrested by the Bureau of Alcohol, Tobacco and Firearms (ATF) agents for firearms violations in Kansas. The defendant signed a waiver of his Miranda rights, and ATF agents then questioned him about a Colorado murder as well as firearms violations. Spring made a statement admitting the murder. Then, the Colorado police then went to Kansas, readvised the defendant of his Miranda rights, and questioned him again about the murder. The Supreme Court upheld the use of his confession. The Court stated that a valid waiver does not require that an individual be informed of all information "useful" in making his decision or all information that might affect his decision to confess. The Court noted that it has never read the Constitution to require that the police supply a suspect with a flow of information to help him calibrate his self-interest in deciding whether to speak or stand by his rights. The Court also noted that a suspect's awareness of all the possible subjects of questioning in advance of interrogation was not relevant to determining whether the suspect voluntarily, knowingly, and intelligently waived his Fifth Amendment privilege.

Fruit of the Poisonous Tree

Failure to give the Miranda warning prior to custodial interrogation alone does not necessitate suppression of all derivative evidence, absent constitutional violation, such as a statement being a product of coercion (*United States v. Medina*, 1989). Attorney and former prosecutor Devailis Rutledge (2004) claims that the Supreme Court has not applied the fruit of the poisonous tree doctrine to violations of the Miranda rule. Rutledge notes that the Miranda rule is an admissibility rule for criminal trial judges, and he quotes *United States v. Patane* (2004) as stating that "the Miranda rule is not a code of police conduct." Rutledge advises police officers that in cases where the Miranda rule has been violated, the resulting statement and the evidence it leads to should be fully documented in arrest reports and the evidence maintained to preserve its admissibility (p. 84).

The Court in *Patane* stated:

> The Miranda rule is a prophylactic employed to protect against violations of the Self-Incrimination Clause. The Self-Incrimination Clause, however, is not implicated by the admission into evidence of the physical fruit of a voluntary statement. Accordingly, there is no justification for extending the Miranda rule to this context. And just as the Self-Incrimination Clause primarily focuses on the criminal trial, so too does the Miranda rule. The Miranda rule is not a code of police conduct, and police do not violate the Constitution (or even the Miranda rule, for that matter) by mere failures to warn.

Involuntary Confessions

The use of improper tactics in conducting interrogation, including psychological coercion, does not render confession involuntary if none of the improper tactics was so inherently coercive as to produce an involuntary statement. However, confessions that are accompanied by physical violence are per se involuntary (*Martin v. Wainwright*, 1985). An involuntary confession may not be used in any manner against the defendant who made the confession.

In *United States v. Moser* (2007), the defendant made a written statement nine hours after his arrest. The statement was not considered as involuntary because his capacity for self-determination was impaired due to the length of his interview and the fact that he ate insufficiently during the interview and slept for only a few hours prior to his arrest. The written statement was voluntary for purposes of the Fifth Amendment because he was permitted to take numerous breaks during his interview, he was encouraged to eat and drink, the defendant never indicated that he was too tired to continue, and the defendant signed a waiver of rights form.

United States v. Miller (1993) involved an FBI agent who was being interrogated and suspected of espionage. The court held that his statement was not involuntary because a Mormon investigator appealed to the agent's Mormon religious beliefs and the agent became tearful after listening to the appeal. The court noted that there was no evidence that Miller's will was overborne.

Where during interrogation the government agent told a defendant charged with making false declarations before court that her life was in danger, that she should not trust anyone outside of government, and that she should obtain relocation through the witness allocation program, and the agents manipulated the defendant's use of methadone and moved her from her residence, compelling her to stay at locations chosen by the agent, a finding was supported that the defendant was subject to psychological coercion that rendered her statements involuntary (*United States v. Eccles*, 1988).

A defendant's postarrest confession of his involvement in a robbery and killing was voluntary where an FBI agent indicated that he might receive lenient treatment if he cooperated because such a statement without coercion did not constitute promise of leniency affecting the voluntariness of the confession (*United States v. Nguyen*, 1998).

The sole concern of the Fifth Amendment privilege against self-incrimination is governmental coercion; the Fifth Amendment privilege is not concerned with moral and psychological pressures to confess emanating from sources other than official coercion. A suspect's perception of coercion flowing from the "voice of God" is a matter to which the federal Constitution does not speak (*Colorado v. Connelly*, 1986).

Commenting on Defendant's Silence

Fifth Amendment protections include forbidding any comment by the prosecution on the accused's silence or that such silence is evidence of guilt. A prosecutor's commenting on the failure of the defendant to explain or to deny by his testimony any evidence or facts in case against him was a violation of the defendant's Fifth Amendment rights (*Griffin v. California*, 1965). A defendant's constitutional privilege against self-incrimination was violated in a state trial by comments of a prosecutor and trial judge to effect that the jury may draw adverse inferences against the accused because of his failure to testify (*Fontaine v. California*, 1968).

Both direct and indirect comments as to an accused's silence that undermine his Fifth Amendment rights will invalidate a conviction, but such comment is the reason for reversal only if the speaker's intention was to focus on that silence or remark and was such that a juror would naturally and necessarily take it as comment on the defendant's failure to testify (*United States v. Garcia*, 1981). A prosecutor's repeated references, in closing remarks, to state's evidence as being "unrefuted" and "uncontradicted" do not violate a defendant's Fifth Amendment rights as constituting comment on her failure to testify (*Lockett v. Ohio*, 1978).

The prosecutor is not permitted to comment upon the silence of a defendant after arrest but before receiving Miranda warnings because, even disregarding the effect of Miranda warnings, postarrest silence is highly ambiguous and lacks significant probative value, the defendant has a right to remain silent at the time of her arrest, and this prohibition is necessary to encourage law enforcement officials to give Miranda warnings promptly (*United States v. Nunez-Rios*, 1980).

The right to remain silent is not a right to actively mislead the jury. For example, evidence that a defendant remained silent after his arrest and receipt of Miranda warnings was admissible for impeachment purposes where defense counsel, in cross-examining a police investigator, attempted to create the false impression that the defendant had actively cooperated with the police at all times (*United States v. Fairchild*, 1975). However, a rape defendant's due process rights were violated by the prosecutor's repeated references to the defendant's postarrest silence with the clear intent of trying to persuade the jury that if the defendant's exculpatory testimony at trial had been true, he would have come forward earlier with his explanation (*Gravley v. Mills*, 1996).

Capstone Case: *Missouri v. Seibert*, 542 U.S. 600 (2004)

Justice Souter announced the judgment of the Court and delivered an opinion, in which Justice Stevens, Justice Ginsburg, and Justice Breyer joined.

This case tests a police protocol for custodial interrogation that calls for giving no warnings of the rights to silence and counsel until interrogation has produced a confession. Although such a statement is generally inadmissible, since taken in violation of *Miranda v. Arizona*, the interrogating officer follows it with Miranda warnings and then leads the suspect to cover the same ground a second time. The question here is the admissibility of the repeated statement. Because this midstream recitation of warnings after interrogation and unwarned confession could not effectively comply with Miranda's constitutional requirement, we hold that a statement repeated after a warning in such circumstances is inadmissible.

Respondent Patrice Seibert's 12-year-old son Jonathan had cerebral palsy, and when he died in his sleep she feared charges of neglect because of bedsores on his body. In her presence, two of her teenage sons and two of their friends devised a plan to conceal the facts surrounding Jonathan's death by incinerating his body in the course of burning the family's mobile home, in which they planned to leave Donald Rector, a mentally ill teenager living with the family, to avoid any appearance that Jonathan had been unattended. Seibert's son Darian and a friend set the fire, and Donald died.

Five days later, the police awakened Seibert at 3 a.m. at a hospital where Darian was being treated for burns. In arresting her, Officer Kevin Clinton followed instructions from Rolla, Missouri, Officer Richard Hanrahan that he refrain from giving Miranda warnings. After Seibert had been taken to the police station and left alone in an interview room for 15 to 20 minutes, Hanrahan questioned her without Miranda warnings for 30 to 40 minutes, squeezing her arm and repeating "Donald was also to die in his sleep." After Seibert finally admitted she knew Donald was meant to die in the fire, she was given a 20-minute coffee and cigarette break. Officer Hanrahan then turned on a tape recorder, gave Seibert the Miranda warnings, and obtained a signed waiver of rights from her. He resumed the questioning with "Ok, 'trice, we've been talking for a little while about what happened on Wednesday the twelfth, haven't we?"

After being charged with first-degree murder for her role in Donald's death, Seibert sought to exclude both her prewarning and postwarning statements. At the suppression hearing, Officer Hanrahan testified that he made a "conscious decision" to withhold Miranda warnings, thus resorting to an interrogation technique he had been taught: question first, then give the warnings, and then repeat the question "until I get the answer that she's already provided once." He acknowledged that Seibert's ultimate statement was "largely a repeat of information ... obtained" prior to the warning.

There are those, of course, who preferred the old way of doing things, giving no warnings and litigating the voluntariness of any statement in nearly every instance. In the aftermath of *Miranda*, Congress even passed a statute seeking to restore that old regime, 18 U.S.C. § 3501, although the Act lay dormant for years until finally invoked and challenged in *Dickerson v. United States*, supra. *Dickerson* reaffirmed *Miranda* and held that its constitutional character prevailed against the statute.

The technique of interrogating in successive, unwarned and warned phases raises a new challenge to *Miranda*. Although we have no statistics on the frequency of this practice, it is not confined to Rolla, Missouri. An officer of that police department testified that the strategy of withholding Miranda warnings until after interrogating and drawing out a confession was promoted not only by his own department, but by a national police training organization and other departments in which he had worked. Consistently with the officer's testimony, the Police Law Institute, for example, instructs that "officers may conduct a two-stage interrogation…." At any point during the pre-Miranda interrogation, usually after arrestees have confessed, officers may then read the Miranda warnings and ask for a waiver. If the arrestees waive their Miranda rights, officers will be able to repeat any subsequent incriminating statements later in court. The upshot of all this advice is a question-first practice of some popularity, as one can see from the reported cases describing its use, sometimes in obedience to departmental policy.

It is not the case, of course, that law enforcement educators en masse are urging that *Miranda* be honored only in the breach. Most police manuals do not advocate the question-first tactic because they understand that *Oregon v. Elstad* involved an officer's good-faith failure to warn.

Missouri argues that a confession repeated at the end of an interrogation sequence envisioned in a question-first strategy is admissible on the authority of *Oregon v. Elstad*, but the argument disfigures that case. In *Elstad*, the police went to the young suspect's house to take him into custody on a charge of burglary. Before the arrest, one officer spoke with the suspect's mother, while the other one joined the suspect in a "brief stop in the living room," where the officer said he "felt" the young man was involved in a burglary. The suspect acknowledged he had been at the scene. This Court noted that the pause in the living room "was not to interrogate the suspect but to notify his mother of the reason for his arrest," and described the incident as having "none of the earmarks of coercion." The Court, indeed, took care to mention that the officer's initial failure to warn was an "oversight" that "may have been the result of confusion as to whether the brief exchange qualified as 'custodial interrogation' or … may simply have reflected … reluctance to initiate an alarming police procedure before an officer had spoken with respondent's mother."

At the opposite extreme are the facts here, which by any objective measure reveal a police strategy adapted to undermine the Miranda warnings. The unwarned interrogation was conducted in the station house, and the questioning was systematic, exhaustive, and managed with psychological skill. When the police were finished there was little, if anything, of incriminating potential left unsaid. The warned phase of questioning proceeded after a pause of only 15 to 20 minutes, in the same place as the unwarned segment. When the same officer who had conducted the first phase recited the Miranda warnings, he said nothing to counter the probable misimpression that the advice that anything Seibert said could be used against her also applied to the details of the inculpatory statement previously elicited. In particular, the police did not advise that her prior statement could not be used. Nothing was said or done to dispel the oddity of warning about legal rights to silence and counsel right after the police had led her through a systematic interrogation, and any uncertainty on her part about a right to stop talking about matters previously discussed would only have been aggravated by the way Officer Hanrahan set the scene by saying "we've been talking for a little while about what happened on Wednesday the twelfth, haven't we?" The impression that the further questioning was a mere continuation of the earlier questions and responses was fostered by references back to the confession already given. It would have been reasonable to regard the two sessions as parts of a continuum, in which it would have been unnatural to refuse to repeat at the second stage what had been said before. These circumstances must be seen as challenging the comprehensibility and efficacy of the Miranda warnings to the point that a reasonable person in the suspect's shoes would not have understood them to convey a message that she retained a choice about continuing to talk.

Strategists dedicated to draining the substance out of *Miranda* cannot accomplish by training instructions what *Dickerson* held Congress could not do by statute. Because the question-first tactic effectively threatens to thwart *Miranda*'s purpose of reducing the risk that a coerced confession would be admitted, and because the facts here do not reasonably support a conclusion that the warnings given could have served their purpose, Seibert's postwarning statements are inadmissible.

Questions in Review

1. When are the police required to advise a person of his or her Miranda rights?
2. What constitutes "in custody" for purposes of the Miranda requirements?
3. What constitutes "interrogation" for purposes of the Miranda requirements?
4. What tricks may be used to get a suspect to confess?
5. Under what circumstances may an involuntary confession be used against a defendant?

Sixth Amendment Issues

7

In all criminal prosecutions, the accused shall enjoy the right to a speedy and public trial, by an impartial jury of the State and district wherein the crime shall have been committed, which district shall have been previously ascertained by law, and to be informed of the nature and cause of the accusation; to be confronted with the witnesses against him; to have compulsory process for obtaining witnesses in his favor, and to have the Assistance of Counsel for his defense.

—U.S. Constitution, Sixth Amendment

Introduction

A careful reading of the Sixth Amendment reveals that it provides seven important rights to an accused in a criminal trial. Each of those rights is discussed in this chapter. The eight rights are as follows:

- Speedy trial
- Public trial
- Impartial jury
- Trial in the judicial district in which the crime was committed
- To be informed of the nature and cause of the accusation
- Right to confront witnesses
- To have a compulsory process for obtaining witnesses in his favor
- To have the assistance of counsel for his defense

Speedy Trial

The right to speedy trial is different from any of the other accused's constitutional rights because there is societal interest in providing a speedy trial that exists separate from, and at times in opposition to, the interests of the accused. In most situations, the greater the delay in a trial, the more likely the accused will not be found guilty because witnesses die, disappear, or forget the facts, and evidence gets lost. Factors that the courts assess in determining whether a defendant has been deprived of his or her Sixth Amendment right to speedy trial include length of delay, reason for delay, defendant's assertion of his or her right, and prejudice to defendant (*Barker v. Wingo*, 1972). There are two speedy trial rights, the constitutional right and the statutory right.

Constitutional Right to a Speedy Trial

The Sixth Amendment's guarantee of a speedy trial is limited by its terms to criminal prosecutions. Juvenile proceedings are not criminal trials or prosecutions for purposes of Sixth Amendment right to a speedy trial (*In re W.*, 1978). It does not apply in probation revocation proceedings because they are not "criminal proceedings" (*United States v. Jackson*, 1979).

The right to speedy trial does not require trial immediately upon return of indictment, nor on arrest made under it, but it does require that trial shall be had as soon as reasonably possible after indictment is found, without depriving prosecution of reasonable time in which to prepare for the trial. The right is relative dependent upon surrounding circumstances (*United States ex rel. Hanson v. Ragen*, 1948).

A 30-month delay between a defendant's initial arrest and his federal indictment did not violate his Sixth Amendment right to a speedy trial where a large portion of the delay resulted from the defendant's own actions or lack of state cooperation, rather than from lack of federal diligence; the defendant did not allege that he unsuccessfully asserted his right to a speedy trial; and he was not prejudiced by lapse of time (*United States v. Bagster*, 1990).

A rape defendant's constitutional right to speedy trial was not violated by an approximately 32-month delay between his rape arrest and the beginning of trial, where approximately 19½ months of the delay consisted of the trial court's order of continuance pending the outcome of the defendant's appeal of his death sentence after a prior murder conviction; he filed no motion asking to go to trial on the rape case; he was incarcerated pursuant to his murder conviction, not because he was awaiting trial on the rape charge; and his anxiety over the upcoming rape trial was probably minimal given that he was facing the death penalty in a murder case (*Fisher v. Hargett*, 1993).

A defendant's right to a speedy trial was violated where the defendant's trial did not occur until two years after the indictment was issued because a two-year delay between indictment and trial was presumptively prejudicial; delay could not be attributed to defendant, as he did not intentionally evade prosecution, and in fact gave the prosecution's investigator his contact information, as well as voluntarily turned himself in when he learned of indictment and accompanying arrest warrant; and defendant properly asserted his right to speedy trial (*United States v. Ingram*, 2006). Another defendant convicted of murder was denied his Sixth Amendment right to a speedy trial due to a 25-month delay between his arrest and trial, because the entire 25-month period was attributable to the government, of which 11 months was significant delay; the defendant was prejudiced because he spent the entire 25-month period in jail, and he asserted his speedy trial rights promptly and frequently (*Graves v. United States*, 1983).

Different weights are assigned by the courts for different reasons for delay; intentional delay by prosecution to hamper defense is weighted more heavily against the government than are more neutral reasons for delay, such as negligence or overcrowded courts, which are counted against government because ultimate responsibility for bring a case to trial rests there; however, delays serving legitimate purposes, such as obtaining missing witness, are not held against the government. Psychological unpreparedness of a nine-year-old victim of sexual assault justifies appropriate delay to permit the victim to become emotionally prepared to face cross-examination (*Isaac v. Perrin*, 1981).

A state has an affirmative duty to make every good faith effort to bring to trial an accused who is incarcerated by federal or state authorities beyond his territorial jurisdiction. For example, the State of Texas had a constitutional duty under the Sixth Amendment to make a diligent good faith effort to bring a prisoner before the Texas court for trial where a prisoner in federal penitentiary in Kansas had been indicted in Texas upon charge of theft, and where he had repeatedly demanded, during the six-year period following his indictment, that he be brought to trial in Texas court (*Smith v. Hooey*, 1969).

Statutory Right to a Speedy Trial

The statutory right to a speedy trial in federal criminal courts is controlled by the Speedy Trial Act of 1974. Most states have a similar statute. The statutory right to a speedy trial under the federal Speedy Trial Act is not as flexible as the constitutional right. In *Zedner v. United States* (2006) defendant Jacob Zedner was indicted in April 1996 for allegedly attempting to open accounts at financial institutions using counterfeit U.S. bonds. In November 1996, the defendant requested an adjournment and signed a waiver of his rights under the Speedy Trial Act "for all time." The question in the case was whether the waiver "for all time" was an effective waiver of his statutory speedy trial rights.

The district court granted him another continuance in January 1997, continuing the case for 91 days. Subsequent proceedings delayed the defendant's trial until 2003. The Supreme Court held that prospective application of the act could not be waived. The statute that provided for waiver of a completed violation of the act due to failure to timely move for dismissal did not permit prospective waivers, and the defendant was not prevented from challenging the excludability of the 1997 continuance, which was not excludable under the act as an ends-of-justice continuance because the district court did not make the express findings required. Failure to make those findings was not subject to harmless-error analysis under Fed. R. Crim. P. 52. Because the 91-day continuance exceeded the 70-day maximum delay, dismissal was required.

Public Trial

The purpose of the Sixth Amendment requirement of a public trial is to guarantee that an accused will be fairly dealt with and not unjustly condemned. Historically secret tribunals have been effective instruments of oppression. Another purpose of requiring a public trial is the reasonable possibility that persons unknown to parties or their counsel, but having knowledge of facts, may be drawn to trial. Also, by subjecting criminal trials to contemporaneous review in the forum of public opinion, the right to public trial prevents abuse of judicial power and instills in public perception that courts are acting fairly (*Rovinsky v. McKaskle*, 1984).

The U.S. Supreme Court noted that "Guarantee of public trial is reflection of notion, deeply rooted in common law, that justice must satisfy appearance of justice" (*Levine v. United States*, 1960, p. 612). Another court stated: "Framers of Sixth Amendment believed it to be essential to preservation of liberty of individual that, subject to certain limitations, members of general public should be admitted to every criminal trial even though it might appear that most of them came only out of morbid curiosity" (*United States v. Kobli*, 1949, p. 921). The right to a public trial also concerns the right to a fair trial (*Walton v. Briley*, 2004).

The right to a public trial is not absolute in the sense that a defendant has no right to have any particular person present under all circumstances during the course of a trial; a judge may remove a particular person on the ground that his or her presence in the courtroom will hinder ascertainment of the truth (*United States ex rel. Laws v. Yeager*, 1971). The concept of a public trial under the Sixth Amendment is so substantial that only in the most exceptional circumstances must closure of a trial to the public even be considered, and in fewer instances compelled; thus, a criminal defendant is guaranteed a public trial, but there is no constitutional guarantee of a closed trial at the defendant's request (*United States v. Powers*, 1980).

An accused who seeks to have a criminal proceeding closed to the public must establish that it is strictly and inescapably necessary to protect a fair trial guarantee; this burden may be discharged by demonstrating substantial probability that irreparable damage to the fair trial right will result from conducting a proceeding in public, substantial probability that alternatives to closure will not protect adequately his right to a fair trial, and substantial probability that closure will be effective in protecting against perceived harm. General statements that the court concludes closure of a criminal proceeding is necessary from balancing of First and Sixth Amendment interests in light of the presence of "probability of publicity" do not afford a basis for determining whether the court applied the correct standard in weighing possible prejudice from open proceedings, or whether the court's conclusion was supported by record (*United States v. Brooklier*, 1982).

In one case, the district court's failure, at the conclusion of a judge-alone trial (bench trial), to announce the verdict in open court, and by instead mailing its decision to the parties, violated the defendant's Sixth Amendment right to an open public trial (*United States v. Canady*, 1997). The public trial requirement of the Sixth Amendment is applicable to states by virtue of the due process clause of the Fourteenth Amendment (*United States ex rel. Bennett v. Rundle* 1969).

The constitutional guarantee of a public trial applies to the entire trial, including that portion devoted to the selection of jury and hearings on motions presented by each party (*United States v. Sorrentino*, 1949). Although the constitutional right of a public trial is substantial, the term *public* is relative, and its construction depends upon various conditions and circumstances; one convicted of raping an eight-year-old child could not claim that he had been denied a "public" trial merely because the court excluded from the trial all spectators except (1) members of the press, (2) members of the bar, (3) relatives or close friends of the defendant, and (4) relatives or close friends of witnesses whose ages were 7, 9, and 11 years; despite those exclusions the trial was considered a public trial (*Geise v. United States*, 1958).

The test for determining whether a defendant's trial is public is not whether the courtroom is large enough to seat everyone who wants to attend, but whether the public has freedom of access to it. A trial held in a small courtroom with only a few open seats for the public is still a public trial (*State v. Jones*, 1979). A trial held within a prison for an offense committed within the prison denied the defendant his fundamental guarantee of the right to a public trial because members of the public did not have access to the court (*State v. Lane*, 1979). However, a defendant whose rape and murder trial was held at a university law center was not denied his right to public trial even though the law center was locked at midnight while the jury was still deliberating on punishment, because securing the building could not be attributed to an intentional act of a court official; no restrictions were placed on the defendant, his counsel, or spectators who were present in the courtroom at the time; and all determinations of guilt had been made by the time the law center was locked. The appellate court noted that the law center was open to the public (*Blackwell v. State*, 1983). The relocation of a trial to a church building to accommodate a larger number of the public to attend was a public trial.

Criminal contempt proceedings do not fall within the meaning of the term *criminal prosecutions* as used in the Sixth Amendment, and there is no Sixth Amendment right to a public trial for contempt proceedings (*Levine v. United States*, 1960). The right to a public trial does not extend to revocation of a probation hearing because such hearing is in the nature of a summary proceeding and is not criminal prosecution (*United States v. Hollien*, 1952).

The Sixth Amendment right to a public trial is also applicable to courts-martial (*United States v. Hershey*, 1985). The right to a public trial does not encompass conferences between court and counsel in a judge's chambers respecting arguments and ruling on a motion for acquittal, where the subject matter of the chamber conference is solely a question of law that could not have been properly heard in the presence of a jury, and therefore the defendant's absence from chambers was not a violation of his right under the Sixth Amendment (*State v. Pullen*, 1970).

When a trial court believes exceptional circumstances exist so as to justify closing a trial even partially to the public, counsel must be informed on record and they must be heard on this question; after so proceeding, the trial court may close limited portions of the trial upon proper determination of strict and inescapable necessity for such a course of action, and closing of a trial to the public without such a finding is per se reversible (*Kleinbart v. United States*, 1978).

The right to a public trial does not preclude the presiding judge from excluding all spectators, including the defendant's family and friends, during particular witness's testimony, when circumstances warrant such action to foster the truth discovery process (*People v. Joseph*, 1983). The Sixth Amendment guarantee of a public trial is a right personal to the accused, but the First Amendment gives the press and public right of access to a trial separate and apart from the accused's Sixth Amendment rights; it is only when necessary for protection of a defendant's fair trial rights that a court may, after proper hearing, bar members of the press and public (*Lexington Herald-Leader Co. v. Meigs*, 1983).

In prosecution for intent to commit rape, exclusion of the defendants' families from the courtroom during the minor victim's testimony did not deprive defendants of their Sixth Amendment right to a public trial, where the trial judge concluded that, given the nature of offenses charged, the victim's age, her apprehension in testifying before family members, and their actions in making faces and giggling during her testimony, justified exclusion and closure was narrowly tailored to protect the victim and elicit her information, affected the defendants' families for only the duration of the victim's testimony, and did not exclude defendants, other members of the public, and the press (*United States v. Sherlock*, 1989).

Spectators admitted to criminal trial are required to observe proper decorum, and if their conduct tends to interfere with administration of justice, they may, of course, be removed. Such removal is not a denial of the accused's Sixth Amendment right to public trial (*United States v. Kobli*, 1949). Without infringing on one's constitutional right to a public trial, aisles and passageways in the courtroom can be kept clear, and when seats of the courtroom are filled, other spectators seeking entry may be excluded (*Davis v. United States*, 1917).

Photo 7.1 Justice Harry Blackmun (1908–1999) was an associate justice of the Supreme Court of the United States from 1970 to 1994. He is best known as the author of the majority opinion in the 1973 *Roe v. Wade* decision, overturning laws restricting abortion in the United States and declaring abortion protected under a constitutional right to privacy. (Photograph by the National Geographic Society, courtesy of the Supreme Court of the United States.)

Impartial Jury

The right to trial by a jury in criminal cases is one of the aspects of due process that is covered by the due process clause of the Fourteenth Amendment and is imposed upon the states (*Duncan v. Louisiana*, 1968). A defendant does not have a corresponding right, however, to refuse a jury trial and demand trial by judge alone (bench trial) (*Smith v. Zimmerman*, 1985). Corporations enjoy the same right as individuals to a trial by an impartial jury (*United States v. R. L. Polk & Co.*, 1971).

Right to Jury Trial

A defendant does not have the right to a jury trial in all cases. State courts must give any defendant charged with serious, as opposed to petty, crime an opportunity to be tried by a jury (*Duncan v. Louisiana*, 1968). There are numerous cases involving what constitutes a serious as opposed to a petty crime. The maximum statutory penalty the defendant could receive is the most relevant objective criterion in determining the Sixth Amendment right to jury trial, but there are other factors to be considered, such as inherent gravity of crime involved (*United States v. Stewart*, 1978). The defendant in a state criminal trial is entitled under the Sixth and Fourteenth Amendments to be tried by jury where statute under which the defendant is charged authorizes imprisonment for more than six months (*Burch v. Louisiana*, 1979).

Under *Burch*, if the defendant is tried for an offense for which he or she could receive more than six months confinement, then the defendant has a right to a jury trial. It is not the sentence that the defendant receives that determines the right to a jury trial, but the maximum sentence that could be given for the crime charged. If an accused is tried for two or more offenses at the same trial and none of the offenses has a maximum sentence of more than six months, then he or she can be refused a jury trial under the federal constitution even if the combined maximum sentences of the combined offenses exceed the six-month threshold. State law may provide, however, that a defendant has a right to a jury trial for even minor offenses. For example, in Texas a defendant has a right to a jury trial on a traffic offense. In California, state defendants have the right to a jury trial in all cases in which the defendants may receive a sentence of confinement. Trial by a military commission of offenses against laws of war is not subject to the constitutional requirement of a trial by jury (*Ex parte Quirin*, 1942).

The Sixth Amendment right to a jury trial was not implicated in a civil *in rem* forfeiture proceeding involving forfeiture of equity in the defendant's real property as proceeds of criminal violations (*United States v. 3814 NW Thurman St.*, 1999). (*In rem* refers to an action not against a person, but against property. For example, in the case just cited, the action was for forfeiture against the house. Anyone with any claimed interest in the house could appear and contest the forfeiture.) In addition, there is no Sixth Amendment right to a jury trial in a denaturalization proceeding (*United States v. Schellong*, 1983).

There is no Sixth Amendment right to trial by jury for persons charged with a first offense of driving under the influence of alcohol under Nevada statute, imposing for such offense a 6-month maximum prison term or 48 hours of community work while identifiably dressed as a DUI offender, plus a maximum $1,000 fine, attendance at an alcohol and abuse course, and loss of license for 90 days; viewed together, statutory penalties are not so severe that the DUI must be deemed a serious offense for purposes of the Sixth Amendment (*Blanton v. North Las Vegas*, 1989). In Nevada, the second offense of DUI within a certain number of years is a felony, and therefore there would be a constitutional right to a jury trial for the second offense.

The due process clause of the Fourteenth Amendment does not require that a juvenile be given a right to a jury trial in the adjudicative phase of a state juvenile court delinquency proceeding, even though an adult charged with the same offense would have a right to trial by jury (*McKeiver v. Pennsylvania*, 1971).

The Sixth Amendment applies to both fact finding necessary to increase the defendant's sentence and fact finding necessary to put him to death (*Ring v. Arizona*, 2002). (In a jury trial, fact finding is the province of a jury and the judge determines the appropriate law to apply in the case.) Any fact (other than prior conviction) that is necessary to support a sentence exceeding the maximum authorized by facts established by a plea of guilty or jury verdict must be admitted by the defendant or proved to the jury beyond reasonable doubt (*United States v. Booker*, 2005). In *Booker*, the Supreme Court held that Sixth Amendment right to trial by jury is violated where under mandatory guidelines the system sentence is increased because of enhancement based on facts found by a judge that were neither admitted by the defendant nor found by jury.

There is no requirement for a jury fact finding for restitution because it is not criminal punishment, but instead is civil remedy that is administered for convenience by courts that have entered criminal convictions, so the Sixth Amendment does not apply. It has accordingly been held that *Booker* does not affect restitution (*United States v. George* 2005).

Impartial Jury

A criminal defendant in a state court is guaranteed an impartial jury by the Sixth Amendment as applicable to states through the Fourteenth Amendment, and principles of due process also guarantee a defendant an impartial jury. An "impartial" jury consists of jurors who will conscientiously apply law and find facts, and simply because the defendant is being tried for a capital crime, he is not entitled to legal presumption or standard that allows jurors to be seated who quite likely will be biased in his favor (*Ristaino v. Ross*, 1976).

The critical question in determining whether a jury in criminal case is impartial is not whether the community remembers the case, but whether jurors at the defendant's trial have such fixed opinions that they cannot judge impartially the guilt of the defendant (*Patton v. Yount*, 1984). The right to an impartial jury does not mean, however, the right to have any particular member of panel sit upon trial unless such a member is accepted and sworn as juror (*Hartzell v. United States*, 1934). If only one juror is improperly influenced, the defendant in criminal case is denied his Sixth Amendment right to an impartial jury (*Styler v. State*, 1980).

For the accused to establish the denial of his right to an impartial jury, he must show either actual juror partiality or circumstances inherently prejudicial to that right (*Brooks v. State*, 1979). A "fair and impartial" trial under constitutional guarantees requires fair, impartial jurors and a trial conducted in an atmosphere free from bias and hatred against the defendant (*Seals v. State*, 1950).

Pretrial Publicity

Newspaper publicity that is not editorialized, that appears to be factually done, and which does not contain inflammatory statements will not constitute showing of prejudice sufficient to deny the defendant his right to an impartial jury. Neither the press nor the public has a right to be contemporaneously informed by police or prosecuting authorities concerning details of evidence being accumulated against a defendant (*Sheppard v. Maxwell*, 1966). The First Amendment right to gather news is not absolute, and it must yield to the accused's Sixth Amendment right to a fair trial; however, restrictions upon the First Amendment right are permissible only to prevent a substantial threat to administration of justice. Due process requires that the accused receive a trial by an impartial jury free from outside influences. Given the pervasiveness of modern communications and the difficulty of effacing prejudicial publicity from minds of jurors, a trial court must take strong measures to ensure that the balance of free press and a fair trial is never weighed against the accused (*United States v. Harrelson*, 1983).

Voir Dire of Jury

Voir dire is the practice of questioning members of the jury panel during jury selection. A jury panel is the group of citizens called and from which a jury is selected. No precise rule prescribes the type of *voir dire* examination that is necessary to protect a defendant's Sixth Amendment rights against prejudicial pretrial publicity; however, when such publicity is great, a trial court should conduct careful, individual examination of each prospective juror, preferably out of the presence of other jurors, and a general question directed to the entire group of prospective jurors is inadequate. Without adequate *voir dire*, a trial judge cannot fulfill his responsibility to remove prospective jurors who may be biased, and defense counsel cannot intelligently exercise peremptory challenges; appellate courts accord district courts broad discretion in determining how best to conduct *voir dire*, subject to limitation that discretion must be exercised consistent with essential demands of fairness. In reviewing a district court's refusal to ask questions during *voir dire*, the central inquiry is whether the trial judge's refusal, coupled with the charge to the jury, adequately protects the defendant from prejudice (*Giese v. United States*, 1979).

Selection of Jurors

Selection of a trial jury from a representative cross section of the community is an essential component of the Sixth Amendment right to a jury trial in a criminal case, and this right cannot be overcome on merely rational grounds for exclusion of class from jury service. A criminal defendant has standing to challenge the exclusion of a particular class of persons in the jury selection process that results in a violation of the requirement of the Sixth Amendment that the jury be selected from a fair cross section of community, whether or not that defendant is member of the excluded class. To establish *prima facie* violation of the Sixth Amendment, a defendant must show that the group alleged to be excluded is "distinctive" in the community, representation of this group in venires from which juries are selected is not fair and reasonable in relation to the number of such persons in community, and this underrepresentation is due to systematic exclusion of the group in the jury selection process. In order for the state to overcome the right to a proper jury drawn from a fair cross section of the community, significant state interest must be manifestly and primarily advanced by those aspects of the jury selection process, such as exemption criteria, that result in disproportionate exclusion of the distinctive group. The Sixth Amendment's guarantee of trial by impartial jury forbids prosecution's peremptory challenges to excuse jurors solely on the basis of their race. To show *prima facie* violation of the right to the possibility of a fair cross section in petit jury, the defendant must show that in his case the group alleged to be excluded is cognizable in the community, and there is substantial likelihood of exclusion having been based on group affiliation rather than because of the juror's possible bias. If the defendant establishes a *prima facie* case, the burden of proof shifts to the state to show that permissible racially neutral selection activity produced the challenged result (*Duren v. Missouri*, 1979).

A jury panel may be challenged on grounds that it overrepresents, rather than excludes, certain economic groups in the community. The purpose of fair cross section protection is to provide the criminal defendant with grand and petit juries that are microcosms of the community. The right to an impartial jury does not require that jurors be mathematically proportioned to the character of the community; there is no requirement that any particular class be represented on every jury (*Adams v. State*, 1982).

A *prima facie* case of discrimination in jury selection is established by showing disparity between the percentage which an ethnic or racial group constitutes the group from which the jury list is drawn and the percentage which that ethnic or racial group constitutes of jury list compiled. Once the defendant establishes a *prima facie* case, the burden shifts to the state to offer a satisfactory explanation of why a disparity exists. To challenge a jury array on racial discrimination grounds, the defendant must establish that the procedure adopted for selection of prospective jurors amounts to "purposeful or deliberate" exclusion of a minority from jury service; mere observation that a particular group is underrepresented on a particular panel does not support constitutional challenge (*United States v. Grose*, 1975).

In *Batson v. Kentucky* (1986), the Supreme Court held that the prohibition against racial and ethnic discrimination applied also to the selection of individual jurors, and that a prosecutor or defense counsel could not use his or her preemptory challenges to exclude members of one racial group. Preemptory challenges refer to the limited number of challenges provided to both the prosecution and defense by which a party can exclude a juror without a specific reason. If the defense or prosecution objects that the other side has used the preemptory challenges to exclude the members of one racial group, then the side that excluded those jurors must provide explanations for the challenges based on something other than the race of the excluded juror. The *Batson* ruling was extended to gender classifications by *J.E.B. v. Alabama* (1994).

Although the English proficiency requirement, which excludes all potential jurors who cannot read, write, or understand the English language with a degree of proficiency sufficient to fill out satisfactorily a juror qualification form or those who cannot speak the English language, operates in a systematic manner in excluding a distinctive group of the community, there is state interest in having a national court system operate in the national language (*United States v. Benmuhar*, 1981).

A state court criminal defendant's right to an impartial jury trial under the Sixth and Fourteenth Amendments is violated by operation of a state's constitutional and statutory provisions that exclude a woman from jury service—unless she has previously filed written declaration of her desire to be subject to service—requiring reversal of the defendant's conviction, where:

- The jury selection system, though not disqualifying women from jury service, results in only very few women, grossly disproportionate to the number of eligible women in community, being called for jury service
- Exclusion of women from jury service by operation of the state's constitutional and statutory provisions may not be justified, so as to overcome the Sixth Amendment right to a proper jury in a criminal case, merely on the ground that subjecting women to jury service would substantially interfere with the distinctive role of women in society (*Taylor v. Louisiana*, 1975)

Attitude toward Death Penalty

Exclusion for cause of a venire member was proper where, although she continually equivocated during her *voir dire* examination, nonetheless she stated at several points that she would not cast her vote as juror in way that would lead to the death penalty.

In prosecution for first-degree murder and other offenses arising out of the bombing of a federal building that resulted in the deaths of 168 persons, the district court did not abuse its discretion, during death penalty *voir dire*, in preventing the defendant from ascertaining whether prospective jurors would automatically vote for the death penalty, and from determining whether their exposure to allegedly prejudicial pretrial publicity had biased them on the issue of punishment, where, although asking at least some of defendant's proposed questions might have been a better course, questions were not constitutionally required to ensure an impartial jury (*United States v. McVeigh*, 1998).

Death penalty imposed or recommended by a jury chosen by excluding veniremen for cause simply because they expressed general objections to death penalty or conscientious or religious scruples against its infliction cannot be carried out, as a jury so chosen is organized to give the death penalty and is not representative of the community (*Witherspoon v. Illinois*, 1968). Under *Witherspoon* doctrine exclusion of jurors unwilling or unable to take oath required by statute, to effect that mandatory penalty of death or life imprisonment would not affect their deliberations on any issue of fact, is violative of the Sixth and Fourteenth Amendments, because statute operates to exclude prospective jurors whose beliefs on the death penalty are not so irrevocably opposed to capital punishment as to frustrate the state's legitimate efforts to administer a constitutionally valid death penalty scheme (*Adams v. Texas*, 1980).

Number of Jurors

Constitutional provision does not mean only a 12-person jury. State statute providing for a 6-person jury in noncapital cases did not violate a defendant's constitutional right to a jury, as constitutional provision does not mean only a 12-person jury (*Williams v. Florida*, 1970). A state criminal trial with a jury of fewer than six persons deprives the accused of a right to trial by jury guaranteed by the Sixth and Fourteenth Amendments (*Ballew v. Georgia*, 1978). The jury must be of sufficient size to promote group deliberation, to insulate members of the jury from outside intimidation, and to provide a representative cross section of the community; a jury of six may adequately perform this function, but a jury may not be fewer than six persons (*People ex rel. Hunter v. District Court of Twentieth Judicial District*, 1981).

Nonunanimous Verdicts in State Courts

An Oregon constitutional provision that conviction of the accused may be secured by 10–2 jury verdict was not violative of the Sixth Amendment as applied to states via the Fourteenth (*Apodaca v. Oregon*, 1972). The conviction of an accused by a nonunanimous six-person jury in a state criminal trial for a nonpetty offense violated the right of an accused to trial by jury under the Sixth and Fourteenth Amendments; conviction for a nonpetty offense by less than all members of a six-person jury threatens preservation of the substance of the jury trial guarantee, and the use of nonunanimous six-person juries cannot be justified on the basis of a state's interest in saving time. A defendant convicted by a six-person jury in a state criminal trial for a nonpetty offense does not have standing to challenge the constitutionality of the provisions of the state's law allowing conviction by a nonunanimous six-person jury, where the defendant has been convicted by a unanimous, rather than by a nonunanimous, six-person jury because the conviction of an accused by a unanimous six-person jury in a state criminal trial for a nonpetty offense does not violate the accused's Sixth and Fourteenth Amendment right to trial by jury (*Burch v. Louisiana*, 1979).

Judge Commenting on Evidence

In federal courts and in some state courts, the judge may comment on the evidence. In other states, the judges are prohibited from making any comments that may be construed by the jury as a statement as to the validity of the evidence. A federal judge in a criminal case may assist the jury in arriving at a just conclusion by explaining and commenting upon evidence, by drawing their attention to parts of it which he or she thinks are important, and by expressing his or her opinion upon facts, if he or she makes it clear to the jury that all matters of fact are submitted to their determination. However, a statement by a judge that the act of the defendant, while testifying, in constantly wiping his hands, indicated that he was lying was prejudicial error and ground for reversal (*Quercia v. United States*, 1933). It was reversible error for a judge to refer to the defense as subterfuge (*Wallace v. United States*, 1923).

Judicial Instructions

A problem that occurs with jury trials is the instructions that a judge must give to the jury prior to the jury's going into closed deliberations. A few of the issues are discussed in this section. For example, in *Sullivan v. Louisiana* (1993) the Supreme Court held that a first-degree murder defendant's Sixth Amendment right to jury trial was denied by the state trial court's giving of constitutionally deficient beyond-reasonable-doubt instruction to the jury.

In state prosecution for burglary and robbery, jury instruction defining "reasonable doubt" as "doubt for which you can give a reason if called upon to do so by a fellow juror," and instructing jurors to "use the same power of reasoning and power of thinking" as they would apply to their "important business affairs," was not constitutionally deficient where, when viewing instruction as a whole, there was no reasonable likelihood that jurors would have understood instruction to increase the degree of doubt necessary for acquittal, that jurors interpreted instruction as shifting the burden of proof away from prosecution, or that jurors understood instruction to permit conviction after anything but process of careful deliberation or upon less than proof beyond a reasonable doubt (*Vargas v. Keane*, 1996, p. 897).

Questioning

The conduct of a judge in cross-examining a defendant and then commenting on his lack of credibility denied a defendant a fair trial and was ground for reversal (*Hunter v. United States*, 1932). The act of a judge in participating in the trial by examination of witnesses and expressing opinion as to facts was a ground for reversal (*Frantz v. United States*, 1933).

A judge's failure to answer a question from the jury during deliberations does not require a new trial where failure to respond is not due to lack of diligence on the court's part, the verdict shows the jury answered the question correctly before reaching a decision, or the jury is in no rush to reach a verdict and could wait until receiving an answer from the court if it continues to be confused (*United States v. Rodriguez*, 1985).

A defendant's Sixth Amendment right to trial by jury was violated when a trial judge answered a jury's questions with facts not in evidence, where the judge's communications with the jury were made outside of the defendant's presence, and where there was no record showing who was present when answers to the jury's questions were determined, nor how whoever was present came up with answers (*United States v. Neff*, 1993).

Urging Jury to Reach Verdict

Often when the jury is deadlocked and cannot arrive at a decision, a trial judge will attempt to persuade the jury to reach a verdict. One of the issues involved in these cases is whether the actions of the judge deprived the defendant of his or her right to a fair trial. For example, the imputation by a judge in addressing a hung jury that some of the members had forgotten their oaths was reversible error (*Kesley v. United States*, 1931). However, the act of a trial judge in refusing to discharge a jury and in urging them to reachi a verdict on account of long duration of the trial was not error (*United States v. Rosso*, 1932). Also, the fact that the trial judge recalled the jury during their deliberation and told them that they should make every possible effort to come to agreement, and that if they could not they would be sent to a hotel and returned in the morning to continue their deliberation was not error (*United States v. Commerford*, 1933).

Penalty for Exercising Right to Jury Trial

A judge cannot penalize a defendant for demanding a trial by jury. Some of the cases involving that issue are discussed in this section.

The sentence imposed by a district court that unconstitutionally penalized the defendant for assertion of his Sixth Amendment right to trial by jury in light of the judge's statements during trial that the defendant had much to lose by exercising his right to trial by jury and statements to the effect that the purpose of the fine was to reimburse the government for the cost of a jury trial (*United States v. Medina-Cervantes*, 1982). However, a district court's refusal to adjust the assault defendant's sentence downward under sentencing guidelines because he did not clearly demonstrate recognition of personal responsibility for his criminal conduct did not unconstitutionally penalize him for exercising his constitutional right to a jury trial (*United States v. Young*, 1989). Also note that a state court's decision that the former state aggravated the murder death penalty law, under which the defendant was sentenced to life without possibility of parole after being convicted of murder and other offenses, and under which possibility of parole from life sentence was available only to a defendant who pleaded guilty, was constitutional and did not violate the defendant's Sixth Amendment right to a jury trial, inter alia, was not contrary to, or an unreasonable application of, clearly established federal law (*Duhaime v. DuCharme*, 2000).

Trial in the Judicial District in Which the Crime Was Committed

The Sixth Amendment provides that the defendant has a right to be tried in the judicial district in which the crime occurred. The locality in which the offense is alleged to have been committed determines, under Constitution, the place and court of trial. Accordingly, a defendant cannot be forced to accept a change of venue against his or her will, but he or she may waive that right (*United States v. Di James*, 1984). Venue refers to the geographical location of the trial. Often an accused will request a change of venue if he or she does not believe that he or she will receive a fair trial in the judicial district where the crime occurred. Because the accused cannot be forced to accept a change of venue, the prosecution has no right to request a change of venue.

The Sixth Amendment right of the accused to be tried in the district in which the crime was committed does not apply to states, and thus a forgery defendant was denied no constitutional right in state prosecution by the state's securing change of venue that caused him to be tried in a county other than one in which the crime was alleged to have occurred (*Caudill v. Scott*, 1988).

Consider this fact situation: The defendant is married and lives in Virginia. His wife goes on vacation to Las Vegas. While she is on vacation, the defendant from Virginia mails her a box of poisonous candy. The defendant had purchased the candy in New York for the purposes of poisoning her. The defendant is tried for her murder. In what state and judicial district may the defendant be tried in? The rule in all federal and state courts is that the defendant may be tried in any jurisdiction in which one of the acts or elements of the offense took place. Accordingly, he could be tried in New York, Virginia, and Nevada. In Virginia, he could be tried under the Commonwealth of Virginia's murder statute; in New York, he could be tried under the New York State statute; and in Nevada, under that state statute. He may also be tried in federal court for violation of federal law in mailing the poisonous candy in the U.S. mails and across state lines.

While the Constitution guarantees a defendant a trial in the state where the crimes have been committed and a jury of that district or state, venue of federal prosecution depends on the situs of crime, but neither the Constitution nor rules of procedure provide criteria for deciding where the crime has been committed. Location of the crime must be ascertained by reference to a statute proscribing a criminal act, and if there is no explicit guidance, situs must be determined from the nature of the crime alleged and the location of act or acts constituting it. The accused need not have been present in the district where the crime was committed (*United States v. Kibler*, 1982).

Probation revocation proceedings do not constitute "criminal prosecutions" for purposes of the Sixth Amendment right to have a trial in the "district wherein the crime shall have been committed," and resentencing after revocation of parole may take place in a district other than where the defendant was originally sentenced (*United States v. Brown*, 1978).

To Be Informed of the Nature and Cause of the Accusation

The right to be informed of the nature and cause of accusation is substantial and cannot be denied. There can be no conviction or punishment for crime without formal and sufficient accusation. Constitutional defect in indictment or information is not cured by verdict (*Grimsley v. United States*, 1931).

A defendant's right to reasonable notice of charges against him was not denied, despite assertion that original and amended felony informations filed against him were defective, where the defendant had received actual notice and clearly understood that he faced a possible life sentence for first-degree murder (*Hulstine v. Morris*, 1987).

A criminal defendant did not have the Sixth Amendment right, upon his arrest, to be informed of reasons for arrest, because, although the Sixth Amendment provides the accused the right to be informed of the nature and cause of accusation, the amendment's protection does not come into play until the government has committed itself to prosecution (*Kladis v. Brezek*, 1987).

The Sixth Amendment makes definiteness an element of every crime, which must be proved. For example, a defendant could not be convicted of contempt of Congress in refusing to answer a question propounded to him by a subcommittee of Congress so imprecise that its intended scope was uncertain and might be differently understood by others, and the fact that the defendant did not complain when before subcommittee that the question was too vague could not constitute a waiver (*O'Connor v. United States*, 1956).

Right to Confront the Witnesses

In *Crawford v. Washington* (2004), Crawford was convicted in a state court of assault but asserted that the admission of his wife's statement to police, after he had invoked state marital privilege to preclude her testimony at trial, violated his constitutional right to confront witnesses against him. The U.S. Supreme Court stated that the wife's statement during interrogation was testimonial in nature and the defendant's right to confront the wife thus clearly included the right to cross-examine the statement, especially in view of the ambiguity in the statement. The right to confrontation was a guarantee that the reliability of the wife's statement be tested by cross-examination. The Court said that procedural guarantee of the right to confront witnesses applies to both federal and state prosecutions. And the right to confront includes the right to cross-examine the witness.

The Court noted that the right to confront one's accusers is a concept that dates back to Roman times and that the founding fathers' immediate source of the concept was the common law. English common law has long differed from continental civil law in regard to the manner in which witnesses give testimony in criminal trials. The common law tradition was one of live testimony in court subject to adversarial testing, while the civil law condones examination in private by judicial officers.

An early state decision (*State v. Webb*, 1794) sheds some light upon the original understanding of the common law right. *Webb*, decided three years after the adoption of the Sixth Amendment, held that depositions could be read against an accused only if they were taken in his presence. The *Webb* court rejected a broader reading of the English authorities, stating: "It is a rule of the common law, founded on natural justice, that no man shall be prejudiced by evidence which he had not the liberty to cross examine" (p. 104).

Does the defendant forfeit the right of confrontation when he kills a potential witness? This issue is discussed in the Giles case.

Giles v. California, 2008 U.S. LEXIS 5264 (2008)

Justice Scalia delivered the opinion of the Court:

We consider whether a defendant forfeits his Sixth Amendment right to confront a witness against him when a judge determines that a wrongful act by the defendant made the witness unavailable to testify at trial.

On September 29, 2002, petitioner Dwayne Giles shot his ex-girlfriend, Brenda Avie, outside the garage of his grandmother's house. No witness saw the shooting, but Giles' niece heard what transpired from inside the house. She heard Giles and Avie speaking in conversational tones. Avie then yelled "Granny" several times and a series of gunshots sounded. Giles' niece and grandmother ran outside and saw Giles standing near Avie with a gun in his hand. Avie, who had not been carrying a weapon, had been shot six times. One wound was consistent with Avie's holding her hand up at the time she was shot, another was consistent with her having turned to her side, and a third was consistent with her having been shot while lying on the ground. Giles fled the scene after the shooting. He was apprehended by police about two weeks later and charged with murder.

At trial, Giles testified that he had acted in self-defense. Giles described Avie as jealous, and said he knew that she had once shot a man, that he had seen her threaten people with a knife, and that she had vandalized his home and car on prior occasions. He said that on the day of the shooting, Avie came to his grandmother's house and threatened to kill him and his new girlfriend, who had been at the house earlier. He said that Avie had also threatened to kill his new girlfriend when Giles and Avie spoke on the phone earlier that day. Giles testified that after Avie threatened him at the house, he went into the garage and retrieved a gun, took the safety off, and started walking toward the back door of the house. He said that Avie charged at him, and that he was afraid she had something in her hand. According to Giles, he closed his eyes and fired several shots, but did not intend to kill Avie.

Prosecutors sought to introduce statements that Avie had made to a police officer responding to a domestic-violence report about three weeks before the shooting. Avie, who was crying when she spoke, told the officer that Giles had accused her of having an affair, and that after the two began to argue, Giles grabbed her by the shirt, lifted her off the floor, and began to choke her. According to Avie, when she broke free and fell to the floor, Giles punched her in the face and head, and after she broke free again, he opened a folding knife, held it about three feet away from her, and threatened to kill her if he found her cheating on him. Over Giles' objection, the trial court admitted these statements into evidence under a provision of California law that permits admission of out-of-court statements describing the infliction or threat of physical injury on a declarant when the declarant is unavailable to testify at trial and the prior statements are deemed trustworthy.

A jury convicted Giles of first-degree murder. He appealed. The California Court of Appeals held that the admission of Avie's unconfronted statements at Giles' trial did not violate the Confrontation Clause as construed by Crawford because Crawford recognized a doctrine of forfeiture by wrongdoing. It concluded that Giles had forfeited his right to confront Avie because he had committed the murder for which he was on trial, and because his intentional criminal act made Avie unavailable to testify.

The Sixth Amendment provides that "in all criminal prosecutions, the accused shall enjoy the right ... to be confronted with the witnesses against him." The Amendment contemplates that a witness who makes testimonial statements admitted against a defendant will ordinarily be present at trial for cross-examination, and that if the witness is unavailable, his prior testimony will be introduced only if the defendant had a prior opportunity to cross-examine him. The State does not dispute here, and we accept without deciding, that Avie's statements accusing Giles of assault were testimonial. But it maintains that the Sixth Amendment did not prohibit prosecutors from introducing the statements because an exception to the confrontation guarantee permits the use of a witness's unconfronted testimony if a judge finds, as the judge did in this case, that the defendant committed a wrongful act that rendered the witness unavailable to testify at trial.

We have previously acknowledged that two forms of testimonial statements were admitted at common law even though they were unconfronted. The first of these were declarations made by a speaker who was both on the brink of death and aware that he was dying. Avie did not make the unconfronted statements admitted at Giles' trial when she was dying, so her statements do not fall within this historic exception.

A second common-law doctrine, which we will refer to as forfeiture by wrongdoing, permitted the introduction of statements of a witness who was "detained" or "kept away" by the "means or procurement" of the defendant. The doctrine has roots in the 1666 decision in Lord Morley's Case, at which judges concluded that a witness's having been "detained by the means or procurement of the prisoner," provided a basis to read testimony previously given at a coroner's inquest. Courts and commentators also concluded that wrongful procurement of a witness's absence was among the grounds for admission of statements made at bail and committal hearings conducted under the Marian statutes, which directed justices of the peace to take the statements of felony suspects and the persons bringing the suspects before the magistrate, and to certify those statements to the court. This class of confronted statements was also admissible if the witness who made them was dead or unable to travel.

The terms used to define the scope of the forfeiture rule suggest that the exception applied only when the defendant engaged in conduct designed to prevent the witness from testifying. The rule required the witness to have been "kept back" or "detained" by "means or procurement" of the defendant.

Cases and treatises of the time indicate that a purpose-based definition of these terms governed. A number of them said that prior testimony was admissible when a witness was kept away by the defendant's "means and contrivance." This phrase requires that the defendant have schemed to bring about the absence from trial that he "contrived."

In sum, our interpretation of the common-law forfeiture rule is supported by (1) the most natural reading of the language used at common law; (2) the absence of common-law cases admitting prior statements on a forfeiture theory when the defendant had not engaged in conduct designed to prevent a witness from testifying; (3) the common law's uniform exclusion of unconfronted inculpatory testimony by murder victims (except testimony given with awareness of impending death) in the innumerable cases in which the defendant was on trial for killing the victim, but was not shown to have done so for the purpose of preventing testimony; (4) a subsequent history in which the dissent's broad forfeiture theory has not been applied. The first two and the last are highly persuasive; the third is in our view conclusive.

We decline to approve an exception to the Confrontation Clause unheard of at the time of the founding or for 200 years thereafter. The judgment of the California Supreme Court is vacated, and the case is remanded for further proceedings not inconsistent with this opinion.

It is so ordered.

To Have a Compulsory Process for Obtaining Witnesses in His Favor

Under the Sixth Amendment, a defendant has the constitutional right to have the compulsory process for obtaining witnesses in his or her favor. The U.S. Supreme Court in *Washington v. Texas* (1967) held that compelling the attendance of witnesses, if necessary, was in plain terms the right to present the defendant's version of the facts as well as the prosecution's to the jury so it might decide where the truth lies. Just as an accused has the right to confront the prosecution's witnesses for the purpose of challenging their testimony, he or she has the right to present his own witnesses to establish a defense. The Court stated that this right was a fundamental element of due process of law.

In the *Washington* case, the defendant claimed that his former girlfriend tricked him into confessing to the murder. After he learned that the cause of the victim's death was inconsistent with his confession, he denied killing the victim. His version of events was corroborated by evidence showing that the girlfriend had told others that she killed the victim. In a prior trial, she was acquitted of the murder charges before the defendant's trial and was granted complete immunity from prosecution. She refused to testify, and the trial court found her in contempt based on this refusal. And the trial court denied the defendant's request to call her to the stand. On appeal, the court held that the trial court's refusal to call the girlfriend to the stand was an abuse of discretion because her testimony was potentially both material and favorable to the defendant, and the defendant was wrongfully denied the benefit of either her testimony or any inference from her refusal to testify in front of the jury. The Court stated that before a defendant had the right to the compulsory process, he must at least make some plausible showing of how the testimony would have been both material and favorable to his defense.

To Have Assistance of Counsel for His Defense

The Sixth Amendment states that in all criminal prosecutions, the accused shall enjoy the right to have the assistance of counsel for his defense. The Supreme Court noted in *Gideon v. Wainwright* (1963) that the importance of the right to assistance of counsel cannot be overstated. The Court stated in our adversarial system of justice that defense counsel is a necessity, not a luxury. Most of the court decisions on the right to counsel concern the failure of the state to appoint counsel for an indigent accused and the issue of effective representation.

There are two separate issues regarding when a defendant has the right to assistance of counsel and when the defendant has a right to an appointed counsel. A defendant has the right to the assistance of counsel at all significant stages of a criminal case. The other issue is: When the defendant cannot afford to hire an attorney, under what circumstances must the government provide him or her with one?

Right to Appointed Counsel

In *Gideon v. Wainwright*, the Supreme Court ruled that an indigent defendant has the right to appointed counsel in any felony case. Later in *Argersinger v. Hamlin* (1972), the Supreme Court ruled that in misdemeanor cases, the indigent accused has a right to appointed counsel in any trial in which a sentence of imprisonment could be imposed upon conviction.

In *Faretta v. California* (1975), the Supreme Court held that a criminal defendant has a Sixth Amendment right to conduct his own defense. The Court stated that the right to counsel is just that—a right to counsel. To thrust a counsel on an unwilling defendant violates his or her rights under the Sixth Amendment.

In *Douglas v. California* (1963), the Court held that an indigent defendant has no right to be represented by appointed counsel on a discretionary appeal. In most states, the defendant has a right to appeal to the first appellate level. In this case, the indigent defendant would have a right to appointed counsel for that "appeal of right" if he or she had a right to appointed counsel at the trial. In most states, an appeal beyond the first appellate level is a discretionary appeal. The discretion is with the appellate court as to whether it wants to accept and decide the defendant's appeal. The *Douglas* case held that the indigent defendant had no right to appointed counsel at this discretionary appeal. In those states that have the death penalty, generally a defendant who receives a death penalty has the right to appeal to the state's highest criminal appeals court, in which case an indigent defendant would have a right to appointed counsel to that court.

When does the right to appointed counsel begin? The Supreme Court in *Mempa v. Rhay* (1967) stated that the right to appointed counsel for an indigent defendant exists during the critical stages of the criminal prosecution. The Court listed these stages of prosecution as critical to the required appointed counsel unless waived by the defendant:

- Identification procedures (except photo lineups)
- Attempts by police or prosecutor to elicit statements from an accused
- First appearance or arraignment
- Preliminary hearing in a case
- Actual trial
- Sentencing procedures

After an indigent accused has been formally charged with a crime, he or she has a right to counsel at any physical lineup under *United States v. Wade* (1967), but if the accused has not formally been charged, there is no right to be present. A defense counsel present at a physical lineup has no official function other than as an observer.

Prior to the initiation of judicial proceedings against an accused, he or she does not have the right to appointed counsel. However, under the *Miranda* case (1966), a person being interrogated while in custody has the right to counsel.

Effective Assistance of Counsel

The right to counsel under the Sixth Amendment includes the right to "effective assistance" of counsel (*Strickland v. Washington*, 1984). Under *Strickland*, incompetency of counsel is to be judged by an objective standard of reasonableness. To establish incompetency under the *Strickland* test, the accused must prove, first, that the counsel was ineffective, and second, that the counsel's performance prejudiced the accused. The Supreme Court in the *Strickland* opinion cautioned the lower courts against second-guessing counsel's performance. The Court also noted that because of the difficulties inherent in making an evaluation of a counsel's duties, a court must indulge in a strong presumption that the counsel's performance falls within the wide range of reasonable professional assistance.

In *Williams v. Taylor* (2000), the Supreme Court restated the *Strickland* rule as follows:

> A violation of the right to the effective assistance of counsel has two components: First, the defendant must show that counsel's performance was deficient. This requires showing that counsel made errors so serious that counsel was not functioning as the "counsel" guaranteed the defendant by U.S. Const. amend. VI. Second, the defendant must show that the deficient performance prejudiced the defense. This requires showing that counsel's errors were so serious as to deprive the defendant of a fair trial, a trial whose result is reliable. To establish ineffectiveness, a defendant must show that counsel's representation fell below an objective standard of reasonableness. To establish prejudice he must show that there is a reasonable probability that, but for counsel's unprofessional errors, the result of the proceeding would have been different. A reasonable probability is a probability sufficient to undermine confidence in the outcome.

Right to Represent Self

If the Sixth Amendment provides that a person has the right to counsel in all criminal proceedings, does it provide the corresponding right to represent oneself? In *Faretta v. California* (1975), the U.S. Supreme Court noted the following:

> Sixth and Fourteenth Amendments of our Constitution guarantee that a person brought to trial in any state or federal court must be afforded the right to the assistance of counsel before he can be validly convicted and punished by imprisonment. This clear constitutional rule has emerged from a series of cases decided here over the last 50 years. The question before us now is whether a defendant in a state criminal trial has a constitutional right to proceed without counsel when he voluntarily and intelligently elects to do so. Stated another way, the question is whether a State may constitutionally haul a person into its criminal courts and there force a lawyer upon him, even when he insists that he wants to conduct his own defense. It is not an easy question, but we have concluded that a State may not constitutionally do so.

The Court held that because rights under Amendment 6 are basic to the adversary system of criminal justice, they are part of the due process of law that is guaranteed by Amendment 14 to defendants in the criminal courts of the states. The rights to notice, confrontation, and compulsory process, when taken together, guarantee that a criminal charge may be answered in a manner now considered fundamental to the fair administration of American justice—through the calling and interrogation of favorable witnesses, the cross-examination of adverse witnesses, and the orderly introduction of evidence. In short, the amendment constitutionalizes the right in an adversary criminal trial to make a defense.

The Court stated in the opinion that the right of self-representation is not a license to abuse the dignity of the courtroom. Neither is it a license not to comply with relevant rules of procedural and substantive law. Thus, whatever else may or may not be open to him on appeal, a defendant who elects to represent himself cannot thereafter complain that the quality of his own defense amounted to a denial of "effective assistance of counsel."

Faretta had also objected to the actions of the trial court in appointing a standby counsel for him. The standby counsel was instructed to sit at the defense desk and be available for consultation by the defendant should Faretta decide that he need consultation. The Court held that a State may, even over objection by the accused, appoint a "standby counsel" to aid the accused if and when the accused requests help and to be available to represent the accused in the event that termination of the defendant's self-representation is necessary.

In *Kane v. Garcia Espitia* (2005), Garcia Espitia, a criminal defendant who chose to proceed *pro se* (without counsel), was convicted in California state court of carjacking and other offenses. He had declined, as was his right, to be represented by a lawyer with unlimited access to legal materials. Espitia claimed he had received no law library access while in jail before trial—despite his repeated requests and court orders to the contrary—and only about four hours of access during trial, just before closing arguments. The United States Court of Appeals for the Ninth Circuit held that the lack of any pretrial access to law books violated the petitioner's constitutional right to represent himself under the Sixth Amendment as established in *Faretta v. California*. The United States Supreme Court held that *Faretta* did not "clearly establish" the law library access right for prisoners. In fact, *Faretta* said nothing about any specific legal aid that the State owed a *pro se* criminal defendant. Thus, the Ninth Circuit, erred in holding, based on *Faretta*, that a violation of a law library access right was a basis for federal habeas relief.

In *Hartman v. State* (2007), a Delaware supreme court held that the defendant was denied his constitutional right of self-representation when the trial court declined to appoint substitute counsel and conducted a hearing on the defendant's motion. At the time of his trial, the defendant was 43, literate, and had a ninth-grade education. He indicated that he knew he could expect no assistance from the judge at trial, that he had no legal training, and that he understood that court rules were very technical. The trial court denied his request for self-representation not on the basis that the defendant had not made a knowledgeable and voluntary waiver, but based on concerns that the trial not be a "sham" or a "charade" or a "public disgrace" and be conducted "appropriately." The state supreme court held that this was error; whether defendant was competent to represent himself was not part of the determination of whether he was knowingly asserting the right to self-representation. As the defendant made a knowing and voluntary waiver of his right to counsel and was adequately informed of the risks of proceeding *pro se*, the trial court was obliged to allow him to represent himself.

The right to self-representation may be waived if not raised before meaningful trial proceedings. In *Upshaw v. State* (2007) a Georgia appellate court faced an interesting question regarding the right of self-representation. Upshaw made his self-representation request after the jury was sworn and the first witness had testified. Under both *Faretta* and Alabama Rules of Criminal Procedure, P. 6.1(b), the trial court was required to be certain that a defendant's waiver of his right to counsel was done knowingly, intelligently, and voluntarily.

Contrary to the defendant's assertions, Upshaw was not allowed to represent himself without the aid of an attorney. He was granted a "hybrid" form of representation in that counsel was directed to assist the defendant. The appellate court held that the failure to conduct a *Faretta* inquiry in a hybrid representation situation was not error if a defendant's role was limited. The defendant's role had been limited. By the time of the defendant's request, counsel had represented the defendant for months, conducted *voir dire*, given the opening argument, and cross-examined the state's first witness. Even after the defendant was allowed to participate in his representation, counsel did the entire cross-examination, conducted the defendant's direct examination, and made the closing argument. The Georgia appellate court affirmed Upshaw's conviction.

Standard of Competence Required for Self-Representation

Because the right of self-representation is not absolute, many states adopt a higher standard of competence for self-representation than for standing trial. That issue was discussed in *Indiana v. Edwards* (2008). In July 1999 Ahmad Edwards, the respondent, tried to steal a pair of shoes from an Indiana department store. After he was discovered, he drew a gun, fired at a store security officer, and wounded a bystander. He was caught and then charged with attempted murder, battery with a deadly weapon, criminal recklessness, and theft. His mental condition subsequently became the subject of three competency proceedings and two self-representation requests, mostly before the same trial judge.

Five months after Edwards' arrest, his court-appointed counsel asked for a psychiatric evaluation. After the hearing psychiatrist and neuropsychologist witnesses (in February 2000 and again in August 2000), the court found Edwards incompetent to stand trial and committed him to Logansport State Hospital for evaluation and treatment. Seven months after his commitment, doctors found that Edwards' condition had improved to the point where he could stand trial. Several months later, however, but still before trial, Edwards' counsel asked for another psychiatric evaluation. In March 2002, the judge held a competency hearing, considered additional psychiatric evidence, and (in April) found that Edwards, while suffering from mental illness, was competent to assist his attorneys in his defense and stand trial for the charged crimes.

Seven months later but still before trial, Edwards' counsel sought yet another psychiatric evaluation of his client. And in April 2003, the court held yet another competency hearing. Edwards' counsel presented further psychiatric and neuropsychological evidence showing that Edwards was suffering from serious thinking difficulties and delusions. A testifying psychiatrist reported that Edwards could understand the charges against him, but he was unable to cooperate with his attorney in his defense because of his schizophrenic illness; his delusions and his marked difficulties in thinking made it impossible for him to cooperate with his attorney. In November 2003, the court concluded that Edwards was not then competent to stand trial and ordered his commitment to a state mental hospital.

In June 2005, about eight months after his commitment, the hospital reported that Edwards' condition had again improved to the point that he had again become competent to stand trial. And almost one year after that Edwards' trial began. Just before trial, Edwards asked to represent himself. He also asked for a continuance, which, he said, he needed to proceed *pro se* (as his own counsel). The court refused the continuance. Edwards then proceeded to trial represented by counsel. The jury convicted him of criminal recklessness and theft but failed to reach a verdict on the charges of attempted murder and battery.

The state decided to retry Edwards on the attempted murder and battery charges. Just before the retrial, Edwards again asked the court to permit him to represent himself. Referring to the lengthy record of psychiatric reports, the trial court noted that Edwards still suffered from schizophrenia and concluded that "with these findings, he's competent to stand trial but I'm not going to find he's competent to defend himself." The trial court denied Edwards' self-representation request. Edwards was represented by appointed counsel at his retrial. The jury convicted Edwards on both of the remaining counts.

Edwards subsequently appealed to Indiana's intermediate appellate court. He argued that the trial court's refusal to permit him to represent himself at his retrial deprived him of his constitutional right of self-representation. The appellate court agreed and ordered a new trial. The matter then went to the Indiana Supreme Court, which agreed with the appellate court that Edwards had been denied the constitutional right to represent himself.

Justice Stephen Breyer delivered the Court's opinion. He stated that *Faretta* did not answer the question before the Court because it did not consider the problem of mental competency (Faretta was "literate, competent, and understanding"), and because *Faretta* itself and later cases have made clear that the right of self-representation is not absolute. He noted that there is no right of self-representation on direct appeal in a criminal case; a trial court may appoint standby counsel over a self-represented defendant's objection; there is no right to abuse the dignity of the courtroom and no right to avoid compliance with relevant rules of procedural and substantive law. The question in the case concerned a mental illness–related limitation on the scope of the self-representation right.

Justice Breyer stated:

> We assume that a criminal defendant has sufficient mental competence to stand trial and that the defendant insists on representing himself during that trial. We ask whether the Constitution permits a State to limit that defendant's self-representation right by insisting upon representation by counsel at trial— on the ground that the defendant lacks the mental capacity to conduct his trial defense unless represented.
>
> Several considerations taken together lead us to conclude that the answer to this question is yes. First, the Court's precedent, while not answering the question, points slightly in the direction of our affirmative answer. The Court's mental competency cases set forth a standard that focuses directly upon a defendant's present ability to consult with his lawyer, a capacity to consult with counsel, and an ability to assist counsel in preparing his defense. It has long been accepted that a person whose mental condition is such that he lacks the capacity to understand the nature and object of the proceedings against him, to consult with counsel, and to assist in preparing his defense may not be subjected to a trial. These standards assume representation by counsel and emphasize the importance of counsel. They thus suggest, though do not hold, that an instance in which a defendant who would choose to forgo counsel at trial presents a very different set of circumstances, which in our view, calls for a different standard.
>
> The nature of the problem before us cautions against the use of a single mental competency standard for deciding both (1) whether a defendant who is represented by counsel can proceed to trial and (2) whether a defendant who goes to trial must be permitted to represent himself. Mental illness itself is not a unitary concept. It varies in degree. It can vary over time. It interferes with an individual's functioning at different times in different ways. The history of this case illustrates the complexity of the problem. In certain instances an individual may well be able to satisfy mental competence standard, for he will be able to work with counsel at trial, yet at the same time he may be unable to carry out the basic tasks needed to present his own defense without the help of counsel. Within each domain of adjudicative competence (competence to assist counsel; decisional competence), the data indicate that understanding, reasoning, and appreciation of the charges against a defendant are separable and somewhat independent aspects of functional legal ability.
>
> For these reasons, the judgment of the Supreme Court of Indiana [ordering a new trial] is vacated.

When the Right to Appointed Counsel Attaches

The right to counsel guaranteed by the Sixth Amendment applies at the first appearance before a judicial officer at which a defendant is told of the formal accusation against him and restrictions are imposed on his liberty.

—Justice David Souter, *Rothgery v. Gillespie County,* **2008**

In *Rothgery v. Gillespie County* (2008), petitioner Rothgery sued respondent Gillespie County pursuant to 42 USCS § 1983, alleging that his Sixth Amendment right to counsel was violated by the county's unwritten policy of denying appointed counsel to indigent defendants out on bond until at least the entry of an information or indictment. Texas police relied on erroneous information that petitioner Rothgery had a previous felony conviction to arrest him as a felon in possession of a firearm. The officers brought Rothgery before a magistrate judge, as required by state law, for a so-called Article 15.17 hearing (Texas Code of Criminal Procedure Annotated Article 15.17), at which the Fourth Amendment probable cause determination was made, bail was set, and Rothgery was formally apprised of the accusation against him. After the hearing, the magistrate judge committed Rothgery to jail, and he was released after posting a surety bond. Rothgery had no money for a lawyer and made several unheeded oral and written requests for appointed counsel. He was subsequently indicted and rearrested, his bail was increased, and he was jailed when he could not post the bail. Subsequently, Rothgery was assigned a lawyer, who assembled the paperwork that prompted the indictment's dismissal.

Rothgery then brought this 42 USC § 1983 action against the respondent county, claiming that if it had provided him a lawyer within a reasonable time after the Article 15.17 hearing, he would not have been indicted, rearrested, or jailed. He asserts that the county's unwritten policy of denying appointed counsel to indigent defendants out on bond until an indictment is entered violated his Sixth Amendment right to counsel.

The issue before the Supreme Court was whether a Texas Code of Criminal Procedure Annotated Article 15.17 hearing marked that point, with the consequent state obligation to appoint counsel within a reasonable time once a request for assistance was made. Prior case law clearly established that the right to counsel attached at the initial appearance before a judicial officer. The Article 15.17 hearing was an initial appearance as the accused was taken before a magistrate judge, informed of the formal accusation against him, and sent to jail until he posted bail. The lower court's attachment standard, which depended on whether a prosecutor had a hand in starting the adversarial judicial proceedings, was wrong. Under the federal standard, an accusation filed with a judicial officer was sufficiently formal, and the government's commitment to prosecute it sufficiently concrete, when the accusation prompted arraignment and restrictions on the accused's liberty to facilitate the prosecution.

The right to counsel guaranteed by the Sixth Amendment applies at the first appearance before a judicial officer at which a defendant is told of the formal accusation against him and restrictions are imposed on his liberty. What counts as a commitment to prosecute is an issue of federal law unaffected by allocations of power among state officials under a state's law. Under the federal standard, an accusation filed with a judicial officer is sufficiently formal, and the government's commitment to prosecute it sufficiently concrete, when the accusation prompts arraignment and restrictions on the accused's liberty to facilitate the prosecution. From that point on, the defendant is faced with the prosecutorial forces of organized society and immersed in the intricacies of substantive and procedural criminal law that define his capacity and control his actual ability to defend himself against a formal accusation that he is a criminal. By that point, it is too late to wonder whether he is accused within the meaning of the Sixth Amendment, and it makes no practical sense to deny it. All of this is equally true whether the machinery of prosecution was turned on by the local police or the state attorney general.

Right to Counsel on Appeal for Indigent Defendants

In *Douglas v. California* (1963), the Supreme Court held that in criminal proceedings, a state must provide counsel for an indigent defendant in a first appeal as of right. Two considerations were key: (1) an appeal "of right" yields an adjudication on the "merits," and (2) first-tier review differs from subsequent appellate stages "at which the claims have once been presented by a lawyer and passed upon by an appellate court." The Court held that a state need not appoint counsel to aid a poor person seeking to pursue a second-tier discretionary appeal to the state's highest court or, thereafter, certiorari review to the Supreme Court. The Court stated that the *Douglas* rationale does not extend to second-tier discretionary review because, at that stage, error correction is not the reviewing court's prime function. Principal criteria for state high court review include whether the issues presented are of significant public interest, whether the cause involves legal principles of major significance to the state's jurisprudence, and whether the decision below is in probable conflict with the high court's precedent. Further, a defendant who has received counsel's aid in a first-tier appeal as a right would be armed with a transcript or other record of trial proceedings, a brief in the appeals court setting forth his claims, and often, that court's opinion disposing of the case.

Guilty Pleas

In order for a guilty plea to be valid, the defendant must be apprised of his constitutional right to jury trial and that his guilty plea waives such right

(*State v. Holsworth*, 1980). A plea of guilty negotiated during plea bargaining waives a right to trial by jury as guaranteed by the Sixth Amendment (*People v. Wei Chen*, 1980). When a defendant changed his plea of not guilty to guilty, denial of his motion for permission to withdraw the plea of guilty was not a denial of his constitutional right to trial by a jury, because a plea of guilty is a waiver of trial, and is in itself a conviction and conclusive (*United States v. Colonna*, 1944).

A defendant cannot be punished by a more severe sentence because he unsuccessfully exercised his constitutional right to stand trial rather than plead guilty; however, if a defendant turns down a plea bargain offered by prosecution, he may not then complain that he received a heavier sentence after trial, absent evidence of vindictiveness or punitive action (*Blackmon v. Wainwright*, 1979).

A defendant who pleads guilty or *nolo contendere* to any criminal offense waives the following fundamental constitutional rights: (1) privilege against self-incrimination, (2) right to trial by jury, (3) right to confront one's accusers, (4) right to insist that prosecution's proof at trial establishes guilt beyond reasonable doubt, (5) right to present witnesses by use of compulsory process, (6) right to testify in defense of charge, and (7) right to a speedy and public trial (*People v. Lesh*, 1983).

The right to withdraw a plea of guilty under appropriate circumstances, even after sentencing, is implicit in the Sixth Amendment of the federal Constitution; manifest injustice, such as unfair conduct of the defense counsel leading to a guilty plea by active inducement, or by inaction when there is duty to speak, is a valid ground for withdrawal of a guilty plea (*Commonwealth v. Hare*, 1977).

Capstone Case: *United States v. Gonzalez-Lopez*, 548 U.S. 140 (2006)

Does the defendant have a right to be represented by the counsel of his or her choice?

Justice Scalia delivered the opinion of the Court:

We must decide whether a trial court's erroneous deprivation of a criminal defendant's choice of counsel entitles him to a reversal of his conviction.

Respondent Gonzalez-Lopez was charged in the Eastern District of Missouri with conspiracy to distribute more than 100 kilograms of marijuana. His family hired attorney John Fahle to represent him. After the arraignment, respondent called a California attorney, Joseph Low, to discuss whether Low would represent him, either in addition to or instead of Fahle. Low flew from California to meet with respondent, who hired him.

Some time later, Low and Fahle represented respondent at an evidentiary hearing before a Magistrate Judge. The Magistrate Judge accepted Low's provisional entry of appearance and permitted Low to participate in the hearing on the condition that he immediately file a motion for admission pro hac vice (A motion for temporary authority to practice in the federal court in Missouri). During the hearing, however, the Magistrate Judge revoked the provisional acceptance on the ground that, by passing notes to Fahle, Low had violated a court rule restricting the cross-examination of a witness to one counsel.

The following week, respondent informed Fahle that he wanted Low to be his only attorney. Low then filed an application for admission pro hac vice. The District Court denied his application without comment. A month later, Low filed a second application, which the District Court again denied without explanation. Low's appeal.

Fahle filed a motion to withdraw as counsel and for a show-cause hearing to consider sanctions against Low. Fahle asserted that, by contacting respondent while respondent was represented by Fahle, Low violated Missouri Rule of Professional Conduct 4-4.2 (1993), which prohibits a lawyer "in representing a client" from "communicating about the subject of the representation with a party ... represented by another lawyer" without that lawyer's consent. Low filed a motion to strike Fahle's motion. The District Court granted Fahle's motion to withdraw and granted a continuance so that respondent could find new representation. Respondent retained a local attorney, Karl Dickhaus, for the trial. The District Court then denied Low's motion to strike and, for the first time, explained that it had denied Low's motions for admission pro hac vice primarily because, in a separate case before it, Low had violated Rule 4-4.2 by communicating with a represented party.

The case proceeded to trial, and Dickhaus represented respondent. Low again moved for admission and was again denied. The court also denied Dickhaus's request to have Low at counsel table with him and ordered Low to sit in the audience and to have no contact with Dickhaus during the proceedings. To enforce the court's order, a United States Marshal sat between Low and Dickhaus at trial. Respondent was unable to meet with Low throughout the trial, except for once on the last night. The jury found respondent guilty.

Respondent appealed, and the Eighth Circuit vacated the conviction. The court first held that the District Court erred in interpreting Rule 4-4.2 to prohibit Low's conduct both in this case and in the separate matter on which the District Court based its denials of his admission motions. The District Court's denials of these motions were therefore erroneous and violated respondent's Sixth Amendment right to paid counsel of his choosing. The court then concluded that this Sixth Amendment violation was not subject to harmless-error review.

The Sixth Amendment provides that "in all criminal prosecutions, the accused shall enjoy the right ... to have the Assistance of Counsel for his defence." We have previously held that an element of this right is the right of a defendant who does not require appointed counsel to choose who will represent him. It is hardly necessary to say that, the right to counsel being conceded, a defendant should be afforded a fair opportunity to secure counsel of his own choice. The Government here agrees, as it has previously, that "the Sixth Amendment guarantees a defendant the right to be represented by an otherwise qualified attorney whom that defendant can afford to hire, or who is willing to represent the defendant even though he is without funds." To be sure, the right to counsel of choice is circumscribed in several important respects. But the Government does not dispute the Eighth Circuit's conclusion in this case that the District Court erroneously deprived respondent of his counsel of choice.

The Government contends, however, that the Sixth Amendment violation is not "complete" unless the defendant can show that substitute counsel was ineffective within the meaning of *Strickland v. Washington*—i.e., that substitute counsel's performance was deficient and the defendant was prejudiced by it. In the alternative, the Government contends that the defendant must at least demonstrate that his counsel of choice would have pursued a different strategy that would have created a reasonable probability that the result of the proceedings would have been different—in other words, that he was prejudiced within the meaning of Strickland by the denial of his counsel of choice even if substitute counsel's performance was not constitutionally deficient. To support these propositions, the Government points to our prior cases, which note that the right to counsel has been accorded not for its own sake, but because of the effect it has on the ability of the accused to receive a fair trial. A trial is not unfair and thus the Sixth Amendment is not violated, the Government reasons, unless a defendant has been prejudiced.

The Sixth Amendment right to counsel of choice, commands, not that a trial be fair, but that a particular guarantee of fairness be provided—to wit, that the accused be defended by the counsel he believes to be best. The Constitution guarantees a fair trial through the Due Process Clauses, but it defines the basic elements of a fair trial largely through the several provisions of the Sixth Amendment, including the Counsel Clause. In sum, the right at stake here is the right to counsel of choice, not the right to a fair trial; and that right was violated because the deprivation of counsel was erroneous. No additional showing of prejudice is required to make the violation complete.

The judgment of the Court of Appeals is affirmed, and the case is remanded for further proceedings consistent with this opinion.

It is so ordered.

Justice Alito, with whom the chief justice, Justice Kennedy, and Justice Thomas join, dissenting:

I disagree with the Court's conclusion that a criminal conviction must automatically be reversed whenever a trial court errs in applying its rules regarding pro hac vice admissions and as a result prevents a defendant from being represented at trial by the defendant's first-choice attorney. Instead, a defendant should be required to make at least some showing that the trial court's erroneous ruling adversely affected the quality of assistance that the defendant received. In my view, the majority's contrary holding is based on an incorrect interpretation of the Sixth Amendment and a misapplication of harmless-error principles. I respectfully dissent.

Questions in Review

1. List the protections provided an accused by the Sixth Amendment.
2. Which one of the Sixth Amendment rights was not applied to the states by the Fourteenth Amendment?
3. What does a court consider in determining whether or not the accused received a speedy trial?
4. Explain the *Strickland* rule for establishing the denial of effective assistance of counsel.
5. If a prosecutor uses all of his or her preemptory challenges to exclude women from the jury and the defense objects, what is required of the prosecutor to exclude those jurors?

The Eighth Amendment

8

Excessive bail shall not be required, nor excessive fines imposed, nor cruel and unusual punishments inflicted.

—**U.S. Constitution, Amendment VIII**

The object of punishment is to prevent evil.

—**Horace Mann (1857)**

Introduction

The Eighth Amendment is one of the shortest amendments, with only 16 words, but it is one of the most litigated. In this chapter, the second clause, "excessive fines" and "cruel and unusual punishments," will be addressed first, and the chapter will conclude with a discussion on the excessive bail clause. In *Ingraham v. Wright* (1977), the Court held that the Eighth Amendment was intended to apply to criminal procedures and did not apply to corporal punishment of students by school administrators.

The second clause of the Eighth Amendment is a punishment clause. As noted by Winston Churchill in 1960: "The mood and temper of the public with regard to the treatment of crime and criminals is one of the most unfailing tests of the civilization of any country" (Kittrie, Zenoff, and Eng, 2002, p. xi).

As Justice Mckenna noted in *Weems v. United States* (1910): "What constitutes a cruel and unusual punishment prohibited by the Eighth Amendment has not been exactly defined and no case has heretofore occurred in this court calling for an exhaustive definition." The Supreme Court has not clearly defined the meaning of the words "cruel and unusual punishment." In *Weems*, the Court noted that the term implies something inhuman and barbarous, torture and the like. *In re Kemmler* (p. 447) the Court stated: "Punishments are cruel when they involve torture or a lingering death; but the punishment of death is not cruel, within the meaning of that word as used in the Constitution."

While the state courts are not entirely in accord as to the meaning of the term, the majority of the cases hold that the words employed in the Constitution signify such punishment as would amount to torture, or which is so cruel as to shock the conscience and reason of men; that something inhuman and barbarous is implied.

Amar (1998) and Justice Hugo Black (Dunne, 1977) both considered that the First Amendment and the Eighth Amendment were historically linked to each other because it appeared that the most cruel punishments in England were against the individuals who spoke out against the government. In *Faretta v. California* (1975), Justice Potter Stewart discussed the case of William Prynne.

According to Justice Stewart, in 1632 English Lawyer William Prynne was informed against for his book called *Histrio Mastix*. In the book, Prynne had spoken out against the English government. His trial was, like the other Star Chamber proceedings, perfectly decent and quiet, but the sentence can be described only as monstrous. He was sentenced to be disbarred and deprived of his university degrees; to stand twice in the pillory, and to have one ear cut off each time; to be fined 5,000 British pounds; and to be perpetually imprisoned, without books, pen, ink, or paper.

Amar (1998, pp. 82–83) discussed the sentence heaped on a political dissenter by an English court in the 1600s. The dissenter was to be drawn upon a hurdle to the place of execution, and there be hanged by the neck, and if alive cut down, and his privy members to be cut off, and his bowels to be taken out of his belly and there burned, and if he is still alive, his head is to be cut off.

Death Penalty as Cruel and Unusual

According to Kittrie et al. (2002, p. 778), the death penalty has received more attention in the United States than any other criminal sanction. The primary dispute concerning the death penalty is whether it violates the prohibition against the cruel and unusual punishment clause of the Eighth Amendment. As of 2008, the Supreme Court has upheld the use of the death penalty under certain circumstances. The United States is the only major Western country that still retains the death penalty. Arguments for abolishing capital punishment include the following:

- There is concern for the conviction of the innocent.
- Capital punishment has not shown to be efficacious in the prevention of crime.
- A democratic state does not have the right to take a person's life.
- Capital punishment is contrary to present-day ethics and morality.
- Capital punishment acts to brutalize society rather than prevent crime.
- It is less costly to keep a person confined in prison for life than to execute the person.
- The retention of capital punishment is contrary to the practice and trends of advanced societies.

Is the Death Penalty Cruel and Unusual?

In the 18th century, there was an average of 12 capital crimes in the colonies. Even as early as 1682, however, there was opposition to the death penalty as noted by William Penn in his "Great Act" (Kittrie et al., 2002, p. 779). In 1972, in the landmark case of *Furman v. Georgia* (1972), the U.S. Supreme Court ruled that the death penalty as applied in various states was arbitrary and capricious, and therefore was cruel and unusual punishment. The states, after *Furman*, who adopted new death penalty statutes, used one of two types: one type provided for a mandatory death penalty for the violation of certain crimes, and the other type provided definite guidelines for assessing the aggravating and mitigating circumstances that provided guidance to the sentencing authority in deciding whether to impose the death penalty.

The Supreme Court in *Roberts v. Louisiana* (1977) and *Woodson v. North Carolina* (1976) held that the mandatory death penalty statutes were unconstitutional. In *Gregg v. Georgia* (1976), the Supreme Court for the first time examined the constitutionality of the death penalty and held that it was not unconstitutional. In *Gregg* (p. 154), the Court stated that: "the death penalty is not a form of punishment that may never be imposed, regardless of the circumstances of the offense, regardless of the character of the offender, and regardless of the procedure followed in reaching the decision to impose it."

The Court noted that the Eighth Amendment has not been regarded as a static concept. As Chief Justice Warren stated, in an often-quoted phrase, "the Amendment must draw its meaning from the evolving standards of decency that mark the progress of a maturing society" (*Furman v. Georgia*, 1972, p. 241). Thus, an assessment of contemporary values concerning the infliction of a challenged sanction is relevant to the application of the Eighth Amendment. The Court in *Gregg* noted that the concerns they expressed in *Furman* that the penalty of death not be imposed in an arbitrary or capricious manner can be met by a carefully drafted statute that ensures that the sentencing authority is given adequate information and guidance. As a general proposition, these concerns are best met by a system that provides for a bifurcated proceeding at which the sentencing authority is apprised of the information relevant to the imposition of sentence and provided with standards to guide its use of the information.

Justice Brennan and Justice Marshall dissented in the *Gregg* case. Brennan expressed the following views:

1. The cruel and unusual punishment clause must draw its meaning from evolving standards of decency that marked the progress of a maturing society.
2. The consideration of "evolving standards of decency" required focusing upon the essence of the death penalty itself, and not primarily or

solely upon the procedure under which the determination to inflict the penalty upon a particular person was made.
3. The death penalty served no penal purpose more effectively than a less severe punishment would have.
4. Our civilization and the law had progressed to the point where the court should hold that the punishment of death, for whatever crime and under all circumstances, was cruel and unusual, in violation of the Eighth and Fourteenth Amendments.

Justice Marshall expressed the view that the death penalty was cruel and unusual punishment prohibited by the Eighth and Fourteenth Amendments because it was excessive, being unnecessary to promote the goal of deterrence of crime or to further any legitimate notion of retribution.

In *Roper v. Simmons* (2005), the Court held that the Eighth and Fourteenth Amendments forbid imposition of the death penalty on offenders who were under the age of 18 when their crimes were committed.

Executing the Mentally Retarded

In *Atkins v. Virginia* (2002), the United States Supreme Court held that the execution of mentally retarded persons violates the prohibition against cruel and unusual punishment contained in the Eighth Amendment. However, the Court provided no implementation guidelines, but rather "left to the states the task of developing appropriate ways to enforce the constitutional restriction upon its execution of sentences" (p. 317).

The Court in *Atkins* noted that the Court's death penalty jurisprudence provides two reasons consistent with the legislative consensus that the mentally retarded should be categorically excluded from execution. First, there is a question as to whether either justification that the Court has recognized as a basis for the death penalty applies to mentally retarded offenders. In *Gregg*, the Court identified retribution and deterrence of capital crimes by prospective offenders as the social purposes served by the death penalty. Unless the imposition of the death penalty on a mentally retarded person measurably contributes to one or both of these goals, the Court concluded that it was nothing more than the purposeless and needless imposition of pain and suffering and, hence, an unconstitutional punishment.

With respect to retribution, the Court concluded that the interest in seeing that the offender gets his "just deserts"—the severity of the appropriate punishment—necessarily depends on the culpability of the offender. Since *Gregg*, its jurisprudence has consistently confined the imposition of the death penalty to a narrow category of the most serious crimes. For example, the Court noted that in *Godfrey v. Georgia* (1980), they set aside a death sentence because the petitioner's crimes did not reflect a consciousness materially more depraved than that of any other person guilty of murder. If the culpability of the average murderer is insufficient to justify the most extreme sanction available to the state, the lesser culpability of the mentally retarded offender surely does not merit that form of retribution. Thus, pursuant to their narrowing jurisprudence, which seeks to ensure that only the most deserving of execution are put to death, exclusion for the mentally retarded is appropriate.

With respect to deterrence, the Court noted that it seemed likely that capital punishment can serve as a deterrent only when murder is the result of premeditation and deliberation. Exempting the mentally retarded from that punishment will not affect the cold calculus that precedes the decision of other potential murderers. The theory of deterrence in capital sentencing is predicated upon the notion that the increased severity of the punishment will inhibit criminal actors from carrying out murderous conduct. Yet it was the same cognitive and behavioral impairments that make these defendants less morally culpable—for example, the diminished ability to understand and process information, to learn from experience, to engage in logical reasoning, or to control impulses—that also make it less likely that they can process the information of the possibility of execution as a penalty and, as a result, control their conduct based upon that information. Nor will exempting the mentally retarded from execution lessen the deterrent effect of the death penalty with respect to offenders who are not mentally retarded. Such individuals are unprotected by the exemption and will continue to face the threat of execution. Thus, the Court concluded that executing the mentally retarded will not measurably further the goal of deterrence.

The Court concluded that the reduced capacity of mentally retarded offenders provides a second justification for a categorical rule making such offenders ineligible for the death penalty. The risk that the death penalty will be imposed in spite of factors may call for a less severe penalty.

Can a state forcibly medicate a prisoner to improve the prisoner's mental condition so that he can be executed? Charles Singleton was convicted in an Arkansas state court of capital murder and aggravated robbery. He received a sentence of death for the murder and a sentence of life imprisonment for the robbery. Singleton was considered mentally incapable of understanding the nature of the death penalty and the execution was delayed. In an attempt to improve his mental condition, the State of Arkansas wanted to force him to take medication, i.e., "medicate to execute." He claimed that the state had no right to forcibly medicate him because the administration of mandatory antipsychotic medication to him was no longer in his medical interest and was therefore unconstitutional, given that he could not be executed if he was incompetent. The U.S. Court of Appeal held that the state's interest in carrying out the sentence outweighed Singleton's interest in avoiding medication, and that his due process interests in life and liberty were foreclosed by the lawfully imposed death sentence and the procedures for imposing medication. The court of appeals stated that the Eighth Amendment did not prohibit executing a prisoner who had become incompetent while on death row but who regained competency through appropriate medical care. The U.S. Supreme Court denied his petition for review by the Supreme Court (*Singleton v. Norris*, 2003).

History of Death Penalty's Methods of Execution

The first case involving the method of execution decided by the U.S. Supreme Court was *Wilkerson v. Utah* in 1879. The Supreme Court in that case had no problems holding that death by firing squad did not amount to cruel and unusual punishment. The defendant, William Wilkerson, probably would have disagreed. On the day of the execution, he was led into the jail yard. He declined a blindfold. When the sheriff gave the order to the firing squad and the squad fired, they missed his heart. He was shot in the arm and torso. It took him 27 minutes to bleed to death in front of the astonished witnesses and a helpless doctor (King, 2008).

William Kemmler of Buffalo, New York, was the first person to be executed via electric chair, on August 6, 1890. The Supreme Court stated in the case, *In re Kemmler* (1890): "Punishments are cruel when they involve torture or a lingering death; but the punishment of death is not cruel, within the meaning of that word as used in the Constitution" (p. 436). On August 6, 1890, Kemmler was strapped into the electric chair and 1,000 volts of current passed through his body. Witnesses reported that they could smell burning flesh in the room, but Kemmler was still breathing and saliva dripped from his mouth as he gasped for air. The witnesses and the sheriff fled from the room. He was given a second surge of current and was pronounced dead eight minutes later (King, 2008).

In 1946, Willie Francis, a stuttering 17-year-old, was scheduled for execution at the Angola Prison in Louisiana. After two unsuccessful attempts, because of faulty wiring, he walked away. It was reported that during one attempt he cried out, "I am not dying." He was removed from the chair and returned to prison, but he was scheduled for execution at a later date. In *Louisiana ex rel. Francis v. Resweber* (1947), the Supreme Court held that he could still be executed. The Court stated that his suggestion

> that because he once underwent the psychological strain of preparation for electrocution, now to require him to undergo this preparation again subjects him to a lingering or cruel and unusual punishment. Even the fact that petitioner has already been subjected to a current of electricity does not make his subsequent execution any more cruel in the constitutional sense than any other execution. The cruelty against which the Constitution protects a convicted man is cruelty inherent in the method of punishment, not the necessary

suffering involved in any method employed to extinguish life humanely. The fact that an unforeseeable accident prevented the prompt consummation of the sentence cannot, it seems to us, add an element of cruelty to a subsequent execution. There is no purpose to inflict unnecessary pain nor any unnecessary pain involved in the proposed execution. The situation of the unfortunate victim of this accident is just as though he had suffered the identical amount of mental anguish and physical pain in any other occurrence, such as, for example, a fire in the cell block. We cannot agree that the hardship imposed upon the petitioner rises to that level of hardship denounced as denial of due process because of cruelty.

On May 9, 1947, Willie Francis was executed.

In April 2008, the U.S. Supreme Court ruled in *Baze v. Rees* (2008) that using a three-drug method of execution did not violate the Eighth Amendment's prohibition against cruel and unusual punishment. In *Baze*, a group of inmates on Kentucky death row petitioned a suit asserting that Kentucky's method of execution by lethal injection violated the Eighth Amendment's ban on cruel and unusual punishments. The U.S. Supreme Court granted review.

The Court noted that in 2008, lethal injection was used for capital punishment by the federal government and 36 states, at least 30 of which (including Kentucky) use the same combination of three drugs: the first, sodium thiopental, induces unconsciousness when given in the specified amounts, and thereby ensures that the prisoner does not experience any pain associated with the paralysis and cardiac arrest caused by the second and third drugs, pancuronium bromide and potassium chloride. Among other things, Kentucky's lethal injection protocol is reserved to qualified personnel having at least one year's professional experience of the responsibility for inserting the intravenous (IV) catheters into the prisoner, leaving it to others to mix the drugs and load them into syringes; specifies that the warden and deputy warden will remain in the execution chamber to observe the prisoner and watch for any IV problems while the execution team administers the drugs from another room; and mandates that if, as determined by the warden and deputy, the prisoner is not unconscious within 60 seconds after the sodium thiopental's delivery, a new dose will be given at a secondary injection site before the second and third drugs are administered.

Chief Justice Roberts stated that as have 35 other states and the federal government, Kentucky has chosen to impose capital punishment for certain crimes. And as is true with respect to each of these states and the federal government, Kentucky has altered its method of execution over time to more humane means of carrying out the sentence. That progress has led to the use of lethal injection by every jurisdiction that imposes the death penalty.

Roberts noted that the petitioners in this case—each convicted of double homicide—acknowledge that the lethal injection procedure, if applied as intended, will result in a humane death. They nevertheless contend that the lethal injection protocol is unconstitutional under the Eighth Amendment's ban on "cruel and unusual punishments," because of the risk that the protocol's terms might not be properly followed, resulting in significant pain. They propose an alternative protocol—one that they concede has not been adopted by any state and has never been tried.

Roberts noted that the trial court held extensive hearings and entered detailed findings of fact and conclusions of law. It recognized that there are no methods of legal execution that are satisfactory to those who oppose the death penalty on moral, religious, or societal grounds, but concluded that Kentucky's procedure complies with the constitutional requirements against cruel and unusual punishment. The Supreme Court agreed that petitioners have not carried their burden of showing that the risk of pain from maladministration of a concededly humane lethal injection protocol, and the failure to adopt untried and untested alternatives constitute cruel and unusual punishment. The judgment below was affirmed.

Roberts noted that by the middle of the 19th century, hanging was the nearly universal form of execution in the United States. In 1888, following the recommendation of a commission empaneled by the governor to find the most humane and practical method known to modern science of carrying into effect the sentence of death, New York became the first state to authorize electrocution as a form of capital punishment. By 1915, 11 other states had followed suit, motivated by the well-grounded belief that electrocution is less painful and more humane than hanging.

According to Roberts, electrocution remained the predominant mode of execution for nearly a century, although several other methods, including hanging, firing squad, and lethal gas, were in use at one time. Following the nine-year hiatus in executions that ended with the decision in *Gregg v. Georgia*, (1976), the state legislatures began responding to public calls to reexamine electrocution as a means of ensuring a humane death. In 1977, legislators in Oklahoma, after consulting with the head of the anesthesiology department at the University of Oklahoma College of Medicine, introduced the first bill proposing lethal injection as the state's method of execution. A total of 36 states adopted lethal injection as the exclusive or primary means of implementing the death penalty, making it by far the most prevalent method of execution in the United States. It was also the method used by the federal government.

Roberts noted that 27 of the 36 states that currently provide for capital punishment require execution by lethal injection as the sole method. Nine states allow for lethal injection in addition to an alternative method, such as electrocution. Nebraska is the only state whose statutes specify electrocution as the sole method of execution, but the Nebraska Supreme Court recently struck down that method under the Nebraska constitution (*State v. Mata*, 2008).

Roberts observed that it was undisputed that the states using lethal injection adopted the protocol first developed by Oklahoma without significant independent review of the procedure; it is equally undisputed that, in moving to lethal injection, the states were motivated by a desire to find a more humane alternative to then-existing methods. Of these 36 states, at least 30 (including Kentucky) use the same combination of three drugs in their lethal injection protocols.

Death Penalty for Crimes Other than Murder

Is it cruel and unusual punishment to execute a child rapist?

Kennedy v. Louisiana, 2008 U.S. LEXIS 5262 (2008)

Decision: The Eighth Amendment bars Louisiana from imposing the death penalty for the rape of a child where the crime did not result, and was not intended to result, in the victim's death.

Louisiana is the only state since 1964 that has sentenced an individual to death for child rape, and the petitioner and another man so sentenced are the only individuals now on death row in the United States for nonhomicide offenses.

Justice Anthony Kennedy delivered the opinion of the Court:

Patrick Kennedy, the petitioner here, seeks to set aside his death sentence under the Eighth Amendment. He was charged by the respondent, the State of Louisiana, with the aggravated rape of his then-8-year-old stepdaughter. After a jury trial petitioner was convicted and sentenced to death under a state statute authorizing capital punishment for the rape of a child under 12 years of age. This case presents the question whether the Constitution bars respondent from imposing the death penalty for the rape of a child where the crime did not result, and was not intended to result, in death of the victim. We hold the Eighth Amendment prohibits the death penalty for this offense. The Louisiana statute is unconstitutional.

Petitioner's crime was one that cannot be recounted in these pages in a way sufficient to capture in full the hurt and horror inflicted on his victim or to convey the revulsion society, and the jury that represents it, sought to express by sentencing petitioner to death.

The Eighth Amendment, applicable to the States through the Fourteenth Amendment, provides that excessive bail shall not be required, nor excessive fines imposed, nor cruel and unusual punishments inflicted. The Amendment proscribes all excessive punishments, as well as cruel and unusual punishments that may or may not be excessive. Whether this requirement has been fulfilled is determined not by the standards that prevailed when the Eighth Amendment was adopted in 1791 but by the norms that currently prevail.

The Amendment draws its meaning from the evolving standards of decency that mark the progress of a maturing society. This is because the standard of extreme cruelty is not merely descriptive, but necessarily embodies a moral judgment. The standard itself remains the same, but its applicability must change as the basic mores of society change.

Evolving standards of decency must embrace and express respect for the dignity of the person, and the punishment of criminals must conform to that rule. As we shall discuss, punishment is justified under one or more of three principal rationales: rehabilitation, deterrence, and retribution. It is the last of these, retribution, that most often can contradict the law's own ends. This is of particular concern when the Court interprets the meaning of the Eighth Amendment in capital cases. When the law punishes by death, it risks its own sudden descent into brutality, transgressing the constitutional commitment to decency and restraint.

For these reasons we have explained that capital punishment must be limited to those offenders who commit a narrow category of the most serious crimes and whose extreme culpability makes them the most deserving of execution.

Applying this principle, we held in *Roper* and *Atkins* that the execution of juveniles and mentally retarded persons are punishments violative of the Eighth Amendment because the offender had a diminished personal responsibility for the crime. The Court further has held that the death penalty can be disproportionate to the crime itself where the crime did not result, or was not intended to result, in death of the victim. In *Coker* for instance, the Court held it would be unconstitutional to execute an offender who had raped an adult woman. And in *Enmund v. Florida*, the Court overturned the capital sentence of a defendant who aided and abetted a robbery during which a murder was committed but did not himself kill, attempt to kill, or intend that a killing would take place. On the other hand, in *Tison v. Arizona*, the Court allowed the defendants' death sentences to stand where they did not themselves kill the victims but their involvement in the events leading up to the murders was active, recklessly indifferent, and substantial.

In these cases the Court has been guided by "objective indicia of society's standards, as expressed in legislative enactments and state practice with respect to executions." The inquiry does not end there, however. Consensus is not dispositive. Whether the death penalty is disproportionate to the crime committed depends as well upon the standards elaborated by controlling precedents and by the Court's own understanding and interpretation of the Eighth Amendment's text, history, meaning, and purpose.

Based both on consensus and our own independent judgment, our holding is that a death sentence for one who raped but did not kill a child, and who did not intend to assist another in killing the child, is unconstitutional under the Eighth and Fourteenth Amendments.

The existence of objective indicia of consensus against making a crime punishable by death was a relevant concern in *Roper, Atkins, Coker,* and *Enmund,* and we follow the approach of those cases here. The history of the death penalty for the crime of rape is an instructive beginning point.

In 1925, 18 States, the District of Columbia, and the Federal Government had statutes that authorized the death penalty for the rape of a child or an adult. Between 1930 and 1964, 455 people were executed for those crimes. To our knowledge the last individual executed for the rape of a child was Ronald Wolfe in 1964.

In 1972, *Furman* invalidated most of the state statutes authorizing the death penalty for the crime of rape; and in *Furman*'s aftermath only six States reenacted their capital rape provisions. Three States—Georgia, North Carolina, and Louisiana—did so with respect to all rape offenses. Three States—Florida, Mississippi, and Tennessee—did so with respect only to child rape. All six statutes were later invalidated under state or federal law.

Louisiana reintroduced the death penalty for rape of a child in 1995. Mistake of age is not a defense, so the statute imposes strict liability in this regard. Five States have since followed Louisiana's lead: Georgia, Montana, Oklahoma, South Carolina, and Texas. Four of these States' statutes are more narrow than Louisiana's in that only offenders with a previous rape conviction are death eligible. Georgia's statute makes child rape a capital offense only when aggravating circumstances are present, including but not limited to a prior conviction.

By contrast, 44 States have not made child rape a capital offense. As for federal law, Congress in the Federal Death Penalty Act of 1994 expanded the number of federal crimes for which the death penalty is a permissible sentence, including certain non-homicide offenses; but it did not do the same for child rape or abuse.

The evidence of a national consensus with respect to the death penalty for child rapists, as with respect to juveniles, mentally retarded offenders, and vicarious felony murderers, shows divided opinion but, on balance, an opinion against it. Thirty-seven jurisdictions—36 States plus the Federal Government—have the death penalty. As mentioned above, only six of those jurisdictions authorize the death penalty for rape of a child. Though our review of national consensus is not confined to tallying the number of States with applicable death penalty legislation, it is of significance that, in 45 jurisdictions, petitioner could not be executed for child rape of any kind.

Rape is without doubt deserving of serious punishment; but in terms of moral depravity and of the injury to the person and to the public, it does not compare with murder, which does involve the unjustified taking of human life. Although it may be accompanied by another crime, rape by definition does not include the death of ... another person. The murderer kills; the rapist, if no more than that, does not. We have the abiding conviction that the death penalty is unique in its severity and irrevocability.

The judgment of the Supreme Court of Louisiana upholding the capital sentence is reversed. This case is remanded for further proceedings not inconsistent with this opinion.

It is so ordered.

Photo 8.1 Associate Justice Thurgood Marshall (July 2, 1908–January 24, 1993) was the first African American to serve on the Supreme Court of the United States. Before becoming a judge, he was the attorney who represented the young black students in *Brown v. Topeka Board of Education*, in which case the Supreme Court ruled that segregation in public schools was unconstitutional. Justice Marshall was appointed to the Supreme Court by President Lyndon B. Johnson and served on the Court for 24 years, compiling a liberal record that included strong support for constitutional protection of individual rights, especially the rights of criminal suspects against the government. Marshall dissented from every denial of certiorari in a capital case and from every decision upholding a sentence of death. (Photograph from the Collection of the Supreme Court of the United States.)

Justice Alito, with whom the chief justice, Justice Scalia, and Justice Thomas joined, dissenting:

> The Court today holds that the Eighth Amendment categorically prohibits the imposition of the death penalty for the crime of raping a child. This is so, according to the Court, no matter how young the child, no matter how many times the child is raped, no matter how many children the perpetrator rapes, no matter how sadistic the crime, no matter how much physical or psychological trauma is inflicted, and no matter how heinous the perpetrator's prior criminal record may be. The Court provides two reasons for this sweeping conclusion: First, the Court claims to have identified "a national consensus" that the death penalty is never acceptable for the rape of a child; second, the Court concludes, based on its "independent judgment," that imposing the death penalty for child rape is inconsistent with "the evolving standards of decency that mark the progress of a maturing society." Because neither of these justifications is sound, I respectfully dissent.

Noncapital Punishments

The historic punishments that were cruel and unusual included "burning at the stake, crucifixion, breaking on the wheel" (*In re Kemmler*, 136 U.S. 436, 446 (1890)), quartering, the rack and thumbscrew (see *Chambers v. Florida*, 309 U.S. 227, 237), and in some circumstances even solitary confinement (see *In re Medley* (1890), 134 U.S. 160, 167–68).

Robinson v. California

> Even one day in prison would be a cruel and unusual punishment for the "crime" of having a common cold.
>
> **—Justice Thurgood Marshall, 1962**

In *Robinson v. California* (1962), a California statute made it a criminal offense for a person to "be addicted to the use of narcotics." The trial judge instructed the jury that Robinson could be convicted under a general verdict if the jury agreed that he either was of the "status" or had committed the "act" denounced by the statute. All that the people must show is either that the defendant did use a narcotic in Los Angeles County, or that while in the City of Los Angeles he was addicted to the use of narcotics.

Justice Marshall, in the Court's opinion, stated that the broad power of a state to regulate the narcotic drugs traffic within its borders was not in issue. He noted that there can be no question of the authority of the state in the exercise of its police power to regulate the administration, sale, prescription, and use of dangerous and habit-forming drugs. Marshall concluded that the right to exercise this power is so manifest in the interest of the public health and welfare, it is unnecessary to enter upon a discussion of it beyond saying that it is too firmly established to be successfully called in question. He stated:

> Although there was evidence in the present case that the appellant had used narcotics in Los Angeles, the jury was instructed that they could convict him even if they disbelieved that evidence. The appellant could be convicted, they were told, if they found simply that the appellant's "status" or "chronic condition" was that of being "addicted to the use of narcotics." And it is impossible to know from the jury's verdict that the defendant was not convicted upon precisely such a finding.
>
> We deal with a statute which makes the "status" of narcotic addiction a criminal offense, for which the offender may be prosecuted "at any time before he reforms." California has said that a person can be continuously guilty of this offense, whether or not he has ever used or possessed any narcotics within the State, and whether or not he has been guilty of any antisocial behavior there. (p. 753)
>
> A State might determine that the general health and welfare require that the victims of these and other human afflictions be dealt with by compulsory treatment, involving quarantine, confinement, or sequestration. But, in the light of contemporary human knowledge, a law which made a criminal offense of such a disease would doubtless be universally thought to be an infliction of cruel and unusual punishment in violation of the Eighth and Fourteenth Amendments.
>
> We hold that a state law which imprisons a person thus afflicted as a criminal, even though he has never touched any narcotic drug within the State or been guilty of any irregular behavior there, inflicts a cruel and unusual punishment in violation of the Fourteenth Amendment. To be sure, imprisonment for ninety days is not, in the abstract, a punishment which is either cruel or unusual. But the question cannot be considered in the abstract. Even one day in prison would be a cruel and unusual punishment for the "crime" of having a common cold.

Under the principles set forth in the *Robinson* case, it would be cruel and unusual to punish a person for being an alcoholic. Is it cruel and unusual to punish an alcoholic for being drunk in public? In *Powell v. Texas* (1968), Powell was convicted, not for being a chronic alcoholic, but for being in public while drunk on a particular occasion, and thus, as distinguished from *Robinson v. California*, was not being punished for a mere status. Powell testified at his trial in an Austin, Texas, state court concerning the history of his drinking problem. He reviewed his many arrests for drunkenness; testified that he was unable to stop drinking; stated that when he was intoxicated he had no control over his actions and could not remember them later, but that he did not become violent; and admitted that he did not remember his arrest on the occasion for which he was being tried. On cross-examination, Powell admitted that he had had one drink on the morning of the trial and had been able to discontinue drinking. Justice Marshall, who also wrote the majority opinion in Powell, stated:

> On its face the present case does not fall within that holding, since Powell was convicted, not for being a chronic alcoholic, but for being in public while drunk on a particular occasion. The State of Texas thus has not sought to punish a mere status, as California did in *Robinson*; nor has it attempted to regulate his behavior in the privacy of his own home. Rather, it has imposed upon Powell a criminal sanction for public behavior which may create substantial health and safety hazards, both for appellant and for members of the general public, and which offends the moral and esthetic sensibilities of a large segment of the community. This seems a far cry from convicting one for being an addict, being a chronic alcoholic, being "mentally ill, or a leper" (Justice Thurgood Marshall in *Robinson v. California*).

Other Cruel and Unusual Punishments

In *Trop v. Dulles* (1958), a native-born American was declared to have lost his U.S. citizenship and become stateless by reason of his conviction by court-martial for wartime desertion. In 1944 Trop was a private in the United States Army, serving in French Morocco. On May 22, he escaped from a stockade at Casablanca, where he had been confined following a previous breach of discipline. The next day Trop and a companion were walking along a road toward Rabat, in the general direction back to Casablanca, when an Army truck approached and stopped. A witness testified that Trop boarded the truck willingly and that no words were spoken. In Rabat Trop was turned over to military police, which ended his "desertion." He had been gone less than a day and had willingly surrendered to an officer on an Army vehicle while he was walking back toward his base.

Trop testified that at the time he and his companion were picked up by the Army truck, "We had decided to return to the stockade. The going was tough. We had no money to speak of, and at the time we were on foot and we were getting cold and hungry." A general court-martial convicted Trop of desertion and sentenced him to three years at hard labor, forfeiture of all pay and allowances, and a dishonorable discharge.

In 1952 Trop applied for a passport. His application was denied on the ground that under the provisions of Section 401(g) of the Nationality Act of 1940, as amended, he had lost his citizenship by reason of his conviction and dishonorable discharge for wartime desertion. The government argues that the sanction of denationalization imposed by Section 401(g) is not a penalty because deportation has not been so considered by this Court. The Court noted that while deportation is undoubtedly a harsh sanction that has a severe penal effect, the Court has in the past sustained deportation as an exercise of the sovereign's power to determine the conditions upon which an alien may reside in this country.

The Court held that Section 401(g) was a penal law, and the Court must face the question whether the Constitution permited Congress to take away citizenship as a punishment for crime. If it is assumed that the power of Congress extends to divestment of citizenship, the problem still remains as to this statute whether denationalization is a cruel and unusual punishment within the meaning of the Eighth Amendment. The Court noted that because wartime desertion is punishable by death, there can be no argument that the penalty of denationalization is excessive in relation to the gravity of the crime. The Court stated that the question before the Court was whether the penalty subjected the individual to a fate forbidden by the principle of civilized treatment guaranteed by the Eighth Amendment.

Justice Warren stated in the Court's opinion:

> The exact scope of the constitutional phrase "cruel and unusual" has not been detailed by this Court. But the basic policy reflected in these words is firmly established in the Anglo-American tradition of criminal justice. The phrase in our Constitution was taken directly from the English Declaration of Rights of 1688, and the principle it represents can be traced back to the Magna Carta. The basic concept underlying the Eighth Amendment is nothing less than the dignity of man. While the State has the power to punish, the Amendment stands to assure that this power be exercised within the limits of civilized standards. Fines, imprisonment and even execution may be imposed depending upon the enormity of the crime, but any technique outside the bounds of these traditional penalties is constitutionally suspect. This Court has had little occasion to give precise content to the Eighth Amendment, and, in an enlightened democracy such as ours, this is not surprising. But when the Court was confronted with a punishment of 12 years in irons at hard and painful labor imposed for the crime of falsifying public records, it did not hesitate to declare that the penalty was cruel in its excessiveness and unusual in its character. *Weems v. United States*, 217 U.S. 349. The Court recognized in that case that the words of the Amendment are not precise, and that their scope is not static. The Amendment must draw its meaning from the evolving standards of decency that mark the progress of a maturing society.
>
> The civilized nations of the world are in virtual unanimity that statelessness is not to be imposed as punishment for crime. It is true that several countries prescribe expatriation in the event that their nationals engage in conduct in derogation of native allegiance. Even statutes of this sort are generally applicable primarily to naturalized citizens. But use of denationalization as punishment for crime is an entirely different matter. The United Nations' survey of the nationality laws of 84 nations of the world reveals that only two countries, the Philippines and Turkey, impose denationalization as a penalty for desertion. In this country the Eighth Amendment forbids this to be done.

Jail and Prison Conditions as Cruel and Unusual

Prison Conditions and Treatment

In *Wilson v. Seiter* (1991), Pearly Wilson complained about the conditions of his confinement and alleged that the conditions violated the cruel and unusual prohibitions in the Eighth Amendment. The Court held that after incarceration, only the unnecessary and wanton infliction of pain constitutes cruel and unusual punishment forbidden by the Eighth Amendment. To be cruel and unusual punishment, conduct that does not purport to be punishment at all must involve more than ordinary lack of due care for the prisoner's interests or safety. It is obduracy and wantonness, not inadvertence or error in good faith, that characterize the conduct prohibited by the cruel and unusual punishments clause, whether that conduct occurs in connection with establishing conditions of confinement, supplying medical needs, or restoring official control over a tumultuous cell block.

The Court noted that the "wantonness" of conduct does not depend upon its effect upon a prisoner. Assuming the conduct is harmful enough to satisfy the objective component of an Eighth Amendment claim, whether it can be characterized as wanton depends upon the constraints facing the official. From that standpoint, there is no significant distinction between claims alleging inadequate medical care and those alleging inadequate "conditions of confinement." Indeed, the medical care a prisoner receives is just as much a "condition" of his confinement as the food he is fed, the clothes he is issued, the temperature he is subjected to in his cell, and the protection he is afforded against other inmates.

The Court also concluded that some conditions of confinement may establish an Eighth Amendment violation in combination when each would not do so alone, but only when they have a mutually enforcing effect that produces the deprivation of a single, identifiable human need such as food, warmth, or exercise.

In *Hudson v. McMillian* (1992), Keith Hudson, a prisoner in a Louisiana state penitentiary, sued three corrections security officers under 42 USCS 1983 in the United States District Court for the Middle District of Louisiana. Claiming that the officers had violated the cruel and unusual punishment clause of the federal Constitution's Eighth Amendment, Hudson alleged that one officer, after arguing with him, punched him in the mouth, eyes, chest, and stomach while another officer held him in place and kicked and punched him from behind, and a third officer, who was the supervisor on duty, watched the beating but merely told the other officers "not to have too much fun." As a result of the beating, Hudson suffered minor bruises and swelling of his face, mouth, and lip, and the blows loosened his teeth and cracked his partial dental plate. He was awarded $800 on his claims and the state appealed. The U.S. Court of Appeals for the Fifth Circuit reversed on the grounds that prisoners who allege use of excessive force in violation of the Eighth Amendment must prove significant injury, and although the officers' use of force was objectively unreasonable and clearly excessive and occasioned unnecessary and wanton infliction of pain, Hudson could not prevail on his claim because his injuries were minor and required no medical attention.

The U.S. Supreme Court disagreed with the Court of Appeals and stated that when prison officials maliciously and sadistically use force to cause harm, contemporary standards of decency always are violated. This is true whether or not significant injury is evident. Otherwise, the Eighth Amendment would permit any physical punishment, no matter how diabolic or inhuman, inflicting less than some arbitrary quantity of injury. Such a result would have been as unacceptable to the drafters of the Eighth Amendment as it is today.

In *Estelle v. Gamble* (1976), Gamble, a prisoner in the Texas prison system, injured his back while performing a prison work assignment. He was placed on various pain relievers but continued to experience pain and refused to return to work because of the pain. After experiencing chest pains he was placed on medication for treatment of irregular cardiac rhythm. Soon thereafter he filed a complaint under 42 USCS § 1983, alleging the doctors and prison personnel subjected him to cruel and unusual punishment in violation of the Eighth Amendment. Gamble based his complaint solely on the lack of diagnosis and inadequate treatment of his back injury.

The Court noted that the government had an obligation to provide medical care for those whom it is punishing by incarceration. An inmate must rely on prison authorities to treat his medical needs; if the authorities fail to do so, those needs will not be met. In the worst cases, such a failure may actually produce physical "torture or a lingering death." The Court noted that the infliction of such unnecessary suffering is inconsistent with contemporary standards of decency as manifested in modern legislation codifying the common law view that it is but just that the public be required to care for the prisoner, who cannot by reason of the deprivation of his liberty, care for himself.

Justice Marshall in the Court opinion stated:

We therefore conclude that deliberate indifference to serious medical needs of prisoners constitutes the unnecessary and wanton infliction of pain. This is true whether the indifference is manifested by prison doctors in their response to the prisoner's needs or by prison guards in intentionally denying or delaying access to medical care or intentionally interfering with the treatment once prescribed. Regardless of how evidenced, deliberate indifference to a prisoner's serious illness or injury states a cause of action under § 1983.

Jails

In *Stevenson v. Anderson* (2001), Billy Stevenson claimed that the jail officials denied him safe and sanitary showers and medical care for serious health impairments caused by the unsafe and unsanitary showers. The district court held that jail officials must provide humane conditions of confinement, ensuring that inmates receive adequate food, clothing, shelter, medical care, and hygiene. The guarantee of "humane conditions of confinement" is found in the due process clause of the Fourteenth Amendment for pretrial detainees and in the cruel and unusual punishment clause of the Eighth Amendment for convicted prisoners. For pretrial detainees, the proper legal standard depends on whether a claim challenges a "jail condition" or whether it alleges an "episodic act or omission." While "jail condition" cases are analyzed under the reasonable relationship test, "episodic" cases are analyzed under the deliberate indifference standard. For convicted prisoners, all "humane conditions of confinement" claims are analyzed under the deliberate indifference standard.

The district court noted that the due process clause forbids punishment of a person held in custody awaiting trial but not yet adjudged guilty of any crime. In determining whether a jail condition amounts to unconstitutional punishment of a pretrial detainee, a court must determine whether the condition is reasonably related to a legitimate, nonpunitive governmental objective. Where a condition is arbitrary or purposeless, a court may permissibly infer that the purpose of the governmental action is unconstitutional punishment.

Court Sentences as Cruel and Unusual

In *Weems v. United States* (1910), the Supreme Court noted that what constituted a cruel and unusual punishment has not been exactly decided. And the possibility that imprisonment in a state prison for a long term of years might be so disproportionate to the offense as to constitute a cruel and unusual punishment has been conceded. Certain tyrannical acts of the English monarchs have also been used to illustrate the meaning of the clause and the extent of its prohibition.

In *Lockyer v. Andrade* (2003), Leandro Andrade was convicted by a jury in a California state court of stealing approximately $150 worth of videotapes from two different stores. The jury found that Andrade had three prior convictions that qualified as serious or violent felonies under the state's "three strikes" law, under which law any felony could constitute the third strike subjecting an accused to a prison term of 25 years to life. Because each of the accused's petty theft convictions triggered a separate application of the three strikes law, the trial judge sentenced the accused to two consecutive prison terms of 25 years to life. Andrade appealed, contending that the sentence violated the Eighth Amendment prohibition against cruel and unusual punishment.

Photo 8.2 Justice John Paul Stevens (1920–) is currently the most senior Associate Justice of the Supreme Court of the United States. He joined the Court in 1975 and is the oldest and longest serving incumbent member of the Court. He was appointed to the court by President Ford and is considered to be on the liberal side of the court. He is the only current Justice to have served on the Burger Court. (Photograph by Steve Petteway, Collection of the Supreme Court of the United States.)

Justice Sandra O'Connor stated in the Court's opinion:

These two incidents were not Andrade's first or only encounters with law enforcement. According to the state probation officer's presentence report, Andrade has been in and out of state and federal prison since 1982. In January 1982, he was convicted of a misdemeanor theft offense and was sentenced to 6 days in jail with 12 months' probation. Andrade was arrested again in

November 1982 for multiple counts of first-degree residential burglary. He pleaded guilty to at least three of those counts, and in April of the following year he was sentenced to 120 months in prison. In 1988, Andrade was convicted in federal court of "transportation of marijuana," and was sentenced to eight years in federal prison. In 1990, he was convicted in state court for a misdemeanor petty theft offense and was ordered to serve 180 days in jail. In September 1990, Andrade was convicted again in federal court for the same felony of "transportation of marijuana," and was sentenced to 2,191 days in federal prison. And in 1991, Andrade was arrested for a state parole violation—escape from federal prison. He was paroled from the state penitentiary system in 1993.

A state probation officer interviewed Andrade after his arrest in this case. The presentence report noted: "The defendant admitted committing the offense. The defendant further stated he went into the K-Mart Store to steal videos. He took four of them to sell so he could buy heroin. He has been a heroin addict since 1977. He says when he gets out of jail or prison he always does something stupid. He admits his addiction controls his life and he steals for his habit."

Andrade claims that his sentence is so grossly disproportionate that it violates the Eighth Amendment. Andrade's position, however, is that our precedents in this area have not been a model of clarity. Indeed, in determining whether a particular sentence for a term of years can violate the Eighth Amendment, we have not established a clear or consistent path for courts to follow.

The gross disproportionality principle reserves a constitutional violation for only the extraordinary case. In applying this principle, it was not an unreasonable application of our clearly established law for the California Court of Appeal to affirm Andrade's sentence of two consecutive terms of 25 years to life in prison.

Bail

The Supreme Court has never decided whether a state was required to have a bail system. It has decided, however, the if a state has a bail system, the bail cannot be excessive or imposed for improper reasons.

Excessive Bail

Bail set at a figure higher than an amount reasonably calculated to assure the presence of an accused is "excessive" under the Eighth Amendment.

—Chief Justice Vinson in *Stack v. Boyle* (1951)

In *Stack v. Boyle* (1951), 12 defendants were arrested on charges of conspiring to violate the Smith Act, and their bail was fixed initially in amounts varying from $2,500 to $100,000. Subsequently, the district court fixed bail pending trial in the uniform amount of $50,000 for each of them. They moved to reduce bail, claiming that it was "excessive" under the Eighth Amendment, and filed supporting statements of fact that were not disputed. The only evidence offered by the government was a certified record showing that four other persons previously convicted under the Smith Act in another district had forfeited bail, and there was no evidence relating them to petitioners.[1]

The Court noted that the right of a defendant to be released before trial is conditioned upon the accused's giving adequate assurance that he will stand trial and submit to sentence if found guilty. And like the ancient practice of securing the oaths of responsible persons to stand as sureties for the accused, the modern practice of requiring a bail bond or the deposit of a sum of money subject to forfeiture serves as additional assurance of the presence of an accused. The Court stated that: "Bail set at a figure higher than an amount reasonably calculated to fulfill this purpose is 'excessive' under the Eighth Amendment."

The Court noted that the function of bail is limited, and that the fixing of bail for any individual defendant must be based upon standards relevant to the purpose of assuring the presence of that defendant. The Court stated:

> The Government asks the courts to depart from the norm by assuming, without the introduction of evidence, that each petitioner is a pawn in a conspiracy and will, in obedience to a superior, flee the jurisdiction. To infer from the fact of indictment alone a need for bail in an unusually high amount is an arbitrary act. Such conduct would inject into our own system of government the very principles of totalitarianism which Congress was seeking to guard against in passing the statute under which petitioners have been indicted.

Until the passage of the Bail Reform Act of 1984, discussed in the next section, the only authority that a judge had to keep an accused in jail awaiting trial was to ensure the accused's presence at trial and that any bail in excess of that amount was excessive.

Protective Custody Awaiting Trial

In *United States v. Salerno* (1987), the Supreme Court reviewed the constitutionality of the Bail Reform Act of 1984, which allows a federal court to detain an arrestee pending trial if the government demonstrates by clear and convincing evidence after an adversary hearing that no release conditions "will reasonably assure ... the safety of any other person and the community." In *Salerno*, the U.S. Court of Appeals for the Second Circuit struck down this provision of the act as unconstitutional, because, in that court's words, this type of pretrial detention violates "substantive due process." The

Supreme Court reversed and held that the act fully comports with constitutional requirements.

The Court noted that the act required a judicial officer to determine whether an arrestee shall be detained. Section 3142(e) provided that "if, after a hearing pursuant to the provisions of subsection (f), the judicial officer finds that no condition or combination of conditions will reasonably assure the appearance of the person as required and the safety of any other person and the community, he shall order the detention of the person prior to trial." Section 3142(f) provided the arrestee with a number of procedural safeguards. He may request the presence of counsel at the detention hearing, he may testify and present witnesses in his behalf, as well as proffer evidence, and he may cross-examine other witnesses appearing at the hearing. If the judicial officer finds that no conditions of pretrial release can reasonably ensure the safety of other persons and the community, he must state his findings of fact in writing, § 3142(i), and support his conclusion with "clear and convincing evidence," § 3142(f).

The Court also noted that the judicial officer was not given unbridled discretion in making the detention determination. Congress has specified the considerations relevant to that decision. These factors include the nature and seriousness of the charges, the substantiality of the government's evidence against the arrestee, the arrestee's background and characteristics, and the nature and seriousness of the danger posed by the suspect's release. Should a judicial officer order detention, the detainee is entitled to expedited appellate review of the detention order.

The Court in upholding the constitutionality of the act stated:

> In our society liberty is the norm, and detention prior to trial or without trial is the carefully limited exception. We hold that the provisions for pretrial detention in the Bail Reform Act of 1984 fall within that carefully limited exception. The Act authorizes the detention prior to trial of arrestees charged with serious felonies who are found after an adversary hearing to pose a threat to the safety of individuals or to the community which no condition of release can dispel. The numerous procedural safeguards detailed above must attend this adversary hearing. We are unwilling to say that this congressional determination, based as it is upon that primary concern of every government—a concern for the safety and indeed the lives of its citizens—on its face violates either the Due Process Clause of the Fifth Amendment or the Excessive Bail Clause of the Eighth Amendment.

Justice Marshall in a bitter dissent in which Justice Brennan joined noted:

> This case brings before the Court for the first time a statute in which Congress declares that a person innocent of any crime may be jailed indefinitely, pending the trial of allegations which are legally presumed to be untrue, if the

Government shows to the satisfaction of a judge that the accused is likely to commit crimes, unrelated to the pending charges, at any time in the future. Such statutes, consistent with the usages of tyranny and the excesses of what bitter experience teaches us to call the police state, have long been thought incompatible with the fundamental human rights protected by our Constitution. Today a majority of this Court holds otherwise. Its decision disregards basic principles of justice established centuries ago and enshrined beyond the reach of governmental interference in the Bill of Rights.

Under the provisions of the federal Bail Reform Act of 1984, a federal court may order that an individual be kept in protective custody while awaiting a federal criminal trial. Note: The burden is on the prosecution to establish by clear and convincing evidence the necessity for the custody. Also note that many states have passed similar bail reform acts based on the federal act, and in those states an accused may be kept in protective custody pursuant to a state statute.

Capstone Case: *Overton v. Bazzetta,* 539 U.S. 126 (2003)

Opinion by Justice Kennedy:

The population of Michigan's prisons increased in the early 1990's. More inmates brought more visitors, straining the resources available for prison supervision and control. In particular, prison officials found it more difficult to maintain order during visitation and to prevent smuggling or trafficking in drugs. Special problems were encountered with the increase in visits by children, who are at risk of seeing or hearing harmful conduct during visits and must be supervised with special care in prison visitation facilities.

The incidence of substance abuse in the State's prisons also increased in this period. Drug and alcohol abuse by prisoners is unlawful and a direct threat to legitimate objectives of the corrections system, including rehabilitation, the maintenance of basic order, and the prevention of violence in the prisons.

In response to these concerns, the Michigan Department of Corrections (MDOC or Department) revised its prison visitation policies in 1995, promulgating the regulations here at issue. One aspect of the Department's approach was to limit the visitors a prisoner is eligible to receive, in order to decrease the total number of visitors.

Under the MDOC's regulations, an inmate may receive visits only from individuals placed on an approved visitor list, except that qualified members of the clergy and attorneys on official business may visit without being listed. The list may include an unlimited number of members of the prisoner's immediate family and ten other individuals the prisoner designates, subject to some restrictions. Minors under the age of 18 may not be placed on the list unless they are the children, stepchildren, grandchildren, or siblings of the inmate.

If an inmate's parental rights have been terminated, the child may not be a visitor. A child authorized to visit must be accompanied by an adult who is an immediate family member of the child or of the inmate or who is the legal guardian of the child. An inmate may not place a former prisoner on the visitor list unless the former prisoner is a member of the inmate's immediate family and the warden has given prior approval.

The Department's revised policy also sought to control the widespread use of drugs and alcohol among prisoners. Prisoners who have committed multiple substance-abuse violations are not permitted to receive any visitors except attorneys and members of the clergy. An inmate subject to this restriction may apply for reinstatement of visitation privileges after two years. Reinstatement is within the warden's discretion.

The respondents are prisoners, their friends, and their family members. They brought this action alleging that the restrictions upon visitation violate the First, Eighth, and Fourteenth Amendments.

Inmates who are classified as the highest security risks, as determined by the MDOC, are limited to noncontact visitation. This case does not involve a challenge to the method for making that determination. By contrast to contact visitation, during which inmates are allowed limited physical contact with their visitors in a large visitation room, inmates restricted to noncontact visits must communicate with their visitors through a glass panel, the inmate and the visitor being on opposite sides of a booth. In some facilities the booths are located in or at one side of the same room used for contact visits. The case before us concerns the regulations as they pertain to noncontact visits.

The United States District Court for the Eastern District of Michigan agreed with the prisoners that the regulations pertaining to noncontact visits were invalid. The Court of Appeals agreed with the District Court that the restrictions on noncontact visits are invalid. This was error. We first consider the contention, accepted by the Court of Appeals, that the regulations infringe a constitutional right of association.

We have said that the Constitution protects "certain kinds of highly personal relationships." And outside the prison context, there is some discussion in our cases of a right to maintain certain familial relationships, including association among members of an immediate family and association between grandchildren and grandparents.

This is not an appropriate case for further elaboration of those matters. The very object of imprisonment is confinement. Many of the liberties and privileges enjoyed by other citizens must be surrendered by the prisoner. An inmate does not retain rights inconsistent with proper incarceration. And, as our cases have established, freedom of association is among the rights least compatible with incarceration. Some curtailment of that freedom must be expected in the prison context.

We do not hold, and we do not imply, that any right to intimate association is altogether terminated by incarceration or is always irrelevant to claims made by prisoners. We need not attempt to explore or define the asserted right of association at any length or determine the extent to which it survives incarceration because the challenged regulations bear a rational relation to legitimate penological interests. This suffices to sustain the regulation in question. Prison administrators had reasonably exercised their judgment as to the appropriate means of furthering penological goals, and that was the controlling rationale for our decision. We must accord substantial deference to the professional judgment of prison administrators, who bear a significant responsibility for defining the legitimate goals of a corrections system and for determining the most appropriate means to accomplish them. The burden, moreover, is not on the State to prove the validity of prison regulations but on the prisoner to disprove it. Respondents have failed to do so here.

In *Turner* we held that four factors are relevant in deciding whether a prison regulation affecting a constitutional right that survives incarceration withstands constitutional challenge: whether the regulation has a "valid, rational connection" to a legitimate governmental interest; whether alternative means are open to inmates to exercise the asserted right; what impact an accommodation of the right would have on guards and inmates and prison resources; and whether there are "ready alternatives" to the regulation.

Turning to the restrictions on visitation by children, we conclude that the regulations bear a rational relation to MDOC's valid interests in maintaining internal security and protecting child visitors from exposure to sexual or other misconduct or from accidental injury. The regulations promote internal security, perhaps the most legitimate of penological goals by reducing the total number of visitors and by limiting the disruption caused by children in particular. Protecting children from harm is also a legitimate goal. The logical connection between this interest and the regulations is demonstrated by trial testimony that reducing the number of children allows guards to supervise them better to ensure their safety and to minimize the disruptions they cause within the visiting areas.

As for the regulation requiring children to be accompanied by a family member or legal guardian, it is reasonable to ensure that the visiting child is accompanied and supervised by those adults charged with protecting the child's best interests. Respondents argue that excluding minor nieces and nephews and children as to whom parental rights have been terminated bears no rational relationship to these penological interests. We reject this contention, and in all events it would not suffice to invalidate the regulations as to all noncontact visits. To reduce the number of child visitors, a line must be drawn, and the categories set out by these regulations are reasonable. Visits are allowed between an inmate and those children closest to him or her—children, grandchildren, and siblings. The prohibition on visitation by children as to whom the inmate no longer has parental rights is simply a recognition by prison administrators of a status determination made in other official proceedings.

MDOC's regulation prohibiting visitation by former inmates bears a self-evident connection to the State's interest in maintaining prison security and preventing future crimes. We have recognized that "communication with other felons is a potential spur to criminal behavior."

Finally, the restriction on visitation for inmates with two substance-abuse violations, a bar which may be removed after two years, serves the legitimate goal of deterring the use of drugs and alcohol within the prisons. Drug smuggling and drug use in prison are intractable problems. Withdrawing visitation privileges is a proper and even necessary management technique to induce compliance with the rules of inmate behavior, especially for high-security prisoners who have few other privileges to lose. In this regard we note that numerous other States have implemented similar restrictions on visitation privileges to control and deter substance-abuse violations.

Respondents argue that the regulation bears no rational connection to preventing substance abuse because it has been invoked in certain instances where the infractions were, in respondents' view, minor. Even if we were inclined, though, to substitute our judgment for the conclusions of prison officials concerning the infractions reached by the regulations, the individual cases respondents cite are not sufficient to strike down the regulations as to all noncontact visits. Respondents also contest the 2-year bar and note that reinstatement of visitation is not automatic even at the end of two years. We agree the restriction is severe. And if faced with evidence that MDOC's regulation is treated as a *de facto* permanent ban on all visitations for certain inmates, we might reach a different conclusion in a challenge to a particular application of the regulation. Those issues are not presented in this case, which challenges the validity of the restriction on noncontact visits in all instances.

Having determined that each of the challenged regulations bears a rational relationship to a legitimate penological interest, we consider whether inmates have alternative means of exercising the constitutional right they seek to assert. Were it shown that no alternative means of communication existed, though it would not be conclusive, it would be some evidence that the regulations were unreasonable. That showing, however, cannot be made. Respondents here do have alternative means of associating with those prohibited from visiting. As was the case in *Pell*, inmates can communicate with those who may not visit by sending messages through those who are allowed to visit. Although this option is not available to inmates barred all visitation after two violations, they and other inmates may communicate with persons outside the prison by letter and telephone. Respondents protest that letter-writing is inadequate for illiterate inmates and for communications with young children. They say, too, that phone calls are brief and expensive, so that these alternatives are not sufficient. Alternatives to visitation need not be ideal, however; they need only be available. Here, the alternatives are of sufficient utility that they give some support to the regulations, particularly in a context where visitation is limited, not completely withdrawn.

Another relevant consideration is the impact that accommodation of the asserted associational right would have on guards, other inmates, the allocation of prison resources, and the safety of visitors. Accommodating respondents' demands would cause a significant reallocation of the prison system's financial resources and would impair the ability of corrections officers to protect all who are inside a prison's walls. When such consequences are present, we are "particularly deferential" to prison administrators' regulatory judgments.

The judgment of the Court of Appeals is reversed.

Questions in Review

1. Under what circumstances has the Supreme Court determined that a death penalty was not cruel and unusual?
2. What is the traditional purpose of bail?
3. What is required before the court will order an accused held in protective custody?
4. What is the test to determine if the failure to provide reasonable medical care to a prisoner is actionable under the Eighth Amendment?
5. Under what circumstances is a court sentence considered cruel and unusual?

Endnote

1. The Smith Act was passed by the U.S. Congress as the Alien Registration Act of 1940. The act made it an offense to advocate or belong to a group that advocated the violent overthrow of the government. The act was designed to punish individuals for belonging to the Communist Party.

The First Amendment 9

Congress shall make no law respecting an establishment of religion, or prohibiting the free exercise thereof; or abridging the freedom of speech, or of the press; or the right of the people peaceably to assemble, and to petition the Government for a redress of grievances.

—First Amendment, U.S. Constitution

Introduction

Supreme Court Justice Byron R. White in *Broadrick v. Oklahoma* (1973) stated:

It has long been recognized that the First Amendment needs breathing space and that statutes attempting to restrict or burden the exercise of First Amendment rights must be narrowly drawn and represent a considered legislative judgment that a particular mode of expression has to give way to other compelling needs of society. As a corollary, the Court has altered its traditional rules of standing to permit—in the First Amendment area—attacks on overly broad statutes with no requirement that the person making the attack demonstrate that his own conduct could not be regulated by a statute drawn with the requisite narrow specificity. Litigants, therefore, are permitted to challenge a statute not because their own rights of free expression are violated, but because of a judicial prediction or assumption that the statute's very existence may cause others not before the court to refrain from constitutionally protected speech or expression.

Supreme Court Justice Anthony M. Kennedy in *United States et al. v. Playboy Entertainment Group, Inc.* stated:

The Constitution exists precisely so that opinions and judgments, including esthetic and moral judgments about art and literature, can be formed, tested, and expressed. What the Constitution says is that these judgments are for the individual to make, not for the Government to decree, even with the mandate or approval of a majority. Technology expands the capacity to choose; and it denies the potential of this revolution if we assume the Government is best positioned to make these choices for us.

The Supreme Court in *Near v. Minnesota* (1931) held that the First Amendment restrictions were within the liberty safeguarded by the due process clause of U.S. Constituion Amendment 14 from invasion by state action. The Court stated that it is impossible to conclude that this essential personal liberty of the citizen was left unprotected by the general guarantee of fundamental rights of person and property. In maintaining this guarantee, the authority of the state to enact laws to promote the health, safety, morals, and general welfare of its people is necessarily admitted. And the limits of this sovereign power must always be determined with appropriate regard to the particular subject of its exercise. The Court concluded in the *Near* case that the liberty of speech, and of the press, is also not an absolute right, and the state may punish its abuse.

Religious Issues

The U.S. Supreme Court has held that government action must have a secular purpose. Although a legislature's stated reasons will generally get deference, the secular purpose required has to be genuine, not a sham, and not merely secondary to a religious objective. As the Court noted in *McCreary County v. ACLU* (2007), the touchstone for the Court's analysis of whether government action has a "secular legislative purpose" is the principle that the First Amendment mandates governmental neutrality between religion and religion, and between religion and nonreligion. When the government acts with the ostensible and predominant purpose of advancing religion, it violates that central establishment clause value of official religious neutrality, there being no neutrality when the government's ostensible object is to take sides. The "purpose" requirement aims at preventing government from abandoning neutrality and acting with the intent of promoting a particular point of view in religious matters. Manifesting a purpose to favor one faith over another, or adherence to religion generally, clashes with the understanding, reached after decades of religious war, that liberty and social stability demand a religious tolerance that respects the religious views of all citizens. By showing a purpose to favor religion, the government sends the message to nonadherents that they are outsiders, not full members of the political community, and an accompanying message to adherents that they are insiders, favored members. Further, the purpose apparent from government action can have an impact more significant than the result expressly decreed.

In the *McCreary County* case, the Court examined the issue of whether the displaying of the Ten Commandants by two counties on the courthouse lawn violated the establishment clause of the first amendment. The Court stated:

> The United States Supreme Court has recognized that the Ten Commandments are an instrument of religion. The question is what viewers may fairly understand to be the purpose of the display. That inquiry, of necessity, turns upon the context in which the contested object appears.

The First Amendment has not one but two clauses tied to religion, the second forbidding any prohibition on the "the free exercise thereof," and sometimes, the two clauses compete. At other times, limits on governmental action that might make sense as a way to avoid establishment could arguably limit freedom of speech when the speaking is done under government auspices. Given the variety of interpretative problems, the principle of neutrality provides a good sense of direction: the government may not favor one religion over another, or religion over irreligion, religious choice being the prerogative of individuals under the Free Exercise Clause.

In a case decided two years earlier, *Van Orden v. Perry* (2005), the Supreme Court upheld the display of the Ten Commandants by the State of Texas. *Van Orden* concerned the 22 acres surrounding the Texas State Capitol, which contained 17 monuments and 21 historical markers commemorating the people, ideals, and events that compose Texan identity. The Court held that the test was not useful in dealing with the sort of passive monument that had been erected on the Texas Capitol grounds. Instead, the Court's analysis was driven both by the nature of the monument and by history. The Court held that the placement of the Ten Commandments monument on the Texas State Capitol grounds was a far more passive use of those texts than the mandatory placement of the text in elementary school classrooms. Indeed, the citizen had apparently walked by the monument for a number of years before bringing this lawsuit. The monument was also quite different from the prayers that had been prohibited in public schools. Texas had treated her Capitol grounds monuments as representing the several strands in the state's political and legal history. The inclusion of the Ten Commandments monument in this group had a dual significance, partaking of both religion and government. The Court concluded that it could not say that Texas's display of the monument violated the establishment clause of the First Amendment.

In *Gonzales v. O Centro Espirita Beneficente Uniao do Vegetal* (2006), the Supreme Court looked at the use by a religion of a controlled substance. In that case, a religious sect with origins in the Amazon Rainforest received communion by drinking a sacramental tea, brewed from plants unique to the region that contain a hallucinogen regulated under the Controlled Substances Act by the federal government.

The government conceded that this practice was a sincere exercise of religion, but nonetheless sought to prohibit the small American branch of the sect from engaging in the practice, on the ground that the Controlled Substances Act barred all uses of the hallucinogen. The sect sued to block enforcement against it of the ban on the sacramental tea.

The government argued that the existence of a congressional exemption for peyote does not indicate that the Controlled Substances Act was amenable to judicially crafted exceptions. See 42 USC § 2000bb-1(c): "A person whose religious exercise has been burdened in violation of this section may assert that violation as a claim or defense in a judicial proceeding and obtain appropriate relief against a government." Congress's role in the peyote exemption—and the executive's; see 21 CFR § 1307.31 (2005)—confirms that the findings in the Controlled Substances Act do not preclude exceptions altogether. It is clear that it is the obligation of the courts to consider whether exceptions are required under the test set forth by Congress:

> Congress has determined that courts should strike sensible balances, pursuant to a compelling interest test that requires the Government to address the particular practice at issue. Applying that test, we conclude that the courts below did not err in determining that the Government failed to demonstrate, at the preliminary injunction stage, a compelling interest in barring the UDV's sacramental use of hoasca.

Freedom of the Press

> The most stringent protection of free speech would not protect a man in falsely shouting fire in a theatre and causing a panic.
>
> **—Justice Oliver Wendell Holmes, *Schenck v. United States* (1919, p. 52)**

In *Schenck v. United States* (1919), Schenck was convicted of obstructing the recruiting or enlistment service by passing out a circular encouraging draft age citizens to refuse to be inducted into the U.S. military. Schenck claimed that he was merely exercising his free speech rights. Justice Holmes stated:

> The most stringent protection of free speech would not protect a man in falsely shouting fire in a theatre and causing a panic. It does not even protect a man from an injunction against uttering words that may have all the effect of force. The question in every case is whether the words used are used in such circumstances and are of such a nature as to create a clear and present danger that they will bring about the substantive evils that Congress has a right to prevent. It is a question of proximity and degree. When a nation is at war many things that might be said in time of peace are such a hindrance to its effort that their utterance will not be endured so long as men fight and that no Court could regard them as protected by any constitutional right. It seems to be admitted that if an actual obstruction of the recruiting service were proved, liability for words that produced that effect might be enforced.

Prior Restraints on Publications

The Supreme Court has placed a heavy burden on anyone trying to institute a prior restraint on the press. In *New York Times Co. v. United States* (1971),

Photo 9.1 Justice William O. Douglas (1898–1980). Associate Justice Douglas was the longest-serving justice in the history of the U.S Supreme Court, with a term lasting 36 years and 209 days. During his term on the Court, he became a spokesman for liberal causes. Justice Douglas had extensive ties with the environmental movement and served on the Board of Directors of the Sierra Club. (Photograph by Harris and Ewing, Collection of the Supreme Court of the United States.)

the federal government sought an injunction to prohibit the publication by *the New York Times* of the contents of a classified study, "History of U.S. Decision-Making Process on Viet Nam Policy." When the district court for the District of Columbia denied injunctive relief, the government appealed. The Supreme Court affirmed the judgment and, in a per curiam opinion that expressed the view of six members of the court, held that the government failed to meet its burden of showing justification for the imposition of a prior restraint of expression. Justices Black and Douglas concurred and stated that under the First Amendment, the press must be left free to publish news, whatever the source, without censorship, injunctions, or prior restraints, and that the guarding of military and diplomatic secrets at the expense of informed representative government was not justified.

Justice Douglas, joined by Justice Black concurring, stated that the First Amendment left no room for governmental restraint on the press, and that the dominant purpose of the First Amendment was to prohibit governmental suppression of embarrassing information.

Justice Brennan, concurring, stated that the First Amendment stood as an absolute bar to the imposition of judicial restraints in circumstances of the kind presented by the present cases.

In *Mills v. Alabama*, 384 U.S. 214 (1966), the Supreme Court held that the State of Alabama violated the U.S. Constitution by making it a crime for the editor of a daily newspaper to write and publish an editorial on election day urging people to vote a certain way on issues submitted to them. And in *Miami Herald Publication Co., Division of Knight Newspapers, Inc. v. Tornillo* (1974), the Court held that Florida's right of reply statute, which provided that a political candidate had the right to demand that a newspaper print any reply of the candidate to criticisms by a newspaper, violated the First Amendment, as it infringed on freedom of the press.

Distribution of Publications

In *Lovell v. Griffin* (1938), the Supreme Court stated that the liberty of the press is not confined to newspapers and periodicals. It necessarily embraces pamphlets and leaflets. These indeed have been historic weapons in the defense of liberty. The press in its historic connotation comprehends every sort of publication that affords a vehicle of information and opinion. Protecting this essential liberty from every sort of infringement is of vital importance. And the liberty to circulate is as essential to that freedom as liberty of publishing; without the circulation, the publication would be of little value. In *Lovell*, the Court held that a municipal ordinance prohibiting the distribution without a permit of circulars, handbooks, advertising, or literature of any kind, whether delivered free or sold, was invalid as infringing the constitutional freedom of the press.

Whitney v. California, 274 U. S. 357 (1927)

Brandenburg v. Ohio, 395 U.S. 444, 89 S. Ct. 1827, 23 L. Ed. 2d. 430 (1969)

The Right to Read Freely

Evans v. Selma Union High School District of Fresno County, 222 P. 801 (Ca. 1924)

Right to Assemble and Free Speech

If all mankind minus one, were of one opinion, and only one person were of the contrary opinion, mankind would be no more justified in silencing that one person, than he, if he had the power, would be justified in silencing mankind.

—John Stuart Mill (1869)

The Commonwealth of Virginia had a statute that prohibited the burning of crosses. Elton Black and several others contended that their cross burning was a symbolic speech and protected by the First Amendment. The Supreme Court considered the issue in *Virginia v. Black* (2004). Black and the others had been convicted in separate cases of burning crosses with the intent to intimidate as proscribed by Virginia Code Annotated § 18.2-423 (1996), which also provided that any cross burning was *prima facie* evidence of intent to intimidate. One had burned a cross during a Ku Klux Klan rally, and the second and third respondents burned a cross in the yard of an African American neighbor who complained about one respondent's use of his backyard as a firing range.

The Supreme Court concluded that the prohibition of cross burning with the intent to intimidate under § 18.2-423 was constitutional because it banned conduct rather than expression. While cross burning could constitute expression, such expressive conduct was not proscribed unless it was done with the intent to intimidate, and targeting cross burning was reasonable because burning a cross was historically a particularly virulent form of intimidation. However, the Supreme Court asserted that the statutory provision that any cross burning was *prima facie* evidence of intent to intimidate, which was interpreted under state law to mean that cross burning by itself could support a conviction without further evidence of intent, was an unconstitutional restraint on speech.

The Court stated in its opinion as follows:

A state may punish those words which by their very utterance inflict injury or tend to incite an immediate breach of the peace. Fighting words, those personally abusive epithets which, when addressed to the ordinary citizen, are, as a matter of common knowledge, inherently likely to provoke violent reaction, are generally proscribable under the First Amendment. Furthermore, the constitutional guarantees of free speech and free press do not permit a state to forbid or proscribe advocacy of the use of force or of law violation except where such advocacy is directed to inciting or producing imminent lawless action and is likely to incite or produce such action. And the First Amendment also permits a state to ban a "true threat." "True threats" encompass those statements where the speaker means to communicate a serious expression of an intent to commit an act of unlawful violence to a particular individual or group of individuals. The speaker need not actually intend to carry out the threat. Rather, a prohibition on true threats protects individuals from the fear of violence and from the disruption that fear engenders, in addition to protecting people from the possibility that the threatened violence will occur. Intimidation in the constitutionally proscribable sense of the word is a type of true threat, where a speaker directs a threat to a person or group of persons with the intent of placing the victim in fear of bodily harm or death.

The First Amendment permits a state to outlaw cross-burnings done with the intent to intimidate because burning a cross is a particularly virulent form of intimidation. Instead of prohibiting all intimidating messages, a state may choose to regulate this subset of intimidating messages in light of cross-burning's long and pernicious history as a signal of impending violence. Thus, just as a state may regulate only that obscenity which is the most obscene due to its prurient content, so too may a state choose to prohibit only those forms of intimidation that are most likely to inspire fear of bodily harm. A ban on cross-burning carried out with the intent to intimidate is proscribable under the First Amendment.

Petitions to the Government

The Supreme Court discussed the right of citizens to petition the government in *City of Cuyahoga Falls v. Buckeye Community Hope Foundation* (2003). The Court noted that a referendum was a basic instrument of democratic government; provisions for referendums demonstrate devotion to democracy, not to bias, discrimination, or prejudice; and that a government may not prohibit the expression of an idea simply because society finds the idea itself offensive or disagreeable dovetails with the notion that all citizens, regardless of the content of their ideas, have the right to petition their government.

In the case, the City of Cuyahoga Falls, Ohio, submitted to voters a facially neutral referendum petition that called for the repeal of a municipal housing ordinance authorizing construction of a low-income housing complex. The voters passed the referendum. Respondents allege that by submitting the petition to the voters and refusing to issue building permits while the petition was pending, the city and its officials violated the equal protection clause.

The Court stated that it was clear that because all power stems from the people, a referendum cannot be characterized as a delegation of power, unlawful unless accompanied by "discernible standards." The people retain the power to govern through referendum with respect to any matter, legislative or administrative, within the realm of local affairs, though the "substantive result" of a referendum may be invalid if it is "arbitrary and capricious." The subjection of the site plan ordinance to the city's referendum process, regardless of whether that ordinance reflected an administrative or legislative

Photo 9.2 Chief Justice John Marshall (1755–1835). Marshall's impact on American constitutional law is peerless. He served for more than 34 years, participating in more than 1,000 decisions and authoring over 500 opinions. He is considered by many as the single most important figure on American constitutional law. (Photograph by Charles St.-Memin, Collection of the Supreme Court of the United States.)

decision, did not constitute per se arbitrary government conduct in violation of due process.

Right of Privacy

Because there is no right to privacy expressly enumerated in the U.S. Constitution, the right is discussed with First Amendment issues because of the similarities between the right of privacy and First Amendment issues. The right of privacy was extensively discussed by the Supreme Court in *Griswold v. Connecticut* (1965).

A Connecticut statute made the use of contraceptives a criminal offense. Griswold and others, a director of a medical clinic and doctors, challenged a decision from the Supreme Court of Errors of Connecticut, which convicted them of violating a state law that prohibited the dispensing or use of birth control devices to or by married couples. The Supreme Court noted that specific guarantees in the Bill of Rights have penumbras, formed by emanations from those guarantees that help give them life and substance. Various guarantees create zones of privacy. The right of association contained in the penumbra of the First Amendment is one. The Third Amendment in its prohibition against the quartering of soldiers in any house in time of peace without the consent of the owner is another facet of that privacy. The Fourth Amendment explicitly affirms the right of the people to be secure in their persons, houses, papers, and effects, against unreasonable searches and seizures. The Fifth Amendment in its self-incrimination clause enables the citizen to create a zone of privacy that government may not force him to surrender to his detriment. The Ninth Amendment provides that the enumeration in the Constitution, of certain rights, shall not be construed to deny or disparage others retained by the people.

The Court noted that the marriage relationship lies within the zone of privacy created by several fundamental constitutional guarantees. Connecticut General Statute § 53-32 (Revision 1958), in forbidding the use of contraceptives rather than regulating their manufacture or sale, seeks to achieve its goals by means having a maximum destructive impact upon that relationship. Such a law cannot stand in light of the rule that a governmental purpose to control or prevent activities constitutionally subject to state regulation may not be achieved by means that sweep unnecessarily broadly and thereby invade the area of protected freedoms. The very idea of allowing the police to search the sacred precincts of marital bedrooms for telltale signs of the use of contraceptives is repulsive to the notions of privacy surrounding the marriage relationship.

In *Stanley v. Georgia* (1969), the Supreme Court looked at the issue of whether an individual had the right to possess obscene photos in his home. An investigation of Stanley's alleged bookmaking activities led to the issuance of a search warrant for his home. Under authority of this warrant, federal and state agents secured entrance. They found very little evidence of bookmaking activity, but while looking through a desk drawer in an upstairs bedroom, one of the federal agents, accompanied by a state officer, found three reels of 8 mm film. Using a projector and screen found in an upstairs living room, they viewed the films. The state officer concluded that they were obscene and seized them. Because a further examination of the bedroom indicated that the appellant occupied it, he was charged with possession of obscene matter and placed under arrest. He was later convicted for "knowingly having possession of obscene matter" in violation of Georgia law.

Justice Marshall, in the Court's opinion, stated that the Constitution protects the right to receive information and ideas. This freedom of speech and press necessarily protects the right to receive. This right to receive information and ideas, regardless of their social worth, is fundamental to our free society. The Court held as follows:

> In the context of this case, a prosecution for mere possession of printed or filmed matter in the privacy of a person's own home, that right takes on an added dimension. For also fundamental is the right to be free, except in very limited circumstances, from unwanted governmental intrusions into one's privacy.
>
> These are the rights that appellant is asserting in the case before us. He is asserting the right to read or observe what he pleases—the right to satisfy his intellectual and emotional needs in the privacy of his own home. He is asserting the right to be free from state inquiry into the contents of his library. Georgia contends that appellant does not have these rights, that there are certain types of materials that the individual may not read or even possess. Georgia justifies this assertion by arguing that the films in the present case are obscene. But we think that mere categorization of these films as "obscene" is insufficient justification for such a drastic invasion of personal liberties guaranteed by the First and Fourteenth Amendments. Whatever may be the justifications for other statutes regulating obscenity, we do not think they reach into the privacy of one's own home. If the First Amendment means anything, it means that a State has no business telling a man, sitting alone in his own house, what books he may read or what films he may watch. Our whole constitutional heritage rebels at the thought of giving government the power to control men's minds.
>
> What we have said in no way infringes upon the power of the State or Federal Government to make possession of other items, such as narcotics, firearms, or stolen goods, a crime. Our holding in the present case turns upon the Georgia statute's infringement of fundamental liberties protected by the First and Fourteenth Amendments. No First Amendment rights are involved in most statutes making mere possession criminal.

The Supreme Court in *Crawford v. Marion County Election Board* (2008) held that Indiana's Senate Enrolled Act 483, which required citizens voting in person to present government-issued photo identification, to the vast majority of Indiana voters was amply justified by the valid interest in protecting the integrity and reliability of the electoral process.

Obscenity

Censorship for political and religious reasons has been traced back to at least Greek and Roman times. In those cultures sexual licentiousness was not censored. The only reported case of prosecution for obscenity in England prior to the 18th Century was the *King v. Sedley* case in 1663. Sir Charles Sedley got drunk with two friends at a tavern. They then climbed to the balcony of the tavern, which overlooked Covent Gardens in London, and removed their clothes and gave speeches laced with profanities. A riot resulted. Sedley and his friend were prosecuted and required to pay a heavy fine (Cohen and Danelski, 2002, p. 353).

The first reported obscenity case in the United States occurred in 1815 in the Commonwealth of Pennsylvania, where the court found that the private showing of a man and woman in an "indecent posture" to be a common law crime. Vermont, in 1821, became the first state to pass an obscenity statute (Cohen and Danelski, 2002, p. 356).

In the *Roth v. United States* (1957) case, the Supreme Court for the first time attempted to define what constitutes obscenity. Roth conducted a business in New York in the publication and sale of books, photographs, and magazines. He used circulars and advertising matter to solicit sales. He was convicted by a jury in the District Court for the Southern District of New York upon 4 counts of a 26-count indictment charging him with mailing obscene circulars and advertising, and an obscene book, in violation of the federal obscenity statute.

In *Roth*, the Court noted that the guarantees of freedom of expression in effect in 10 of the 14 states that by 1792 had ratified the Constitution, gave no absolute protection for every utterance. Thirteen of the 14 states provided for the prosecution of libel, and all of those states made either blasphemy or profanity, or both, statutory crimes. As early as 1712, Massachusetts made it criminal to publish "any filthy, obscene, or profane song, pamphlet, libel or mock sermon" in imitation or mimicking of religious services. Thus, profanity and obscenity were related offenses.

The Court concluded that in light of this history, it was apparent that the unconditional phrasing of the First Amendment was not intended to protect every utterance. This phrasing did not prevent the Court from concluding that libelous utterances are not within the area of constitutionally protected speech. At the time of the adoption of the First Amendment, obscenity law was not as fully developed as libel law, but there was sufficiently contemporaneous evidence to show that obscenity, too, was outside the protection intended for speech and press. The protection given speech and press was fashioned to ensure unfettered interchange of ideas for the bringing about of political and social changes desired by the people. Justice Brennan stated:

> All ideas having even the slightest redeeming social importance—unorthodox ideas, controversial ideas, even ideas hateful to the prevailing climate of opinion—have the full protection of the guaranties, unless excludable because they encroach upon the limited area of more important interests. But implicit

in the history of the First Amendment is the rejection of obscenity as utterly without redeeming social importance. This rejection for that reason is mirrored in the universal judgment that obscenity should be restrained, reflected in the international agreement of over 50 nations, in the obscenity laws of all of the 48 States, and in the 20 obscenity laws enacted by the Congress from 1842 to 1956.

There are certain well-defined and narrowly limited classes of speech, the prevention and punishment of which have never been thought to raise any Constitutional problem. These include the lewd and obscene. It has been well observed that such utterances are no essential part of any exposition of ideas, and are of such slight social value as a step to truth that any benefit that may be derived from them is clearly outweighed by the social interest in order and morality.

We hold that obscenity is not within the area of constitutionally protected speech or press.

In *Miller v. California* (1973), Chief Justice Burger, expressing the views of five members of the court, held the following:

1. Obscene material was not protected by the First Amendment.
2. The proper First Amendment standards to be applied by the states in determining whether particular material was obscene and subject to regulation were as follows:
   a. Whether the average person, applying contemporary community standards, would find that the work, taken as a whole, appealed to the prurient interest
   b. Whether the work could be depicted or described, in a patently offensive way, as sexual conduct specifically defined by the applicable state law, as written or authoritatively construed
   c. Whether the work, taken as a whole, lacked serious literary, artistic, political, or scientific value
3. There was no requirement that the material must be shown to be utterly without redeeming social value.
4. The requirement that state law, as written or construed, must specifically define the sexual conduct as to which depiction or description was proscribed, provided fair notice as to what public and commercial activities would bring prosecution.
5. Obscenity was to be determined by applying "contemporary community standards," not "national standards"—there thus having been no constitutional error in instructing the jury in the instant case to apply state community standards.

The Supreme Court in *United States v. Williams*, 128 S. Ct. 1830 (2007), held that offers to provide or requests to obtain child pornography were categorically excluded from First Amendment protection; therefore, 18

USCS § 2252A(a)(3)(B), which criminalized pandering of child pornography, was constitutional and the decision overturning the defendant's conviction was reversed.

Students and the First Amendment

Freedom of Expression in Schools

In *Tinker v. Des Moines Independent Community School District* (1969), the U.S. Supreme Court held that school officials did not violate the First Amendment by suspending a student who refused to take down a pro-drug banner at a school-sponsored event; the student's freedom of expression claim failed because school officials were entitled to take steps to safeguard those entrusted to their care from speech that could reasonably be regarded as encouraging illegal drug use.

School Assignments

In *Parents Involved in Community School v. Seattle School District No. 1*, 127 S. Ct. 2738 (2007), the Supreme Court held that Seattle students were denied equal protection under the U.S. Constitution, because the school districts, which did not operate legally segregated schools, improperly classified students by race and relied upon the classification in making school assignments in a nonindividualized, mechanical way as a decisive factor. The Seattle school district was attempting to establish a racial mixture of students in each school.

Public Funding of Education

In *Zelman v. Simmons-Harris* (2002), Ohio had established a program to provide educational choices to families with children who reside in the Cleveland City School District. Studies had indicated that Cleveland's public schools were among the worst-performing public schools in the nation. The Ohio program provided tuition aid for students wanting to attend either public or private school of their parent's choosing and tutorial aid for students who chose to remain enrolled in public school. The Court concluded that the program was neutral with respect to religion. It provided benefits directly to a wide spectrum of individuals, defined only by financial need and residence in a particular school district. It permitted individuals to exercise genuine choice among options public and private, secular and religious. The program was therefore a program of private choice and did not offend the establishment clause.

Use of School Property

In *Good News Club v. Milford Central School* (2001), a school had opened its facilities to activities that served a variety of purposes, including discussions of subjects such as child rearing and the development of character and morals. But school policy prohibited use by any organization for religious purposes. A club with religious affiliation applied to use the facilities for afterschool meetings. The school denied the request because the proposed use was the equivalent of religious worship. The students on behalf of the club sued the school, alleging free speech violations. The Court held that school had engaged in impermissible viewpoint discrimination when it excluded the club from the afterschool forum. Such violations were not justified by the school's concern that permitting the club's activities would violate the establishment clause; the meetings were held after school hours, not sponsored by the school, and open to any student who obtained parental consent.

The general rule on the use of school property appears to be that the school can prohibit all use by clubs, etc., but cannot pick and choose based on the whether the use involves a religious purpose.

School Prayers

In *Santa Fe Independent School District v. Doe* (2000), the Supreme Court held that a school district's policy permitting student-led, student-initiated prayer prior to school football games violated the establishment clause of the U.S. Constitution. The Court noted the principle that while the government may accommodate the free exercise of religion, this right does not supersede the fundamental limitations imposed by the establishment clause of U.S. Constitution Amendment 1. The Court concluded that it was beyond dispute that, at a minimum, the Constitution guarantees that government may not coerce anyone to support or participate in religion or its exercise, or otherwise act in a way that establishes a state religion or religious faith, or tends to do so.

Prisoners and the First Amendment

Regulation of Incoming Publications

In *Thornburgh v. Abbott* (1989), Abbott and other federal prison inmates filed suit in the United States District Court for the District of Columbia, alleging that prison officials had violated the inmates' rights under the federal Constitution's First Amendment by, among other things, rejecting certain publications that had been sent to the inmates from outside the prison. When the class action had not yet been tried, the Federal Bureau of Prisons promulgated regulations dealing with the rejection of publications. One provision permits a federal prison inmate to subscribe to or to receive a publication—defined as a book, a single issue of a magazine or newspaper, or other materials such as advertising brochures, fliers, and catalogs—without prior approval. However, this right was restricted by further provisions that authorize a warden to reject a publication if it was determined to be detrimental to the security, good order, or discipline of the institution, or if it might facilitate criminal activity, contain a nonexhaustive list of criteria that may support rejection of a publication, or require the warden to review separately each issue of a subscription publication, and provide procedural safeguards for both the recipient and the sender. The inmates and publishers alleged that these regulations were invalid on their face and as applied to rejections of publications. The inmates and publishers also challenged a practice known as the all-or-nothing rule, under which prison officials reject in its entirety any incoming publication that contains material that is excludible under the bureau's regulations.

The Supreme Court has held that prison regulations concerning the rejection of incoming publications, or of any incoming correspondence sent by prisoners or nonprisoners, do not violate First Amendment rights if such regulations are reasonably related to legitimate penological interests, the regulations at issue satisfied this standard of review, the all-or-nothing rule was not an exaggerated response to prison concerns so as to violate the First Amendment, and prison officials were not obligated to adopt a proposed less restrictive alternative to the rule, and remand was necessary for an examination of the validity of the regulations as applied to any of the 46 publications as to which there remained a live controversy.

In *Beard v. Banks*, 548 U.S. 521 (2006), the Supreme Court held that a state prison regulation prohibiting certain particularly difficult inmates from having access to newspapers, magazines, and photographs did not violate the First Amendment, because there was evidence that the regulation was necessary to motivate better behavior, and this rationale provided sufficient justification for the policy.

Prisoner's Mail

The Supreme Court discussed the right to regulate prisoner's mail in *Procunier v. Martinez* (1974). The Court held that the censorship of prisoner mail was justified if the following criteria are met. The regulation or practice in question must further an important or substantial governmental interest unrelated to the suppression of expression. Prison officials may not censor inmate correspondence simply to eliminate unflattering or unwelcome opinions or factually inaccurate statements. Rather, they must show that a regulation authorizing mail censorship furthers one or more of the substantial governmental interests of security, order, and rehabilitation. The limitation of First Amendment freedoms must be no greater than is necessary or essential to the protection of the particular governmental interest involved. Thus, a restriction on inmate correspondence that furthers an important or substantial interest of penal administration will nevertheless be invalid if its sweep is unnecessarily broad. This does not mean that prison administrators may be required to show with certainty that adverse consequences would flow from the failure to censor a particular letter. Some latitude in anticipating the probable consequences of allowing certain speech in a prison environment is essential to the proper discharge of an administrator's duty.

Right of Association

In *Turner v. Safley* (1987), the Supreme Court addressed the right of inmates to marry. The Court held that the right to marry, like many other rights, is subject to substantial restrictions as a result of incarceration. Many important attributes of marriage remain, however, after taking into account the limitations imposed by prison life. First, inmate marriages, like others, are expressions of emotional support and public commitment. These elements are an important and significant aspect of the marital relationship. In addition, many religions recognize marriage as having spiritual significance; for some inmates and their spouses, therefore, the commitment of marriage may be an exercise of religious faith as well as an expression of personal dedication. Third, most inmates eventually will be released by parole or commutation, and therefore most inmate marriages are formed in the expectation that they ultimately will be fully consummated. Finally, marital status often is a precondition to the receipt of government benefits (e.g., Social Security benefits), property rights (e.g., tenancy by the entirety, inheritance rights), and other, less tangible benefits (e.g., legitimation of children born out of wedlock). These incidents of marriage, like the religious and personal aspects of the marriage commitment, are unaffected by the fact of confinement or the pursuit of legitimate corrections goals.

Capstone Case: *Morse v. Frederick*, 127 S. Ct. 2618 (2007)

Chief Justice John Roberts delivered the opinion of the Court:

> At a school-sanctioned and school-supervised event, a high school principal saw some of her students unfurl a large banner conveying a message she reasonably regarded as promoting illegal drug use. Consistent with established school policy prohibiting such messages at school events, the principal directed the students to take down the banner. One student—among those

who had brought the banner to the event—refused to do so. The principal confiscated the banner and later suspended the student. The Ninth Circuit held that the principal's actions violated the First Amendment, and that the student could sue the principal for damages.

Our cases make clear that students do not "shed their constitutional rights to freedom of speech or expression at the schoolhouse gate." At the same time, we have held that "the constitutional rights of students in public school are not automatically coextensive with the rights of adults in other settings," and that the rights of students "must be applied in light of the special characteristics of the school environment." Consistent with these principles, we hold that schools may take steps to safeguard those entrusted to their care from speech that can reasonably be regarded as encouraging illegal drug use. We conclude that the school officials in this case did not violate the First Amendment by confiscating the pro-drug banner and suspending the student responsible for it.

On January 24, 2002, the Olympic Torch Relay passed through Juneau, Alaska, on its way to the winter games in Salt Lake City, Utah. The torchbearers were to proceed along a street in front of Juneau-Douglas High School (JDHS) while school was in session. Petitioner Deborah Morse, the school principal, decided to permit staff and students to participate in the Torch Relay as an approved social event or class trip. Students were allowed to leave class to observe the relay from either side of the street. Teachers and administrative officials monitored the students' actions.

Respondent Joseph Frederick, a JDHS senior, was late to school that day. When he arrived, he joined his friends (all but one of whom were JDHS students) across the street from the school to watch the event. Not all the students waited patiently. Some became rambunctious, throwing plastic cola bottles and snowballs and scuffling with their classmates. As the torchbearers and camera crews passed by, Frederick and his friends unfurled a 14-foot banner bearing the phrase: "BONG HiTS 4 JESUS." The large banner was easily readable by the students on the other side of the street.

Principal Morse immediately crossed the street and demanded that the banner be taken down. Everyone but Frederick complied. Morse confiscated the banner and told Frederick to report to her office, where she suspended him for 10 days. Morse later explained that she told Frederick to take the banner down because she thought it encouraged illegal drug use, in violation of established school policy.

Frederick administratively appealed his suspension, but the Juneau School District Superintendent upheld it, limiting it to time served (8 days). In a memorandum setting forth his reasons, the superintendent determined that Frederick had displayed his banner "in the midst of his fellow students, during school hours, at a school-sanctioned activity." He further explained that Frederick "was not disciplined because the principal of the school 'disagreed' with his message, but because his speech appeared to advocate the use of illegal drugs."

The superintendent continued:

> The common-sense understanding of the phrase "bong hits" is that it is a reference to a means of smoking marijuana. Given Frederick's inability or unwillingness to express any other credible meaning for the phrase, I can only agree with the principal and countless others who saw the banner as advocating the use of illegal drugs. Frederick's speech was not political. He was not advocating the legalization of marijuana or promoting a religious belief. He was displaying a fairly silly message promoting illegal drug usage in the midst of a school activity, for the benefit of television cameras covering the Torch Relay. Frederick's speech was potentially disruptive to the event and clearly disruptive of and inconsistent with the school's educational mission to educate students about the dangers of illegal drugs and to discourage their use.

Relying on the decision in *Fraser, supra*, the superintendent concluded that the principal's actions were permissible because Frederick's banner was "speech or action that intrudes upon the work of the schools." The Juneau School District Board of Education upheld the suspension.

Frederick then filed suit under 42 U.S.C. § 1983, alleging that the school board and Morse had violated his First Amendment rights. He sought declaratory and injunctive relief, unspecified compensatory damages, punitive damages, and attorney's fees. The District Court granted summary judgment for the school board and Morse, ruling that they were entitled to qualified immunity and that they had not infringed Frederick's First Amendment rights. The court found that Morse reasonably interpreted the banner as promoting illegal drug use—a message that "directly contravened the Board's policies relating to drug abuse prevention." Under the circumstances, the court held that "Morse had the authority, if not the obligation, to stop such messages at a school-sanctioned activity."

The Ninth Circuit reversed. Deciding that Frederick acted during a "school-authorized activity," and "proceeding on the basis that the banner expressed a positive sentiment about marijuana use," the court nonetheless found a violation of Frederick's First Amendment rights because the school punished Frederick without demonstrating that his speech gave rise to a "risk of substantial disruption." The court further concluded that Frederick's right to display his banner was so "clearly established" that a reasonable principal in Morse's position would have understood that her actions were unconstitutional, and that Morse was therefore not entitled to qualified immunity.

We granted certiorari on two questions: whether Frederick had a First Amendment right to wield his banner, and, if so, whether that right was so clearly established that the principal may be held liable for damages. We resolve the first question against Frederick, and therefore have no occasion to reach the second.

At the outset, we reject Frederick's argument that this is not a school speech case—as has every other authority to address the question. The event occurred during normal school hours. It was sanctioned by Principal Morse "as an approved social event or class trip," and the school district's rules expressly provide that pupils in "approved social events and class trips are subject to district rules for student conduct." Teachers and administrators were interspersed among the students and charged with supervising them. The high school band and cheerleaders performed. Frederick, standing among other JDHS students across the street from the school, directed his banner toward the school, making it plainly visible to most students. Under these circumstances, we agree with the superintendent that Frederick cannot "stand in the midst of his fellow students, during school hours, at a school-sanctioned activity and claim he is not at school." There is some uncertainty at the outer boundaries as to when courts should apply school-speech precedents.

The message on Frederick's banner is cryptic. It is no doubt offensive to some, perhaps amusing to others. To still others, it probably means nothing at all. Frederick himself claimed "that the words were just nonsense meant to attract television cameras." But Principal Morse thought the banner would be interpreted by those viewing it as promoting illegal drug use, and that interpretation is plainly a reasonable one.

As Morse later explained in a declaration, when she saw the sign, she thought that "the reference to a 'bong hit' would be widely understood by high school students and others as referring to smoking marijuana." She further believed that "display of the banner would be construed by students, District personnel, parents and others witnessing the display of the banner, as advocating or promoting illegal drug use"—in violation of school policy.

We agree with Morse. At least two interpretations of the words on the banner demonstrate that the sign advocated the use of illegal drugs. First, the phrase could be interpreted as an imperative: "Take bong hits …"—a message equivalent, as Morse explained in her declaration, to "smoke marijuana" or "use an illegal drug." Alternatively, the phrase could be viewed as celebrating drug use—"bong hits are a good thing," or "we take bong hits"—and we discern no meaningful distinction between celebrating illegal drug use in the midst of fellow students and outright advocacy or promotion.

The pro-drug interpretation of the banner gains further plausibility given the paucity of alternative meanings the banner might bear. The best Frederick can come up with is that the banner is "meaningless and funny." Gibberish is surely a possible interpretation of the words on the banner, but it is not the only one, and dismissing the banner as meaningless ignores its undeniable reference to illegal drugs.

The question thus becomes whether a principal may, consistent with the First Amendment, restrict student speech at a school event, when that speech is reasonably viewed as promoting illegal drug use. We hold that she may.

In *Tinker*, this Court made clear that "First Amendment rights, applied in light of the special characteristics of the school environment, are available to teachers and students." *Tinker* involved a group of high school students who decided to wear black armbands to protest the Vietnam War. School officials learned of the plan and then adopted a policy prohibiting students from wearing armbands. When several students nonetheless wore armbands to school, they were suspended. The students sued, claiming that their First Amendment rights had been violated, and this Court agreed.

Tinker held that student expression may not be suppressed unless school officials reasonably conclude that it will "materially and substantially disrupt the work and discipline of the school." The essential facts of *Tinker* are quite stark, implicating concerns at the heart of the First Amendment. The students sought to engage in political speech, using the armbands to express their "disapproval of the Vietnam hostilities and their advocacy of a truce, to make their views known, and, by their example, to influence others to adopt them." Political speech, of course, is "at the core of what the First Amendment is designed to protect." The only interest the Court discerned underlying the school's actions was the "mere desire to avoid the discomfort and unpleasantness that always accompany an unpopular viewpoint," or "an urgent wish to avoid the controversy which might result from the expression." That interest was not enough to justify banning "a silent, passive expression of opinion, unaccompanied by any disorder or disturbance."

This Court's next student speech case was *Fraser*. Matthew Fraser was suspended for delivering a speech before a high school assembly in which he employed what this Court called "an elaborate, graphic, and explicit sexual metaphor." Analyzing the case under *Tinker*, the District Court and Court of Appeals found no disruption, and therefore no basis for disciplining *Fraser*. This Court reversed, holding that the "School District acted entirely within its permissible authority in imposing sanctions upon *Fraser* in response to his offensively lewd and indecent speech."

The mode of analysis employed in *Fraser* is not entirely clear. The Court was plainly attuned to the content of Fraser's speech, citing the "marked distinction between the political 'message' of the armbands in *Tinker* and the sexual content of Fraser's speech." But the Court also reasoned that school boards have the authority to determine "what manner of speech in the classroom or in school assembly is inappropriate." There is no suggestion that school officials attempted to regulate Fraser's speech because they disagreed with the views he sought to express.

We need not resolve this debate to decide this case. For present purposes, it is enough to distill from *Fraser* two basic principles. First, *Fraser's* holding demonstrates that "the constitutional rights of students in public school are not automatically coextensive with the rights of adults in other settings." Had Fraser delivered the same speech in a public forum outside the school context, it would have been protected. Second, *Fraser* established that the mode of analysis set forth in *Tinker* is not absolute. Whatever approach *Fraser* employed, it certainly did not conduct the "substantial disruption" analysis prescribed by *Tinker.*

Our most recent student speech case, *Kuhlmeier,* concerned "expressive activities that students, parents, and members of the public might reasonably perceive to bear the imprimatur of the school." Staff members of a high school newspaper sued their school when it chose not to publish two of their articles. The Court of Appeals analyzed the case under *Tinker,* ruling in favor of the students because it found no evidence of material disruption to classwork or school discipline. This Court reversed, holding that "educators do not offend the First Amendment by exercising editorial control over the style and content of student speech in school-sponsored expressive activities so long as their actions are reasonably related to legitimate pedagogical concerns."

Drawing on the principles applied in our student speech cases, we have held in the Fourth Amendment context that "while children assuredly do not shed their constitutional rights ... at the schoolhouse gate, ... the nature of those rights is what is appropriate for children in school." In particular, "the school setting requires some easing of the restrictions to which searches by public authorities are ordinarily subject." Fourth Amendment rights, no less than First and Fourteenth Amendment rights, are different in public schools than elsewhere. While schoolchildren do not shed their constitutional rights when they enter the schoolhouse, Fourth Amendment rights ... are different in public schools than elsewhere; the reasonableness inquiry cannot disregard the schools' custodial and tutelary responsibility for children.

The "special characteristics of the school environment," and the governmental interest in stopping student drug abuse—reflected in the policies of Congress and myriad school boards, including JDHS—allow schools to restrict student expression that they reasonably regard as promoting illegal drug use. *Tinker* warned that schools may not prohibit student speech because of "undifferentiated fear or apprehension of disturbance" or "a mere desire to avoid the discomfort and unpleasantness that always accompany an unpopular viewpoint." The danger here is far more serious and palpable. The particular concern of presenting student drug abuse is at issue here, and this concern is embodied in established school policy,

School principals have a difficult job, and a vitally important one. When Frederick suddenly and unexpectedly unfurled his banner, Morse had to decide to act—or not act—on the spot. It was reasonable for her to conclude that the banner promoted illegal drug use—in violation of established school policy—and that failing to act would send a powerful message to the students in her charge, including Frederick, about how serious the school was about the dangers of illegal drug use. The First Amendment does not require schools to tolerate at school events student expression that contributes to those dangers.

The judgment of the United States Court of Appeals for the Ninth Circuit is reversed, and the case is remanded for further proceedings consistent with this opinion.

Questions in Review

1. What are the important restrictions on government action set forth in the First Amendment?
2. What are the limitations on providing public financial aid to religious schools?
3. What rights does a prisoner retain while in prison?
4. Under what circumstances may the government prevent the publication in a newspaper of material that is unfavorable to the government?
5. What constitutes obscenity?

Civil Liability and the Criminal Justice Professional

10

Introduction

In this chapter, the Supreme Court's decisions involving the issue of civil liability and the criminal justice professional are examined. Most issues concerning liability of criminal justice professionals involve a civil action under 42 USC § 1983. Professionals are also liable under the common law actions (torts) of assault and battery, unlawful imprisonment, false arrest, and defamation of character. 42 USCS § 1983 gives remedy—action at law, suit in equity, or other proper proceeding for redress—to parties deprived of constitutional rights, privileges, and immunities by an official's abuse of his position (*Monroe v. Pape*, 1961). The general guidelines of the common law actions and § 1983 are very similar with the exception that under 1983, the individual suing (plaintiff) must show that the wrongdoer (tort feasor) was acting under the "color of law."

Federal Civil Rights

The Supreme Court noted in *Mitchum v. Foster* (1972) that the purpose of a federal civil rights statute (42 USCS § 1983) authorizing action at law, suit in equity, or other proper proceedings for redress of deprivation, under color of state law, of rights secured by federal Constitution and federal laws, is to interpose federal courts between states and people, as guardians of people's federal rights, and thus to protect people from unconstitutional action under color of state law, whether that action be executive, legislative, or judicial. In carrying out this purpose, Congress, by expressly authorizing suit in equity as one means of redress, has plainly authorized federal courts to issue injunctions in § 1983 actions.

To state claim for deprivation of rights under 42 USCS § 1983, the plaintiff must show that (1) conduct complained of was committed by person acting under color of law; (2) defendants' conduct in fact deprived them of rights, privileges, or immunities secured by the Constitution or laws of the United States; (3) defendants' conduct caused deprivation of federal constitutional rights; and (4) defendants' conduct must have been intentional or grossly negligent, or have amounted to reckless or callous indifference to constitutional rights of others (*Neris v. Vivoni*, 2003).

42 U.S. Code § 1983: Civil Action for Deprivation of Rights

Every person who, under color of any statute, ordinance, regulation, custom, or usage, of any State or Territory or the District of Columbia, subjects, or causes to be subjected, any citizen of the United States or other person within the jurisdiction thereof to the deprivation of any rights, privileges, or immunities secured by the Constitution and laws, shall be liable to the party injured in an action at law, suit in equity, or other proper proceeding for redress, except that in any action brought against a judicial officer for an act or omission taken in such officer's judicial capacity, injunctive relief shall not be granted unless a declaratory decree was violated or declaratory relief was unavailable. For the purposes of this section, any Act of Congress applicable exclusively to the District of Columbia shall be considered to be a statute of the District of Columbia.

Under Color of Law

Misuse of power, possessed by virtue of state law and made possible only because the wrongdoer is clothed with the authority of state law, is action taken under color of state law.

—**Justice Flex Frankfurter,** *United States v. Classic,* **1941**

Excessive Force Used in an Arrest

In *Brosseau v. Haugen* (2004), Officer Rochelle Brosseau, a member of the Puyallup, Washington Police Department, was attempting to arrest Kenneth Haugen, who had locked himself in his vehicle. Haugen ignored the officer's commands, issued at gunpoint, to get out of the vehicle. The officer shattered the driver's side window by hitting it with her handgun. She unsuccessfully attempted to grab the keys and struck the victim on the head with her gun. Haugen, still undeterred, succeeded in starting the vehicle and began to move away. The officer fired one shot through a window of the vehicle, hitting the victim in the back. She later explained that she shot him because she was fearful for other officers she believed were in the immediate area on foot, as well as for the occupied vehicles in the victim's path and any other citizens who might have been in the area.

The Supreme Court held that this area was one in which the result depended very much on the facts of each case. Furthermore, the cases suggested that the officer's actions fell in the hazy border between excessive and acceptable force and did not clearly establish that the officer's conduct had violated the Fourth Amendment rights of Haugen.

The Court noted that it had clearly established the general proposition that use of force is contrary to the Fourth Amendment if it is excessive under

objective standards of reasonableness. The contours of the right must be sufficiently clear that a reasonable official would understand that what he is doing
violates that right. The relevant, dispositive inquiry in determining whether a
right is clearly established is whether it would be clear to a reasonable officer
that his conduct was unlawful in the situation he confronted.

The Court concluded that it was not clear that the officer had used excessive force. The Court noted that courts found no Fourth Amendment violation when an officer shot a fleeing suspect who presented a risk to others.
And where an officer and suspect engaged in a car chase, which appeared to
be at an end when the officer cornered the suspect at the back of a dead-end
residential street. The suspect, however, freed his car and began speeding
down the street. At this point, the officer fired a shot, which killed the suspect. The court held the officer's decision was reasonable and thus did not
violate the Fourth Amendment. It noted that the suspect, like Haugen here,
had proven he would do almost anything to avoid capture and that he posed
a major threat to, among others, the officers at the end of the street.

In *Saucier v. Katz* (2001), the Supreme Court stated that claims of excessive force in the context of arrests or investigatory stops should be analyzed
under the Fourth Amendment's "objective reasonableness standard," not
under substantive due process principles. Because police officers are often
forced to make split-second judgments—in circumstances that are tense,
uncertain, and rapidly evolving—about the amount of force that is necessary
in a particular situation, the reasonableness of the officer's belief as to the
appropriate level of force should be judged from that on-scene perspective.
The test cautions against the "20/20 vision of hindsight" in favor of deference
to the judgment of reasonable officers on the scene.

Use of Deadly Force

The Supreme Court, in *Tennessee v. Garner* (1985), held that the use of deadly
force to prevent the escape of all felony suspects, whatever the circumstances,
is constitutionally unreasonable. It is not better that all felony suspects die
than that they escape. Where the suspect poses no immediate threat to the
officer and no threat to others, the harm resulting from failing to apprehend
him does not justify the use of deadly force to do so. A police officer may not
seize an unarmed, nondangerous suspect by shooting him dead. Where the
officer has probable cause to believe that the suspect poses a threat of serious physical harm, either to the officer or to others, it is not constitutionally
unreasonable to prevent escape by using deadly force. Thus, if the suspect
threatens the officer with a weapon or there is probable cause to believe that
he has committed a crime involving the infliction or threatened infliction
of serious physical harm, deadly force may be used if necessary to prevent
escape, and if, where feasible, some warning has been given.

Private Correctional Officers

In *Richardson v. McKnight*, 521 U.S. 399 (U.S. 1997), respondent McKnight, a prisoner at a Tennessee correctional center whose management had been privatized, filed this constitutional tort action under 42 USC § 1983 for physical injuries inflicted by petitioner prison guards. The District Court denied the petitioners' motion to dismiss, finding that, because they were employed by a private prison management firm, they were not entitled to qualified immunity from § 1983 lawsuits. The court of appeals affirmed. The Supreme Court agreed and held that prison guards employed by a private firm are not entitled to a qualified immunity from suit by prisoners charging a § 1983 violation. Private actors are not automatically immune from suit, and § 1983 immunity does not automatically follow § 1983 liability. Private prison guards, unlike those who work directly for the government, do not enjoy immunity from suit in a § 1983 case. Officers who seek exemption from personal liability have the burden of showing that such an exemption is justified.

False Arrest Statute of Limitations

In *Wallace v. Kato* (U.S. 2007), after Andre Wallace's murder conviction was overturned based on a lack of probable cause for arrest and the charges were dismissed, he sued the arresting police officers under 42 USCS § 1983 for false imprisonment. The Court held that the statute of limitations for a 42 USCS § 1983 claim seeking damages for a false arrest in violation of the Fourth Amendment, where the arrest is followed by criminal proceedings, begins to run at the time the claimant becomes detained pursuant to the legal process, not when the conviction was reversed. The Court held that the statute of limitations had expired and dismissed the action.

Abusive Interrogations

In *Chavez v. Martinez* (2003), while respondent Martinez was being treated for gunshot wounds received during an altercation with police, he was interrogated by petitioner Chavez, a patrol supervisor. Martinez admitted that he used heroin and had taken an officer's gun during the incident. At no point was Martinez given Miranda warnings. Although he was never charged with a crime, and his answers were never used against him in any criminal proceeding, Martinez filed a 42 USC § 1983 suit, maintaining, among other things, that Chavez's actions violated his Fifth Amendment right not to be "compelled in any criminal case to be a witness against himself," and his Fourteenth Amendment substantive due process right to be free from coercive questioning.

Justice Thomas, joined by the Chief Justice, Justice O'Connor, and Justice Scalia, concluded that Chavez had not deprived Martinez of his Fifth Amendment rights. An officer is entitled to qualified immunity if his alleged conduct did not violate a constitutional right. The Court noted that the text of the Fifth Amendment's self-incrimination clause is not violated by mere compulsive questioning. A criminal case at the very least requires the initiation of legal proceedings, and police questioning does not constitute such a case. Statements compelled by police interrogation may not be used against a defendant in a criminal case, but it is not until such use that the self-incrimination clause is violated. In deciding whether an officer is entitled to qualified immunity, the Court noted that it must first determine whether the officer's alleged conduct violated a constitutional right. If not, the officer is entitled to qualified immunity, and we need not consider whether the asserted right was "clearly established." The Court concluded that Martinez's allegations fail to state a violation of his constitutional rights. Martinez was never made to be a "witness" against himself because his statements were never admitted as testimony against him in a criminal case. Nor was he ever placed under oath and exposed to the cruel trilemma of self-accusation, perjury, or contempt.

The Court noted that rules designed to safeguard a constitutional right do not extend the scope of the constitutional right itself, just as violations of judicially crafted prophylactic rules do not violate the constitutional rights of any person. The Court explained that it had allowed the Fifth Amendment privilege to be asserted by witnesses in noncriminal cases to safeguard the core constitutional right defined by the self-incrimination clause—the right not to be compelled in any criminal case to be a witness against oneself. The Court has likewise established the Miranda exclusionary rule as a prophylactic measure to prevent violations of the right protected by the text of the self-incrimination clause—the admission into evidence in criminal cases of confessions obtained through coercive custodial questioning. This case clearly indicates that Miranda violations are not actionable under § 1983.

The Court cautioned that their views on the proper scope of the Fifth Amendment's self-incrimination clause does not mean that police torture or other abuse that results in a confession is constitutionally permissible so long as the statements are not used at trial; it simply means that the Fourteenth Amendment's due process clause, rather than the Fifth Amendment's self-incrimination clause, would govern the inquiry in those cases and provide relief in appropriate circumstances.

Violations of Constitutional Rights in a Foreign Country

In *Sosa v. Alvarez-Machain* (2004), the Drug Enforcement Administration (DEA) approved using petitioner Sosa and other Mexican nationals to abduct respondent Alvarez-Machain (Alvarez), also a Mexican national, from

Mexico to stand trial in the United States for a DEA agent's torture and murder. After his acquittal, Alvarez sued the United States for false arrest under the Federal Tort Claims Act (FTCA), which waives sovereign immunity in suits for personal injury caused by the negligent or wrongful act or omission of any government employee while acting within the scope of his office or employment. The Court held that the FTCA did not apply to violations of constitutional rights that occurred in a foreign jurisdiction.

General Rules of Liability

The general rules of liability are as follows:

- Judges are immune from liability for damages for acts committed within their judicial jurisdiction.
- This immunity applies even when the judge is accused of acting maliciously and corruptly, and it is not for the protection or benefit of a malicious or corrupt judge, but for the benefit of the public, whose interest it is that the judges should be at liberty to exercise their functions with independence and without fear of consequences.
- A peace officer who arrests someone with probable cause is not liable for false arrest simply because the innocence of the suspect is later proved.
- A policeman's lot is not so unhappy that he must choose between being charged with dereliction of duty if he does not arrest when he has probable cause, and being mulcted in damages if he does.
- The same consideration would seem to require excusing him from liability for acting under a statute that he reasonably believed to be valid but that was later held unconstitutional, on its face or as applied.
- The defense of good faith and probable cause, which may be available to police officers in the common law action for false arrest and imprisonment, is also available to them in an action under 42 USCS § 1983.

Liability of Federal Agents under 42 USCS § 1983

The liability of federal law enforcement officers for violating a person's constitutional rights when conducting an illegal search was discussed in the case of *Bivens v. Six Unknown Named Agents of Federal Bureau of Narcotics* (1971).*

---

* The name of this case has been the subject of much discussion. How can the "named agents" be unknown?

Mr. Justice Brennan delivered the opinion of the Court in *Bivens*:

In *Bell v. Hood*, 327 U.S. 678 (1946), we reserved the question whether violation of a command by a federal agent acting under color of his authority gives rise to a cause of action for damages consequent upon his unconstitutional conduct. Today we hold that it does.

This case has its origin in an arrest and search carried out on the morning of November 26, 1965. Petitioner's complaint alleged that on that day respondents, agents of the Federal Bureau of Narcotics acting under claim of federal authority, entered his apartment and arrested him for alleged narcotics violations. The agents manacled petitioner in front of his wife and children, and threatened to arrest the entire family. They searched the apartment from stem to stern. Thereafter, petitioner was taken to the federal courthouse in Brooklyn, where he was interrogated, booked, and subjected to a visual strip search.

As our cases make clear, the Fourth Amendment operates as a limitation upon the exercise of federal power regardless of whether the State in whose jurisdiction that power is exercised would prohibit or penalize the identical act if engaged in by a private citizen. It guarantees to citizens of the United States the absolute right to be free from unreasonable searches and seizures carried out by virtue of federal authority. And where federally protected rights have been invaded, it has been the rule from the beginning that courts will be alert to adjust their remedies so as to grant the necessary relief.

A violation of the Fourth Amendment protection against unreasonable searches and seizures by a federal agent acting under color of his authority gives rise to a cause of action for damages consequent upon his unconstitutional conduct. Where legal rights have been invaded, and a federal statute provides for a general right to sue for such invasion, federal courts may use any available remedy to make good the wrong done.

Officer's Duty to Arrest

If an officer has a duty to arrest someone and fails to do so, is the officer liable when the individual later commits a crime?

That was the question in the case of *Town of Castle Rock v. Gonzales* (U.S. 2005). Mrs. Gonzales was going through a bitter divorce with her children's father. The local state court had issued a restraining order against the father ordering him to leave her and children alone. Mrs. Gonzales made numerous calls to the police and demanded that they arrest the ex-husband. The police failed to do so even when she reported that the father had taken the children. Later the father killed the children and Mrs. Gonzales filed a civil suit against the town. In her 42 USCS § 1983 suit, she claimed that the defendant's city violated the Fourteenth Amendment's due process clause when police officers failed to act on repeated reports that the father took their children, resulting in the children's murders.

The Court noted that in each and every state there are long-standing statutes that, by their terms, seem to preclude nonenforcement by the police. However, for a number of reasons, including their legislative history, insufficient resources, and sheer physical impossibility, it has been recognized that such statutes cannot be interpreted literally. They clearly do not mean that a police officer may not lawfully decline to make an arrest. As to third parties in these states, the full-enforcement statutes simply have no effect, and their significance is further diminished.

Colorado law, according to the Court, has not created a personal entitlement to enforcement of restraining orders. It does not appear that state law truly made such enforcement mandatory. A well-established tradition of police discretion has long coexisted with apparently mandatory arrest statutes. The Court concluded that against that backdrop, a true mandate of police action would require some stronger indication than the Colorado statute's direction to "use every reasonable means to enforce a restraining order" or even to "arrest or seek a warrant." A Colorado officer would likely have some discretion to determine that—despite probable cause to believe a restraining order has been violated—the violation's circumstances or competing duties counsel decisively against enforcement in a particular instance. The practical necessity for discretion is particularly apparent in a case such as this, where the suspected violator is not actually present and his whereabouts are unknown. In such circumstances, the statute does not appear to require officers to arrest, but only to seek a warrant. That, however, would be an entitlement to nothing but procedure, which cannot be the basis for a property interest.

Even if the statute could be said to make enforcement mandatory, that would not necessarily mean that the respondent has an entitlement to enforcement. Her alleged interest stems not from common law or contract, but only from a state's statutory scheme. If she was given a statutory entitlement, the Court would expect to see some indication of that in the statute itself. Although the statute spoke of protected persons such as the respondent, it did so in connection with matters other than a right to enforcement. Most importantly, it spoke directly to the protected person's power to initiate contempt proceedings if the order was issued in a civil action, which contrasts tellingly with its conferral of a power merely to request initiation of criminal contempt proceedings—and even more dramatically with its complete silence about any power to request (much less demand) that an arrest be made.

Liability of a Public Agency for Failure to Train Its Police Officers

In *City of Canton v. Harris* (1989), respondent Geraldine Harris was arrested by officers of the Canton Police Department. Mrs. Harris was brought to the police station in a patrol wagon.

When she arrived at the station, Mrs. Harris was found sitting on the floor of the wagon. She was asked if she needed medical attention, and responded with an incoherent remark. After she was brought inside the station for processing, Mrs. Harris slumped to the floor on two occasions. Eventually, the police officers left Mrs. Harris lying on the floor to prevent her from falling again. No medical attention was ever summoned for Mrs. Harris. After about an hour, Mrs. Harris was released from custody, and taken by an ambulance (provided by her family) to a nearby hospital. There, Mrs. Harris was diagnosed as suffering from several emotional ailments; she was hospitalized for one week and received subsequent outpatient treatment for an additional year.

Some time later, Mrs. Harris commenced this action alleging many state law and constitutional claims against the City of Canton and its officials. Among these claims was one seeking to hold the city liable under 42 USC § 1983 for its violation of Mrs. Harris's right, under the due process clause of the Fourteenth Amendment, to receive necessary medical attention while in police custody.

The Court discussed the city's liability under 42 USCS § 1983 for failure to train its police force. The Court stated that a municipality can be found liable under 42 USCS § 1983 only where the municipality itself causes the constitutional violation at issue. Respondeat superior or vicarious liability [liability based on the fact that the party employed the officers] will not attach under § 1983. The Court noted that it is only when the execution of the government's policy or custom inflicts the injury that the municipality may be held liable under § 1983.

The inadequacy of police training may serve as the basis for 42 USCS § 1983 liability only where the failure to train amounts to deliberate indifference to the rights of persons with whom the police come into contact. The rule that a city is not liable under 42 USCS § 1983 unless a municipal policy causes a constitutional deprivation will not be satisfied by merely alleging that the existing training program for a class of employees, such as police officers, represents a policy for which the city is responsible. The issue is whether that training program is adequate, and if it is not, the question becomes whether such inadequate training can justifiably be said to represent "city policy."

It may happen that in light of the duties assigned to specific officers or employees, the need for more or different training is so obvious, and the inadequacy so likely to result in the violation of constitutional rights, that the policymakers of the city can reasonably be said to have been deliberately indifferent to the need. In that event, the failure to provide proper training may fairly be said to represent a policy for which the city is responsible, and for which the city may be held liable if it actually causes injury.

In resolving the issue of a city's liability, the focus must be on adequacy of the training program in relation to the tasks the particular officers must perform. That a particular officer may be unsatisfactorily trained will not alone suffice to fasten liability on the city, for the officer's shortcomings may have resulted from factors other than a faulty training program. Neither will it suffice to prove that an injury or accident could have been avoided if an officer had had better or more training, sufficient to equip him to avoid the particular injury-causing conduct.

For liability to attach, the identified deficiency in a city's training program must be closely related to the ultimate injury.

The question is whether the injury could have been avoided had the employee been trained under a program that was not deficient in the identified respect. Predicting how a hypothetically well-trained officer would have acted under the circumstances may not be an easy task for the fact finder, particularly because matters of judgment may be involved, and because officers who are well trained are not free from error and perhaps might react very much like the untrained officer in similar circumstances. But judge and jury, doing their respective jobs, will be adequate to the task.

Immunity from Liability

In this section, the immunity from liability protections are discussed. Basically, immunity is a defense to a civil action for violations of a person's right or damages to a person's property. The *Pierson v. Ray* (1967) case examined the liability of local police officers and judges under the Civil Rights Act of 1871 (42 USC § 1983.1). Petitioners (individuals who were suing police officers and a judge) were members of a group of 15 white and Negro Episcopal clergymen who attempted to use segregated facilities at an interstate bus terminal in Jackson, Mississippi, in 1961. They were arrested by respondents Ray, Griffith, and Nichols (Jackson policeofficers) and charged with violating the Mississippi Code, which made it a misdemeanor for anyone to congregate with others in a public place under circumstances such that a breach of the peace may be occasioned thereby and refuse to move on when ordered to do so by a police officer.

Petitioners waived a jury trial and were convicted of the offense by respondent Spencer, a municipal judge. They were each given the maximum sentence of four months in jail and a fine of $200. On appeal petitioner Jones was accorded a trial *de novo* in the county court, and after the city produced its evidence the court granted his motion for a directed verdict. The cases against the other petitioners were then dropped.

Having been vindicated in the county court, petitioners brought an action for damages in the U.S. District Court for the Southern District of Mississippi alleging that respondents had violated 18 U.S. Code § 1983 by arresting them, and that respondents were liable at common law for false arrest and imprisonment. A jury returned verdicts for respondents on both counts. On appeal, the Court of Appeals for the Fifth Circuit held that Judge Spencer was immune from liability under both § 1983 and the common law of Mississippi for acts committed within his judicial jurisdiction. As to the police officers, the court noted that the Mississippi Code was held unconstitutional as applied to similar facts in *Thomas v. Mississippi*, 380 U.S. 524 (1965). The Court held that under the count based on the common law of Mississippi, the policemen would not be liable if they had probable cause to believe that the statute had been violated, because Mississippi law does not require police officers to predict at their peril which state laws are constitutional and which are not. Apparently dismissing the common law claim, the court of appeals reversed and remanded for a new trial on the § 1983 claim against the police officers because defense counsel had been allowed to cross-examine the ministers on various irrelevant and prejudicial matters, particularly including an alleged convergence of their views on racial justice with those of the Communist Party. At the new trial, however, the court held that the ministers could not recover if it were proved that they went to Mississippi anticipating that they would be illegally arrested because such action would constitute consent to the arrest under the principle of he who consents to a wrong cannot be injured.

All witnesses including the police officers agreed that the ministers entered the waiting room peacefully and engaged in no boisterous or objectionable conduct while in the "White Only" area. There was conflicting testimony on the number of bystanders present and their behavior. Petitioners testified that there was no crowd at the station, that no one followed them into the waiting room, and that no one uttered threatening words or made threatening gestures. The police testified that some 25 to 30 persons followed the ministers into the terminal, that persons in the crowd were in a very dissatisfied and ugly mood, and that they were mumbling and making unspecified threatening gestures. The police did not describe any specific threatening incidents, and testified that they took no action against any persons in the crowd who were threatening violence because they had determined that the ministers were the cause of the violence if any might occur, although the ministers were concededly orderly and polite and the police did not claim that it was beyond their power to control the allegedly disorderly crowd. The arrests and convictions were followed by this lawsuit.

Chief Justice Earl Warren stated in delivering the Court's opinion:

We find no difficulty in agreeing with the Court of Appeals that Judge Spencer is immune from liability for damages for his role in these convictions. The record is barren of any proof or specific allegation that Judge Spencer played any role in these arrests and convictions other than to adjudge petitioners guilty when their cases came before his court. Few doctrines were more solidly established at common law than the immunity of judges from liability for damages for acts committed within their judicial jurisdiction, as this Court recognized when it adopted the doctrine. This immunity applies even when the judge is accused of acting maliciously and corruptly, and it is not for the protection or benefit of a malicious or corrupt judge, but for the benefit of the public, whose interest it is that the judges should be at liberty to exercise their functions with independence and without fear of consequences. It is a judge's duty to decide all cases within his jurisdiction that are brought before him, including controversial cases that arouse the most intense feelings in the litigants. His errors may be corrected on appeal, but he should not have to fear that unsatisfied litigants may hound him with litigation charging malice or corruption. Imposing such a burden on judges would contribute not to principled and fearless decision-making but to intimidation.

The common law has never granted police officers an absolute and unqualified immunity, and the officers in this case do not claim that they are entitled to one. Their claim is rather that they should not be liable if they acted in good faith and with probable cause in making an arrest under a statute that they believed to be valid. Under the prevailing view in this country a peace officer who arrests someone with probable cause is not liable for false arrest simply because the innocence of the suspect is later proved. A policeman's lot is not so unhappy that he must choose between being charged with dereliction of duty if he does not arrest when he has probable cause, and being mulcted in damages if he does. Although the matter is not entirely free from doubt, the same consideration would seem to require excusing him from liability for acting under a statute that he reasonably believed to be valid but that was later held unconstitutional, on its face or as applied. The defense of good faith and probable cause, which the Court of Appeals found available to the officers in the common-law action for false arrest and imprisonment, is also available to them in the action under § 1983. This holding does not, however, mean that the count based thereon should be dismissed.

The Court of Appeals ordered dismissal of the common-law count on the theory that the police officers were not required to predict our decision in *Thomas v. Mississippi*. We agree that a police officer is not charged with predicting the future course of constitutional law. But the petitioners in this case did not simply argue that they were arrested under a statute later held unconstitutional. They claimed and attempted to prove that the police officers arrested them solely for attempting to use the "White Only" waiting room, that no crowd was present, and that no one threatened violence or seemed about to cause a disturbance. The officers did not defend on the theory that they believed in good faith that it was constitutional to arrest the ministers solely for using the waiting room. Rather, they claimed and attempted to prove that they did not arrest the ministers for the purpose of preserving the custom of segregation in Mississippi, but solely for the purpose of preventing violence. They testified, in contradiction to the ministers, that a crowd gathered and that imminent violence was likely. If the jury believed the testimony of the officers and disbelieved that of the ministers, and if the jury found that the officers reasonably believed in good faith that the arrest was constitutional, then a verdict for the officers would follow even though the arrest was in fact unconstitutional. The jury did resolve the factual issues in favor of the officers but, for reasons previously stated, its verdict was influenced by irrelevant and prejudicial evidence. Accordingly, the case must be remanded to the trial court for a new trial.

In *Briscoe v. Lahue*, 460 U.S. 325 (U.S. 1983), the Court noted that common law provided absolute immunity from subsequent damages liability for all persons—governmental or otherwise—who are integral parts of the judicial process. And 42 USCS § 1983 does not authorize a damages claim against private witnesses or against judges or prosecutors in the performance of their respective duties. When a police officer appears as a witness, he may reasonably be viewed as acting like any other witness sworn to tell the truth, in which event he can make a strong claim to witness immunity; alternatively, he may be regarded as an official performing a critical role in the judicial process, in which event he may seek the benefit afforded to other governmental participants in the same proceeding. Nothing in the language of § 1983 suggests that such a witness belongs in a narrow, special category lacking protection against damages suits. Nothing in the legislative history of § 1983 points to a different conclusion.

Prosecutors

In *Buckley v. Fitzsimmons* (1993), the Court held that the actions of a prosecutor are not absolutely immune merely because they are performed by a prosecutor. Qualified immunity represents the norm for executive officers, so when a prosecutor functions as an administrator rather than as an officer of the court, he is entitled only to qualified immunity. There is a difference between the advocate's role in evaluating evidence and interviewing witnesses as he prepares for trial, on the one hand, and the detective's role in searching for the clues and corroboration that might give him probable cause to recommend that a suspect be arrested, on the other hand. When a prosecutor performs the investigative functions normally performed by a detective or police officer, it is neither appropriate nor justifiable that, for the same act, immunity should protect the one and not the other. Thus, if a prosecutor plans and executes a raid on a suspected weapons cache, he has no greater claim to complete immunity than activities of police officers allegedly acting under his direction.

Capstone Case: *Wilson v. Layne,* 526 U.S. 603, 628 (1999)

Chief Justice Rehnquist delivered the opinion of the Court:

> While executing an arrest warrant in a private home, police officers invited representatives of the media to accompany them. We hold that such a "media ride along" does violate the Fourth Amendment, but that because the state of the law was not clearly established at the time the search in this case took place, the officers are entitled to the defense of qualified immunity.
>
> In early 1992, the Attorney General of the United States approved "Operation Gunsmoke," a special national fugitive apprehension program in which United States Marshals worked with state and local police to apprehend dangerous criminals. The "Operation Gunsmoke" policy statement explained that the operation was to concentrate on "armed individuals wanted on federal and/or state and local warrants for serious drug and other violent felonies." This effective program ultimately resulted in over 3,000 arrests in 40 metropolitan areas.
>
> One of the dangerous fugitives identified as a target of "Operation Gunsmoke" was Dominic Wilson, the son of petitioners Charles and Geraldine Wilson. Dominic Wilson had violated his probation on previous felony charges of robbery, theft, and assault with intent to rob, and the police computer listed "caution indicators" that he was likely to be armed, to resist arrest, and to "assault police." The computer also listed his address as 909 North StoneStreet Avenue in Rockville, Maryland. Unknown to the police, this was actually the home of the petitioners, Dominic Wilson's parents. Thus, in April 1992, the Circuit Court for Montgomery County issued three arrest warrants for Dominic Wilson, one for each of his probation violations. The warrants were each addressed to any duly authorized peace officer, and commanded such officers to arrest him and bring him immediately before the Circuit Court to answer an indictment as to his probation violation. The warrants made no mention of media presence or assistance.
>
> In the early morning hours of April 16, 1992, a Gunsmoke team of Deputy United States Marshals and Montgomery County Police officers assembled to execute the Dominic Wilson warrants. The team was accompanied by a reporter and a photographer from the *Washington Post,* who had been invited by the Marshals to accompany them on their mission as part of a Marshal's Service ride-along policy.
>
> At around 6:45 a.m., the officers, with media representatives in tow, entered the dwelling at 909 North StoneStreet Avenue in the Lincoln Park neighborhood of Rockville. Petitioners Charles and Geraldine Wilson were still in bed when they heard the officers enter the home. Petitioner Charles Wilson, dressed only in a pair of briefs, ran into the living room to investigate.

Discovering at least five men in street clothes with guns in his living room, he angrily demanded that they state their business, and repeatedly cursed the officers. Believing him to be an angry Dominic Wilson, the officers quickly subdued him on the floor. Geraldine Wilson next entered the living room to investigate, wearing only a nightgown. She observed her husband being restrained by the armed officers.

When their protective sweep was completed, the officers learned that Dominic Wilson was not in the house, and they departed. During the time that the officers were in the home, the *Washington Post* photographer took numerous pictures. The print reporter was also apparently in the living room observing the confrontation between the police and Charles Wilson. At no time, however, were the reporters involved in the execution of the arrest warrant. The *Washington Post* never published its photographs of the incident.

Petitioners sued the law enforcement officials in their personal capacities for money. They contended that the officers' actions in bringing members of the media to observe and record the attempted execution of the arrest warrant violated their Fourth Amendment rights.

The petitioners sued the federal officials under *Bivens* and the state officials under § 1983. Both *Bivens* and § 1983 allow a plaintiff to seek money damages from government officials who have violated his Fourth Amendment rights. But government officials performing discretionary functions generally are granted a qualified immunity and are shielded from liability for civil damages insofar as their conduct does not violate clearly established statutory or constitutional rights of which a reasonable person would have known.

Although this case involves suits under both § 1983 and *Bivens*, the qualified immunity analysis is identical under either cause of action. A court evaluating a claim of qualified immunity must first determine whether the plaintiff has alleged the deprivation of an actual constitutional right at all, and if so, proceed to determine whether that right was clearly established at the time of the alleged violation. This order of procedure is designed to spare a defendant not only unwarranted liability, but unwarranted demands customarily imposed upon those defending a long drawn-out lawsuit. Deciding the constitutional question before addressing the qualified immunity question also promotes clarity in the legal standards for official conduct, to the benefit of both the officers and the general public. We now turn to the Fourth Amendment question.

In 1604, an English court made the now-famous observation that "the house of everyone is to him as his castle and fortress, as well for his defence against injury and violence, as for his repose." In his *Commentaries on the Laws of England*, William Blackstone noted that

> "the law of England has so particular and tender a regard to the immunity of a man's house, that it stiles it his castle, and will never suffer it to be violated with impunity: agreeing herein with the sentiments of antient Rome.... For this reason no doors can in general be broken open to execute any civil process; though, in criminal causes, the public safety supersedes the private." William Blackstone, 4 *Commentaries on the Laws of England* 223 (1765–1769)

The Fourth Amendment embodies this centuries-old principle of respect for the privacy of the home. Physical entry of the home is the chief evil against which the wording of the Fourth Amendment is directed.

Our decisions have applied these basic principles of the Fourth Amendment to situations, like those in this case, in which police enter a home under the authority of an arrest warrant in order to take into custody the suspect named in the warrant. We noted that although clear in its protection of the home, the common-law tradition at the time of the drafting of the Fourth Amendment was ambivalent on the question of whether police could enter a home without a warrant. We were ultimately persuaded that the overriding respect for the sanctity of the home that has been embedded in our traditions since the origins of the Republic meant that absent a warrant or exigent circumstances, police could not enter a home to make an arrest. We decided that "an arrest warrant founded on probable cause implicitly carries with it the limited authority to enter a dwelling in which the suspect lives when there is reason to believe the suspect is within."

Here, of course, the officers had such a warrant, and they were undoubtedly entitled to enter the Wilson home in order to execute the arrest warrant for Dominic Wilson. But it does not necessarily follow that they were entitled to bring a newspaper reporter and a photographer with them. If the scope of the search exceeds that permitted by the terms of a validly issued warrant or the character of the relevant exception from the warrant requirement, the subsequent seizure is unconstitutional. While this does not mean that every police action while inside a home must be explicitly authorized by the text of the warrant, the Fourth Amendment does require that police actions in execution of a warrant be related to the objectives of the authorized intrusion.

Certainly the presence of reporters inside the home was not related to the objectives of the authorized intrusion. Respondents concede that the reporters did not engage in the execution of the warrant, and did not assist the police in their task. The reporters therefore were not present for any reason related to the justification for police entry into the home—the apprehension of Dominic Wilson.

This is not a case in which the presence of the third parties directly aided in the execution of the warrant. Where the police enter a home under the authority of a warrant to search for stolen property, the presence of third parties for the purpose of identifying the stolen property has long been approved by this Court and our common-law tradition.

Respondents argue that the presence of the *Washington Post* reporters in the Wilsons' home nonetheless served a number of legitimate law enforcement purposes. They first assert that officers should be able to exercise reasonable discretion about when it would further their law enforcement mission to permit members of the news media to accompany them in executing a warrant. But this claim ignores the importance of the right of residential privacy at the core of the Fourth Amendment. It may well be that media ride-alongs further the law enforcement objectives of the police in a general sense, but that is not the same as furthering the purposes of the search. Were such generalized "law enforcement objectives" themselves sufficient to trump the Fourth

Amendment, the protections guaranteed by that Amendment's text would be significantly watered down.

Finally, respondents argue that the presence of third parties could serve in some situations to minimize police abuses and protect suspects, and also to protect the safety of the officers. While it might be reasonable for police officers to themselves videotape home entries as part of a "quality control" effort to ensure that the rights of homeowners are being respected, or even to preserve evidence, such a situation is significantly different from the media presence in this case. The *Washington Post* reporters in the Wilsons' home were working on a story for their own purposes. They were not present for the purpose of protecting the officers, much less the Wilsons. A private photographer was acting for private purposes, as evidenced in part by the fact that the newspaper and not the police retained the photographs. Thus, although the presence of third parties during the execution of a warrant may in some circumstances be constitutionally permissible, the presence of these third parties was not.

We hold that it is a violation of the Fourth Amendment for police to bring members of the media or other third parties into a home during the execution of a warrant when the presence of the third parties in the home was not in aid of the execution of the warrant.

Since the police action in this case violated the petitioners' Fourth Amendment right, we now must decide whether this right was clearly established at the time of the search. As noted above, government officials performing discretionary functions generally are granted a qualified immunity and are shielded from liability for civil damages insofar as their conduct does not violate clearly established statutory or constitutional rights of which a reasonable person would have known. What this means in practice is that whether an official protected by qualified immunity may be held personally liable for an allegedly unlawful official action generally turns on the objective legal reasonableness of the action, assessed in light of the legal rules that were clearly established at the time it was taken.

We hold that it was not unreasonable for a police officer in April 1992 to have believed that bringing media observers along during the execution of an arrest warrant (even in a home) was lawful. First, the constitutional question presented by this case is by no means open and shut. The Fourth Amendment protects the rights of homeowners from entry without a warrant, but there was a warrant here. The question is whether the invitation to the media exceeded the scope of the search authorized by the warrant. Accurate media coverage of police activities serves an important public purpose, and it is not obvious from the general principles of the Fourth Amendment that the conduct of the officers in this case violated the Amendment.

For the foregoing reasons, the judgment of the Court of Appeals is affirmed. [The officers were held not liable for the violation.]

Questions in Review

1. Explain the meaning of the term *under color of law.*
2. Under what circumstances may an officer use deadly force to prevent the escape of a prisoner?
3. What are the required elements of a § 1983 claim for damages?
4. What is meant by the term *qualified immunity*?
5. Why should police officers be liable for money damages when they arrest someone?

Terrorism and the Writ of Habeas Corpus

11

That is a matter yet to be determined. We hold that petitioners (terrorist prisoners) may invoke the fundamental procedural protections of habeas corpus. The laws and Constitution are designed to survive, and remain in force, in extraordinary times. Liberty and security can be reconciled; and in our system they are reconciled within the framework of the law. The Framers decided that habeas corpus, a right of first importance, must be a part of that framework, a part of that law.

—**Associate Supreme Court Justice Anthony Kennedy in**
***Boumediene v. Bush* (2008)**

The Nation will live to regret what the Court has done today. I dissent.

—**Chief Justice John Roberts in *Boumediene v. Bush* (2008)**

Introduction

In this chapter, the writ of habeas corpus, often referred to as the Great Writ, and terrorism will be examined. Probably one of the most important decisions made by the Supreme Court in recent years was the *Boumediene v. Bush* (2008) case. That case is set forth in this chapter because its decision provides the guideline and rules involving the writ and terrorism. The *Boumediene* case concerned the issue of whether the prisoners being detained by the United States at the Guantanamo Bay prison as international terrorists were constitutionally entitled to bring habeas corpus proceedings in federal court to challenge the legality of their detention. At the time of the actions, some of the prisoners had been held for six years without an opportunity to challenge the legality of their detention. The case was decided by a 5–4 decision. The justices with the majority were Anthony Kennedy, John Paul Stevens, David Souter, Ruth Ginsberg, and Steven Breyer. The dissenters were Chief Justice John Roberts and Associate Justices Antonin Scalia, Clarence Thomas, and Samuel Alito.

Boumediene v. Bush **Case**

The basic issue before the Supreme Court was should the prisoners being held at Guantanamo have protection of the writ of habeas corpus to test the legality of their confinement?

Boumediene v. Bush, 2008 U.S. LEXIS 4887 (2008)

Justice Anthony Kennedy delivered the opinion of the Court.

Petitioners are aliens designated as enemy combatants and detained at the United States Naval Station at Guantanamo Bay, Cuba. There are others detained there, also aliens, who are not parties to this suit.

Black's Law Dictionary 728 (8th ed., 2004) defines habeas corpus as a writ employed to bring a person before a court, most frequently to ensure that the party's imprisonment or detention is not illegal.

In deciding the constitutional questions now presented we must determine whether petitioners are barred from seeking the writ or invoking the protections of the Suspension Clause either because of their status, i.e., petitioners' designation by the Executive Branch as enemy combatants, or their physical location, i.e., their presence at Guantanamo Bay. The Government contends that noncitizens designated as enemy combatants and detained in territory located outside our Nation's borders have no constitutional rights and no privilege of habeas corpus. Petitioners contend they do have cognizable constitutional rights and that Congress, in seeking to eliminate recourse to habeas corpus as a means to assert those rights, acted in violation of the Suspension Clause.

We begin with a brief account of the history and origins of the writ. Our account proceeds from two propositions. First, protection for the privilege of habeas corpus was one of the few safeguards of liberty specified in a Constitution that, at the outset, had no Bill of Rights. In the system conceived by the Framers the writ had a centrality that must inform proper interpretation of the Suspension Clause. Second, to the extent there were settled precedents or legal commentaries in 1789 regarding the extraterritorial scope of the writ or its application to enemy aliens, those authorities can be instructive for the present cases.

The Framers viewed freedom from unlawful restraint as a fundamental precept of liberty, and they understood the writ of habeas corpus as a vital instrument to secure that freedom. Experience taught, however, that the common-law writ all too often had been insufficient to guard against the abuse of monarchial power. That history counseled the necessity for specific language in the Constitution to secure the writ and ensure its place in our legal system.

Magna Carta decreed that no man would be imprisoned contrary to the law of the land. No free man shall be taken or imprisoned or dispossessed, or outlawed, or banished, or in any way destroyed, nor will we go upon him, nor send upon him, except by the legal judgment of his peers or by the law of the land. Important as the principle was, the Barons at Runnymede prescribed no specific legal process to enforce it. Gradually the writ of habeas corpus became the means by which the promise of Magna Carta was fulfilled.

The development was painstaking, even by the centuries-long measures of English constitutional history. The writ was known and used in some form at least as early as the reign of Edward I. Yet at the outset it was used to protect not the rights of citizens but those of the King and his courts. The early courts were considered agents of the Crown, designed to assist the King in the exercise of his power. Thus the writ, while it would become part of the foundation of liberty for the King's subjects, was in its earliest use a mechanism for securing compliance with the King's laws.

Over time it became clear that by issuing the writ of habeas corpus common-law courts sought to enforce the King's prerogative to inquire into the authority of a jailer to hold a prisoner.

Even so, from an early date it was understood that the King, too, was subject to the law. As the writers said of Magna Carta, it means this, that the king is and shall be below the law. And, by the 1600's, the writ was deemed less an instrument of the King's power and more a restraint upon it.

Still, the writ proved to be an imperfect check. Even when the importance of the writ was well understood in England, habeas relief often was denied by the courts or suspended by Parliament. Denial or suspension occurred in times of political unrest, to the anguish of the imprisoned and the outrage of those in sympathy with them.

A notable example from this period was Darnel's Case. The events giving rise to the case began when, in a display of the Stuart penchant for authoritarian excess, Charles I demanded that Darnel and at least four others lend him money. Upon their refusal, they were imprisoned. The prisoners sought a writ of habeas corpus; and the King filed a return in the form of a warrant signed by the Attorney General. The court held this was a sufficient answer and justified the subjects' continued imprisonment.

There was an immediate outcry of protest. The House of Commons promptly passed the Petition of Right, which condemned executive imprisonment without any cause shown, and declared that no freeman in any such manner as is before mentioned shall be imprisoned or detained. Yet a full legislative response was long delayed. The King soon began to abuse his authority again, and Parliament was dissolved. When Parliament reconvened in 1640, it sought to secure access to the writ by statute. The Act of 1640 expressly authorized use of the writ to test the legality of commitment by command or warrant of the King or the Privy Council. Civil strife and the Interregnum soon followed, and not until 1679 did Parliament try once more to secure the writ, this time through the Habeas Corpus Act of 1679. The Act, was later described by Blackstone as the "stable bulwark of our liberties."

This history was known to the Framers. It no doubt confirmed their view that pendulum swings to and away from individual liberty were endemic to undivided, uncontrolled power. The Framers' inherent distrust of governmental power was the driving force behind the constitutional plan that allocated powers among three independent branches. This design serves not only to make Government accountable but also to secure individual liberty. Because the Constitution's separation-of-powers structure, like the substantive guarantees of the Fifth and Fourteenth Amendments, protects persons as well as citizens, foreign nationals who have the privilege of litigating in our courts can seek to enforce separation-of-powers principles.

That the Framers considered the writ a vital instrument for the protection of individual liberty is evident from the care taken to specify the limited grounds for its suspension: "The Privilege of the Writ of Habeas Corpus shall not be suspended, unless when in Cases of Rebellion or Invasion the public Safety may require it." Art. I, § 9, cl. 2. The word "privilege" was used, perhaps, to avoid mentioning some rights to the exclusion of others. Indeed, the only mention of the term "right" in the Constitution, as ratified, is in its clause giving Congress the power to protect the rights of authors and inventors. See Art. I, § 8, cl. 8.

Surviving accounts of the ratification debates provide additional evidence that the Framers deemed the writ to be an essential mechanism in the separation-of-powers scheme. In a critical exchange with Patrick Henry at the Virginia ratifying convention Edmund Randolph referred to the Suspension Clause as an "exception" to the "power given to Congress to regulate courts." A resolution passed by the New York ratifying convention made clear its understanding that the Clause not only protects against arbitrary suspensions of the writ but also guarantees an affirmative right to judicial inquiry into the causes of detention. Alexander Hamilton likewise explained that by providing the detainee a judicial forum to challenge detention, the writ preserves limited government.

As he explained in *The Federalist* No. 84:

> The practice of arbitrary imprisonments, have been, in all ages, the favorite and most formidable instruments of tyranny. The observations of the judicious Blackstone are well worthy of recital: To bereave a man of life or by violence to confiscate his estate, without accusation or trial, would be so gross and notorious an act of despotism as must at once convey the alarm of tyranny throughout the whole nation; but confinement of the person, by secretly hurrying him to jail, where his sufferings are unknown or forgotten, is a less public, a less striking, and therefore a more dangerous engine of arbitrary government. And as a remedy for this fatal evil he is everywhere peculiarly emphatical in his encomiums on the habeas corpus act, which in one place he calls the BULWARK of the British Constitution.

Post-1789 habeas developments in England, though not bearing upon the Framers' intent, do verify their foresight. Those later events would underscore the need for structural barriers against arbitrary suspensions of the writ. Just as the writ had been vulnerable to executive and parliamentary encroachment on both sides of the Atlantic before the American Revolution, despite the Habeas Corpus Act of 1679, the writ was suspended with frequency in England during times of political unrest after 1789. Parliament suspended the writ for much of the period from 1792 to 1801, resulting in rampant arbitrary imprisonment.

In our own system the Suspension Clause is designed to protect against these cyclical abuses. The Clause protects the rights of the detained by a means consistent with the essential design of the Constitution. It ensures that, except during periods of formal suspension, the Judiciary will have a time-tested device, the writ, to maintain the delicate balance of governance that is itself the surest safeguard of liberty. The Clause protects the rights of the detained by affirming the duty and authority of the Judiciary to call the jailer to account. The essence of habeas corpus is an attack by a person in custody upon the legality of that custody. The important fact to be observed in regard to the mode of procedure upon this habeas writ is, that it is directed to, and served upon, not the person confined, but his jailer. The separation-of-powers doctrine, and the history that influenced its design, therefore must inform the reach and purpose of the Suspension Clause.

The broad historical narrative of the writ and its function is central to our analysis, but we seek guidance as well from founding-era authorities address-ing the specific question before us: whether foreign nationals, apprehended and detained in distant countries during a time of serious threats to our Nation's security, may assert the privilege of the writ and seek its protection. The Court has been careful not to foreclose the possibility that the protections of the Suspension Clause have expanded along with post-1789 developments that define the present scope of the writ. But the analysis may begin with precedents as of 1789, for the Court has said that at the absolute minimum the Clause pro-tects the writ as it existed when the Constitution was drafted and ratified.

We know that at common law a petitioner's status as an alien was not a cat-egorical bar to habeas corpus relief. We know as well that common-law courts entertained habeas petitions brought by enemy aliens detained in England—"entertained" at least in the sense that the courts held hearings to determine the threshold question of entitlement to the writ.

Drawing from its position that at common law the writ ran only to territo-ries over which the Crown was sovereign, the Government says the Suspension Clause affords petitioners no rights because the United States does not claim sovereignty over the place of detention.

Guantanamo Bay is not formally part of the United States. And under the terms of the lease between the United States and Cuba, Cuba retains "ultimate sovereignty" over the territory while the United States exercises "complete jurisdiction and control." Under the terms of the 1934 Treaty, however, Cuba effectively has no rights as a sovereign until the parties agree to modification of the 1903 Lease Agreement or the United States abandons the base.

The United States contends, nevertheless, that Guantanamo is not within its sovereign control. This was the Government's position well before the events of September 11, 2001. And in other contexts the Court has held that questions of sovereignty are for the political branches to decide.

We therefore do not question the Government's position that Cuba, not the United States, maintains sovereignty, in the legal and technical sense of the term, over Guantanamo Bay. But this does not end the analysis. Our cases do not hold it is improper for us to inquire into the objective degree of control the Nation asserts over foreign territory. As commentators have noted, sover-eignty is a term used in many senses and is much abused.

Fundamental questions regarding the Constitution's geographic scope first arose at the dawn of the 20th century when the Nation acquired noncontiguous Territories: Puerto Rico, Guam, and the Philippines—ceded to the United States by Spain at the conclusion of the Spanish-American War—and Hawaii—annexed by the United States in 1898. At this point Congress chose to discontinue its previous practice of extending constitutional rights to the territories by statute.

In a series of opinions later known as the Insular Cases, the Court addressed whether the Constitution, by its own force, applies in any territory that is not a State. The Court held that the Constitution has independent force in these territories, a force not contingent upon acts of legislative grace. Yet it took note of the difficulties inherent in that position.

The Government presents no credible arguments that the military mission at Guantanamo would be compromised if habeas corpus courts had jurisdiction to hear the detainees' claims. And in light of the plenary control the United States asserts over the base, none are apparent to us.

There is no indication, furthermore, that adjudicating a habeas corpus petition would cause friction with the host government. No Cuban court has jurisdiction over American military personnel at Guantanamo or the enemy combatants detained there. While obligated to abide by the terms of the lease, the United States is, for all practical purposes, answerable to no other sovereign for its acts on the base. Were that not the case, or if the detention facility were located in an active theater of war, arguments that issuing the writ would be "impracticable or anomalous" would have more weight. Under the facts presented here, however, there are few practical barriers to the running of the writ. To the extent barriers arise, habeas corpus procedures likely can be modified to address them.

It is true that before today the Court has never held that noncitizens detained by our Government in territory over which another country maintains de jure sovereignty have any rights under our Constitution. But the cases before us lack any precise historical parallel. They involve individuals detained by executive order for the duration of a conflict that, if measured from September 11, 2001, to the present, is already among the longest wars in American history. The detainees, moreover, are held in a territory that, while technically not part of the United States, is under the complete and total control of our Government. Under these circumstances the lack of a precedent on point is no barrier to our holding.

We hold that Art. I, § 9, cl. 2, of the Constitution has full effect at Guantanamo Bay. If the privilege of habeas corpus is to be denied to the detainees now before us, Congress must act in accordance with the requirements of the Suspension Clause.

We do not endeavor to offer a comprehensive summary of the requisites for an adequate substitute for habeas corpus. We do consider it uncontroversial, however, that the privilege of habeas corpus entitles the prisoner to a meaningful opportunity to demonstrate that he is being held pursuant to "the erroneous application or interpretation" of relevant law.

In light of our conclusion that there is no jurisdictional bar to the District Court's entertaining petitioners' claims the question remains whether there are prudential barriers to habeas corpus review under these circumstances.

The real risks, the real threats, of terrorist attacks are constant and not likely soon to abate. The ways to disrupt our life and laws are so many and unforeseen that the Court should not attempt even some general catalogue of crises that might occur. Certain principles are apparent, however. Practical considerations and exigent circumstances inform the definition and reach of the law's writs, including habeas corpus. The cases and our tradition reflect this precept.

The determination by the Court of Appeals that the Suspension Clause and its protections are inapplicable to petitioners was in error. The judgment of the Court of Appeals is reversed. The cases are remanded to the Court of Appeals with instructions that it remand the cases to the District Court for proceedings consistent with this opinion.

It is so ordered.

Chief Justice Roberts, with whom Justice Scalia, Justice Thomas, and Justice Alito join, dissenting, wrote:

Today the Court strikes down as inadequate the most generous set of procedural protections ever afforded aliens detained by this country as enemy combatants. The political branches crafted these procedures amidst an ongoing military conflict, after much careful investigation and thorough debate. The Court rejects them today out of hand, without bothering to say what due process rights the detainees possess, without explaining how the statute fails to vindicate those rights, and before a single petitioner has even attempted to avail himself of the law's operation. And to what effect? The majority merely replaces a review system designed by the people's representatives with a set of shapeless procedures to be defined by federal courts at some future date. One cannot help but think, after surveying the modest practical results of the majority's ambitious opinion, that this decision is not really about the detainees at all, but about control of federal policy regarding enemy combatants.

The majority is adamant that the Guantanamo detainees are entitled to the protections of habeas corpus—its opinion begins by deciding that question. I regard the issue as a difficult one, primarily because of the unique and unusual jurisdictional status of Guantanamo Bay. I nonetheless agree with Justice Scalia's analysis of our precedents and the pertinent history of the writ, and accordingly join his dissent. The important point for me, however, is that the Court should have resolved these cases on other grounds. Habeas is most fundamentally a procedural right, a mechanism for contesting the legality of executive detention. The critical threshold question in these cases, prior to any inquiry about the writ's scope, is whether the system the political branches designed protects whatever rights the detainees may possess. If so, there is no need for any additional process, whether called "habeas" or something else.

The Nation will live to regret what the Court has done today. I dissent.

Subsequent Proceedings

On June 23, 2008, just 11 days after the Supreme Court issued its decision in *Boumediene v. Bush*, the U.S. Court of Appeals for the District of Columbia held that the U.S. military had improperly labeled a Chinese Muslim held at Guantanamo Bay an "enemy combatant," and it ordered that he be released, transferred, or granted a new hearing. The ruling by the U.S. Court of Appeals marked the first time a federal court has weighed in on the issue of a Guantanamo detainee's classification and granted him the opportunity to try to secure his release through civilian courts.

The detainee, Huzaifa Parhat, had been detained for more than six years. He was one of 17 Uighur Muslims, an ethnic minority in China, who are still being held at Guantanamo even though the U.S. government had acknowledged that the group posed no threat to U.S. security. In a one-paragraph notice, the three judges on the appellate panel said they could not discuss their order publicly because it contained classified information and that a declassified version would be available later. The panel of three appellate justices who decided the case consisted of a justice appointed by President Reagan, one appointed by President Clinton, and one appointed by President George W. Bush.

Parhat and the other Uighurs were captured in Afghanistan after the September 11 attacks. He has insisted that he sought refuge there from an oppressive Chinese government and never fought against the United States. The U.S. government had no evidence suggesting that he ever intended to fight, but it designated him an enemy combatant because of alleged links to the East Turkestan Islamic Movement, a separatist group demanding independence from China that Washington says has links to Al Qaeda.

Questions in Review

1. What was the basis of the majority's opinion?
2. What was the rationale of the dissenters' opinion?
3. How do you feel? Should the prisoners being held in Guantanamo Bay have rights to contest the legality of their detention by a writ of habeas corpus?

Glossary

Acquittal: Judgment that a criminal defendant has not been proved guilty beyond a reasonable doubt, in other words, a verdict of "not guilty."

Affidavit: A written statement of facts confirmed by the oath of the party making it, before a notary or officer having authority to administer oaths.

Affirmed: In the practice of the court of appeals, it means that the court of appeals has concluded that the lower court decision is correct and will stand as rendered by the lower court.

Answer: The formal written statement by a defendant responding to a civil complaint and setting forth the grounds for his defense.

Appeal: A request made after a trial by a party that has lost on one or more issues that a higher court (appellate court) review the trial court's decision to determine if it was correct. To make such a request is "to appeal" or "to take an appeal." One who appeals is called the "appellant"; the other party is the "appellee."

Arraignment: A proceeding in which an individual who is accused of committing a crime is brought into court, told of the charges, and asked to plead guilty or not guilty.

Bail: Security given for the release of a criminal defendant or witness from legal custody (usually in the form of money) to secure his appearance on the day and time set by the court.

Bench trial: Trial without a jury in which a judge decides which party prevails.

Brief: A written statement submitted by each party in a case that explains why the court should decide the case, or particular issues in a case, in that party's favor.

Capital offense: A crime punishable by death.

Case law: The law as reflected in the written decisions of the courts.

Chambers: A judge's office, typically including workspace for the judge's law clerks and secretary.

Clerk of court: An officer appointed by the judges of the court to assist in managing the flow of cases through the court, maintain court records, handle financial matters, and provide other administrative support to the court.

Common law: The legal system that originated in England and is now in use in the United States that relies on the articulation of legal principles in a historical succession of judicial decisions. Common law principles can be changed by legislation.

Complaint: A written statement filed by the plaintiff that initiates a civil case, stating the wrongs allegedly committed by the defendant and requesting relief from the court. In criminal cases that are tried without a grand jury indictment, the complaint is a document that formally states the charges against the defendant.

Court reporter: A person who makes a word-for-word record of what is said in court, generally by using a stenographic machine, shorthand, or audio recording, and then produces a transcript of the proceedings upon request.

Deposition: An oral statement made before an officer authorized by law to administer oaths. Such statements are often taken to examine potential witnesses, to obtain discovery, or to be used later in trial. *See* discovery.

Discovery: The process by which lawyers learn about their opponent's case in preparation for trial. Typical tools of discovery include depositions, interrogatories, requests for admissions, and requests for documents. All of these devices help the lawyer learn the relevant facts and collect and examine any relevant documents or other materials.

Docket: A log containing the complete history of each case in the form of brief chronological entries summarizing the court proceedings.

En banc: "In the bench" or "as a full bench." Refers to court sessions with the entire membership of a court participating rather than the usual number. U.S. circuit courts of appeals usually sit in panels of three judges, but all the judges in the court may decide certain matters together. They are then said to be sitting "en banc" (occasionally spelled "in banc").

Equitable: Pertaining to civil suits in equity rather than in law. In English legal history, the courts of law could order the payment of damages and could afford no other remedy. A separate court of equity could order someone to do something or to cease to do something. *See*, e.g., injunction. In American jurisprudence, the federal courts have both legal and equitable power, but the distinction is still an important one. For example, a trial by jury is normally available in law cases but not in equity cases.

Evidence: Information presented in testimony or in documents that is used to persuade the fact finder (judge or jury) to decide the case in favor of one side or the other.

Federal question jurisdiction: Jurisdiction given to federal courts in cases involving the interpretation and application of the U.S. Constitution, acts of Congress, and treaties.

Felony: A serious crime carrying a penalty of more than a year in prison. *See also* misdemeanor.

File: To place a paper in the official custody of the clerk of court to enter into the files or records of a case.

Grand jury: A body of 16 to 23 citizens who listen to evidence of criminal allegations, which is presented by the prosecutors, and determine whether there is probable cause to believe an individual committed an offense. *See also* indictment and U.S. attorney.

Habeas corpus: A writ (court order) that is usually used to bring a prisoner before the court to determine the legality of his imprisonment. Someone imprisoned in state court proceedings can file a petition in federal court for a writ of habeas corpus, seeking to have the federal court review whether the state has violated his or her rights under the U.S. Constitution. Federal prisoners can file habeas petitions as well. A writ of habeas corpus may also be used to bring a person in custody before the court to give testimony or to be prosecuted.

Hearsay: Statements by a witness who did not see or hear the incident in question but heard about it from someone else. Hearsay is usually not admissible as evidence in court.

Impeachment: 1. The process of calling a witness's testimony into doubt. For example, if the attorney can show that the witness may have fabricated portions of his testimony, the witness is said to be "impeached." 2. The constitutional process whereby the House of Representatives may "impeach" (accuse of misconduct) high officers of the federal government, who are then tried by the Senate.

Indictment: The formal charge issued by a grand jury stating that there is enough evidence that the defendant committed the crime to justify having a trial; it is used primarily for felonies. *See also* information.

In forma pauperis: "In the manner of a pauper." Permission given by the court to a person to file a case without payment of the required court fees because the person cannot pay them.

Information: A formal accusation by a government attorney that the defendant committed a misdemeanor. *See* also indictment.

Injunction: A court order prohibiting a defendant from performing a specific act, or compelling a defendant to perform a specific act.

Interrogatories: Written questions sent by one party in a lawsuit to an opposing party as part of pretrial discovery in civil cases. The party receiving the interrogatories is required to answer them in writing under oath.

Judgment: The official decision of a court finally resolving the dispute between the parties to the lawsuit.

Jurisdiction: 1. The legal authority of a court to hear and decide a case. 2. The geographic area over which the court has authority to decide cases.

Jurisprudence: The study of law and the structure of the legal system.

Jury: The group of persons selected to hear the evidence in a trial and render a verdict on matters of fact. *See also* grand jury.

Jury instructions: A judge's directions to the jury before it begins deliberations regarding the factual questions it must answer and the legal rules that it must apply.

Magistrate judge: A judicial officer of a district court who conducts initial proceedings in criminal cases, decides criminal misdemeanor cases, conducts many pretrial civil and criminal matters on behalf of district judges, and decides civil cases with the consent of the parties.

Misdemeanor: An offense punishable by one year of imprisonment or less. *See also* felony.

Mistrial: An invalid trial, caused by fundamental error. When a mistrial is declared, the trial must start again with the selection of a new jury.

Motion: A request by a litigant to a judge for a decision on an issue relating to the case.

***Nolo contendere*:** No contest. A plea of *nolo contendere* has the same effect as a plea of guilty, as far as the criminal sentence is concerned, but may not be considered an admission of guilt for any other purpose.

Opinion: A judge's written explanation of the decision of the court. Because a case may be heard by three or more judges in the court of appeals, the opinion in appellate decisions can take several forms. If all the judges completely agree on the result, one judge will write the opinion for all. If all the judges do not agree, the formal decision will be based upon the view of the majority, and one member of the majority will write the opinion. The judges who did not agree with the majority may write separately in dissenting or concurring opinions to present their views. A dissenting opinion disagrees with the majority opinion because of the reasoning or the principles of law the majority used to decide the case. A concurring opinion agrees with the decision of the majority opinion, but offers further comment or clarification, or even an entirely different reason for reaching the same result. Only the majority opinion can serve as binding precedent in future cases. *See also* precedent.

Oral argument: An opportunity for lawyers to summarize their position before the court and also to answer the judges' questions.

Panel: 1. In appellate cases, a group of judges (usually three) assigned to decide the case. 2. In the jury selection process, the group of potential jurors. 3. The list of attorneys who are both available and qualified to serve as court-appointed counsel for criminal defendants who cannot afford their own counsel.

Party: One of the litigants. At the trial level, the parties are typically referred to as the plaintiff and defendant. On appeal, they are known as the appellant and appellee, or in some cases involving administrative agencies, as the petitioner and respondent.

Petit jury (or trial jury): A group of citizens who hears the evidence presented by both sides at trial and determine the facts in dispute. Federal criminal juries consist of 12 persons. Federal civil juries consist of at least six persons. *See also* jury and grand jury.

Petty offense: A misdemeanor punishable by six months or less in prison.

Plaintiff: The person who files the complaint in a civil lawsuit.

Plea: In a criminal case, the defendant's statement pleading "guilty" or "not guilty" in answer to the charges. *See also nolo contendere.*

Pleadings: Written statements filed with the court that describe a party's legal or factual assertions about the case.

Precedent: A court decision in an earlier case with facts and legal issues similar to those of a dispute currently before a court. Judges will generally "follow precedent"—meaning that they use the principles established in earlier cases to decide new cases that have similar facts and raise similar legal issues. A judge will disregard precedent if a party can show that the earlier case was wrongly decided, or that it differed in some significant way from the current case.

Presentence report: A report prepared by a court's probation officer, after a person has been convicted of an offense, summarizing for the court the background information needed to determine the appropriate sentence.

Pretrial conference: A meeting of the judge and lawyers to plan the trial, to discuss which matters should be presented to the jury, to review proposed evidence and witnesses, and to set a trial schedule.

Pretrial services: A department of the district court that conducts an investigation of a criminal defendant's background to help a judge decide whether to release the defendant into the community before trial.

Probation: 1. A sentencing alternative to imprisonment in which the court releases convicted defendants under supervision of a probation officer, who makes certain that the defendant follows certain rules (e.g., gets a job, gets drug counseling). 2. A department of the court that prepares a presentence report.

Probation officer: Officers of the probation office of a court. Probation officer duties include conducting presentence investigations, preparing presentence reports on convicted defendants, and supervising released defendants.

Procedure: The rules for conducting a lawsuit; there are rules of civil procedure, criminal procedure, evidence, bankruptcy, and appellate procedure.

Pro per: A slang expression sometimes used to refer to a *pro se* litigant. It is a corruption of the Latin phrase *in propria persona.*

Pro se: A Latin term meaning "on one's own behalf"; in courts, it refers to persons who present their own cases without lawyers.

Reversal: The act of an appellate court setting aside the decision of a trial court. A reversal is often accompanied by a remand to the lower court for further proceedings.

Sentence: The punishment ordered by a court for a defendant convicted of a crime.

Sentencing guidelines: A set of rules and principles established by a sentencing commission that trial judges use to determine the sentence for a convicted defendant.

Service of process: The delivery of writs or summonses to the appropriate party.

Sequester: To separate. Sometimes juries are sequestered from outside influences during their deliberations.

Statute of limitations: A law that sets the deadline by which prosecution must start in a criminal case.

Subpoena: A command, issued under authority of a court or other authorized government entity, to a witness to appear and give testimony.

Subpoena *duces tecum*: A command to a witness to appear and produce documents.

Summary judgment: A decision made on the basis of statements and evidence presented for the record without a trial. It is used when it is not necessary to resolve any factual disputes in the case. Summary judgment is granted when—on the undisputed facts in the record—one party is entitled to judgment as a matter of law.

Temporary restraining order: Prohibits a person from taking an action that is likely to cause irreparable harm. This differs from an injunction in that it may be granted immediately, without notice to the opposing party and without a hearing. It is intended to last only until a hearing can be held. Sometimes referred to as a T.R.O.

Testimony: Evidence presented orally by witnesses during trials or before grand juries.

Tort: A civil wrong or breach of a duty to another person. The "victim" of a tort may be entitled to sue for the harm suffered. Victims of crimes may also sue in tort for the wrongs done to them. Most tort cases are handled in state court, except when the tort occurs on federal property (e.g., a military base), when the government is the defendant, or when there is diversity of citizenship between the parties.

Transcript: A written, word-for-word record of what was said, either in a proceeding, such as a trial, or during some other formal conversation, such as a hearing or oral deposition.

Uphold: The appellate court agrees with the lower court decision and allows it to stand. *See* affirmed.

U.S. attorney: A lawyer appointed by the president in each judicial district to prosecute and defend cases for the federal government. The U.S. attorney employs a staff of assistant U.S. attorneys who appear as the government's attorneys in individual cases.

Venue: The geographical location in which a case is tried.

Verdict: The decision of a trial jury or a judge that determines the guilt or innocence of a criminal defendant, or that determines the final outcome of a civil case.

Voir dire: The process by which judges and lawyers select a trial jury from among those eligible to serve, by questioning them to make certain that they would fairly decide the case. *Voir dire* means "to speak the truth."

Warrant: A written order authorizing official action by law enforcement officials, usually directing them to arrest the individual named in the warrant. A search warrant orders that a specific location be searched for items, which if found, can be used in court as evidence.

Writ: A formal written command or order, issued by the court, requiring the performance of a specific act.

Writ of certiorari: An order issued by the U.S. Supreme Court directing the lower court to transmit records for a case that it will hear on appeal.

References

Publications

Amar, Akhil R. (1998). *The Bill of Rights.* New Haven, CT: Yale University Press.

Black's law dictionary. (1961). 6th ed. St. Paul, MN: West.

Cohen, William, and David J. Danelski. (2002). *Constitutional law: Civil liberty and individual rights.* 5th ed. New York: Foundation Press.

Dunne, Gerald T. (1977). *Hugo Black and the judicial revolution.* New York: Simon & Schuster.

Hendrie, Edward D. (1998, April). Curtilage: The expectation of privacy in the yard. *FBI Law Enforcement Bulletin,* pp. 25–28.

King, Gilbert. (2008). *The execution of Willie Francis: Race, murder and the search for justice in the American South.* New York: Basic Civitas Books.

Kittrie, Nicholas, Elyce Zenoff, and Vincent Eng. (2002). *Sentencing, sanctions, and corrections.* New York: Foundation Press.

Levy, Leonard. (1988). *Original intent and the framers' Constitution.* New York: Macmillan.

Mill, John Stuart. (1869). *On liberty.* London: Longman, Roberts & Green. Reprinted, New York: Bartleby.com, 1999.

Orth, John V. (2003). *Due process of law.* Lawrence: University of Kansas Press.

Padover, Saul K. (1943). *The complete Jefferson.* New York: Duell, Sloan & Pearce.

Roberson, Cliff. (2003). *Criminal procedure today.* 2nd ed. Upper Saddle River, NJ: Prentice-Hall.

Rutledge, Devailis. (2004, September). Does Miranda bear poisonous fruit. *Police Magazine,* pp. 82–84.

Supreme Historical Society (2007). *The Supreme Court of the United States* (revised), Washington, DC: Supreme Court Historical Society.

Statutes or Laws Cited

Federal

Civil Rights Act of 1871 (42 USC § 1983.1)

Migratory Bird Treaty Act of July 3, 1918, 40 Statute 75

Title III of the Omnibus Crime Control and Safe Streets Act of 1968

18 U.S. Code § 922(q)(1)(A)

18 U.S. Code § 2252A(a)(3)(B)

18 U.S. Code § 2518
18 U.S. Code § 3052
18 U.S. Code § 3553(a)(4) and (5)
21 Code of Federal Regulations § 1307.31 (2005)
42 U.S. Code § 1983
49 Code of Federal Regulations § 24291 (1984)
Federal Rules of Criminal Procedure P. 52

Alabama

Alabama Rules of Criminal Procedures § 6.1(b)

California

California Penal Code 261.5

New York State

New York Penal Law § 1141(2)

Texas

Texas Code Criminal Procedure Annotated Article 15.17

Virginia

Virginia Code, Annotated, § 18.2-423 (1996)

Local Ordinances

Rockford, Illinois, Code of Ordinances, ch. 28, § 18.1(i)
Rockford, Illinois, Code of Ordinances, ch. 28, § 19.2(a)

Cases Cited

Adams v. State, 431 N.E.2d 820 (1982, Ind.)
Adams v. Texas, 448 U.S. 38 (1980)
Adams v. Williams, 407 U.S. 143 (1972)
Adamson v. California, 332 U.S. 46 (1947)
Agnello v. United States, 269 U.S. 20 (1925)
Aguilar v. Texas, 378 U.S. 108 (1964)
Albert v. Montgomery, 732 F.2d 865 (1984, CA11 Ga.)
Alexander v. Connecticut, 917 F.2d 747(1990, CA2 Conn.)
Apodaca v. Oregon, 406 U.S. 404 (1972)

Argersinger v. Hamlin, 407 U.S. 25 (1972)
Arizona v. Evans, 514 U.S. 1 (1995)
Ashe v. Swensen, 1970
Ashwander v. Tennessee Valley Authority, 297 U.S. 288 (1936)
Atkins v. Virginia, 536 U.S. 304 (2002)
Atwater v. City of Lago Vista, 149 L. ed. 2d 549 (2001)
Bacon v. Patera, 772 F.2d 259 (1985, CA6 Ohio)
Ballew v. Georgia, 435 U.S. 223 (1978)
Barker v. Wingo, 407 U.S. 514 (1972)
Barrett v. City of Allentown, 152 FRD 50 (1993, E.D. Pa.)
Barron v. Baltimore, 32 U.S. 243 (1833)
Batson v. Kentucky, 476 U.S. 79 (1986)
Baumann v. United States, 692 F.2d 565 (1982, CA9 Ariz.)
Baze v. Rees, 2008 U.S. LEXIS 3476 (2008)
Beard v. Banks, 548 U.S. 521 (2006)
Beard v. Whitmore Lake School District, 402 F.3d 598 (6th Cir. 2005)
Bell v. Hood, 327 U.S. 678 (1946)
Benton v. Maryland, 395 U.S. 784 (1969)
Berna v. State, 282 Ark 563, 670 S.W.2d 434 (1984)
Bivens v. Six Unknown Named Agents of Federal Bureau of Narcotics, 403 U.S. 388
    (1971)
Blackledge v. Perry, 417 U.S. 21 (1974)
Blackmon v. Wainwright, 608 F.2d 183 (1979, CA5 Fla.)
Blackwell v. State 663 P.2d 12 (1983, Okla. Crim.)
Blanton v. North Las Vegas, 489 U.S. 538 (1989)
Boumediene v. Bush, 2008 U.S. LEXIS 4887 (2008)
Brede v. Powers, 263 U.S. 4 (1923)
Brendlin v. California, 127 S. Ct. 2400 (2007)
Briley v. Booker, 746 F.2d 225 (1984, CA4 Va.)
Brinegar v. United States, 338 U.S. 160 (1949)
Briscoe v. Lahue, 460 U.S. 325 (1983)
Broadrick v. Oklahoma, 413 U.S. 601 (1973)
Brooks v. State, 244 Ga 574 (1979)
Brosseau v. Haugen, 543 U.S. 194 (2004)
Brown v. Illinois, 422 U.S. 590 (1975)
Buchannon v. Wainwright, 474 F.2d 1006 (1973, CA5 Fla.)
Buckley v. Fitzsimmons, 509 U.S. 259 (1993)
Burch v. Louisiana, 441 U.S. 130 (1979)
Burks v. United States, 437 U.S. 1 (1978)
California v. Beheler, 463 U.S. 1121 (1983)
California v. Byers, 402 U.S. 424 (1971)
California v. Prysock, 453 U.S. 355 (1981)
California v. Carney, 471 U.S. 386 (1985)
California v. Ciraolo, 476 U.S. 207 (1986)
California v. Greenwood, 486 U.S. 35 (1988)
California v. Hodari D., 499 U.S. 621 (1991)
Cason v. Cook, 810 F.2d 188 (1987, CA8 Iowa)
Caudill v. Scott, 857 F.2d 344. (1988, CA6 Ky.)

Chambers v. Florida, 309 U.S. 227 (1940)

Chavez v. Martinez, 538 U.S. 760 (2003)

Chavez-Raya v. Immigration and Naturalization Service, 519 F.2d 397 (1975, CA7)

Chicago, Burlington, and Quincy R.R. v. Chicago, 166 U.S. 226 (1897)

Chimel v. California, 395 U.S. 752 (1969)

City of Canton v. Harris, 489 U.S. 378 (1989)

City of Cuyahoga Falls v. Buckeye Community Hope Foundation, 538 U.S. 188 (2003)

Clark v. Murphy, 331 F.3d 1062 (2003, CA9 Ariz.)

Colorado v. Bannister, 449 U.S. 1 (1980)

Colorado v. Connelly, 479 U.S. 157 (1986)

Colorado v. Spring, 479 U.S. 564 (1987)

Colten v. Kentucky, 407 U.S. 104 (1972)

Commonwealth v. Allen, 395 Mass. 448, 480 N.E.2d 630 (1985)

Commonwealth v. Hare, 475 Pa. 234 (1977)

Commonwealth v. Johnson, 921 A.2d 1221 (Pa. Super. Ct. 2007)

Commonwealth v. McCree, 592 Pa. 238, 924 A.2d 621 (2007)

Commonwealth v. Vitello, 367 Mass. 224 (1975)

Commonwealth v. Wallace, 493 N.E.2d 216 (1986)

Connally v. General Construction Co., 269 U.S. 385 (1926)

Craig v. Boren, 429 U.S. 190 (1976)

Crawford v. Marion County Election Board, 128 S. Ct. 1610 (2008)

Crawford v. Washington, 541 U.S. 36 (2004)

Cutshall v. Sundquist, 193 F.3d 466 (1999, CA6 Tenn.)

D'Aguanno v. Gallagher, 50 F.3d 877 (1995, CA11 Fla.)

Davis v. United States, 247 F. 394 (1917, CA8 Okla.)

Davis v. United States, 512 U.S. 452 (1994)

Davis v. Washington, 547 U.S. 813 (2006)

Dejonge v. Oregon, 299 U.S. 353 (1937)

Delaware v. Prouse, 440 U.S. 648 (1979)

Dickerson v. United States, 530 U.S. 428 (2000)

District of Columbia v. Heller, 2008 U.S. LEXIS 5268 (2008)

Doe v. Norris, 751 SW2d 834 (1986, Tenn.)

Douglas v. California, 372 U.S. 353 (1963)

Draper v. United States, 358 U.S. 307 (1959)

Duhaime v. DuCharme, 200 F.3d 597 (2000, CA9 Wash.)

Duke v. United States, 301 U.S. 492 (1937)

Duncan v. Louisiana, 391 U.S. 145 (1968)

Duren v. Missouri, 439 U.S. 357(1979)

Edwards v. Arizona, 451 U.S. 477 (1981)

Elkins v. United States, 364 U.S. 206 (1960)

Engblom v. Carey, 677 F.2d 957 (1982, CA2 N.Y.)

Enmund v. Florida, 458 U.S. 782 (1982)

Escobedo v. Illinois, 378 U.S. 478 (1964)

Estelle v. Gamble, 429 U.S. 97 (1976)

Ex parte Lange, 85 U.S. 163 (1874)

Ex parte Quirin, 317 U.S. 1 (1942)

Ex parte Wilson, 114 U.S. 417 (1885)

Eyman v. Alford, 448 F.2d 306 (1969, CA9 Ariz.)

Fare v. Michael C., 442 U.S. 707 (1979)

Faretta v. California, 422 U.S. 806 (1975)

Fiehe v. R. E. Householder Co., 125 So. 2 (1929, Fla.)

Fisher v. Hargett, 997 F.2d 1095 (1993, CA5 Miss.)

Fisher v. United States, 425 U.S. 391 (1976)

Flittie v. Solem, 775 F.2d 933 (1985, CA8 S.D.)

Florida v. Bostick, 501 U.S. 429 (1991)

Florida v. Jimeno, 500 U.S. 248 (1991)

Fontaine v. California, 390 U.S. 593 (1968)

Franks v. Delaware, 438 U.S. 154 (1978)

Frantz v. United States, 62 F.2d 737 (1933, CA6 Mich.)

Fuentes v. Shevin, 407 U.S. 67 (1972)

Fulmer v. Jensen, 221 Neb. 582, 379 N.W.2d 736 (1986)

Furman v. Georgia, 408 U.S. 238 (1972)

Garcia v. Dykstra, 2008 Fed. App. 0074N (2008, 6th Cir.)

Garcia v. San Antonio Metropolitan Transit Authority, 469 U.S. 528 (1985)

Geise v. United States, 262 F.2d 151 (1958, CA9 Alaska)

Gibson v. Commonwealth, 653 S.E.2d 626 (2007)

Gideon v. Wainwright, 372 U.S. 335 (1963)

Giese v. United States, 444 U.S. 979 (1979)

Giles v. California, 2008 U.S. LEXIS 5264 (2008)

Gitlow v. New York, 268 U.S. 652 (1925)

Godfrey v. Georgia, 446 U.S. 420, 64 L. Ed. 2d 398, 100 S. Ct. 1759 (1980)

Gonzales v. O Centro Espirita Beneficente Uniao do Vegetal, 546 U.S. 418 (2006)

Good News Club v. Milford Central School, 533 U.S. 98 (2001)

Graves v. United States, 467 A.2d 712 (1983, Dist. Col. App.)

Gravley v. Mills, 87 F.3d 779 (1996, CA6 Tenn.)

Grayned v. City of Rockford, 408 U.S. 104 (1972)

Gregg v. Georgia, 428 U.S. 153 (1976)

Griffin v. California, 380 U.S. 609 (1965)

Grimsley v. United States, 50 F.2d 509 (1931, CA5 Fla.)

Griswold v. Connecticut, 381 U.S. 479 (1965)

Groh v. Ramirez, 540 U.S. 551 (2004)

Harris v. New York, 401 U.S. 222 (1971)

Hartman v. State, 918 A.2d 1138, 2007 Del. LEXIS 102 (2007)

Hartzell v. United States, 72 F.2d 569 (1934, CA8 Iowa)

Hatcher v. State, 274 Ind. 230, 410 N.E.2d 1187 (1980)

Hester v. United States, 265 U.S. 57 (1924)

Hiibel v. Sixth Judicial Dist. Court, 542 U.S. 177 (2004)

Hill v. California, 401 U.S. 797 (1971)

Hoag v. New Jersey, 356 U.S. 464 (1958)

Hudson v. McMillian, 503 U.S. 1 (1992)

Hudson v. Michigan, 547 U.S. 586 (2006)

Hulstine v. Morris, 819 F.2d 861 (1987, CA8 Mo.)

Hunter v. United States, 62 F.2d 217 (1932, CA5 Tex.)

Hurtado v. California, 110 U.S. 516 (1884)

Illinois v. Gates, 462 U.S. 213 (1983)

Illinois v. Perkins, 496 U.S. 292 (1990)

Immigration and Naturalization Service v. Lopez-Mendoza, 468 U.S. 1032 (1984)
In re Kemmler, 136 U.S. 436 (1890)
In re Medley, 134 U.S. 160 (1890)
In re W., 391 A.2d 1385 (1978, Dist. Col. App.)
Indiana v. Edwards, 2008 U.S. LEXIS 5031 (2008)
Ingraham v. Wright, 430 U.S. 651 (1977)
Isaac v. Perrin, 659 F.2d 279 (1981, CA1 N.H.)
J.E.B. v. Alabama, 511 U.S. 127 (1994)
Johnson v. New Jersey, 384 U.S. 719 (1966)
Joint Anti-Fascist Refugee Committee v. McGrath, 341 U.S. 123 (1951)
Jones v. Breed, 497 F.2d 1160 (1974, CA9 Cal.)
Jones v. United States, 362 U.S. 257 (1960)
Kane v. Garcia Espitia, 546 U.S. 9 (2005)
Kansas v. Colorado, 206 U.S. 46 (1907)
Katz v. United States, 389 U.S. 347 (1967)
Kennedy v. Louisiana, 2008 U.S. LEXIS 5262 (2008)
Kern v. State, 426 N.E.2d 385 (1981, Ind.)
Kesley v. United States, 47 F.2d 453 (1931, CA5 Fla.)
Kladis v. Brezek, 823 F.2d 1014 (1987, CA7 Ill.)
Kleinbart v. United States, 388 A.2d 878 (1978, Dist. Col. App.)
Klopfer v. North Carolina, 386 U.S. 213 (1967)
Kruelski v. Conn. Superior Court, 316 F.3d 103 (2003, CA2 Conn.)
Levine v. United States, 362 U.S. 610 (1960)
Lexington Herald-Leader Co. v. Meigs, 660 S.W.2d 658 (1983, Ky.)
Lindsley v. Natural Carbonic Gas Co., 220 U.S. 61 (1911)
Lockett v. Ohio, 438 U.S. 586 (1978)
Lockyer v. Andrade, 538 U.S. 63 (2003)
Louisiana ex rel. Francis v. Resweber, 329 U.S. 459 (1947)
Love v. Pepersack, 47 F.3d 120 (1995, CA4 Md.)
Lovell v. Griffin, 303 U.S. 444 (1938)
Loving v. Virginia, 388 U.S. 1 (1967)
Mackin v. United States, 117 U.S. 348 (1886)
Malloy v. Hogan, 378 U.S. 1 (1968)
MAPCO, Inc. v. Carter, 573 F.2d 1268 (1978, Em. Ct. App.)
Mapp v. Ohio, 367 U.S. 643 (1961)
Marshall v. Kansas City, 355 S.W.2d 877 (1962, Mo.)
Martin v. Hunter's Lessee, 14 U.S. 304 (1816)
Martin v. Wainwright, 770 F.2d 918 (1985, CA11 Fla.)
Maryland v. Garrison, 480 U.S. 79 (1987)
Massiah v. United States, 377 U.S. 201 (1964)
McClinnahan v. United States, 454 A.2d 1340 (1982, Dist. Col. App.)
McCreary County v. ACLU, 545 U.S. 844 (2007)
McDonald v. United States, 335 U.S. 451 (1948)
McKeiver v. Pennsylvania, 403 U.S. 528 (1971)
Medina v. California, 505 U.S. 437 (1992)
Mempa v. Rhay, 389 U.S. 128 (1967)
Miami Herald Publication Co., Division of Knight Newspapers, Inc. v. Tornillo, 418 U.S. 241 (1974)

Michael M. v. Superior Court of Sonoma County, 450 U.S. 464 (1981)

Michigan v. Jackson, 475 U.S. 625 1986)

Miller v. California, 413 U.S. 15 (1973)

Mills v. Alabama, 384 U.S. 214 (1966)

Minnesota v. Carter, 525 U.S. 83 (1998)

Miranda v. Arizona, 384 U.S. 436 (1966)

Missouri v. Holland, 252 U.S. 416 (1920)

Missouri v. Seibert, 542 U.S. 600 (2004)

Mitchum v. Foster, 407 U.S. 225 (1972)

Monroe v. Pape, 365 U.S. 167 (1961)

Moore v. Ballone, 658 F.2d 218 (1981, CA4 Va.)

Morrissey v. Brewer, 408 U.S. 471 (1972)

Morse v. Frederick, 127 S. Ct. 2618 (2007)

Murray v. United States, 487 U.S. 533 (1988)

National Paint and Coatings Association v. City of Chicago, 45 F.3d 1124 (1995, 7th Cir.)

Near v. Minnesota, 283 U.S. 697 (1931)

Neris v. Vivoni, 249 F. Supp. 2d 146 (2003, DC Puerto Rico)

New Jersey v. T. L. O., 469 U.S. 325 (1985)

New State Ice Co. v. Liebmann, 285 U.S. 262 (1932)

New York Times Co. v. United States, 403 U.S. 713 (1971)

New York v. Quarles, 467 U.S. 649 (1984)

Nix v. Williams, 467 U.S. 431 (1984)

O'Connor v. United States, 99 U.S. App. D.C. 373 (1956, App. D.C.)

Ohio v. Johnson, 467 U.S. 493 (1984)

Oliver v. United States, 466 U.S. 170 (1984)

One 1958 Plymouth Sedan v. Pennsylvania, 380 U.S. 693 (1965)

Oregon v. Bradshaw, 462 U.S. 1039 (1983)

Oregon v. Elstad, 470 U.S. 298 (1985)

Overton v. Bazzetta, 539 U.S. 126 (2003)

Palko v. Connecticut, 302 U.S. 319 (1937)

Papachristou v. City of Jacksonville, 405 U.S. 156 (1972)

Parklane Hosiery Co. v. Shore, 439 U.S. 322 (1979)

Pasdon v. City of Peabody, 417 F.3d 225 (2005, CA1 Mass.)

Patton v. Yount, 467 U.S. 1025 (1984)

Pennsylvania Board of Probation and Parole v. Scott, 524 U.S. 357 (1998)

Pennsylvania v. Bruder, 488 U.S. 9 (1988)

People ex rel. Hunter v. District Court of Twentieth Judicial District, 634 P.2d 44 (1981, Colo.)

People v. Huffman, 61 N.Y.2d 795 (1984)

People v. Joseph, 59 N.Y.2d 496 (1983)

People v. Lesh, 668 P.2d 1362 (1983, Colo.)

People v. Lowe, 200 Colo. 470, 616 P.2d 118 (1980)

People v. Roark, 643 P.2d 756 (1982, Colo.)

People v. Wei Chen, 430 N.Y.S.2d 469 (1980)

People v. Burgner, 41 Cal. 3d. 505 (1986)

People v. Superior Court of San Mateo County, 35 Cal. App. 3d 1 (1973, Cal. App. 1st Dist.)

People v. Weathington, 76 Ill. App. 3d 173 (1979, Ill. App. Ct.)
Pierson v. Ray, 386 U.S. 547 (1967)
Pointer v. Texas, 380 U.S. 400 (1965)
Powell v. Alabama, 287 U.S. 45 (1932)
Powell v. Texas, 392 U.S. 514 (1968)
Procunier v. Martinez, 416 U.S. 396 (1974)
Quercia v. United States, 289 U.S. 466 (1933)
Quinn v. United States, 349 U.S. 155 (1955)
Ramon by Ramon v. Soto, 916 F.2d 1377 (1989, CA9 Ariz.)
Richardson v. McKnight, 521 U.S. 399 (1997)
Richmond Newspapers, Inc. v. Virginia, 448 U.S. 555 (1980)
Ring v. Arizona, 536 U.S. 584 (2002)
Ristaino v. Ross, 424 U.S. 589 (1976)
Roberson v. Commonwealth, 185 S.W.3d 634 (2006, Ky.)
Roberson v. State, 42 Fla. 223 (1900)
Roberts v. Louisiana, 431 U.S. 633 (1977)
Robinson v. California, 370 U.S. 660 (1962)
Rochin v. California, 342 U.S. 165 (1952)
Roe. v. Wade, 410 U.S. 113 (1973)
Roper v. Simmons, 543 U.S. 551 (2005)
Roth v. United States, 354 U.S. 476 (1957)
Rothgery v. Gillespie County, 2008 U.S. LEXIS 5057 (2008)
Rovinsky v. McKaskle, 722 F.2d 197 (1984, CA5 Tex.)
Russell v. United States, 369 U.S. 749 (1962)
Samson v. California, 547 U.S. 843 (2006)
Sanchez-Llamas v. Oregon, 548 U.S. 331 (2006)
Sanders v. United States, 396 F.2d 221 (1968, CA5 Fla.)
Santa Fe Independent School District v. Doe, 530 U.S. 290 (2000)
Saucier v. Katz, 533 U.S. 194 (2001)
Schenck v. United States, 249 U.S. 47 (1919)
Schilb v. Kuebel, 404 U.S. 357 (1971)
Schmerber v. California, 384 U.S. 757 (1966)
Schneckloth v. Bustamonte, 412 U.S. 218 (1973)
Seals v. State, 208 Miss. 236 (1950)
Sheppard v. Maxwell, 384 U.S. 333 (1966)
Sherbrooke v. City of Pelican Rapids, 2008 U.S. App. LEXIS 972 (2008, 8th Cir.)
Silverthorne Lumber Co. v. United States, 251 U.S. 385 (1920)
Singleton v. Board of Education, 894 F. Supp. 386, 391 (1995, D. Kan.)
Singleton v. Norris, 319 F.3d 1018 (2003, 8th Cir. Ark.)
Skinner v. Railway Labor Executives' Association, 489 U.S. 602 (1989)
Smith v. Hooey, 393 U.S. 374 (1969)
Smith v. Zimmerman, 768 F.2d 69 (1985, CA3 Pa.)
Snyder v. Massachusetts, 291 U.S. 97 (1934)
Spinelli v. United States, 393 U.S. 410 (1969)
Sosa v. Alvarez-Machain, 542 U.S. 692 (2004)
Stack v. Boyle, 342 U.S. 1 (1951)
Stanley v. Georgia, 394 U.S. 557 (1969)

State ex rel. Juckett v. Evergreen District Court, 100 Wash. 2d 824, 675 P.2d 599 (1984)

State v. Bomboy, 161 P.3d 898 (2007, N.M. Ct. App.)

State v. Buchholz, 11 Ohio St. 3d 24 (1984)

State v. Fields, 294 N.W.2d 404 (1980, N.D.)

State v. Green, 232 S.W.2d 897, 903 (1950, Mo.)

State v. Halvorson, 346 N.W.2d 704 (1984, N.D.)

State v. Holsworth, 93 Wash. 2d 148 (1980)

State v. Jones 281 N.W.2d 13 (1979, Iowa)

State v. Lane 60 Ohio St. 2d 112 (1979)

State v. Lombard, 146 Vt. 411, 505 A.2d 1182 (1985)

State v. Mata, 275 Neb. 1, 745 N.W.2d 229, 2008 WL 351695 (2008, Neb.)

State v. Munson, 339 Mont. 68, 169 P.3d 364 (2007)

State v. Oyenusi, 903 A.2d 467 (2006, N.J. App. Div.)

State v. Philbrick, 436 A.2d 844 (1981, Me.)

State v. Pullen, 266 A.2d 222 (1970, Me.)

State v. Ronngren, 361 N.W.2d 224 (1985, N.D.)

State v. Rupp, 282 N.W.2d 125 (1979, Iowa)

State v. Russo, 67 Hawaii 126, 681 P.2d 553 (1984)

State v. Thibodeau, 496 A.2d 635 (1985, Me.)

State v. Webb, 2 N. C. 103 (1794)

State Department of Revenue v. Oliver, 636 P.2d 1156 (1981, Alaska)

Stevenson v. Anderson, 2001 U.S. Dist. LEXIS 21478 (2001, N.D. Tex.)

Stoner v. California, 376 U.S. 483 (1964)

Strickland v. Washington, 466 U.S. 668 (1984)

Styler v. State, 417 A.2d 948 (1980, Del.)

Sullivan v. Louisiana, 508 U.S. 275 (1993)

Swisher v. Brady, 438 U.S. 204 (1978)

Swofford v. Mandrell, 969 F.2d 547 (1992, CA7)

Szlemko v. State, 2007 Ark. App. LEXIS 362 (2007, Ark. Ct. App.)

Taylor v. Louisiana, 419 U.S. 522 (1975)

Tennessee v. Garner, 471 U.S. 1 (1985)

Terry v. Ohio, 392 U.S. 1 (1968)

Thomas v. Mississippi, 380 U.S. 524 (1965)

Thomerson v. State, 274 Ark. 17, 621 S.W.2d 690 (1981)

Thornburgh v. Abbott, 490 U.S. 401 (1989)

Tinker v. Des Moines Independent Community School District, 393 U.S. 503 (1969)

Tison v. Arizona, 481 U.S. 137 (1987)

Town of Castle Rock v. Gonzales, 545 U.S. 748 (2005)

Trop v. Dulles, 356 U.S. 86 (1958)

Turner v. Safley, 482 U.S. 78 (1987)

Ullmann v. United States, 350 U.S. 422 (1956)

United States ex rel. Bennett v. Rundle, 419 F.2d 599 (1969, CA3 Pa.)

United States ex rel. Hanson v. Ragen, 166 F.2d 608 (1948, CA7 Ill.)

United States ex rel. Henne v. Fike, 563 F.2d 809 (1977, CA7 Ill.)

United States ex rel. Laws v. Yeager, 448 F.2d 74 (1971, CA3 N.J.)

United States v. 3814 NW Thurman St., 164 F.3d 1191 (1999, CA9 Or.)

United States v. Abdus-Price, 2008 U.S. App. LEXIS 5144 (2008, D.C. Cir.)

United States v. Ali, 68 F.3d 1468 (1995, CA2 N.Y.)

United States v. Bagster, 915 F.2d 607 (1990, CA10, Okla.)

United States v. Ball, 163 U.S. 662 (1896)

United States v. Banks, 2008 U.S. App. LEXIS 2508 (2008b, 10th Cir.)

United States v. Banks, 2008 U.S. App. LEXIS 326 (2008a, 8th Cir.)

United States v. Bencs, 28 F.3d 555 (1994, CA6 Ohio)

United States v. Benmuhar, 658 F.2d 14 (1981, CA1 Puerto Rico)

United States v. Bishop, 66 F.3d 569 (1995, CA3 N.J.)

United States v. Booker, 160 L. Ed. 2d 621 (2005)

United States v. Booker, 2008 U.S. App. LEXIS 5810 (2008, 3d Cir. N.J.)

United States v. Borchardt, 809 F.2d 1115 (1987, CA5 Tex.)

United States v. Boston, 718 F.2d 1511 (1983, CA10 Okla.)

United States v. Bridges, 499 F.2d 179 (1974, CA7 Ill.)

United States v. Brooklier, 685 F.2d 1162 (1982, CA9 Cal.)

United States v. Brown, 583 F.2d 915 (1978, CA7 Ill.)

United States v. Cabrera-Sarmiento, 533 F. Supp. 799 (1982, SD Fla.)

United States v. Calandra, 414 U.S. 338 (1974)

United States v. Canady, 126 F.3d 352 (1997, CA2 N.Y.)

United States v. Carmona, 873 F.2d 569 (1989, CA2 N.Y.)

United States v. Ceccolini, 435 U.S. 268 (1977)

United States v. Chemaly, 741 F.2d 1346 (1984, 11th Cir.)

United States v. Classic, 313 U.S. 299 (1941)

United States v. Colonna, 142 F.2d 210 (1944, CA3 N.J.)

United States v. Commerford, 64 F.2d 28 (1933, CA2 N.Y.)

United States v. Cook, 311 F. Supp. 618 (1970, WD Pa.)

United States v. Cortez, 449 U.S. 411 (1981)

United States v. Cos, 2006 U.S. Dist. LEXIS 95396 (2006, D.N.M.)

United States v. Cruikshank, 92 U.S. 542, 2 Otto 542, 23 L. Ed. 588 (1876)

United States v. Danks, 221 F.3d 1037 (1999, 8th Cir.)

United States v. Darby, 312 U.S. 100 (1941)

United States v. Decoud, 456 F.3d 996 (2006, 9th Cir.)

United States v. DeLuca, 269 F.3d 1128 (2001, 10th Cir.)

United States v. Di James, 731 F.2d 758 (1984, CA11 Ga.)

United States v. Dorsey, 418 F.3d 1038 (2005, 9th Cir.)

United States v. Doyle, 129 F.3d 1372 (1997, 10th Cir.)

United States v. Duarte, 160 F.3d 80 (1998, CA1 Mass.)

United States v. Eccles, 850 F.2d 1357 (1988, 9th Cir.)

United States v. Edwards, 415 U.S. 800 (1974)

United States v. Edwards, 885 F.2d 377 (1989, CA7 Wis.)

United States v. Fairchild, 505 F.2d 1378 (1975, CA5 Tex.)

United States v. Feldman, 788 F.2d 544 (1986, CA9 Cal.)

United States v. Gambale, 610 F. Supp. 1515 (1985, D. Mass.)

United States v. Garcia, 655 F.2d 59 (1981, CA5 Fla.)

United States v. Gecas, 120 F.3d 1419 (1997, CA11 Fla.)

United States v. George, 403 F.3d 470 (2005, CA7 Wis.)

United States v. Godsey, 224 Fed. Appx. 896 (2007, 11th Cir. Ala.)

United States v. Gonzales,121 F.3d 928 (1997, CA5 Tex.)

United States v. Gonzalez, 512 F.3d 285 (2008, 6th Cir. Ohio)

United States v. Gonzalez, 71 F.3d 819 (1996, 11th Cir.)

United States v. Gonzalez-Lopez, 548 U.S. 140 (2006)

United States v. Grose, 525 F.2d 1115 (1975, CA7 Wis.)

United States v. Guerrero-Hernandez, 95 F.3d 983 (1996, CA10 N.M.)

United States v. Hall, 2008 U.S. App. LEXIS 5866 (2008, 3d Cir. Pa.)

United States v. Harrelson, 713 F.2d 1114 (1983, CA5 Tex.)

United States v. Haswood, 350 F.3d 1024 (2003, CA9 Ariz.)

United States v. Hershey, 20 M.J. 433 (1985, CMA)

United States v. Hidalgo, 7 F.3d 1566 (1993, 11th Cir.)

United States v. Hollien, 105 F. Supp. 987 (1952, DC Mich.)

United States v. Hubbell, 530 U.S. 27 (2000)

United States v. Ingram, 446 F.3d 1332 (2006, CA11 Fla.)

United States v. International Brotherhood of Teamsters, 941 F.2d 1292 (1991, CA2 N.Y.)

United States v. Jackson, 590 F.2d 121 (1979, CA5 Ga.)

United States v. Janis, 428 U.S. 433 (1976)

United States v. Johnson, 364 F.3d 1185 (2004, 10th Cir.)

United States v. Jordan, 557 F.2d 1081 (1977, CA5 Tex.)

United States v. Kapperman, 764 F.2d 786 (1985, 11th Cir.)

United States v. Kibler, 667 F.2d 452 (1982, CA4 Md.)

United States v. Knights, 534 U.S. 112 (2001)

United States v. Kobli, 172 F.2d 919 (1949, CA3 Pa.)

United States v. Leon, 468 U.S. 897 (1984)

United States v. Mahmood, 415 F. Supp. 2d 13 (2006, DC Mass.)

United States v. McRae, 156 F.3d 708 (1998, 6th Cir.)

United States v. McVeigh, 153 F.3d 1166 (1998, CA10 Colo.)

United States v. Medina, 709 F.2d 155 (1983, CA2 N.Y.)

United States v. Medina, 887 F.2d 528 (1989, CA5)

United States v. Medina-Cervantes, 690 F.2d 715 (1982, CA9 Cal.)

United States v. Mettetal, 2000 U.S. Dist. LEXIS 21604 (2000, W.D. Va.)

United States v. Miller, 471 U.S. 130 (1985)

United States v. Miller, 984 F.2d 1028 (1993, CA9 Cal.)

United States v. Moser, 2007 U.S. App. LEXIS 19064 (2007, CA4 Md.)

United States v. Nava-Ramirez, 210 F.3d 1128 (2000, 10th Cir.)

United States v. Neff, 10 F.3d 1321 (1993, CA7 Ill.)

United States v. Newman, 685 F.2d 90 (1982, 3d Cir.)

United States v. Nguyen, 155 F.3d 1219 (1998, CA10 Kan.)

United States v. Nunez-Rios, 622 F.2d 1093 (1980, CA2 N.Y.)

United States v. Oddo, 133 Fed. Appx. 632 (2005, CA11 Fla.)

United States v. Olivares-Rangel, 458 F.3d 1104 (2007, 10th Cir.)

United States v. Pandilidis, 524 F.2d 644 (1975, CA6 Ohio)

United States v. Parker, 368 F.3d 963 (2004, CA7 Ill.)

United States v. Patane, 159 L. Ed. 2d 667 (2004)

United States v. Pollard, 215 F.3d 643 (2000, 6th Cir.)

United States v. Ponder, 240 Fed. Appx. 17 (2007, 6th Cir.)

United States v. Powers, 482 F.2d 941 (1973, CA8 Minn.)

United States v. Powers, 622 F.2d 317 (1980, CA8 Iowa)

United States v. R. L. Polk and Co., 438 F.2d 377 (1971, CA6 Mich.)
United States v. Ramirez-Sandoval, 872 F.2d 1392 (1989, 9th Cir.)
United States v. Reyes, 157 F.3d 949 (1998, 2d Cir.)
United States v. Reyes, 225 F.3d 71 (2000, CA1 Me.)
United States v. Ritter, 416 F.3d 256 (2005, 3d Cir.)
United States v. Rodriguez, 765 F.2d 1546 (1985, CA11 Fla.)
United States v. Romero, 897 F.2d 47 (1990, CA2 N.Y.)
United States v. Ross, 456 U.S. 798 (1982)
United States v. Rosso, 58 F.2d 197 (1932, CA2 N.Y.)
United States v. Salerno, 481 U.S. 739 (1987)
United States v. Scalf, 725 F.2d 1272 (1984, CA10 Okla.)
United States v. Schellong, 717 F.2d 329 (1983, CA7 Ill.)
United States v. Sherlock, 865 F.2d 1069 (1989, CA9 Ariz.)
United States v. Silvestri, 790 F.2d 186 (1986, CA1 Mass.)
United States v. Sorrentino 175 F.2d 721 (1949, CA3 Pa.)
United States v. Stewart, 568 F.2d 501 (1978, CA6 Tenn.)
United States v. Streifel, 781 F.2d 953 (1986, CA1 Me.)
United States v. Stroman, 500 F.3d 61 (2007)
United States v. Susini, 2008 U.S. App. LEXIS 584 (2008, 11th Cir.)
United States v. Thomas, 447 F.3d 1191 (2006, 9th Cir.)
United States v. Thompson, 475 F.2d 1359 (1973, CA5 Tex.)
United States v. Villa-Chaparro, 115 F.3d 797 (1997, 10th Cir.)
United States v. Wade, 388 U.S. 218 (1967)
United States v. Washington, 431 U.S. 181 (1977)
United States v. White, 322 U.S. 694 (1944)
United States v. Whitson, 587 F.2d 948 (1978, CA9 Cal.)
United States v. Williams, 128 S.Ct. 1830 (2007)
United States v. Williams, 504 U.S. 36 (1992)
United States v. Young, 875 F.2d 1357 (1989, CA8 S.D.)
United States v. Ziegler, 474 F.3d 1184 (2007, 9th Cir.)
Upshaw v. State, 2007 Ala. Crim. App. LEXIS 145 (2007)
Vandergriff v. City of Chattanooga, 44 F. Supp. 2d 927 (1998, E.D. Tenn.)
Van Orden v. Perry, 545 U.S. 677 (2005)
Vargas v. Keane, 86 F.3d 1273 (1996, CA2 N.Y.)
Virginia v. Black, 538 U.S. 343 (2004)
Virginia v. Moore, 2008 U.S. LEXIS 3674 (2008)
Wallace v. Kato, 549 U.S. 384 (2007)
Wallace v. United States, 291 F. 972 (1923, CA6 Tenn.)
Walton v. Briley, 361 F.3d 431 (2004, CA7 Ill.)
Warner v. McCunney, 2008 U.S. App. LEXIS 279 (2008, 3d Cir. Pa.)
Washington v. Texas, 388 U.S. 14 (1967)
Watson v. Jago, 558 F.2d 330 (1977, CA6 Ohio)
Weeks v. United States, 232 U.S. 383 (1914)
Weems v. United States, 217 U.S. 349 (1910)
Whiteley v. Warden, Wyoming State Penitentiary, 401 U.S. 560 (1971)
Wilkerson v. Utah, 99 U.S. 130 (1879)
Williams v. Ellington, 936 F.2d 881 (1991, 6th Cir. Ky.)
Williams v. Florida, 399 U.S. 78 (1970)

Williams v. Taylor, 529 U.S. 362 (2000)
Williamson v. Parke, 963 F.2d 863 (1992, CA6 Ky.)
Wilson v. Layne, 526 U.S. 603 (1999)
Wilson v. Seiter, 501 U.S. 294 (1991)
Winters v. New York, 333 U.S. 507 (1948)
Witherspoon v. Illinois, 391 U.S. 510 (1968)
Wolf v. Colorado, 338 U.S. 25 (1949)
Wong Sun v. United States, 371 U.S. 471 (1963)
Woodson v. North Carolina, 428 U.S. 280 (1976)
Zedner v. United States, 547 U.S. 489 (2006)
Zelman v. Simmons-Harris, 536 U.S. 639 (2002)

Appendix A: U.S. Constitution

Preamble

We the People of the United States, in Order to form a more perfect Union, establish Justice, insure domestic Tranquility, provide for the common defense, promote the general Welfare, and secure the Blessings of Liberty to ourselves and our Posterity, do ordain and establish this Constitution for the United States of America.

Article I [The Legislative Branch]

Section 1 [The Legislature]

All legislative Powers herein granted shall be vested in a Congress of the United States, which shall consist of a Senate and House of Representatives.

Section 2 [The House]

The House of Representatives shall be composed of Members chosen every second Year by the People of the several States, and the Electors in each State shall have the Qualifications requisite for Electors of the most numerous Branch of the State Legislature.

No Person shall be a Representative who shall not have attained to the Age of twenty five Years, and been seven Years a Citizen of the United States, and who shall not, when elected, be an Inhabitant of that State in which he shall be chosen.

Representatives and direct Taxes shall be apportioned among the several States which may be included within this Union, according to their respective Numbers, which shall be determined by adding to the whole Number of free Persons, including those bound to Service for a Term of Years, and excluding Indians not taxed, three fifths of all other Persons. [The previous sentence was modified by the 14th Amendment, Section 2.] The actual Enumeration shall be made within three Years after the first Meeting of the Congress of the United States, and within every subsequent Term of ten Years, in such

Manner as they shall by Law direct. The Number of Representatives shall not exceed one for every thirty Thousand, but each State shall have at Least one Representative; and until such enumeration shall be made, the State of New Hampshire shall be entitled to chuse three, Massachusetts eight, Rhode Island and Providence Plantations one, Connecticut five, New York six, New Jersey four, Pennsylvania eight, Delaware one, Maryland six, Virginia ten, North Carolina five, South Carolina five and Georgia three.

When vacancies happen in the Representation from any State, the Executive Authority thereof shall issue Writs of Election to fill such Vacancies.

The House of Representatives shall chuse their Speaker and other Officers; and shall have the sole Power of Impeachment.

Section 3 [The Senate]

The Senate of the United States shall be composed of two Senators from each State, chosen by the Legislature thereof [The words were modified by 17th Amendment, Section 1.], for six Years; and each Senator shall have one Vote.

Immediately after they shall be assembled in Consequence of the first Election, they shall be divided as equally as may be into three Classes. The Seats of the Senators of the first Class shall be vacated at the Expiration of the second Year, of the second Class at the Expiration of the fourth Year, and of the third Class at the Expiration of the sixth Year, so that one third may be chosen every second Year; and if Vacancies happen by Resignation, or otherwise, during the Recess of the Legislature of any State, the Executive thereof may make temporary Appointments until the next Meeting of the Legislature, which shall then fill such Vacancies. [The final clause was superseded by the 17th Amendment, Section 2.]

No person shall be a Senator who shall not have attained to the Age of thirty Years, and been nine Years a Citizen of the United States, and who shall not, when elected, be an Inhabitant of that State for which he shall be chosen.

The Vice President of the United States shall be President of the Senate, but shall have no Vote, unless they be equally divided.

The Senate shall chuse their other Officers, and also a President pro tempore, in the absence of the Vice President, or when he shall exercise the Office of President of the United States.

The Senate shall have the sole Power to try all Impeachments. When sitting for that Purpose, they shall be on Oath or Affirmation. When the President of the United States is tried, the Chief Justice shall preside: And no Person shall be convicted without the Concurrence of two thirds of the Members present.

Judgment in Cases of Impeachment shall not extend further than to removal from Office, and disqualification to hold and enjoy any Office of honor, Trust or Profit under the United States: but the Party convicted shall nevertheless be liable and subject to Indictment, Trial, Judgment and Punishment, according to Law.

Section 4 [Elections, Meetings]

The Times, Places and Manner of holding Elections for Senators and Representatives, shall be prescribed in each State by the Legislature thereof; but the Congress may at any time by Law make or alter such Regulations, except as to the Places of Chusing Senators.

The Congress shall assemble at least once in every Year, and such Meeting shall [be on the first Monday in December,] unless they shall by Law appoint a different Day. [The words in parentheses were superseded by the 20th Amendment, Section 2.]

Section 5 [Membership, Rules, Journals, Adjournment]

Each House shall be the Judge of the Elections, Returns and Qualifications of its own Members, and a Majority of each shall constitute a Quorum to do Business; but a smaller Number may adjourn from day to day, and may be authorized to compel the Attendance of absent Members, in such Manner, and under such Penalties as each House may provide.

Each House may determine the Rules of its Proceedings, punish its Members for disorderly Behavior, and, with the Concurrence of two thirds, expel a Member.

Each House shall keep a Journal of its Proceedings, and from time to time publish the same, excepting such Parts as may in their Judgment require Secrecy; and the Yeas and Nays of the Members of either House on any question shall, at the Desire of one fifth of those Present, be entered on the Journal.

Neither House, during the Session of Congress, shall, without the Consent of the other, adjourn for more than three days, nor to any other Place than that in which the two Houses shall be sitting.

Section 6 [Compensation]

The Senators and Representatives shall receive a Compensation for their Services, to be ascertained by Law, and paid out of the Treasury of the United States. [The preceding words were modified by the 27th Amendment.] They shall in all Cases, except Treason, Felony and Breach of the Peace, be privileged from Arrest during their Attendance at the Session of their respective Houses, and in going to and returning from the same; and for any Speech or Debate in either House, they shall not be questioned in any other Place.

No Senator or Representative shall, during the Time for which he was elected, be appointed to any civil Office under the Authority of the United

States, which shall have been created, or the Emoluments whereof shall have been increased during such time; and no Person holding any Office under the United States, shall be a Member of either House during his Continuance in Office.

Section 7 [Revenue Bills, Legislative Process, Presidential Veto]

All Bills for raising Revenue shall originate in the House of Representatives; but the Senate may propose or concur with Amendments as on other Bills.

Every Bill which shall have passed the House of Representatives and the Senate, shall, before it become a Law, be presented to the President of the United States; If he approve he shall sign it, but if not he shall return it, with his Objections to that House in which it shall have originated, who shall enter the Objections at large on their Journal, and proceed to reconsider it. If after such Reconsideration two thirds of that House shall agree to pass the Bill, it shall be sent, together with the Objections, to the other House, by which it shall likewise be reconsidered, and if approved by two thirds of that House, it shall become a Law. But in all such Cases the Votes of both Houses shall be determined by Yeas and Nays, and the Names of the Persons voting for and against the Bill shall be entered on the Journal of each House respectively. If any Bill shall not be returned by the President within ten Days (Sundays excepted) after it shall have been presented to him, the Same shall be a Law, in like Manner as if he had signed it, unless the Congress by their Adjournment prevent its Return, in which Case it shall not be a Law.

Every Order, Resolution, or Vote to which the Concurrence of the Senate and House of Representatives may be necessary (except on a question of Adjournment) shall be presented to the President of the United States; and before the Same shall take Effect, shall be approved by him, or being disapproved by him, shall be repassed by two thirds of the Senate and House of Representatives, according to the Rules and Limitations prescribed in the Case of a Bill.

Section 8 [Powers of Congress]

The Congress shall have Power To lay and collect Taxes, Duties, Imposts and Excises, to pay the Debts and provide for the common Defence and general Welfare of the United States; but all Duties, Imposts and Excises shall be uniform throughout the United States;

To borrow Money on the credit of the United States;

To regulate Commerce with foreign Nations, and among the several States, and with the Indian Tribes;

To establish an uniform Rule of Naturalization, and uniform Laws on the subject of Bankruptcies throughout the United States;

To coin Money, regulate the Value thereof, and of foreign Coin, and fix the Standard of Weights and Measures;

To provide for the Punishment of counterfeiting the Securities and current Coin of the United States;

To establish Post Offices and post Roads;

To promote the Progress of Science and useful Arts, by securing for limited Times to Authors and Inventors the exclusive Right to their respective Writings and Discoveries;

To constitute Tribunals inferior to the supreme Court;

To define and punish Piracies and Felonies committed on the high Seas, and Offenses against the Law of Nations;

To declare War, grant Letters of Marque and Reprisal, and make Rules concerning Captures on Land and Water;

To raise and support Armies, but no Appropriation of Money to that Use shall be for a longer Term than two Years;

To provide and maintain a Navy;

To make Rules for the Government and Regulation of the land and naval Forces;

To provide for calling forth the Militia to execute the Laws of the Union, suppress Insurrections and repel Invasions;

To provide for organizing, arming, and disciplining, the Militia, and for governing such Part of them as may be employed in the Service of the United States, reserving to the States respectively, the Appointment of the Officers, and the Authority of training the Militia according to the discipline prescribed by Congress;

To exercise exclusive Legislation in all Cases whatsoever, over such District (not exceeding ten Miles square) as may, by Cession of particular States, and the Acceptance of Congress, become the Seat of the Government of the United States, and to exercise like Authority over all Places purchased by the Consent of the Legislature of the State in which the Same shall be, for the Erection of Forts, Magazines, Arsenals, dock-Yards, and other needful Buildings,—And

To make all Laws which shall be necessary and proper for carrying into Execution the foregoing Powers, and all other Powers vested by this Constitution in the Government of the United States, or in any Department or Officer thereof.

Section 9 [Limits on Congress]

The Migration or Importation of such Persons as any of the States now existing shall think proper to admit, shall not be prohibited by the Congress prior to the Year one thousand eight hundred and eight, but a Tax or duty may be imposed on such Importation, not exceeding ten dollars for each Person.

The Privilege of the Writ of Habeas Corpus shall not be suspended, unless when in Cases of Rebellion or Invasion the public Safety may require it.

No Bill of Attainder or ex post facto Law shall be passed.

No capitation, or other direct, Tax shall be laid, unless in Proportion to the Census or Enumeration herein before directed to be taken. [Section clarified by the 16th Amendment.]

No Tax or Duty shall be laid on Articles exported from any State.

No Preference shall be given by any Regulation of Commerce or Revenue to the Ports of one State over those of another: nor shall Vessels bound to, or from, one State, be obliged to enter, clear, or pay Duties in another.

No Money shall be drawn from the Treasury, but in Consequence of Appropriations made by Law; and a regular Statement and Account of the Receipts and Expenditures of all public Money shall be published from time to time.

No Title of Nobility shall be granted by the United States: And no Person holding any Office of Profit or Trust under them, shall, without the Consent of the Congress, accept of any present, Emolument, Office, or Title, of any kind whatever, from any King, Prince or foreign State.

Section 10 [Powers Prohibited of States]

No State shall enter into any Treaty, Alliance, or Confederation; grant Letters of Marque and Reprisal; coin Money; emit Bills of Credit; make any Thing but gold and silver Coin a Tender in Payment of Debts; pass any Bill of Attainder, ex post facto Law, or Law impairing the Obligation of Contracts, or grant any Title of Nobility.

No State shall, without the Consent of the Congress, lay any Imposts or Duties on Imports or Exports, except what may be absolutely necessary for executing its inspection Laws: and the net Produce of all Duties and Imposts, laid by any State on Imports or Exports, shall be for the Use of the Treasury of the United States; and all such Laws shall be subject to the Revision and Controul of the Congress.

No State shall, without the Consent of Congress, lay any Duty of Tonnage, keep Troops, or Ships of War in time of Peace, enter into any Agreement or Compact with another State, or with a foreign Power, or engage in War, unless actually invaded, or in such imminent Danger as will not admit of delay.

Article II [The Executive Branch]

Section 1 [The President]

The executive Power shall be vested in a President of the United States of America. He shall hold his Office during the Term of four Years, and, together with the Vice President, chosen for the same Term, be elected, as follows:

Each State shall appoint, in such Manner as the Legislature thereof may direct, a Number of Electors, equal to the whole Number of Senators and Representatives to which the State may be entitled in the Congress: but no Senator or Representative, or Person holding an Office of Trust or Profit under the United States, shall be appointed an Elector.

The Electors shall meet in their respective States, and vote by Ballot for two persons, of whom one at least shall not be an Inhabitant of the same State with themselves. And they shall make a List of all the Persons voted for, and of the Number of Votes for each; which List they shall sign and certify, and transmit sealed to the Seat of the Government of the United States, directed to the President of the Senate. The President of the Senate shall, in the Presence of the Senate and House of Representatives, open all the Certificates, and the Votes shall then be counted. The Person having the greatest Number of Votes shall be the President, if such Number be a Majority of the whole Number of Electors appointed; and if there be more than one who have such Majority, and have an equal Number of Votes, then the House of Representatives shall immediately chuse by Ballot one of them for President; and if no Person have a Majority, then from the five highest on the List the said House shall in like Manner chuse the President. But in chusing the President, the Votes shall be taken by States, the Representation from each State having one Vote; a quorum for this Purpose shall consist of a Member or Members from two thirds of the States, and a Majority of all the States shall be necessary to a Choice. In every Case, after the Choice of the President, the Person having the greatest Number of Votes of the Electors shall be the Vice President. But if there should remain two or more who have equal Votes, the Senate shall chuse from them by Ballot the Vice President. [This clause is superseded by the 12th Amendment.]

The Congress may determine the Time of chusing the Electors, and the Day on which they shall give their Votes; which Day shall be the same throughout the United States.

No Person except a natural born Citizen, or a Citizen of the United States, at the time of the Adoption of this Constitution, shall be eligible to the Office of President; neither shall any Person be eligible to that Office who shall not have attained to the Age of thirty five Years, and been fourteen Years a Resident within the United States.

In Case of the Removal of the President from Office, or of his Death, Resignation, or Inability to discharge the Powers and Duties of the said Office, the same shall devolve on the Vice President, and the Congress may by Law provide for the Case of Removal, Death, Resignation or Inability, both of the President and Vice President, declaring what Officer shall then act as President, and such Officer shall act accordingly, until the Disability be removed, or a President shall be elected. [This clause was modified by the 20th and 25th Amendments.]

The President shall, at stated Times, receive for his Services, a Compensation, which shall neither be increased nor diminished during the Period for which he shall have been elected, and he shall not receive within that Period any other Emolument from the United States, or any of them.

Before he enter on the Execution of his Office, he shall take the following Oath or Affirmation: "I do solemnly swear (or affirm) that I will faithfully execute the Office of President of the United States, and will to the best of my Ability, preserve, protect and defend the Constitution of the United States."

Section 2 [Civilian Power over Military, Cabinet, Pardon Power, Appointments]

The President shall be Commander in Chief of the Army and Navy of the United States, and of the Militia of the several States, when called into the actual Service of the United States; he may require the Opinion, in writing, of the principal Officer in each of the executive Departments, upon any Subject relating to the Duties of their respective Offices, and he shall have Power to Grant Reprieves and Pardons for Offences against the United States, except in Cases of Impeachment.

He shall have Power, by and with the Advice and Consent of the Senate, to make Treaties, provided two thirds of the Senators present concur; and he shall nominate, and by and with the Advice and Consent of the Senate, shall appoint Ambassadors, other public Ministers and Consuls, Judges of the supreme Court, and all other Officers of the United States, whose Appointments are not herein otherwise provided for, and which shall be established by Law: but the Congress may by Law vest the Appointment of such inferior Officers, as they think proper, in the President alone, in the Courts of Law, or in the Heads of Departments.

The President shall have Power to fill up all Vacancies that may happen during the Recess of the Senate, by granting Commissions which shall expire at the End of their next Session.

Section 3 [State of the Union, Convening Congress]

He shall from time to time give to the Congress Information of the State of the Union, and recommend to their Consideration such Measures as he shall judge necessary and expedient; he may, on extraordinary Occasions, convene both Houses, or either of them, and in Case of Disagreement between them, with Respect to the Time of Adjournment, he may adjourn them to such Time as he shall think proper; he shall receive Ambassadors and other public Ministers; he shall take Care that the Laws be faithfully executed, and shall Commission all the Officers of the United States.

Section 4 [Disqualification]

The President, Vice President and all civil Officers of the United States, shall be removed from Office on Impeachment for, and Conviction of, Treason, Bribery, or other high Crimes and Misdemeanors.

Article III [The Judicial Branch]

Section 1 [Judicial Powers]

The judicial Power of the United States, shall be vested in one supreme Court, and in such inferior Courts as the Congress may from time to time ordain and establish. The Judges, both of the supreme and inferior Courts, shall hold their Offices during good Behavior, and shall, at stated Times, receive for their Services a Compensation which shall not be diminished during their Continuance in Office.

Section 2 [Trial by Jury, Original Jurisdiction, Jury Trials]

The judicial Power shall extend to all Cases, in Law and Equity, arising under this Constitution, the Laws of the United States, and Treaties made, or which shall be made, under their Authority;—to all Cases affecting Ambassadors, other public Ministers and Consuls;—to all Cases of admiralty and maritime Jurisdiction;—to Controversies to which the United States shall be a Party;—to Controversies between two or more States;—between a State and Citizens of another State;—between Citizens of different States;—between Citizens of the same State claiming Lands under Grants of different States, and between a State, or the Citizens thereof, and foreign States, Citizens or Subjects. [This section was modified by the 11th Amendment.]

In all Cases affecting Ambassadors, other public Ministers and Consuls, and those in which a State shall be Party, the supreme Court shall have original Jurisdiction. In all the other Cases before mentioned, the supreme Court shall have appellate Jurisdiction, both as to Law and Fact, with such Exceptions, and under such Regulations as the Congress shall make.

The Trial of all Crimes, except in Cases of Impeachment, shall be by Jury; and such Trial shall be held in the State where the said Crimes shall have been committed; but when not committed within any State, the Trial shall be at such Place or Places as the Congress may by Law have directed.

Section 3 [Treason Note]

Treason against the United States, shall consist only in levying War against them, or in adhering to their Enemies, giving them Aid and Comfort.

No Person shall be convicted of Treason unless on the Testimony of two Witnesses to the same overt Act, or on Confession in open Court.

The Congress shall have power to declare the Punishment of Treason, but no Attainder of Treason shall work Corruption of Blood, or Forfeiture except during the Life of the Person attainted.

Article IV [The States]

Section 1 [Each State to Honor All Others]

Full Faith and Credit shall be given in each State to the public Acts, Records, and judicial Proceedings of every other State. And the Congress may by general Laws prescribe the Manner in which such Acts, Records and Proceedings shall be proved, and the Effect thereof.

Section 2 [State Citizens, Extradition]

The Citizens of each State shall be entitled to all Privileges and Immunities of Citizens in the several States.

A Person charged in any State with Treason, Felony, or other Crime, who shall flee from Justice, and be found in another State, shall on Demand of the executive Authority of the State from which he fled, be delivered up, to be removed to the State having Jurisdiction of the Crime.

Section 3 [New States]

New States may be admitted by the Congress into this Union; but no new State shall be formed or erected within the Jurisdiction of any other State; nor any State be formed by the Junction of two or more States, or Parts of States, without the Consent of the Legislatures of the States concerned as well as of the Congress.

The Congress shall have Power to dispose of and make all needful Rules and Regulations respecting the Territory or other Property belonging to the United States; and nothing in this Constitution shall be so construed as to Prejudice any Claims of the United States, or of any particular State.

Section 4 [Republican Government]

The United States shall guarantee to every State in this Union a Republican Form of Government, and shall protect each of them against Invasion; and on Application of the Legislature, or of the Executive (when the Legislature cannot be convened) against domestic Violence.

Article V [Amendment]

The Congress, whenever two thirds of both Houses shall deem it necessary, shall propose Amendments to this Constitution, or, on the Application of the Legislatures of two thirds of the several States, shall call a Convention for proposing Amendments, which, in either Case, shall be valid to all Intents and Purposes, as Part of this Constitution, when ratified by the Legislatures of three fourths of the several States, or by Conventions in three fourths thereof, as the one or the other Mode of Ratification may be proposed by the Congress; Provided that no Amendment which may be made prior to the Year One thousand eight hundred and eight shall in any Manner affect the first and fourth Clauses in the Ninth Section of the first Article; and that no State, without its Consent, shall be deprived of its equal Suffrage in the Senate.

Article VI [Debts, Supremacy, Oaths]

All Debts contracted and Engagements entered into, before the Adoption of this Constitution, shall be as valid against the United States under this Constitution, as under the Confederation.

This Constitution, and the Laws of the United States which shall be made in Pursuance thereof; and all Treaties made, or which shall be made, under the Authority of the United States, shall be the supreme Law of the Land; and the Judges in every State shall be bound thereby, any Thing in the Constitution or Laws of any State to the Contrary notwithstanding.

The Senators and Representatives before mentioned, and the Members of the several State Legislatures, and all executive and judicial Officers, both of the United States and of the several States, shall be bound by Oath or Affirmation, to support this Constitution; but no religious Test shall ever be required as a Qualification to any Office or public Trust under the United States.

Article VII [Ratification]

The Ratification of the Conventions of nine States, shall be sufficient for the Establishment of this Constitution between the States so ratifying the Same. Done in Convention by the Unanimous Consent of the States present the Seventeenth Day of September in the Year of our Lord one thousand seven hundred and Eighty seven and of the Independence of the United States of America the Twelfth. In witness whereof We have hereunto subscribed our Names.

G. Washington—President and deputy from Virginia
New Hampshire—John Langdon, Nicholas Gilman
Massachusetts—Nathaniel Gorham, Rufus King
Connecticut—Wm. Saml. Johnson, Roger Sherman
New York—Alexander Hamilton
New Jersey—Wil. Livingston, David Brearley, Wm. Paterson, Jona. Dayton
Pensylvania—B. Franklin, Thomas Mifflin, Robt. Morris, Geo. Clymer,
    Thos. FitzSimons, Jared Ingersoll, James Wilson, Gouv Morris
Delaware—Geo. Read, Gunning Bedford jun, John Dickinson, Richard
    Bassett, Jaco. Broom
Maryland—James McHenry, Dan of St. Tho. Jenifer, Danl. Carroll
Virginia—John Blair, James Madison Jr.
North Carolina—Wm. Blount, Richd Dobbs Spaight, Hu Williamson
South Carolina—J. Rutledge, Charles Cotesworth Pinckney, Charles
    Pinckney, Pierce Butler
Georgia—William Few, Abr. Baldwin
Attest: William Jackson, Secretary

The Amendments

Amendment 1 [Freedom of religion, press, expression; ratified December
    15, 1791.]

Congress shall make no law respecting an establishment of religion, or prohibiting the free exercise thereof; or abridging the freedom of speech, or of
the press; or the right of the people peaceably to assemble, and to petition the
Government for a redress of grievances.

Amendment 2 [Right to bear arms; ratified December 15, 1791.]

A well regulated Militia, being necessary to the security of a free State, the
right of the people to keep and bear Arms, shall not be infringed.

Amendment 3 [Quartering of soldiers; ratified December 15, 1791.]

No Soldier shall, in time of peace be quartered in any house, without the consent of the Owner, nor in time of war, but in a manner to be prescribed by
law.

Amendment 4 [Search and seizure; ratified December 15, 1791.]

The right of the people to be secure in their persons, houses, papers, and
effects, against unreasonable searches and seizures, shall not be violated, and

no Warrants shall issue, but upon probable cause, supported by Oath or affirmation, and particularly describing the place to be searched, and the persons or things to be seized.

Amendment 5 [Trial and punishment, compensation for takings; ratified December 15, 1791.]

No person shall be held to answer for a capital, or otherwise infamous crime, unless on a presentment or indictment of a Grand Jury, except in cases arising in the land or naval forces, or in the Militia, when in actual service in time of War or public danger; nor shall any person be subject for the same offence to be twice put in jeopardy of life or limb; nor shall be compelled in any criminal case to be a witness against himself, nor be deprived of life, liberty, or property, without due process of law; nor shall private property be taken for public use, without just compensation.

Amendment 6 [Right to speedy trial, confrontation of witnesses; ratified December 15, 1791]

In all criminal prosecutions, the accused shall enjoy the right to a speedy and public trial, by an impartial jury of the State and district wherein the crime shall have been committed, which district shall have been previously ascertained by law, and to be informed of the nature and cause of the accusation; to be confronted with the witnesses against him; to have compulsory process for obtaining witnesses in his favor, and to have the Assistance of Counsel for his defence.

Amendment 7 [Trial by jury in civil cases; ratified December 15, 1791]

In Suits at common law, where the value in controversy shall exceed twenty dollars, the right of trial by jury shall be preserved, and no fact tried by a jury, shall be otherwise re-examined in any Court of the United States, than according to the rules of the common law.

Amendment 8 [Cruel and unusual punishment; ratified December 15, 1791]

Excessive bail shall not be required, nor excessive fines imposed, nor cruel and unusual punishments inflicted.

Amendment 9 [Construction of Constitution; ratified December 15, 1791]

The enumeration in the Constitution, of certain rights, shall not be construed to deny or disparage others retained by the people.

Amendment 10 [Powers of the states and people; ratified December 15, 1791]

The powers not delegated to the United States by the Constitution, nor prohibited by it to the States, are reserved to the States respectively, or to the people.

Amendment 11 [Judicial limits; ratified February 7, 1795]

The Judicial power of the United States shall not be construed to extend to any suit in law or equity, commenced or prosecuted against one of the United States by Citizens of another State, or by Citizens or Subjects of any Foreign State.

Amendment 12 [Choosing the president, vice-president; ratified June 15, 1804]

The Electors shall meet in their respective states, and vote by ballot for President and Vice-President, one of whom, at least, shall not be an inhabitant of the same state with themselves; they shall name in their ballots the person voted for as President, and in distinct ballots the person voted for as Vice-President, and they shall make distinct lists of all persons voted for as President, and of all persons voted for as Vice-President and of the number of votes for each, which lists they shall sign and certify, and transmit sealed to the seat of the government of the United States, directed to the President of the Senate;

The President of the Senate shall, in the presence of the Senate and House of Representatives, open all the certificates and the votes shall then be counted;

The person having the greatest Number of votes for President, shall be the President, if such number be a majority of the whole number of Electors appointed; and if no person have such majority, then from the persons having the highest numbers not exceeding three on the list of those voted for as President, the House of Representatives shall choose immediately, by ballot, the President. But in choosing the President, the votes shall be taken by states, the representation from each state having one vote; a quorum for this purpose shall consist of a member or members from two-thirds of the states, and a majority of all the states shall be necessary to a choice. And if the House of Representatives shall not choose a President whenever the right of choice shall devolve upon them, before the fourth day of March next following, then the Vice-President shall act as President, as in the case of the death or other constitutional disability of the President.

The person having the greatest number of votes as Vice-President, shall be the Vice-President, if such number be a majority of the whole number of Electors appointed, and if no person have a majority, then from the two highest numbers on the list, the Senate shall choose the Vice-President; a quorum for the purpose shall consist of two-thirds of the whole number of Senators, and a majority of the whole number shall be necessary to a choice. But no person constitutionally ineligible to the office of President shall be eligible to that of Vice-President of the United States.

Amendment 13 [Slavery abolished; ratified December 6, 1865]

1. Neither slavery nor involuntary servitude, except as a punishment for crime whereof the party shall have been duly convicted, shall exist within the United States, or any place subject to their jurisdiction.
2. Congress shall have power to enforce this article by appropriate legislation.

Amendment 14 [Citizenship rights; ratified July 9, 1868]

1. All persons born or naturalized in the United States, and subject to the jurisdiction thereof, are citizens of the United States and of the State wherein they reside. No State shall make or enforce any law which shall abridge the privileges or immunities of citizens of the United States; nor shall any State deprive any person of life, liberty, or property, without due process of law; nor deny to any person within its jurisdiction the equal protection of the laws.
2. Representatives shall be apportioned among the several States according to their respective numbers, counting the whole number of persons in each State, excluding Indians not taxed. But when the right to vote at any election for the choice of electors for President and Vice-President of the United States, Representatives in Congress, the Executive and Judicial officers of a State, or the members of the Legislature thereof, is denied to any of the male inhabitants of such State, being twenty-one years of age, and citizens of the United States, or in any way abridged, except for participation in rebellion, or other crime, the basis of representation therein shall be reduced in the proportion which the number of such male citizens shall bear to the whole number of male citizens twenty-one years of age in such State.
3. No person shall be a Senator or Representative in Congress, or elector of President and Vice President, or hold any office, civil or military, under the United States, or under any State, who, having previously taken an oath, as a member of Congress, or as an officer of the United States, or as a member of any State legislature, or as an executive or judicial officer of any State, to support the Constitution of the United States, shall have engaged in insurrection or rebellion against the same, or given aid or comfort to the enemies thereof. But Congress may by a vote of two-thirds of each House, remove such disability.
4. The validity of the public debt of the United States, authorized by law, including debts incurred for payment of pensions and bounties for services in suppressing insurrection or rebellion, shall not be questioned. But neither the United States nor any State shall assume or pay any debt or obligation incurred in aid of insurrection or rebellion

against the United States, or any claim for the loss or emancipation of any slave; but all such debts, obligations and claims shall be held illegal and void.

5. The Congress shall have power to enforce, by appropriate legislation, the provisions of this article.

Amendment 15 [Race no bar to vote; ratified February 3, 1870]

1. The right of citizens of the United States to vote shall not be denied or abridged by the United States or by any State on account of race, color, or previous condition of servitude.

2. The Congress shall have power to enforce this article by appropriate legislation.

Amendment 16 [Status of income tax clarified; ratified February 3, 1913]

The Congress shall have power to lay and collect taxes on incomes, from whatever source derived, without apportionment among the several States, and without regard to any census or enumeration.

Amendment 17 [Senators elected by popular vote; ratified April 8, 1913]

The Senate of the United States shall be composed of two Senators from each State, elected by the people thereof, for six years; and each Senator shall have one vote. The electors in each State shall have the qualifications requisite for electors of the most numerous branch of the State legislatures.

When vacancies happen in the representation of any State in the Senate, the executive authority of such State shall issue writs of election to fill such vacancies: *Provided*, That the legislature of any State may empower the executive thereof to make temporary appointments until the people fill the vacancies by election as the legislature may direct.

This amendment shall not be so construed as to affect the election or term of any Senator chosen before it becomes valid as part of the Constitution.

Amendment 18 [Liquor abolished; ratified January 16, 1919; repealed by Amendment 21, December 5, 1933]

1. After one year from the ratification of this article the manufacture, sale, or transportation of intoxicating liquors within, the importation thereof into, or the exportation thereof from the United States and all territory subject to the jurisdiction thereof for beverage purposes is hereby prohibited.

2. The Congress and the several States shall have concurrent power to enforce this article by appropriate legislation.

3. This article shall be inoperative unless it shall have been ratified as an amendment to the Constitution by the legislatures of the several States, as provided in the Constitution, within seven years from the date of the submission hereof to the States by the Congress.

Amendment 19 [Women's suffrage; ratified August 18, 1920]

The right of citizens of the United States to vote shall not be denied or abridged by the United States or by any State on account of sex.

Congress shall have power to enforce this article by appropriate legislation.

Amendment 20 [Presidential, congressional terms; ratified January 23, 1933]

1. The terms of the President and Vice President shall end at noon on the 20th day of January, and the terms of Senators and Representatives at noon on the 3d day of January, of the years in which such terms would have ended if this article had not been ratified; and the terms of their successors shall then begin.
2. The Congress shall assemble at least once in every year, and such meeting shall begin at noon on the 3d day of January, unless they shall by law appoint a different day.
3. If, at the time fixed for the beginning of the term of the President, the President elect shall have died, the Vice President elect shall become President. If a President shall not have been chosen before the time fixed for the beginning of his term, or if the President elect shall have failed to qualify, then the Vice President elect shall act as President until a President shall have qualified; and the Congress may by law provide for the case wherein neither a President elect nor a Vice President elect shall have qualified, declaring who shall then act as President, or the manner in which one who is to act shall be selected, and such person shall act accordingly until a President or Vice President shall have qualified.
4. The Congress may by law provide for the case of the death of any of the persons from whom the House of Representatives may choose a President whenever the right of choice shall have devolved upon them, and for the case of the death of any of the persons from whom the Senate may choose a Vice President whenever the right of choice shall have devolved upon them.
5. Sections 1 and 2 shall take effect on the 15th day of October following the ratification of this article.
6. This article shall be inoperative unless it shall have been ratified as an amendment to the Constitution by the legislatures of three-

fourths of the several States within seven years from the date of its submission.

Amendment 21 [Amendment 18 repealed; ratified December 5, 1933]

1. The eighteenth article of amendment to the Constitution of the United States is hereby repealed.
2. The transportation or importation into any State, Territory, or possession of the United States for delivery or use therein of intoxicating liquors, in violation of the laws thereof, is hereby prohibited.
3. The article shall be inoperative unless it shall have been ratified as an amendment to the Constitution by conventions in the several States, as provided in the Constitution, within seven years from the date of the submission hereof to the States by the Congress.

Amendment 22 [Presidential term limits; ratified February 27, 1951]

1. No person shall be elected to the office of the President more than twice, and no person who has held the office of President, or acted as President, for more than two years of a term to which some other person was elected President shall be elected to the office of the President more than once. But this Article shall not apply to any person holding the office of President, when this Article was proposed by the Congress, and shall not prevent any person who may be holding the office of President, or acting as President, during the term within which this Article becomes operative from holding the office of President or acting as President during the remainder of such term.
2. This article shall be inoperative unless it shall have been ratified as an amendment to the Constitution by the legislatures of three-fourths of the several States within seven years from the date of its submission to the States by the Congress.

Amendment 23 [Presidential vote for District of Columbia; ratified March 29, 1961]

1. The District constituting the seat of Government of the United States shall appoint in such manner as the Congress may direct: A number of electors of President and Vice President equal to the whole number of Senators and Representatives in Congress to which the District would be entitled if it were a State, but in no event more than the least populous State; they shall be in addition to those appointed by the States, but they shall be considered, for the purposes of the election of President and Vice President, to be electors appointed by

a State; and they shall meet in the District and perform such duties as provided by the twelfth article of amendment.

2. The Congress shall have power to enforce this article by appropriate legislation.

Amendment 24 [Poll tax barred; ratified January 23, 1964]

1. The right of citizens of the United States to vote in any primary or other election for President or Vice President, for electors for President or Vice President, or for Senator or Representative in Congress, shall not be denied or abridged by the United States or any State by reason of failure to pay any poll tax or other tax.

2. The Congress shall have power to enforce this article by appropriate legislation.

Amendment 25 [Presidential disability and succession; ratified February 10, 1967]

1. In case of the removal of the President from office or of his death or resignation, the Vice President shall become President.

2. Whenever there is a vacancy in the office of the Vice President, the President shall nominate a Vice President who shall take office upon confirmation by a majority vote of both Houses of Congress.

3. Whenever the President transmits to the President pro tempore of the Senate and the Speaker of the House of Representatives his written declaration that he is unable to discharge the powers and duties of his office, and until he transmits to them a written declaration to the contrary, such powers and duties shall be discharged by the Vice President as Acting President.

4. Whenever the Vice President and a majority of either the principal officers of the executive departments or of such other body as Congress may by law provide, transmit to the President pro tempore of the Senate and the Speaker of the House of Representatives their written declaration that the President is unable to discharge the powers and duties of his office, the Vice President shall immediately assume the powers and duties of the office as Acting President.

Thereafter, when the President transmits to the President pro tempore of the Senate and the Speaker of the House of Representatives his written declaration that no inability exists, he shall resume the powers and duties of his office unless the Vice President and a majority of either the principal officers of the executive department or of such other body as Congress may by law provide, transmit within four days to the President pro tempore of the Senate and the Speaker of the House of Representatives their written declaration that the President is unable to discharge the powers and duties of his office. Thereupon Congress shall decide the issue, assembling within forty-eight hours for that purpose if not in session. If the Congress, within twenty-one days after receipt of the latter written declaration, or, if Congress is not in session, within twenty-one days after Congress is required to assemble, determines by two-thirds vote of both Houses that the President is unable to discharge the powers and duties of his office, the Vice President shall continue to discharge the same as Acting President; otherwise, the President shall resume the powers and duties of his office.

Amendment 26 [Voting age set to 18 years; ratified July 1, 1971]

1. The right of citizens of the United States, who are eighteen years of age or older, to vote shall not be denied or abridged by the United States or by any State on account of age.
2. The Congress shall have power to enforce this article by appropriate legislation.

Amendment 27 [Limiting congressional pay increases; ratified May 7, 1992]

No law, varying the compensation for the services of the Senators and Representatives, shall take effect, until an election of Representatives shall have intervened.

Appendix B:
Search Warrants

STATE OF COLORADO)
) ss.

COUNTY OF WELD)   **RETURN AND INVENTORY**

The undersigned officer, being sworn says: On the 21ˢᵗ day of March, 2007, I duly executed the within Search Warrant by taking into my possession from the place named in said Warrant, certain property and the following is a true, complete and correct Inventory of the property as taken:

SEE ATTACHED INVENTORY SHEET.

I further certify that said Inventory was made by me in the presence of Detective Dennis Lobato and that a copy of said Warrant and a Receipt for the property taken was given by me to Deborah Smith, the person who owned the property taken.

Michael D. Prill/Detective

Sworn and subscribed to before me this 22 day of March, 2007.

NOTARY PUBLIC/DEPUTY CLERK
my commission expires 4-25-10

The inventory shall be made in the presence of the applicant for the warrant and the person from whose possession or premises or vehicle the property was taken, if they are present, or in the presence of at least one credible person other than the applicant for the warrant or the person from whose possession or premises or vehicle the property was taken.

SEE RULE 41 (c)(d), Colorado Rules of Criminal Procedure.

RECEIPT

On the ____ day of _____ 2007, I received the items listed in the foregoing Inventory.

_____
OFFICER *

GREELEY POLICE DEPARTMENT
SEARCH WARRANT INVENTORY

CR # _07-1317_   DATE: _032107_   START TIME: _1600 Hrs_   END TIME: _1630 Hrs_

LOCATION: ██████████████████ Greeley, Co.

OFFICERS ON SCENE: _M. Prill 209,   D. Lobato 202, J. Bush 150,_

ITEM #	PROPERTY DESCRIPTION	LOCATION	OFFICER
1	TOSHIBA LAPTOP COMPUTER 1805-9204, SN# Z1023097P	FRONT, OFFICE, 1ST LOCATION / ON DESK	Prill
2	TOSHIBA CHARGER, FUR LAPTOP		
3	OFFICE DEPOT CD; GMATTING'S 804	" " TOP LEFT DESK DRAWER	
4	AARP LETTER	" " MIDDLE DESK DRAWER	
5	Phillips CD " GRACE MANUELS	" " TOP FILING CABINET DRAWER	
6	HEWLETT COMPUTER TOWER 8775C	" " CLOSET	
7	(PRESARIO) COMPUTER TOWER COMPAQ 3443	" " CLOSET	
8	(PRESARIO) COMPAQ SN# 1X13JD4JAZTN	DOWNSTAIRS, LIVING ROOM	D. LOBATO

OFFICERS SIGNATURES: _[signatures]_ W.S.
_B150_

GPD 2136 (10/00)   PAGE _1_ OF _1_

STATE OF COLORADO)
) ss.
COUNTY OF WELD)

IN THE _DISTRICT_ COURT
NINETEENTH JUDICIAL DISTRICT
NO. _07 CR_ DIVISION _1_

SEARCH WARRANT

THE PEOPLE OF THE STATE OF COLORADO.

TO: Any officer authorized by law to execute a search warrant in the County wherein the property is located.

Michael D. Prill, having this date filed an Affidavit for a Search Warrant in conformity with the provisions of Colorado Rules of Criminal Procedure, 41(b) and (c), for the following described property, to-wit:

1. Any and all computer systems and computer equipment to include, but not limited to, central processing units and circuit boards attached or unattached to the computer system.
2. Any and all storage media to include, but not limited to, floppy diskettes, hard disk drives, removable disk drive cartridges and drives, magnetic computer tapes, compact disks, and any other device capable of storing information in a magnetic/optical form, whether internal or external to the computer system, attached or unattached to the computer system.
3. Paper and documents showing residency

Believed to be situated at the place known as:

Upon one or more grounds as set forth in Rule 41(b), Colorado Rules of Criminal Procedure, namely:

(1)   Is stolen or embezzled;
(2)   Is designed or intended for use or which is or has been used as a means of committing a criminal offense or the possession of which is illegal;
(3)   Would be material evidence in a subsequently criminal prosecution;

The names of persons whose affidavits have been taken in support hereof are: **Michael D. Prill**, and I am satisfied that there is probable cause to believe that the property so described is located on the person, premises or in the vehicle above described, YOU ARE THEREFORE COMMANDED to search forthwith the person, place, or vehicle above described, for the property described at any time, day or night. This Warrant shall be executed within ten (10) days of the date the Warrant is issued. The return shall be made promptly and shall be accompanied by a written inventory of all property taken. You shall deliver to the person from whom the property is taken or from whose premises or vehicle the property is taken a copy of this Warrant together with a receipt for the property taken or, in lieu thereof, to leave the copy and receipt at the place from which the property is taken; and to deliver to the issuing judge a written inventory of the property with the return of this Warrant.

Dated this _21_ day of March 2007, at Weld County, Colorado, at _2:20_ A.M. (P.M.)

Further orders which the court deems necessary: _This AFFIDAVIT AND SEARCH WARRANT WILL REMAIN SEALED UNTIL APRIL 26, 2007 @ 4:00pm OR FURTHER ORDER OF THE Court_

_____
                           JUDGE

IN THE ___*District*___ COURT, IN

AND FOR THE COUNTY OF WELD,

BEFORE JUDGE ___*Roger A. Klein*___

FD IN WELD COUN.
COMBINED COURTS

2007 MAR 21 PM 2: 30

**AFFIDAVIT FOR
SEARCH WARRANT
UNDER RULE 16**

Your affiant, **Michael D. Prill,** being first duly sworn, upon his oath says: that he has reason to believe that in the property known as:

There is now located certain property, to-wit:

1. Any and all computer systems and computer equipment to include, but not limited to, central processing units and circuit boards attached or unattached to the computer system.
2. Any and all storage media to include, but not limited to, floppy diskettes, hard disk drives, removable disk drive cartridges and drives, magnetic computer tapes, compact disks, and any other device capable of storing information in a magnetic/optical form, whether internal or external to the computer system, attached or unattached to the computer system.
3. Paper and documents showing residency

Which property:
(1)   Is stolen or embezzled.
(2)   Is designed or intended for use or which is or has been used as a means of committing a criminal offense or the possession of which is illegal;
(3)   Would be material evidence in a subsequent criminal prosecution;

Based upon the following facts:

Your affiant is a police officer for the City of Greeley Police Department and has gained the following information from reading the reports and speaking to fellow officers, from reading the statements of the victim and witnesses and through personal investigation.

On January 23, 2007 at 1815 hours, Greeley Police officers were dispatched to a reported shooting in the parking lot of 2505 S. 11th Avenue, Greeley, Weld, Colorado. The address is the location of the Colorado State Employee's Credit Union.

Officers found a female lying on the ground in the parking lot. The female was bleeding profusely from a head wound and showed no signs of life. Responding medical personnel rushed the victim to North Colorado Medical Center where she was pronounced deceased.

The victim was identified as Heather Garraus. Heather Garraus is married to Ignacio Garraus. Ignacio Garraus is a Greeley Police Officer. Within the last two years Ignacio Garraus had a sexual affair with a Shawna Nelson. Towards the end of the affair Shawna Nelson became pregnant and bore a child. Shawna Nelson alleged the child was Ignacio Garraus'. Shawna Nelson is the wife of Kenneth Nelson, a Weld County Sherriff's Deputy.

During the subsequent investigation Greeley Police Detectives collected evidence indicating Shawna Nelson murdered Heather Garraus. Shawna Nelson was taken into custody for the homicide. Shawna Nelson provided a statement to Detectives; your affiant monitored that interview and listened to her statement. An arrest warrant was secured for Shawna Nelson, who was later booked into the Weld County Jail. On January 31st 2007 Shawna Nelson was transferred to the custody of the Larimer County Jail.

During the initial stages of the investigation Detectives contacted Deborah Smith at her home, ▮▮▮▮▮▮▮▮ ▮▮▮▮▮Greeley, Weld, Colorado. Deborah Smith is the older sister of Shawna Nelson. Smith lives two homes east of the Nelson residence. During that interview Smith provided a home phone number of ▮▮▮▮▮▮▮

On January 29th 2007 a search warrant was secured for the home of Shawna Nelson. During that search warrant your affiant walked to Deborah Smiths residence and met with Kenneth Nelson, to release property to him. Arriving at the address the door was opened by Deborah Smith. Your affiant spoke briefly with Smith who called Kenneth Nelson to the door.

Your affiant has monitored all telephone calls made by Shawna Nelson from the Larimer County Jail. Your affiant has listened to countless telephone calls made by Shawna Nelson since her arrest. Your affiant recognized Shawna Nelson's voice on each of these calls. Nearly every call made by Shawna Nelson has been dialed to either the Nelsons home, or to Deborah Smith's home telephone number ▮▮▮▮▮▮▮. Your affiant recognized Deborah Smith's voice during those calls made to Smiths telephone number from Shawna Nelson.

On February 4th 2007 Shawna Nelson called Deborah Smiths telephone number twice in quick succession. During these calls Shawna Nelson directed Deborah Smith to access the internet and log into Shawna Nelson's Verizon wireless photograph account, called "Pix Place." Verizon wireless customers have the ability to electronically store photographs outside of their cellular phones within the individual customer's Verizon account. Pix Place is essentially an on-line photo album maintained by Verizon wireless.

During these calls Shawna Nelson directed Deborah Smith to Nelsons Pix Place account, providing Smith with Nelson's password to the account. Once into the account Nelson guided Smith through Nelson's Pix Place account and the photographs contained within. Nelson described to Smith a list of photographs in the account, under each of Nelson's children names.

Shawna Nelson told Deborah Smith that selecting these listed photographs will access even more photographs stored in the account. Nelson told Smith to select the photographs "that I don't want anymore" and asked Smith if she knows which ones Nelson is referring to. Smith said yes.

Shawna Nelson tells Deborah Smith to "just get rid of" the photographs Nelson is referring to. Initially Smith is reluctant telling Nelson she can't, "I'm going to get in trouble." Smith told Nelson "they will know about this." Shawna Nelson told Smith she didn't want Kenneth Nelson to ever see the pictures. After a pause Smith is heard saying, "Oh my god."

After nearly a minute and a half pause Deborah Smith asked how to enlarge these pictures to "see what I'm looking at." Shawna explains how. After another pause Smith is heard sighing. Shawna Nelson told Smith not to show the pictures to Kenneth Nelson and Smith replied, "believe me I won't, I won't." Nelson told Smith she doesn't want the photographs anymore and Smith says she understands.

On February 7th 2007 a production of records for Shawna Nelsons Verizon wireless Pix Place account was secured and executed. On February 20th 2007 Verizon wireless advised your affiant a Pix Place account exists for Nelson, but no photographs of any kind were presently in the account.

Your affiant discussed this evidence with Detective Trevor Anderson, a forensic computer analyst with the Greeley Police Department. Detective Anderson advised the history of Deborah Smiths visit to the Verizon Pix Place account would be maintained in the computer's memory. In addition, Detective Anderson advised it is possible to retrieve the images viewed by Smith while at the account; even if those images were deleted during the internet session to the account. Detective Anderson stated; however, that over time this information would be permanently deleted as more recently deleted data is compiled.

Your affiant respectfully requests this affidavit, and search warrant, be sealed at the present time. The on-going conversations monitored through the inmate telephone calls, made by Shawna Nelson, have continued to provide Detectives with an unending wealth of evidence regarding this homicide investigation. Not the least of which is the contradictory evidence provided by Shawna Nelson during these calls. In addition, the investigation of Deborah Smiths possible tampering of evidence relevant to this case is on-going.

The release of the information contained within this affidavit would effectively cease all discussions of this case, and the collection of new leads and evidence would come to an end. Your affiant respectfully requests these documents remained sealed until further order by the court, following an advisement with Detectives with the Greeley Police Department.

The release of the information would jeopardize the ongoing investigation in that release of the information to the public may affect investigators' abilities to locate and interview witnesses, may result in the destruction or concealment of evidence, may impact the statements of witnesses and may cause potential suspects to flee to avoid arrest or prosecution. Release of the said documents is therefore not in the public's interest.

24-72-305(5) C.R.S. authorizes the Court to deny disclosure of any criminal justice records on the grounds that said disclosure would be contrary to the public interest and specifically authorizes the Court to deny access to records of investigations conducted by or of intelligence information or security procedures of any district attorney or police department. Disclosure of the appendices would, for the reasons set forth above, be contrary to the public interest.

Dated this _____ day of March 2007.

_____
Michael D. Prill
AFFIANT

This Affidavit, consisting of **3** pages, was subscribed and sworn to before me this __2/__ day of ___MARCH___ 2007.

_____
JUDGE

STATE OF COLORADO)
) ss.
COUNTY OF WELD   )

RETURN AND INVENTORY

FILED IN WELD COUNTY COMBINED COURTS

The undersigned officer, being sworn says: On the 26ᵗ day of March, 2007, I duly executed the within Search Warrant by taking into my possession from the place named in said Warrant, certain property and the following is a true, complete and correct Inventory of the property as taken:

SEE ATTACHED INVENTORY SHEET.

I further certify that said Inventory was made by me in the presence of ___Geee Thorp___ and that a copy of said Warrant and a Receipt for the property taken was given by me to ___Kathy Domesla___, the evidence custodian.

Sworn and subscribed to before me this **3ᵉᵈ** day of ___APRIL___, 2007.

Christy R. Hardwick
NOTARY PUBLIC/DEPUTY CLERK

The inventory shall be made in the presence of the applicant for the warrant and the person from whose possession or premises or vehicle the property was taken, if they are present, or in the presence of at least one credible person other than the applicant for the warrant or the person from whose possession or premises or vehicle the property was taken.

SEE RULE 41 (c)(d), Colorado Rules of Criminal Procedure.

RECEIPT

On the ____ day of _____ 2007, I received the items listed in the foregoing Inventory.

_____
OFFICER #

*THIS INFORMATION INCLUDES DETAILS OF THE FOUR
HARD DRIVE IMAGES PRODUCED AS A RESULT OF THIS
SEARCH WARRANT* 251

C
_____

```
Name:              DebLaptop (G200856#1)
ActualDate:        03/26/07 01:11:14PM
TargetDate:        03/26/07 01:11:14PM
FilePath:          L:\Image\DebLaptop.E01
Case Number:       GP07-1317 D Smith Laptop
Evidence Number:   DebLaptop
Examiner Name:     T. Anderson
Notes:
Drive Type:        DRIVEFIXED
File Integrity:    Completely Verified, 0 Errors
Acquisition Hash:  58FE15AEADAFD0CDC2D22A63B57BEF2D
Verify Hash:       58FE15AEADAFD0CDC2D22A63B57BEF2D
EnCase Version:    5.05e
System Version:    Windows XP
Fastbloced:        No
Is Physical:       Yes
Compression:       Good
Total Sectors:     39070080
```

C
_____

```
Name:              200856#2
ActualDate:        04/02/07 08:44:27AM
TargetDate:        04/02/07 08:44:27AM
FilePath:          L:\G200856#2\Image\G200856#2.E01
Case Number:       200856#2
Evidence Number:   200856#2
Examiner Name:     T. Anderson
Notes:
Drive Type:        DRIVEFIXED
File Integrity:    Completely Verified, 0 Errors
Acquisition Hash:  275A9C083894254A27B89D514907537F
Verify Hash:       275A9C083894254A27B89D514907537F
EnCase Version:    5.05e
System Version:    Windows XP
Fastbloced:        No
Is Physical:       Yes
Compression:       Good
Total Sectors:     120060864
```

C
_____

```
Name:              G200856#3
ActualDate:        04/02/07 11:01:16AM
TargetDate:        04/02/07 11:01:16AM
FilePath:          L:\G200856#3\Image\G200856#3.E01
Case Number:       200856#3
Evidence Number:   G200856#3
Examiner Name:     T. Anderson
Notes:
Drive Type:        DRIVEFIXED
File Integrity:    Completely Verified, 0 Errors
Acquisition Hash:  935077B5F5B9E854CF7CAE74F1E86571
Verify Hash:       935077B5F5B9E854CF7CAE74F1E86571
EnCase Version:    5.05e
System Version:    Windows XP
Fastbloced:        No
Is Physical:       Yes
Compression:       Good
Total Sectors:     25075008
```

C
_____

```
Name:              G200856#4
ActualDate:        04/03/07 07:51:53AM
TargetDate:        04/03/07 07:51:53AM
FilePath:          L:\G200856#4\Image\G200856#4.E01
Case Number:       200856#4
Evidence Number:   G200856#4
Examiner Name:     T. Anderson
Notes:
Drive Type:        DRIVEFIXED
File Integrity:    Completely Verified, 0 Errors
Acquisition Hash:  13CAA8A7A19C5DFFA364F58D421D1509
Verify Hash:       13CAA8A7A19C5DFFA364F58D421D1509
EnCase Version:    5.05e
System Version:    Windows XP
Fastbloced:        No
Is Physical:       Yes
Compression:       Good
Total Sectors:     78177792
```

D
_____

```
Unable to open registry on volume D
```

STATE OF COLORADO   )   IN THE ___District___ COURT
) ss.   NINETEENTH JUDICIAL DISTRICT
COUNTY OF WELD)   NO. 07cr128 DIVISION ONE

SEARCH WARRANT

THE PEOPLE OF THE STATE OF COLORADO:

TO: Any officer authorized by law to execute a search warrant in the County wherein the property is located.

Gregory Tharp, having this date filed an Affidavit for a Search Warrant in conformity with the provisions of Colorado Rules of Criminal Procedure, 41(b) and (c), for the following described property, to-wit:

1) Any and all computer systems and computer equipment to include, but not limited to, central processing units and circuit boards attached or unattached to the computer system.

2) Any and all storage media to include, but not limited to, floppy diskettes, hard disk drives, removable disk drive cartridges and drives, magnetic computer tapes, compact disks, and any other device capable of storing information in a magnetic/optical form, whether internal or external to the computer system, attached or unattached to the computer system.

3) Any and all computer peripheral devices attached or unattached to the computer to include but not limited to computer monitors, printers, keyboards, modems, or other physical devices which serve to transmit or receive information to and from the computer.

4) Any and all computer programs or software used in the operation of the computer system, used to transmit or receive information, used to display or print graphics or other types of files, and all other computer programs and software associated with the computer system to include all programs stored on the computer, floppy disk, CD's, or other storage media.

5) Any and all documents which serve the purpose of explaining the way in which the computer hardware, programs, and data are used, including manuals for computer equipment or software, printouts of computer programs, data files, or other information which has been or continues to be stored electronically or magnetically in the computer system.

6) Any and all correspondence, diaries, memoirs, journals, personal reminiscences, electronic mail (e-mail), letters, notes, memorandum, or other communications in written or printed form, as these items pertain to allegations set forth in this affidavit.

7) Any and all passwords, encryption keys, access codes or other security or privacy devices, whether of a physical, written or oral form, used to encrypt, encode, or otherwise limit access to information, files, programs, accounts or other data associated with or stored any computer.

8) Any proof of ownership, maintenance, control, or use of electronic or computer related equipment, programs, data, or documentation at that address including correspondence, invoices, or similar items.

9) Your affiant is seeking permission for Detective Trevor Anderson to examine the computers and storage devices for any and all data, correspondence, electronic mail, voice messages, letters, notes, ledgers, spreadsheets, documents, memorandum, image, video, sound or graphic files:

Which relate to or identify persons who possessed, accessed, or viewed evidentiary material related to this case or to Shawna Nelson or to Deborah Smith.

Any and all passwords, encryption keys, access codes or other security or privacy devices, whether of a physical, written or oral form, used to encrypt, encode, or otherwise limit access to information, files, programs, accounts or other data associated with or stored on the computer.

Any proof of ownership, maintenance or control of the computer related equipment, programs, data, correspondence, invoices, registration keys, or similar items.

Any and all diaries, memoirs, journals, personal reminiscences, correspondence, letters, notes, memorandum, stories, electronic mail or other communications in written or oral form, stored on the computer evidence seized as those items relate to the allegations.

The specific items to be examined include:
G200856 #1 Toshiba Laptop Computer
G200856 #2 Hewlet Packard 8775C Computer
G200856 #3 Compaq 3443 Computer
G200856 #4 Compaq 5008us Computer

These items were seized on March 21, 2007 from the residence at ▮▮▮▮▮▮▮▮ Greeley, Weld, Colorado as a result of a search warrant service.

Upon examination, these items may be found to contain additional items as described above.

known to be situated (on the person) (at the place) or (in the vehicle) known as:
The Greeley Police secure evidence facility
919 7th Street
Greeley, Weld County, Colorado

Upon one or more grounds as set forth in Rule 41(b), Colorado Rules of Criminal Procedure, namely:

( )   Is stolen or embezzled;
(X)   Is designed or intended for use or which is or has been used as a means of committing a criminal offense or the possession of which is illegal;
(X)   Would be material evidence in a subsequently criminal prosecution;

The names of persons whose affidavits have been taken in support hereof are: **Gregory P. Tharp**, and I am satisfied that there is probable cause to believe that the property so described is located on the person, premises or in the vehicle above described, YOU ARE THEREFORE COMMANDED to search forthwith the person, place, or vehicle above described, for the property described at any time, day or night. This Warrant shall be executed within ten (10) days of the date the Warrant is issued. The return shall be made promptly and shall be accompanied by a written inventory of all property taken. You shall deliver to the person from whom the property is taken or from whose premises or vehicle the property is taken a copy of this Warrant together with a receipt for the property taken or, in lieu thereof, to leave the copy and receipt at the place from which the property is taken; and to deliver to the issuing judge a written inventory of the property with the return of this Warrant.

Dated this ___26___ day of March 2007, at Weld County, Colorado, at _12:00_ A.M. (P.M.)

Further orders which the court deems necessary: THIS SEARCH WARRANT + SUPPORTING AFFIDAVIT SHALL REMAIN SEALED UNTIL APRIL 26, 2007 @ 4:00 pm

_____
JUDGE

IN THE ⎽⎽⎽⎽⎽⎽⎽COURT, IN

AND FOR THE COUNTY OF WELD, ,

BEFORE JUDGE ⎽⎽⎽⎽⎽⎽⎽⎽⎽⎽

**AFFIDAVIT FOR
SEARCH WARRANT
UNDER RULE 16**

Your affiant, **Gregory P. Tharp**, being first duly sworn, upon his oath says: that he has reason to believe that in
the property known as:

    G200856 #1 Toshiba Laptop Computer
    G200856 #2 Hewlet Packard 8775C Computer
    G200856 #3 Compaq 3443 Computer
    G200856 #4 Compaq 5008us Computer

    Currently located at the Greeley Police secure evidence facility
    919 7th Street
    Greeley, Weld County, Colorado

There is now located certain property, to-wit:

1) Any and all computer systems and computer equipment to include, but not limited to, central
processing units and circuit boards attached or unattached to the computer system.

2) Any and all storage media to include, but not limited to, floppy diskettes, hard disk drives, removable
disk drive cartridges and drives, magnetic computer tapes, compact disks, and any other device
capable of storing information in a magnetic/optical form, whether internal or external to the
computer system, attached or unattached to the computer system.

3) Any and all computer peripheral devices attached or unattached to the computer to include but not
limited to computer monitors, printers, keyboards, modems, or other physical devices which serve to
transmit or receive information to and from the computer.

4) Any and all computer programs or software used in the operation of the computer system, used to
transmit or receive information, used to display or print graphics or other types of files, and all other
computer programs and software associated with the computer system to include all programs stored
on the computer, floppy disk, CD's, or other storage media.

5) Any and all documents which serve the purpose of explaining the way in which the computer
hardware, programs, and data are used, including manuals for computer equipment or software,
printouts of computer programs, data files, or other information which has been or continues to be
stored electronically or magnetically in the computer system.

6) Any and all correspondence, diaries, memoirs, journals, personal reminiscences, electronic mail (e-
mail), letters, notes, memorandum, or other communications in written or printed form, as these items
pertain to allegations set forth in this affidavit.

7) Any and all passwords, encryption keys, access codes or other security or privacy devices, whether of
a physical, written or oral form, used to encrypt, encode, or otherwise limit access to information,
files, programs, accounts or other data associated with or stored any computer.

8) Any proof of ownership, maintenance, control, or use of electronic or computer related equipment, programs, data, or documentation at that address including correspondence, invoices, or similar items.

9) Your affiant is seeking permission for Detective Trevor Anderson to examine the computers and storage devices for any and all data, correspondence, electronic mail, voice messages, letters, notes, ledgers, spreadsheets, documents, memorandum, image, video, sound or graphic files:

Which relate to or identify persons who possessed, accessed, or viewed evidentiary material related to this case or to Shawna Nelson or to Deborah Smith.

Any and all passwords, encryption keys, access codes or other security or privacy devices, whether of a physical, written or oral form, used to encrypt, encode, or otherwise limit access to information, files, programs, accounts or other data associated with or stored on the computer.

Any proof of ownership, maintenance or control of the computer related equipment, programs, data, correspondence, invoices, registration keys, or similar items.

Any and all diaries, memoirs, journals, personal reminiscences, correspondence, letters, notes, memorandum, stories, electronic mail or other communications in written or oral form, stored on the computer evidence seized as those items relate to the allegations.

The specific items to be examined include:
G200856 #1 Toshiba Laptop Computer
G200856 #2 Hewlet Packard 8775C Computer
G200856 #3 Compaq 3443 Computer
G200856 #4 Compaq 5008us Computer

These items were seized on March 21, 2007 from the residence at ▉▉▉▉▉▉▉▉, Greeley, Weld, Colorado as a result of a search warrant service.

Upon examination, these items may be found to contain additional items as described above.

Upon one or more grounds as set forth in Rule 41(b), Colorado Rules of Criminal Procedure, namely:

( ) Is stolen or embezzled;
(X) Is designed or intended for use or which is or has been used as a means of committing a criminal offense or the possession of which is illegal;
(X) Would be material evidence in a subsequently criminal prosecution;

Based upon the following facts:

Your affiant is an investigator for the City of Greeley Police Department and has gained the following information from reading the reports and speaking to fellow officers, from reading the statements of the victim and witnesses and through personal investigation.

On January 23, 2007 at 1815 hours, Greeley Police officers were dispatched to a reported shooting in the parking lot of 2505 S. 11th Avenue, Greeley, Weld, Colorado. The address is the location of the Colorado State Employee's Credit Union.

Officers found a female lying on the ground in the parking lot. The female was bleeding profusely from a head wound and showed no signs of life. Responding medical personnel rushed the victim to North Colorado Medical Center where she was pronounced deceased.

The victim was identified as Heather Garraus. Heather Garraus is married to Ignacio Garraus. Ignacio Garraus is a Greeley Police Officer. Within the last two years Ignacio Garraus had a sexual affair with Shawna Nelson. Towards the end of the affair Shawna Nelson became pregnant and bore a child. Shawna Nelson alleged the child was Ignacio Garraus'. Shawna Nelson is the wife of Kenneth Nelson, a Weld County Sherriff's Deputy.

During the subsequent investigation Greeley Police Detectives collected evidence indicating Shawna Nelson murdered Heather Garraus. Shawna Nelson was taken into custody for the homicide. An arrest warrant was secured for Shawna Nelson, who was later booked into the Weld County Jail. On January 31ʳᵗ 2007 Shawna Nelson was transferred to the custody of the Larimer County Jail.

During the initial stages of the investigation Detectives contacted Deborah Smith at her home, ██████████ ██████ Greeley, Weld, Colorado. Deborah Smith is the older sister of Shawna Nelson. Smith lives two homes east of the Nelson residence. During that interview Smith provided a home phone number ██████████████

On January 29ᵗʰ 2007 a search warrant was secured for the home of Shawna Nelson. During that search warrant Detective Mike Prill walked to Deborah Smiths residence and met with Kenneth Nelson, to release property to him. Arriving at the address the door was opened by Deborah Smith. Your affiant spoke briefly with Smith who called Kenneth Nelson to the door.

Detective Mike Prill has monitored all telephone calls made by Shawna Nelson from the Larimer County Jail. Detective Mike Prill has listened to countless telephone calls made by Shawna Nelson since her arrest. Detective Mike Prill recognized Shawna Nelson's voice on each of these calls. Nearly every call made by Shawna Nelson has been dialed to either the Nelsons home, or to Deborah Smith's home telephone number ██████████████. Detective Mike Prill recognized Deborah Smith's voice during those calls made to Smiths telephone number from Shawna Nelson.

On February 4ᵗʰ 2007 Shawna Nelson called Deborah Smith's telephone number twice in quick succession. During these calls Shawna Nelson directed Deborah Smith to access the Internet and log into Shawna Nelson's Verizon wireless photograph account, called "Pix Place." Verizon wireless customers have the ability to electronically store photographs outside of their cellular phones within the individual customer's Verizon account. Pix Place is essentially an on-line photo album maintained by Verizon wireless.

During these calls Shawna Nelson directed Deborah Smith to Nelsons Pix Place account, providing Smith with Nelson's password to the account. Once into the account Nelson guided Smith through Nelson's Pix Place account and the photographs contained within. Nelson described to Smith a list of photographs in the account, under each of Nelson's children names.

Shawna Nelson told Deborah Smith that selecting these listed photographs will access even more photographs stored in the account. Nelson told Smith to select the photographs "that I don't want anymore" and asked Smith if she knows which ones Nelson is referring to. Smith said yes.

Shawna Nelson tells Deborah Smith to "just get rid of" the photographs Nelson is referring to. Initially Smith is reluctant telling Nelson she can't, "I'm going to get in trouble." Smith told Nelson "they will know about this." Shawna Nelson told Smith she didn't want Kenneth Nelson to ever see the pictures. After a pause Smith is heard saying, "Oh my god."

After nearly a minute and a half pause Deborah Smith asked how to enlarge these pictures to "see what I'm looking at." Shawna explains how. After another pause Smith is heard sighing. Shawna Nelson told Smith not to show the pictures to Kenneth Nelson and Smith replied, "believe me I won't, I won't." Nelson told Smith she doesn't want the photographs anymore and Smith says she understands.

On February 7th 2007 a production of records for Shawna Nelsons Verizon wireless Pix Place account was secured and executed. On February 20th 2007 Verizon wireless advised your affiant a Pix Place account exists for Nelson, but no photographs of any kind were presently in the account.

Detective Mike Prill discussed this evidence with Detective Trevor Anderson, a forensic computer analyst with the Greeley Police Department. Detective Anderson advised the history of Deborah Smiths visit to the Verizon Pix Place account would be maintained in the computer's memory. In addition, Detective Anderson advised it is possible to retrieve the images viewed by Smith while at the account; even if those images were deleted during the Internet session to the account. Detective Anderson stated; however, that over time this information would be permanently deleted as more recently deleted data is compiled.

Your affiant respectfully requests this affidavit, and search warrant, be sealed at the present time. The on-going conversations monitored through the inmate telephone calls, made by Shawna Nelson, have continued to provide Detectives with an unending wealth of evidence regarding this homicide investigation. Not the least of which is the contradictory evidence provided by Shawna Nelson during these calls. In addition, the investigation of Deborah Smiths possible tampering of evidence relevant to this case is on-going.

The release of the information contained within this affidavit would effectively cease all discussions of this case, and the collection of new leads and evidence would come to an end. Your affiant respectfully requests these documents remained sealed until further order by the court, following an advisement with Detectives with the Greeley Police Department.

The release of the information would jeopardize the ongoing investigation in that release of the information to the public may affect investigators' abilities to locate and interview witnesses, may result in the destruction or concealment of evidence, may impact the statements of witnesses and may cause potential suspects to flee to avoid arrest or prosecution. Release of the said documents is therefore not in the public's interest.

24-72-305(5) C.R.S. authorizes the Court to deny disclosure of any criminal justice records on the grounds that said disclosure would be contrary to the public interest and specifically authorizes the Court to deny access to records of investigations conducted by or of intelligence information or security procedures of any district attorney or police department. Disclosure of the appendices would, for the reasons set forth above, be contrary to the public interest.

Dated this _____ day of March 2007.

_____
Gregory P. Tharp, Affiant

This Affidavit, consisting of 4 pages, was subscribed and sworn to before me this _____ day of _____ 2007.

_____
JUDGE

Appendix C:
Grand Jury Indictment,
August 2005 Term—
at Alexandria, Virginia

THE GRAND JURY CHARGES THAT:

General Allegations

At all times material to this indictment:

1. Defendant LAWRENCE ANTHONY FRANKLIN was employed by the United States government at the Department of Defense (DoD) in the Office of the Secretary of Defense (OSD), International Security Affairs (ISA), Office of Near East and South Asia, Office of Northern Gulf Affairs, Iran desk, and held a Top Secret security clearance with access to Sensitive Compartmented Information (SCI). FRANKLIN'S office was located within the Pentagon, in the Eastern District of Virginia. FRANKLIN was also a Colonel in the United States Air Force Reserve (USAFR).

2. Throughout his employment with the United States government, FRANKLIN repeatedly signed written agreements acknowledging his duty to safeguard classified information:
    - On or about July 31, 1979, FRANKLIN signed a Defense Intelligence Agency (DIA) Secrecy Agreement, by which he acknowledged that he would never divulge any classified information relating to the national security without prior consent of the Director of the Defense Intelligence Agency or his designated representative. FRANKLIN further acknowledged that the burden was his to ascertain whether information is classified and who is authorized to receive it. FRANKLIN acknowledged that he had read and understood the provisions of the Espionage Act, including 18 U.S.C. § 793, 794 and 798.
    - On or about December 8, 1999, FRANKLIN signed a Classified Information Nondisclosure Agreement, a Standard Form 312 (SF312). In that document FRANKLIN acknowledged that he

was aware that the unauthorized disclosure of classified information by him could cause irreparable injury to the United States or could be used to advantage by a foreign nation and that he would never divulge classified information to an unauthorized person. He further acknowledged that he would never divulge classified information unless he had officially verified that the recipient was authorized by the United States to receive it. Additionally, he agreed that if he was uncertain about the classification status of information, he was required to confirm from an authorized official that the information is unclassified before he could disclose it.

- On or about June 5, 2001, FRANKLIN orally attested that he fully understood his responsibility to protect national security information and would adhere to the provisions of the SF-321. By doing so, FRANKLIN again acknowledged that he was aware that the unauthorized disclosure of classified information by him could cause irreparable injury to the United States yr [sic] could be used to advantage by a foreign nation and that he would never divulge classified information to an unauthorized person. He again acknowledged that he would never divulge classified information unless he had officially verified that the recipient was authorized by the United States to receive it. Additionally, he again agreed that if he was uncertain about the classification status of information, he was required to confirm from an authorized official that the information is unclassified before he could disclose it. He again acknowledged that any unauthorized disclosure of classified information by him may constitute a violation, or violations of criminal laws, including 18 U.S.C. § 793, 794 and 798 and 50 U.S.C. § 783.

- On or about July 17, 2001, FRANKLIN signed an SCI Nondisclosure Statement in conjunction with his employment at the DoD/OSD. FRANKLIN acknowledged that he was granted access to classified information protected as SCI and that he received a security indoctrination addressing the nature and protection of SCI information. In this document, FRANKLIN again acknowledged that he had been advised that the unauthorized disclosure of SCI by him could cause irreparable injury to the United States or be used to advantage by a foreign nation— He agreed he would never divulge anything marked as SCI or that he knew to be SCI to anyone who is not authorized to receive it without prior written authorization from the United States government. He acknowledged that he was obligated by law and regulation not to disclose any classified information in an unauthorized fashion. FRANKLIN again acknowledged that unauthorized disclosure of that information "may constitute violations of United States criminal laws, including the provisions of Sections 793, 794, 798, and 952, Title 18, United States Code."

3. At no time was FRANKLIN authorized to release classified information to co-defendants ROSEN and WEISSMAN, except with respect to Overt Acts 43 and 44 in Count One. At no time was FRANKLIN ever authorized to de-classify classified information.

4. Defendant STEVEN J. ROSEN was employed as the Director of Foreign Policy Issues for the American Israel Public Affairs Committee (AIPAC) in Washington, D.C. ROSEN was hired by AIPAC in or about July 1982. AIPAC, according to its website, is "America's ProIsrael Lobby." AIPAC lobbies the U.S. Congress and Executive Branch agencies on various issues related to Israel and U.S. foreign policy in the Middle East. As the Director of Foreign Policy Issues, ROSEN lobbied on behalf of AIPAC, primarily with officials within the Executive Branch of the U.S. government. During the time period of this indictment, ROSEN did not have a U.S. government security clearance and was not authorized to receive or possess U.S. government classified information.

5. From 1978–1982, ROSEN was a Social Scientist at the RAND Corporation (RAND) in Santa Monica, California. ROSEN was initially granted a U.S. government secret security clearance on or about August 31, 1978, for his work at RAND. ROSEN was later authorized to hold a Top Secret U.S. government security clearance on or about July 18, 1979. These clearances were issued by the Defense Industrial Security Clearance Organization (DISCO), which processes security clearances for U.S. government contractors.

6. Based upon the Top Secret security clearance granted to ROSEN by DISCO on July 18, 1979, the Central Intelligence Agency (CIA) granted ROSEN a Secret Industrial security clearance on July 17, 1980 for CIA contracts on which he would work while at RAND Corporation. On August [8], [sic] 1980, ROSEN signed the requisite U.S. government secrecy agreement (Form 10-71 1 060). In that document, ROSEN acknowledged that he had read and understood the provisions of the espionage laws (sections 793, 794 and 798 of Title 18, United States Code) concerning the disclosure of information relating to the national defense and that he was familiar with the penalties provided for any violation thereof. Additionally, he agreed that he would never divulge, publish or reveal either by word, conduct, or any other means, such information or intelligence unless specifically authorized to do so by an authorized representative of the U.S. government. Further, ROSEN indicated he understood that

this agreement would remain binding upon him after termination of his relationship with the U.S. government. ROSEN's Secret Industrial security clearance for work on the CIA contracts was terminated on or about July 6, 1982.

7. Defendant KEITH WEISSMAN was employed as the Senior Middle East Analyst in the Foreign Policy Issues department at AIPAC. WEISSMAN was lured by AIPAC in 1993. While employed at AIPAC, WEISSMAN worked closely with STEVEN ROSEN in lobbying on behalf of AIPAC, primarily with officials within the Executive Branch of the U.S. government. WEISSMAN did not have a U.S. government security clearance and was not authorized to receive or possess U.S. government classified information.

8. Pursuant to Executive Order 12958, as amended by Executive Order 13292, national security information is classified as "Top Secret," "Secret" or "Confidential[.]" The designation "Top Secret" applies to information, the unauthorized disclosure of which reasonably could be expected to cause exceptionally grave damage to the national security. The designation "Secret" applies to information, the unauthorized disclosure of which reasonably could be expected to cause serious damage to national security. The designation "Confidential" applies to information, the unauthorized disclosure of which reasonably could be expected to cause damage to national security. Access to classified information at any level may be further restricted through compartmentation in SCI categories. Classified information, of any designation, may only be shared with persons determined by an appropriate U.S. government official to be eligible for access to classified information, who have signed an approved non-disclosure agreement and who possess a need to know. If a person is not eligible to receive classified information, classified information may not be disclosed to that person.

COUNT ONE

Conspiracy to [C]ommunicate National Defense Information

THE GRAND JURY FURTHER CHARGES THAT:

Between in [o]n [*sic*] or about April 1999 and continuing until on or about August 27, 2004, in the Eastern District of Virginia and elsewhere, defendants LAWRENCE ANTHONY FRANKLIN, STEVEN J. ROSEN, and KEITH WEISSMAN did unlawfully, knowingly and willfully conspire, confederate and agree together and with others, known and unknown to the Grand Jury, to commit the following offenses against the United States:

1) having lawful possession of, access to, and control over information relating to the national defense, did willfully communicate, deliver and transmit that information directly and indirectly to a person or persons not entitled to receive it, having reason to believe that said information could be used to the injury of the United States and to the advantage of a[n]y [sic] foreign nation, a violation of Title 18, United States Code, Section 793(d); and

2) having unauthorized possession of, access to, and control over information relating to the national defense, did willfully communicate, deliver and transmit that information directly and indirectly to a person or persons not entitled to receive it, having reason to believe that said information could be used to the injury of *the* United States and to the advantage of any foreign nation, a violation of Title 18, United States Code, Section 793(e).

WAYS, MANNER AND MEANS OF THE CONSPIRACY

A. It was part of the conspiracy that, in an effort to influence persons within and outside the United States government, ROSEN and WEISSMAN would cultivate relationships with FRANKLIN and others and would use their contacts within the U.S. government and elsewhere to gather sensitive U.S. government information, including classified information relating to the national defense, for subsequent unlawful communication, delivery and transmission to persons not entitled to receive it.

B. It was further part of the conspiracy that FRANKLIN would use his position as a desk officer in the Office of the Secretary of Defense to [g]ather [sic] information relating to the national defense, for subsequent unlawful communication, delivery and transmission to ROSEN and WEISSMAN and others not entitled to receive it.

C. It was further part of the conspiracy that FRANKLIN, ROSEN and WEISSMAN would meet at locations in the Eastern District of Virginia and elsewhere, to exchange information, including classified information relating to the national defense.

D. It was further part of the conspiracy that FRANKLIN would unlawfully deliver, communicate and transmit classified national defense information in an effort to advance his own personal foreign policy agenda and influence persons within and outside the United States government.

E. It was further part of the conspiracy that ROSEN and WEISSMAN, without lawful authority, would communicate to persons not entitled to receive it, classified information relating to the national defense.

OVERT ACTS

In furtherance of the conspiracy and to effect the object thereof, defendants FRANKLIN, ROSEN, and WEISSMAN did commit overt acts in the Eastern District of Virginia and elsewhere, including but not limited to the following:

1. On or about April 13, 1999, ROSEN had a conversation with Foreign Official 1 (FO-1) and told FO-1 that he (ROSEN) had "picked up a[n] [sic] extremely sensitive piece of intelligence" which ROSEN described as codeword protected intelligence. ROSEN then disclosed to FO-1 national defense information concerning terrorist activities in Central Asia.

2. On or about May 12, 1999, ROSEN and FO-1 met for lunch and further discussed the disclosure ROSEN made on April 13, 1999.

3. On or about June 11, 1999, WEISSMAN had a conversation with FO-1 and told FO-1 that a "Secret FBI, classified FBI report" on the Khobar Towers bombing had been prepared and that he (WEISSMAN) had gotten this information from three different sources, including United States government officials.

4. On or about June 11, 1999, WEISSMAN had another conversation with FO-1 and told FO-1 that he (WEISSMAN) had gotten a member of the media interested in the abovereferenced [sic] classified FBI report on the Khobar Towers bombing[.]

5. On or about December 12, 2000, ROSEN and WEISSMAN met with a United States government official (USGO-1). Following the meeting, ROSEN had a conversation with a member of the media to whom he gave information about classified United States strategy options against a Middle Eastern country and the internal United Sta[t]es government deliberations on those options. USGO-1, with whom ROSEN and WEISSMAN met, had access to the classified information ROSEN disclosed.

6. On or about January 18, 2002, ROSEN met with another United States government official (USGO-2). After the meeting and on that same day, a memorandum containing information ROSEN had obtained from USGO-2 was sent to fellow AIPAC employees. The memorandum contained classified information provided by USGO-2.

7. On or about January 23, 2002, ROSEN had a conversation with a foreign national and disclosed classified information provided to ROSEN by USGO-2 during their January 18, 20[0]2 [sic] meeting.

8. On or about March 12, 2002, ROSEN and USGO-2 met and discussed classified information regarding Al-Qaeda.

9. On or about March 13, 2002, ROSEN disclosed to a fellow AIPAC employee classified information regarding Al-Qaeda that had been provided by USGO-2.

10. On or about March 14, 2002, ROSEN met with Foreign Official 2 (FO-2) and disclosed classified information regarding Al-Qaeda, previously provided by USGO-2 on March 12, 2002.

11. On or about August 5, 2002, ROSEN called a Department of Defense employee (DoD employee A) at the Pentagon and asked for the name of someone in OSD ISA with an expertise on Iran and was given the name of defendant LAWRENCE FRANKLIN.

12. On or about August 15, 2002, after FRANKLIN called ROSEN and left a message saying that he had heard that ROSEN was interested in issues concerning Iran, ROSEN called FRANKLIN and left his cell phone number and said he would like to meet.

13. On or about August 20, 2002, FRANKLIN and ROSEN spoke on the telephone and arranged to meet the next day. ROSEN advised that he was bringing his colleague, KEITH WEISSMAN.

14. On or about August 21, 2002, FRANKLIN called ROSEN, and they agreed to postpone their meeting. FRANKLIN advised ROSEN that he had seven or eight issues he wanted to discuss with him, and the issues were not limited to Iran.

15. On or about February 7, 2003, FRANKLIN and a DoD employee (DoD employee B) agreed to meet with ROSEN and WEISSMAN.

16. On or about February 12, 2003, in a telephone conversation with another individual while en route to the meeting with FRANKLIN, ROSEN stated that he was excited to meet with a "Pentagon guy" because this person was a "real insider."

17. On or about February 12, 2003, FRANKLIN, DoD employee B, ROSEN, and WEISSMAN met for breakfast at a restaurant in Arlington, Virginia, whereupon FRANKLIN disclosed to ROSEN and WEISSMAN national defense information relating to a classified draft internal United States government policy document concerning a Middle Eastern country. FRANKLIN told ROSEN and WEISSMAN that he had also prepared a separate document in connection with this policy document.

18. On or about February 12, 2003, ROSEN and WEISSMAN discussed the information FRANKLIN had given as it related to a draft article written by a journalist concerning United States foreign policy toward a country in the Middle East. ROSEN questioned the accuracy of the journalist's information.

19. On or about February 14, 2003, FRANKLIN and ROSEN discussed FRANKLIN's prospects f[o]r [sic] a position on the National Security Council (NSC) staff, and ROSEN told FRANKLIN that by working at the NSC that he would be "by the elbow of the President." FRANKLIN asked ROSEN to "put in a good word" for him, and ROSEN said, "I'll do what I can." ROSEN ended the conversation by

telling FRANKLIN that he hoped they would keep in touch and that breakfast was a real "eye-opener."

20. On or about March 7, 2003, ROSEN called FRANKLIN at the Pentagon and arranged to meet early one morning at Union Station, in Washington, D.C.

21. On or about March 10, 2003, FRANKLIN[,] ROSEN and WEISSMAN met at Union Station early in the morning. In the course of the meeting, the three men moved from one restaurant to another restaurant and then finished the meeting in an empty restaurant,

22. On or about March 12, 2003, FRANKLIN called ROSEN from his office in the Pentagon and left a message saying that he was trying to fax a document to ROSEN and WEISSMAN but was unable to do so and wanted to make sure ROSEN was present to receive it.

23. On or about March 13, 2003, FRANKLIN spoke with ROSEN and was provided with ROSEN's home fax number. FRANKLIN told ROSEN that he preferred to send the fax to ROSEN's residence.

24. On or about March 13, 2003, ROSEN met FO-2, who was assigned to a foreign embassy in Washington, D.C. ROSEN disclosed to FO-2 information related to the classified draft internal United States government policy document that he had discussed with FRANKLIN. ROSEN also told FO-2 about the internal deliberations of United States government officials concerning the policy document that FRANKLIN had disclosed to ROSEN and WEISSMAN.

25. On or about March 13, 2003, after his breakfast with FO-2, ROSEN had a conversation with FO-1, who was from the same embassy as FO-2. ROSEN asked FO-1 if he had heard, from FO-2, "the interesting report" he had given him concerning the classified draft internal policy document. ROSEN then discussed the specifics in the document with FO-1. ROSEN and FO-1 also discussed whether a specific United States government official was aware of this information and how the deliberations would proceed.

26. On or about March 13, 2003, WEISSMAN had a separate conversation with FO-1. WEISSMAN asked FO-1, "Have you talked to Steve about Iran lately?" WEISSMAN related that "we" had heard from a "friend of ours in the Pentagon" about a national intelligence document— WEISSMAN discussed specifics about the classified draft internal policy document and the internal deliberations of United States government officials.

27. On [o]r [sic] about March 13, 2003, ROSEN disclosed to a senior fellow at a Washington, D.C. think tank the information relating to the classified draft internal policy document concerning a Middle Eastern country and the internal deliberations of United States government officials that had been provided to ROSEN by FRANKLIN.

ROSEN disclosed details from the document and encouraged the official to use his contacts to investigate further. The senior fellow advised ROSEN that he would follow up and see what he could do.

28. On or about March 17, 2003, FRANKLIN faxed, from the Pentagon to ROSEN's office fax machine, a document he had typed himself. The contents of this document appeared in the classified appendix to the classified draft internal policy document FRANKLIN had previously discussed with ROSEN and WEISSMAN on February 12, 2003.

29. On or about March 18, 2003, in a conversation with a member of the media about the classified draft internal policy document, ROSEN stated, "I'm not supposed to know this," and that it was a "considerable story." He encouraged the member of the media to pursue the story.

30. On or about May 30, 2003, in a conversation with another member of the media, ROSEN discussed the classified draft internal policy document and internal United States government deliberations about the document.

31. On or about June 3, 2003, WEISSMAN called FRANKLIN and left a message. Without naming the country, he said that he and ROSEN wanted to meet and talk about "our favorite country."

32. On or about June 24, 2003, WEISSMAN called FRANKLIN and asked FRANKLIN to obtain a document for him. While the document itself was not classified, WEISSMAN told FRANKLIN that he knew "the Agency" had a copy. FRANKLIN told WEISSMAN he would try to get WEISSMAN a copy and that he had a friend at the CIA if he could not get it anywhere else.

33. On or about June 24, 2003, ROSEN and WEISSMAN talked about arranging to have lunch with FRANKLIN.

34. On or about June 26, 2003, FRANKLIN, ROSEN and WEISSMAN met for lunch at a restaurant in Arlington, Virginia. FRANKLIN told ROSEN, "You set the agenda." ROSEN stated that he knew that "the constraints" under which FRANKLIN met with them were difficult. The three discussed the previously described classified draft internal policy document, as well as a newspaper article which described the document as classified, and the state of internal United States government deliberations.

35. On or about June 26, 2003, during the aforementioned meeting, FRANKLIN disclosed to ROSEN and WEISSMAN classified information related to potential attacks upon United States forces in Iraq. FRANKLIN told ROSEN and WEISSMAN that the information was "highly classified" and asked them not to use it.

36. On or about June 26, 2003, ROSEN and WEISSMAN spoke about the luncheon they had earlier attended with FRANKLIN. ROSEN specifically noted the information FRANKLIN had identified as

highly classified and stated that it was "quite a story." ROSEN also told WEISSMAN, "Well, look, it seems to me that this channel is one to keep wide open insofar as possible." WEISSMAN replied that he was taking FRANKLIN to a baseball game. ROSEN replied, "Smart guy. That's the thing to do."

37. On or about June 30, 2003, WEISSMAN and FRANKLIN, together, attended a major league baseball game in Baltimore, Maryland.

38. On or about October 24, 2003, FRANKLIN and Foreign Official 3 (FO-3) had a telephone conversation during which they discussed the status of the previously described classified draft internal policy document. FO-3 said he had information that work on the "policy" had stopped, and FRANKLIN confirmed that there had been "nothing on any calendar in regard to that" document.

39. On or about May 21, 2004, FRANKLIN verbally provided to reporters from a national news organization Top Secret/SCI national defense information concerning meetings involving two Middle Eastern officials. Shortly thereafter, the news organization, quoting FRANKLIN, broadcast a report that an unidentified source had specified that the U.S. government had obtained intelligence pertaining to these meetings and further provided details based on information FRANKLIN had supplied to the reporters.

40. On [o]r [sic] about June 30, 2004, FRANKLIN, without lawful authority, possessed at his residence in Kearneysville, West Virginia, Top Secret and Secret documents containing national defense information.

41. On or about July 9, 2004, WEISSMAN agreed to meet with Lawrence FRANKLIN, who, unbeknown to WEISSMAN, had begun cooperating with the government.

42. On or about July 9, 2004, after being informed of WEISSMAN's scheduled meeting with FRANKLIN, ROSEN asked WEISSMAN to later advise him as to what FRANKLIN had to say at the meeting.

43. On or about July 9, 2004, in Arlington, Virginia, WEISSMAN met with FRANKLIN and received from him classified national defense information involving United States intelligence related to certain Middle Eastern countries.

44. On or about July 21, 2004, in Arlington, Virginia, WEISSMAN met with FRANKLIN and obtained from FRANKLIN classified national defense information concerning a foreign government's covert actions in Iraq. Before disclosing the information, FRANKLIN warned WEISSMAN that the information he was about to receive was highly classified "Agency stuff" and that WEISSMAN could get into trouble by having the information.

45. On or about July 21, 2004, after meeting with FRANKLIN, WEISSMAN immediately returned to his office, met with ROSEN,

and disclosed to ROSEN the classified national defense information he had received from FRANKLIN.

46. On or about July 21, 2004, ROSEN and WEISSMAN had a conversation with FO-3 during which they disclosed classified national information obtained from Franklin earlier that day. ROSEN told FO-3 that the information being disclosed was "Agency" information.

47. On or about July 21, 2004, ROSEN and WEISSMAN had a conversation with a member of the media during which they disclosed classified national defense information provided by FRANKLIN earlier that day. ROSEN told the member of the media that he could not ask about the source of the information, but that the information was "Agency" information and that the source of the information was "an American intelligence source" with whom ROSEN and WEISSMAN had dealt with in the past and was "100 percent credible."

48. On or about July 21, 2004, WEISSMAN disclosed to another AIPAC employee classified national defense information provided by FRANKLIN earlier that day. In his disclosure, WEISSMAN described the information as having come from "an American intelligence source."

49. On or about August 3, 2004, WEISSMAN contacted ROSEN and advised ROSEN that he had been contacted by the FBI. ROSEN advised WEISSMAN that he, too, had been contacted by the FBI. During their conversation, ROSEN and WEISSMAN discussed whether the FBI contact was about "something they picked up at work" and whether the FBI had discovered their contact with the member of the media, referenced above.

50. On or about August 3, 2004, following his above-referenced contact with WEISSMAN, ROSEN was interviewed by FBI agents and falsely told the agents that FRANKLIN had never discussed classified information with him and had never provided him with classified information.

51. On or about August 3, 2004, following his interview with FBI agents, ROSEN contacted WEISSMAN and told him that the FBI talked with him about FRANKLIN.

52. On or about August 9, 2004, WEISSMAN was interviewed by FBI agents and falsely told the agents that FRANKLIN had never discussed classified information with him and had never provided him with classified information.

53. On or about August 20, 2004, WEISSMAN contacted another member of the media and disclosed to that person classified national defense information obtained on July 21, 2004 from Franklin. WEISSMAN further advised that he was trying to arrange a meeting between FRANKLIN and the member of the media.

54. On or about August 27, 2004, in an interview with FBI agents, ROSEN falsely stated that Franklin had never given him classified information and that he (ROSEN) did not know of anyone to whom FRANKLIN had given classified information.
55. On or about August 27, 2004, following his false statements to FBI agents that day, ROSEN contacted FO-2 and asked to meet with FO-2 or FO-3 about a "serious matter." ROSEN also told FO-2 that the FBI had "made some allegations which are important" and added that he did not want to "discuss it on the phone" and did not want to go to FO-2's embassy office.
56. On or about August 27, 2004, following the above-referenced conversation with FO-2, ROSEN went to a restaurant in Washington, D.C. near FO-2's embassy office. Once there, ROSEN approached FO-2 inside the restaurant. The two then proceeded outside where they engaged in conversation.
57. On or about August 27, 2004, WEISSMAN falsely told FBI agents that he did not know if FRANKLIN had disclosed classified information to him.

(In violation of Title 18, United States Code, Section 793(g))

COUNT TWO

Communication of National Defense Information

THE GRAND ([JU]RY [sic] FURTHER CHARGES THAT:
On or about February 12, 2003, in Arlington, Virginia, within the Eastern District of Virginia, defendant LAWRENCE ANTHONY FRANKLIN, lawfully having possession of, access to, control over, and being entrusted with information relating to the national defense, which information the defendant had reason [t]o [sic] believe could be used to the injury of the United States and to the advantage of a foreign nation, did unlawfully, knowingly and willfully communicate, deliver and transmit such information to a person or persons not entitled to receive it.

(In violation of Title 18, United States Code, Section 793(d))

COUNT THREE

Communication of National Defense Information

THE GRAND JURY FURTHER CHARGES THAT:

On or about March 17, 2003, in Arlington, Virginia, within the Eastern District of Virginia and elsewhere, defendant LAWRENCE ANTHONY FRANKLIN, lawfully having possession of, access to, control over, and being entrusted with a document, writing and note relating to the national defense, did unlawfully, knowingly and willfully communicate, deliver and transmit said document, writing and note to a person or persons not entitled to receive it, namely defendant STEVEN J. ROSEN, who did unlawfully, knowingly and willfully aid and abet FRANKLIN in the communication, delivery and transmission of said document, writing and note.

(In violation of Title 18, United States Code, Sections 793(d) and 2)

COUNT FOUR

Communication of National Defense Information

THE GRAND JURY FURTHER CHARGES THAT:

On or about June 26, 2003, in Arlington, Virginia, within the Eastern District of Virginia, defendant LAWRENCE ANTHONY FRANKLIN, lawfully having possession of, access to, control over, and being entrusted with information relating to the national defense, which information the defendant had reason to believe could be used to the injury of the United States and to the advantage of a foreign nation, did unlawfully, knowingly and willfully communicate, deliver and transmit such information to a person or persons not entitled to receive it.

(In violation of Title 18, United States Code, Section 793(d))

COUNT FIVE

Conspiracy to Communicate Classified Information

THE GRAND JURY FURTHER CHARGES THAT:

General Allegations

1. Foreign Official 3 (FO-3) is a diplomatic staff member of the embassy of Foreign Nation A located in Washington, D.C. FO-3 is not a United States citizen.

2. At no time relevant to this indictment was defendant FRANKLIN assigned or instructed to meet with FO-3 in the Washington, D.C. area as part of his OSD or USAFR employment. At no time relevant to this indictment was defendant FRANKLIN authorized to disclose classified information to FO-3.

The Offense

Between on or about August [15], [*sic*] 2002 and continuing until on or about June 30, 2004, in the Eastern District of Virginia and elsewhere, defendant LAWRENCE ANTHONY FRANKLIN, an employee of the United States, did unlawfully and knowingly conspire, confederate, and agree, with persons known and unknown [to] [*sic*] the Grand jury, to commit the following offense against the United States: to communicate in a manner and by a means, to a person whom defendant FRANKLIN knew and had reason to believe was an agent and representative of a foreign government, information of a kind which had been classified by the head of a United States agency with the approval of the President, as affecting the security of the United States, said defendant having known and having had reason to know that such information had been so classified, a violation of Title 50, United States Code, Section 783(a).

WAYS[,] MANNER AND MEANS OF THE CONSPIRACY

A. It was part of the conspiracy that FRANKLIN would use his position as a desk officer in the Office of the Secretary of Defense to gather information, classified as affecting the security of the United States, for subsequent unlawful communication to FO-3 from Foreign Nation A.

B. It was further part of the conspiracy that FRANKLIN would communicate by telephone with FO-3 to arrange meetings, share information, set agendas for meetings and act upon requests for additional information. It was part of the conspiracy to develop a trustworthy relationship between the conspirators and foster an environment in which the defendant felt free to disclose classified information.

C. It was further part of the conspiracy that FRANKLIN and FO-3 would meet at locations in the Eastern District of Virginia and elsewhere, to exchange information, including classified information affecting the security of the United States.

D. It was further part of the conspiracy that FRANKLIN would communicate classified information to FO-3 in an effort to enhance his own standing, advance his own personal foreign policy agenda, and influence persons within and outside the United States government.

OVERT ACTS

In furtherance of the conspiracy and to effect the object thereof, defendant LAWRENCE ANTHONY FRANKLIN and FO-3 did commit overt acts in the Eastern District of Virginia and elsewhere, including but not limited to the following:

1. On or about August 15, 2002, defendant FRANKLIN met with FO-3 at a restaurant in Washington, D.C. FO-3 explained to FRANKLIN that he was the "policy" person at the embassy and he would be the appropriate person with whom the defendant should talk.
2. On or about September 13, 2002, FRANKLIN communicated with one of his contacts at Foreign Nation A's embassy. That contact directed him to FO-3. The defendant and FO-3 exchanged phone calls in September, October, and November in an effort to set up a meeting. FRANKLIN called FO-3 at his office located at the embassy, and FO-3 called the defendant at his office at the Pentagon.
3. On or about January 30, 2003, the defendant and FO-3 met near Foreign Nation A's embassy in Washington, D.C. The subject of the discussion at this meeting was a Middle Eastern country's nuclear program.
4. [O]n [sic] or about February, March, and April of 2003, FRANKLIN and [FO-3] [sic] spoke by telephone and set up appointments to meet. The defendant called FO-3 from his office in the Pentagon.
5. On or about May 2, 2003, FRANKLIN met with FO-3 at the Pentagon Officer's Athletic Club (POAC), located adjacent to the Pentagon, within the Eastern District of Virginia. At this meeting, the two discussed foreign policy issues and senior United Stales government officials.
6. On or about May 23, 2003, FRANKLIN again met FO-3 at the POAC. At this meeting, the two discussed issues concerning a Middle Eastern country and its nuclear program and the views held by Europe and certain United States government agencies with regard to that issue. Following this meeting, the defendant drafted an Action Memo to his supervisors, incorporating suggestions made by FO-3 during the meeting.
7. On or about June 3, 2003, FRANKLIN met with FO-3 at the POAC, and the discussion centered on a specific person, not in the United Stat[e]s [sic] government, and her thoughts concerning the nuclear program of the Middle Eastern country and, separately, certain charity, efforts in Foreign Nation A.
8. On or about July 11, 2003, FRANKLIN met with FO-3 at the POAC and discussed certain charity work being done in a foreign nation.
9. On or about August 8, 2003, the defendant met with FO-3.
10. On or about August 29, 2003, the defendant met with FO-3 at the POAC.

11. On or about October 9, 2003, FRANKLIN met with FO-3 at a sandwich shop near the United States Department of State headquarters. The defendant asked FO-3 to provide him with a letter for his daughter, to aid her in her travels to the Middle East and Foreign Nation A.

12. On or about January 15, 2004, FRANKLIN met FO-3 and again asked FO-3 to provide some type of letter for his daughter for her travel to the Middle East, including Foreign Nation A.

3. [sic] On or about February 13, 2004, FRANKLIN met FO-3 at the POAC. At this meeting, FO-3 suggested to the defendant that he should meet with a person previously associated with an intelligence agency of Foreign Nation A who was then running a think tank in Foreign Nation A. FO-3 also gave the defendant a gift card.

14. On or about February 20, 2004, FRANKLIN met in the cafeteria at the Pentagon with this person previously associated with an intelligence agency of Foreign Nation A and discussed a Middle Eastern country's nuclear program.

15. [O]n or about late February 2004, the defendant and FO-3 exchanged telephone calls about certain foreign organizations.

16. On or about May 13, 2004, FO-3 faxed a letter from his embassy office to FRANKLIN's Pentagon fax relating to the defendant's daughter's travel to Foreign Nation A.

17. On or about June 8, 2004, FRANKLIN and FO-3 met at a coffee house in Washington, D.C. At this meeting, the defendant provided FO-3 with classified information he had learned from a classified United States government document related to a Middle Eastern country's activities in Iraq. The defendant was not authorized to disclose this classified information to FO-3.

18. On June 23, 2004, FRANKLIN met FO-3 [a]nd [sic] another official from Foreign Nation A at the Pentagon. The parties discussed the military situation in Iraq. The defendant provided FO-3 with an unclassified copy of a speech and list of questions that a senior United States government official was to give that day or the next before the Congressional Foreign Affairs Committee.

19. Between December 2003 and June 2004, at an unknown location, FRANKLIN disclosed to FO-3 classified United States government information relating to a weapons test conducted by a Middle Eastern country.

(In violation of Title 18, United States Code, Section 371.).

A TRUE BILL

FOREPERSON

Index